The NEW ENCYCLOPEDIA *of* SOUTHERN CULTURE

VOLUME 13 : GENDER

Volumes to appear in

The New Encyclopedia of Southern Culture

are:

Agriculture and Industry   *Law and Politics*

Art and Architecture   *Literature*

Education   *Media*

Environment   *Music*

Ethnicity   *Myth, Manners, and Memory*

Folk Art   *Race*

Folklife   *Recreation*

Foodways   *Religion*

Gender   *Science and Medicine*

Geography   *Social Class*

History   *Urbanization*

Language   *Violence*

The NEW

ENCYCLOPEDIA *of* SOUTHERN CULTURE

CHARLES REAGAN WILSON General Editor

JAMES G. THOMAS JR. Managing Editor

ANN J. ABADIE Associate Editor

VOLUME 13

Gender

NANCY BERCAW & TED OWNBY

Volume Editors

Sponsored by

THE CENTER FOR THE STUDY OF SOUTHERN CULTURE

at the University of Mississippi

THE UNIVERSITY OF NORTH CAROLINA PRESS

Chapel Hill

This book was published with the
assistance of the Anniversary Endowment Fund
of the University of North Carolina Press.

Designed by Richard Hendel
Set in Minion types by Tseng Information Systems, Inc.
Manufactured in the United States of America
The paper in this book meets the guidelines for permanence and
durability of the Committee on Production Guidelines for Book
Longevity of the Council on Library Resources.
The University of North Carolina Press has been a member of the
Green Press Initiative since 2003.
Library of Congress Cataloging-in-Publication Data
Gender / Nancy Bercaw and Ted Ownby, volume editors.
p. cm. — (The new encyclopedia of Southern culture ; v. 13)
"Sponsored by The Center for the Study of Southern Culture at the
University of Mississippi."
Includes bibliographical references and index.
ISBN 978-0-8078-3287-5 (alk. paper) —
ISBN 978-0-8078-5948-3 (pbk. : alk. paper)
1. Sex role—Southern States—Encyclopedias. 2. Women—
Southern States—History—Encyclopedias. 3. Feminism—
Southern States—Encyclopedias. 4. Popular culture—Southern
States—Encyclopedias. 5. Southern States—Social conditions—
Encyclopedias. 6. Southern States—Civilization—Encyclopedias.
I. Bercaw, Nancy. II. Ownby, Ted. III. University of Mississippi.
Center for the Study of Southern Culture. IV. Series.
F209 .N47 2006 vol. 13
[HQ1075.5.U6]
975.003 s—dc22
2008365936
The *Encyclopedia of Southern Culture*, sponsored by the Center for
the Study of Southern Culture at the University of Mississippi, was
published by the University of North Carolina Press in 1989.
cloth   13 12 11 10 09   5 4 3 2 1
paper   13 12 11 10 09   5 4 3 2 1

Tell about the South. What's it like there.

What do they do there. Why do they live there.

Why do they live at all.

WILLIAM FAULKNER

Absalom, Absalom!

CONTENTS

In 1989 years of planning and hard work came to fruition when the University of North Carolina Press joined the Center for the Study of Southern Culture at the University of Mississippi to publish the *Encyclopedia of Southern Culture.* While all those involved in writing, reviewing, editing, and producing the volume believed it would be received as a vital contribution to our understanding of the American South, no one could have anticipated fully the widespread acclaim it would receive from reviewers and other commentators. But the *Encyclopedia* was indeed celebrated, not only by scholars but also by popular audiences with a deep, abiding interest in the region. At a time when some people talked of the "vanishing South," the book helped remind a national audience that the region was alive and well, and it has continued to shape national perceptions of the South through the work of its many users—journalists, scholars, teachers, students, and general readers.

As the introduction to the *Encyclopedia* noted, its conceptualization and organization reflected a cultural approach to the South. It highlighted such issues as the core zones and margins of southern culture, the boundaries where "the South" overlapped with other cultures, the role of history in contemporary culture, and the centrality of regional consciousness, symbolism, and mythology. By 1989 scholars had moved beyond the idea of cultures as real, tangible entities, viewing them instead as abstractions. The *Encyclopedia*'s editors and contributors thus included a full range of social indicators, trait groupings, literary concepts, and historical evidence typically used in regional studies, carefully working to address the distinctive and characteristic traits that made the American South a particular place. The introduction to the *Encyclopedia* concluded that the fundamental uniqueness of southern culture was reflected in the volume's composite portrait of the South. We asked contributors to consider aspects that were unique to the region but also those that suggested its internal diversity. The volume was not a reference book of southern history, which explained something of the design of entries. There were fewer essays on colonial and antebellum history than on the postbellum and modern periods, befitting our conception of the volume as one trying not only to chart the cultural landscape of the South but also to illuminate the contemporary era.

When C. Vann Woodward reviewed the *Encyclopedia* in the *New York Review of Books*, he concluded his review by noting "the continued liveliness of interest in the South and its seeming inexhaustibility as a field of study." Research on the South, he wrote, furnishes "proof of the value of the *Encyclopedia* as a scholarly undertaking as well as suggesting future needs for revision or supplement to keep up with ongoing scholarship." The two decades since the publication of the *Encyclopedia of Southern Culture* have certainly suggested that Woodward was correct. The American South has undergone significant changes that make for a different context for the study of the region. The South has undergone social, economic, political, intellectual, and literary transformations, creating the need for a new edition of the *Encyclopedia* that will remain relevant to a changing region. Globalization has become a major issue, seen in the South through the appearance of Japanese automobile factories, Hispanic workers who have immigrated from Latin America or Cuba, and a new prominence for Asian and Middle Eastern religions that were hardly present in the 1980s South. The African American return migration to the South, which started in the 1970s, dramatically increased in the 1990s, as countless books simultaneously appeared asserting powerfully the claims of African Americans as formative influences on southern culture. Politically, southerners from both parties have played crucial leadership roles in national politics, and the Republican Party has dominated a near-solid South in national elections. Meanwhile, new forms of music, like hip-hop, have emerged with distinct southern expressions, and the term "dirty South" has taken on new musical meanings not thought of in 1989. New genres of writing by creative southerners, such as gay and lesbian literature and "white trash" writing, extend the southern literary tradition.

Meanwhile, as Woodward foresaw, scholars have continued their engagement with the history and culture of the South since the publication of the *Encyclopedia*, raising new scholarly issues and opening new areas of study. Historians have moved beyond their earlier preoccupation with social history to write new cultural history as well. They have used the categories of race, social class, and gender to illuminate the diversity of the South, rather than a unified "mind of the South." Previously underexplored areas within the field of southern historical studies, such as the colonial era, are now seen as formative periods of the region's character, with the South's positioning within a larger Atlantic world a productive new area of study. Cultural memory has become a major topic in the exploration of how the social construction of "the South" benefited some social groups and exploited others. Scholars in many disciplines have made the southern identity a major topic, and they have used a variety of methodologies to suggest what that identity has meant to different social groups. Literary critics have adapted cultural theories to the South and have raised the issue of postsouthern literature to a major category of concern as well as exploring the links between the literature of the American South and that of the Caribbean. Anthropologists have used different theoretical formulations from literary critics, providing models for their fieldwork in southern communities. In the past 30 years anthropologists have set increasing numbers of their ethnographic studies in the South, with many of them now exploring topics specifically linked to southern cultural issues. Scholars now place the Native American story, from prehistory to the contemporary era, as a central part of southern history. Comparative and interdisciplinary approaches to the South have encouraged scholars to look at such issues as the borders and boundaries of the South, specific places and spaces with distinct identities within the American South, and the global and transnational Souths, linking the American South with many formerly colonial societies around the world.

The first edition of the *Encyclopedia of Southern Culture* anticipated many of these approaches and indeed stimulated the growth of Southern Studies as a distinct interdisciplinary field. The Center for the Study of Southern Culture has worked for more than a quarter century to encourage research and teaching about the American South. Its academic programs have produced graduates who have gone on to write interdisciplinary studies of the South, while others have staffed the cultural institutions of the region and in turn encouraged those institutions to document and present the South's culture to broad public audiences. The center's conferences and publications have continued its long tradition of promoting understanding of the history, literature, and music of the South, with new initiatives focused on southern foodways, the future of the South, and the global Souths, expressing the center's mission to bring the best current scholarship to broad public audiences. Its documentary studies projects build oral and visual archives, and the New Directions in Southern Studies book series, published by the University of North Carolina Press, offers an important venue for innovative scholarship.

Since the *Encyclopedia of Southern Culture* appeared, the field of Southern Studies has dramatically developed, with an extensive network now of academic and research institutions whose projects focus specifically on the interdisciplinary study of the South. The Center for the Study of the American South at the University of North Carolina at Chapel Hill, led by Director Harry Watson and Associate Director and *Encyclopedia* coeditor William Ferris, publishes the lively journal *Southern Cultures* and is now at the organizational center of many other Southern Studies projects. The Institute for Southern Studies at the University of South Carolina, the Southern Intellectual History Circle, the Society for the Study of Southern Literature, the Southern Studies Forum of the European American Studies Association, Emory University's SouthernSpaces.org, and the South Atlantic Humanities Center (at the Virginia Foundation for the Humanities, the University of Virginia, and Virginia Polytechnic Institute and State University) express the recent expansion of interest in regional study.

Observers of the American South have had much to absorb, given the rapid pace of recent change. The institutional framework for studying the South is broader and deeper than ever, yet the relationship between the older verities of regional study and new realities remains unclear. Given the extent of changes in the American South and in Southern Studies since the publication of the *Encyclopedia of Southern Culture*, the need for a new edition of that work is clear. Therefore, the Center for the Study of Southern Culture has once again joined the University of North Carolina Press to produce *The New Encyclopedia of Southern Culture*. As readers of the original edition will quickly see, *The New Encyclopedia* follows many of the scholarly principles and editorial conventions established in the original, but with one key difference; rather than being published in a single hardback volume, *The New Encyclopedia* is presented in a series of shorter individual volumes that build on the 24 original subject categories used in the *Encyclopedia* and adapt them to new scholarly developments. Some earlier *Encyclopedia* categories have been reconceptualized in light of new academic interests. For example, the subject section originally titled "Women's Life" is reconceived as a new volume, *Gender*, and the original "Black Life" section is more broadly interpreted as a volume on race. These changes reflect new analytical concerns that place the study of women and blacks in broader cultural systems, reflecting the emergence of, among other topics, the study of male culture and of whiteness. Both volumes draw as well from the rich recent scholarship on women's life and black life. In addition, topics with some thematic coherence are combined in a volume, such as *Law and Politics* and *Agriculture and Industry*. One new topic, *Foodways*, is the basis of a separate volume, reflecting its new prominence in the interdisciplinary study of southern culture.

Numerous individual topical volumes together make up *The New Encyclopedia of Southern Culture* and extend the reach of the reference work to wider audiences. This approach should enhance the use of the *Encyclopedia* in academic courses and is intended to be convenient for readers with more focused interests within the larger context of southern culture. Readers will have handy access to one-volume, authoritative, and comprehensive scholarly treatments of the major areas of southern culture.

We have been fortunate that, in nearly all cases, subject consultants who offered crucial direction in shaping the topical sections for the original edition have agreed to join us in this new endeavor as volume editors. When new volume editors have been added, we have again looked for respected figures who can provide not only their own expertise but also strong networks of scholars to help develop relevant lists of topics and to serve as contributors in their areas. The reputations of all our volume editors as leading scholars in their areas encouraged the contributions of other scholars and added to *The New Encyclopedia's* authority as a reference work.

The New Encyclopedia of Southern Culture builds on the strengths of articles in the original edition in several ways. For many existing articles, original authors agreed to update their contributions with new interpretations and theoretical perspectives, current statistics, new bibliographies, or simple factual developments that needed to be included. If the original contributor was unable to update an article, the editorial staff added new material or sent it to another scholar for assessment. In some cases, the general editor and volume editors selected a new contributor if an article seemed particularly dated and new work indicated the need for a fresh perspective. And importantly, where new developments have warranted treatment of topics not addressed in the original edition, volume editors have commissioned entirely new essays and articles that are published here for the first time.

The American South embodies a powerful historical and mythical presence, both a complex environmental and geographic landscape and a place of the imagination. Changes in the region's contemporary socioeconomic realities and new developments in scholarship have been incorporated in the conceptualization and approach of *The New Encyclopedia of Southern Culture*. Anthropologist Clifford Geertz has spoken of culture as context, and this encyclopedia looks at the American South as a complex place that has served as the context for cultural expression. This volume provides information and perspective on the diversity of cultures in a geographic and imaginative place with a long history and distinctive character.

The *Encyclopedia of Southern Culture* was produced through major grants from the Program for Research Tools and Reference Works of the National Endowment for the Humanities, the Ford Foundation, the Atlantic-Richfield Foundation, and the Mary Doyle Trust. We are grateful as well to the College of Liberal Arts at the University of Mississippi for support and to the individual donors to the Center for the Study of Southern Culture who have directly or indirectly supported work on *The New Encyclopedia of Southern Culture*. We thank the volume editors for their ideas in reimagining their subjects and the contributors of articles for their work in extending the usefulness of the book in new ways. We acknowledge the support and contributions of the faculty and staff at the Center for the Study of Southern Culture. Finally, we want especially to honor the work of William Ferris and Mary Hart on the *Encyclopedia of Southern Culture*. Bill, the founding director of the Center for the Study of Southern Culture, was coeditor, and his good work recruiting authors, editing text, selecting images, and publicizing the volume among a wide network of people was, of course, invaluable. Despite the many changes in the new encyclopedia, Bill's influence remains. Mary "Sue" Hart was also an invaluable member of the original encyclopedia team, bringing the careful and precise eye of the librarian, and an iconoclastic spirit, to our work.

INTRODUCTION

Gender is a central category of analysis in understanding the American South. The "Women's Life" section of the original *Encyclopedia of Southern Culture* focused attention on previously neglected issues of women's culture and identity, but in considering this volume of *The New Encyclopedia of Southern Culture* the editors believed that we needed to reconceptualize many of the issues raised in that section. Work on the "masculine" and the "feminine" grew exponentially after publication of the original encyclopedia, and that scholarship complicates our understanding of men's and women's lives in the South. As Ted Ownby and Nancy Bercaw note in their overview essay, gender analysis destabilizes discourse about the South, upsetting conventional wisdom. Southern culture looks different than it did in earlier eras because scholars are giving more serious consideration to the conflicts and tensions that are inherent in the cultural constructions that men and women have made over centuries.

The power of gendered terminology is apparent in the importance of the term "patriarchy" as a way to bridge class and regional gaps within the South in order to emphasize shared values around male dominance of the household. "Family," with its culturally sanctioned antebellum roles for men, women, children, and slaves, proved a related imaginative construct that ideologues used to justify the slave society, and, later, "family values" would prove a resonant contemporary idea for conservative southern Christians.

This volume charts ways that men and women have had differing experiences of manhood and womanhood. The expectations, opportunities, and limitations of white plantation owners, slave field hands, and small yeoman farmers established enduring parameters and boundaries for men's understanding of their roles as fathers or husbands. The domestic worker and the woman she worked for might share the kitchen, but they did so in complex relationships of intimacy and power. Native American men and women and Latino men and women surely have had differing gender experiences from other people in the South, based on their positioning in southern society. The public and private contexts made a difference in how men and women played gender roles, and the regional context resulted in many southern women having differing ideas about feminism than women in other parts of the nation had.

This volume is particularly important in illuminating a major goal of *The New Encyclopedia*, namely to show—within the systematic categorization of a reference work—that topics and themes have overlapped in southern culture. Despite neat classifications needed for clarity, topics range across not only disciplinary boundaries but thematic ones as well. In particular, gender entries have close relationships with those on race and social class, and gender themes pervade encyclopedia entries in every volume. Articles in this volume delineate gendered meanings in such major historical events as the Civil War and the civil rights movement. Public policy issues such as abortion and citizenship have clear gendered meanings that are brought out in separate entries on those topics. Gender studies has built on earlier works on regional mythology to examine such central iconic representations as belles and ladies, mammies, and maiden aunts, all covered herein. Gender influences cultural expressions, as seen in thematic entries on autobiography, blues, country music, and photography. A judicious selection of topical entries illustrates the breadth of gender's meanings. Readers will meet politicians, writers, musicians, social reformers, educators, religious leaders, television celebrities, and memoirists, each of which reveals differing conceptions of gender's impact. Gender studies finds meaning in a historical incident (the capture of Jefferson Davis), a slogan (I AM A MAN), and a television show (*Designing Women*).

The overview essay stresses that gender studies is often about process, and this volume is timely in presenting the latest scholarship of a field that has grown to be of crucial significance in understanding evolving southern culture.

The NEW ENCYCLOPEDIA *of* SOUTHERN CULTURE

VOLUME 13 : GENDER

GENDER

This volume presents both the obvious and the somewhat hidden issues involving gender in southern cultural life. The obvious points are moments and images when gender was clearly relevant—characters like Scarlett O'Hara and Uncle Tom, justifications for violence and arguments for and against woman suffrage, slogans such as "I AM A MAN." The less obvious issues involve the roles gender plays in almost any question. If women make up most of the workers in some jobs and a small minority of other jobs, or if wages and salaries or levels of poverty are substantially different for men, the issues of work and reward have gender components. If women make up small percentages of southern legislatures and if men make up large percentages of convicted felons, the issues of law and politics have gender components. And if the language people use suggests that some behavior is male and some is female (or, to use perhaps even more complicated terms, masculine or feminine), the very words people use raise important questions about gender.

The list could go on. This collection of encyclopedia entries is fairly large, but it could be far larger, because one can find gender components in virtually any element of human life. This means we have had to make choices that we hope will reflect the many, and often unexpected, ways that gender enters southern lives and culture.

This volume builds on and replaces the section from the original *Encyclopedia of Southern Culture* called "Women's Life," edited by Carol Ruth Berkin. This transition from women's studies to gender highlights what is new about this volume and, in doing so, dramatizes an important shift in scholarship. Women's studies emerged in the 1960s and 1970s as a series of ways to document and often celebrate the lives of people more or less ignored by generations of scholars, who tended to study the lives of the men who were in charge. Much of the early scholarship stressed, even in the names of books and articles, that the goal was to bring to light experiences that had too long been invisible.

Considering the pervasiveness of the belle, the mammy, and the hillbilly granny in popular culture, it is hard to imagine that the southern woman could ever have been invisible. Indeed, women have often seemed to represent the essence of the South. "Dixie, after all," Tara McPherson reminds us, "is a woman's name." Yet despite the close association of southern culture with women, only a handful of scholars studied southern women (either real or imagined) before the 1980s. The first edition of the *Encyclopedia of Southern Culture* helped make that new scholarship visible by recognizing the work of established scholars and introducing new ones. The section "Women's Life" covered a growing academic field that has, in the past generation, helped stimulate the largely new field of gender studies.

To many people, "women's history" was a welcome term. On the other hand, "gender" tends to be a scholar's term that many people outside academia find troubling, vague, or irrelevant. The term "gender" complicates many people's assumptions that the world is divided into females and males. Yet it was precisely this point that makes the term so useful in studying the South. Southern women did not seem to fit the molds established by the leading scholars in American women's history. For much of the region's history, a few southern women were feminists—but only a few. More interesting, southern women defined feminism in different terms than most Americans. Almost none were abolitionists. Southern women did not go to work in factories before the Civil War and form sisterly bonds. Few elite white women created or joined reform organizations. In fact, slavery ensured that sisterly bonds between races or classes remained unthinkable, literally beyond the ken of most southerners. The southern experience challenged any simple assumptions of a universal woman's experience or a shared women's culture. Slavery, for example, forced a rethinking of motherhood when historians and writers, such as Toni Morrison in *Beloved*, considered what it meant for an enslaved woman to bring a child into the world. Feminist assertions in the South tend to take their own forms; southern feminists may say that the personal is political, or they may say, as Loretta Lynn sang, "Now I've got the pill." In short, southern women's history severely complicated women's history, but gender helped.

The concept of gender has forced scholars to rethink important differences in southern women's lives because as Elsa Barkley Brown reminds us, "all women do not have the same gender." The study of southern women made the truth of this statement apparent. Certainly an enslaved woman would not have agreed with a plantation mistress about what it meant to be a mother, wife, or citizen. Nor would a Cherokee woman likely agree with a white woman about a woman's place within a family—or even who and what constituted a family. And history and literature tell us that most southern women have not agreed with most northern women about the meaning of feminism. In other words, one cannot neatly divide the world into males and females because men do not experience or understand manhood in the same way and women do not live womanhood in the same way.

Perhaps as much as anything, gender scholars have worked to destabilize

Doris Ullman photograph of a young woman, Brasstown, N.C., 1930s
(Doris Ullman, Art Department, Berea College, Berea, Ky.)

concepts—men or women or African Americans or whites or Latin Americans or southerners or northerners or gays or straight people. Studying gender usually means studying instability and therefore often means emphasizing processes and conflict. Gender studies tends to suggest that things are in process, that concepts and norms and identities that people often take for granted are in fact the results of past contests and may very well be a matter of winning contests still going on or—more intriguingly—winning them before they start. Compared to tendencies in women's studies, gender studies tends not to celebrate but instead to analyze how notions of gender structure social relations.

But gender studies does in fact share at least three crucial points with much of women's studies. First, its scholars seek to bring to light the differences between cultural images and everyday realities rooted in unjust power relations. A turning point in southern women's history was Anne Firor Scott's significantly titled *The Southern Lady: From Pedestal to Politics* (1970). Current scholarship that sees politics in everything would say that the notion of the pedestal was part of a political discourse, designed to use cultural imagery to buck up the existing system. The same scholars would likely argue that the activism of women who became involved in temperance, child labor, suffrage, and other reforms represented a new form of political action—not a new entrance into the political sphere. But many of those differences are relatively minor, and the goals are somewhat similar.

Second, both women's studies and gender studies tend to emphasize that experience is far deeper than it seems. Both say that gender ideals tend to serve certain purposes for certain people and that we should not take them as reality. Both believe that ideals often include lies—lies told for particular purposes. As Carol Ruth Berkin wrote in the introduction to the "Women's Life" section of the *Encyclopedia of Southern Culture*, "The powerful images of 'Miss Scarlett' and 'Mammy' were based on the power of the elite planter class who created these ideals." Recent scholars tend to study how people use such ideals, negotiate within them, or reject them, but they emphasize those images as part of ongoing processes of power and experience.

Third, women's studies and gender studies are comfortable suggesting, as Berkin did in the first edition of this encyclopedia, that "no easily identifiable 'southern woman' exists." Southern experience is simply too varied and too complex to be one, or even a handful, of ideal types. The current scholarship reflects the freedom in moving beyond the typical narrative. Many entries in this volume begin less from the perspective of those who came to dominate the South (the planter class and its inheritors) than from the perspective of other southerners—American Indians, poor whites, Latin Americans, and African

Americans—who were dealing with and often contesting that domination. The shift in perspective illuminates familiar and less familiar subjects, helping us to see the South in new ways. Both fields recognize the importance of going beyond simply adding new voices. Instead, they ask us to recognize how new voices substantially shift the foundation of what we know.

Attention to gender continues to reshape the way we think about big moments in southern culture: the origins of slavery, the experience of slavery, the Civil War, Reconstruction, Jim Crow, and the civil rights movement. So much has been written about these big topics that one might assume there is nothing more to say or to discover. Yet it would be fair to say that gender studies encourages scholars to ask and answer new questions. For example, why would a hardworking, hill-country, subsistence farmer support slavery and identify with a wealthy slaveholder who rarely worked with his hands and placed himself above the hardworking farmer? Stephanie McCurry, using a gender analysis, carefully examined the words, actions, and politics of South Carolina to conclude that both men saw themselves as masters of their households. Both groups spoke of duty and responsibility toward their households, and both understood that marriage and manhood gave them these rights and obligations. The hardworking farmer, as master of his wife and children, spoke the same language as the master of a complex plantation household composed largely of enslaved people. Their shared identity as the male heads of households united them in unexpected ways that transcended social differences.

Another example shows how gender studies has enriched, without overturning, one of the most persistent arguments by a southern historian. In classic books published in the 1950s, C. Vann Woodward argued that the passage of segregation laws, disfranchisement laws, and constitutional provisions represented a new way, more or less designed by political leaders, for various groups of white southerners to band together when the Populist movement threatened to unite white and African American farming people around shared goals as working farmers. Gender scholars have generally agreed with Woodward's main assumptions—southern history was full of conflict and possibility and new restrictions emerged as a political effort to shore up white unity at the expense of African Americans' rights and lives. But gender scholars have added new stories—that the lynching and rioting that started in the late 1890s occurred in large part because white elites used the concept of unleashed black male sexual excess to overcome Populist threats, that such elites called on heavily gendered notions of manners and civility to differentiate between those who deserved citizenship and those who did not, and that many African Americans responded with new calls for respectable behavior that emphasized Victorian family standards, restricted women from pursuing any overtly political behavior, and made new calls for prohibition.

Attention to gender also brings new subjects to the table—foodways, recreation, health, and the ways people communicate. Some of these topics were for years part of small and marginalized subfields of scholarship, but gender scholarship has helped make them almost as central to scholarly work as they are to real life. Recent work in African American gender scholarship emphasizes the significance of silence and the need to address troubling subjects—rape, sexual harassment, domestic violence—as well as joyful ones—courtship, dress, dance. Through concepts such as the "politics of respectability," "the culture of dissemblance," and the "pleasures of resistance," African American gender scholars ask us to be mindful of the cultural weight attached to the topics we choose to study. The "culture of dissemblance," for example, refers to black women's deliberate avoidance (or dissemblance) of any topic regarding African American women's bodies because of America's long history of sexual stereotyping. Foodways scholars connect the production and consumption of food to cultural images like mothers, grandmothers, and domestic workers—all of them loaded with meanings for considering the relationship between gender and identity. Scholarship on sports analyzes the acceptable forms of competition in a society and raises questions about gender and race and, particularly, about the physical body. Scholarship on health asks us to consider which bodies are the most vulnerable to biomedical experimentation and how the legacy of such experimentation shapes some black southerners' perceptions and avoidance of health care professionals.

The men's studies movement, always far smaller than women's studies, has had significant effects on southern scholarship. It is tempting but incorrect to say that prior to the 1960s virtually all southern scholarship was men's scholarship—tempting because men dominated the profession and also because those men tended to write about other men, especially those who were in charge of something. But that assertion would be misleading, because gender scholars have tended to study how people used the notion of manhood to keep or challenge authority. In the past generation, questions of the meanings or usefulness of concepts like paternalism, patriarchy, honor, and manly independence have been crucial to scholarship on the South. Gender studies has also helped expand the range of subjects into the emotions and sports and recreation—topics that scholars missed if they concentrated exclusively on how people got power, used power, and kept power.

Scholars generally agree that the times they live in help to determine the topics they research, their questions, and often their answers. One of the changes

Young Florida cowgirls posing in Jacksonville studio, 1930s (Florida State Archives, Tallahassee)

between the 1980s South and the contemporary South is the growth and con-fidence of the Religious Right, whose leaders and followers have argued that there is only one proper definition of family life—that is, one man and one woman married and raising their children and, at least according to many reli-gious conservatives, women playing a subservient role to men. Most gender scholars disagree with essentialist arguments that there are fixed definitions of anything, but in the wake of the feminist movement they have been especially interested in deconstructing the notion of "the family" as an institution that could only conform or aspire to Victorian norms. Thus, scholars have studied single women, communal family arrangements, households that unite many people with no biological or permanent connections, and, recently, gay, lesbian, and transgendered individuals, whose lives show the variety of choices people make and also cast doubt on conceptions of gender or family life as the only standard for social organization.

The subjects discussed in this volume display the ways gender scholarship has reshaped the study of the South. Numerous topics covered in other vol-umes of the *New Encyclopedia of Southern Culture* receive treatment here from the perspective of gender scholarship. As a volume on culture, it pays particu-lar attention to ideals, images, and stereotypes, and the range and number of gender ideals, images, and stereotypes in the South is extraordinary. Too many people think of "ladies" and "gentlemen" as the most important or even prototypical southern images and ideals. The term "paternalist" is more common among academics than nonacademics, but it carries plenty of weight as image or stereotype, if not much any longer as an ideal. Like the term "paternalist," the old term "yeoman" is male, without a frequently used female equivalent. "Bubba" is a derogatory if comic and generally good-natured term for males, almost all of them white. The terms "good old boy" and "good old girl," also generally terms for white southerners, tend to be friendly enough terms, although "redneck," long a largely male image before country singer Gretchen Wilson turned "Redneck Woman" into a bit of an anthem, suggests something angrier, more defensive, and maybe more prone to violence. The term "hillbilly" tends to be more male than female, probably because images of laziness make more sense for men than for overworked women with lots of children. But southern culture has plenty of images for white women as well. The debutante and the beauty queen. The resolute migrant mother of FSA photographs. Steel magnolias. And if white southerners suffer from a surplus of images, African Americans, especially African American men, are among the most heavily imaged people in American history. Uncle Tom, both admired and condemned. Jim Crow himself, an overdressed dandy. Mammy and Aunt Jemima. The kneeling slave holding up chains, asking for help. The black beast rapist. John Henry, with superhuman strength. The Superwoman who holds things together inside and outside the home and maybe also in church. The welfare queen. The ramblin' blues man, maybe a genius, always mysterious. The dignified leader, usually an educator or minister, teaching or preaching uplift. The gang member, the convict.

Some images that are less clearly identified with the South have plenty of popularity in thinking about the region as well. Southern men long loved the image of the dignified and dutiful military figure, an image long associated with white men who liked to remember or imagine themselves with high rank, complicated first by African Americans returning from a series of wars and demanding justice and more recently by wars in which both men and women could be either heroic, or in the cases of William Calley or Lynndie England of Abu Ghraib infamy, destructive. The upright lawyer—whether Faulkner's Gavin Stevens, who tended to talk himself out of any real action, or Harper Lee's Atticus Finch, with his belief in the potential for justice and human decency—is a recurring and often controversial figure. The character of the minister, apparently upright but with the potential for hypocrisy and even lechery, runs from southwestern humorists to Jimmy Swaggart, although this image has

Country storekeeper, Regantown, Miss., 1975
(William R. Ferris Collection, Southern Folklife
Collection, Wilson Library, University of North
Carolina at Chapel Hill)

plenty of representatives outside the South. Other gendered southern images seem exclusive to parts of the South: Pocahontas in Virginia, singing cowboys, old ideas of Appalachian cultural purity or cultural separation or inbreeding, coastal lifeguards and bathing beauties, the Evangeline myth in southern Louisiana, and gender inversion rituals in New Orleans.

This volume studies images, their creation, the multiple meanings they may have for different people, and sometimes their accuracy or falsehood, but it is also committed to studying topics that may not be common in the public discussion of the South. So, if picking up a book on gender in southern culture means reading about familiar topics, it should also mean reading about abortion, and the myth of matriarchy, and migrant workers. And since reading southern fiction often seems to bring up a recurring set of familiar characters, gender scholars have been at the forefront in saying we need to look for new patterns in literature as well as history. Patricia Yaeger, troubled by the frequency with which people who write about southern fiction seem to concentrate on a few stock images, has offered a new set of tendencies that come from women's fiction. She refers to an "anti-autochthonous ideal" in which the earth, far from an agrarian image of nurturing human life, forces people off the land, and she sees in literature "exploding bodies" that dramatize instability and impermanence. Scholars who write about African American memoirs have demonstrated how female autobiographers confound the norms of their genre by tending to emphasize talking back as resistance and a creative commitment to redefining families rather than the older expectations of individual flights to freedom. Unlike past scholars who might have started with, say, William Faulkner, the Vanderbilt Agrarians, and Richard Wright to exemplify southern writing, today's students of southern literature are less likely to put any single author at the center of southern culture, preferring instead to hear multiple voices. But any short list would include Alice Walker, with her concept of "womanism," and Kaye Gibbons, with her character Ellen Foster, who gave herself her last name out of a desire to become a foster child.

If gender studies scholarship suggests the instability of most ideas, it needs also to admit its own impermanence—perhaps difficult in the case of an encyclopedia. Many of us grew up with the idea of encyclopedias—long rows of books full of wisdom and respectability—as the ultimate sources of authority. But a scholarly term like "gender," a term that tends to be best when studying cultural life as part of ongoing, complicated, destabilizing processes, may be better at raising questions than at reaching conclusions of a sort some readers may expect from a book called an encyclopedia. We see this not as a problem but as an exciting challenge. Perhaps future scholars will seek a more stable concept as the basis for organizing their work, or perhaps scholarship that addresses gender will become so commonplace that future encyclopedias will not even need to highlight the topic. What seems certain at the present moment is that the study of gender, as reflected in this volume, has succeeded in altering, and perhaps even revolutionizing, the ways we think about southern culture.

TED OWNBY
NANCY BERCAW
University of Mississippi

Houston Baker and Dana D. Nelson, *Violence, the Body, and "The South"* (2001); Peter W. Bardaglio, *Reconstructing the Household: Families, Sex, and the Law in the Nineteenth-Century South* (1998); Elsa Barkley Brown, "'What Has Happened Here': The Politics of Difference in Women's History and Feminist Politics," *Feminist Studies* (September 1992); Nancy Bercaw, ed., *Gender and the Southern Body Politic* (2000); Stephen Berry, *Princes of Cotton: Four Diaries of Young Men in the South, 1848–1860* (2007); Kathleen M. Brown, *Good Wives, Nasty Wenches, and Anxious Patriarchs: Gender, Race, and Power in Colonial Virginia* (1996); Stephanie M. H. Camp, *Closer to Freedom: Enslaved Women and Everyday Resistance in the Plantation South* (2004); Hazel V. Carby, *Reconstructing Womanhood: The Emergence of the Afro-American Woman Novelist* (1989); Catherine Clinton, *The Plantation Mistress: Woman's World in the Old South* (1984); Catherine Clinton and Nina Silber, eds., *Divided Houses: Gender and the Civil War* (1992); Jane Dailey, Glenda Gilmore, and Bryant Simon, eds., *Jumpin' Jim Crow: Southern Politics from Civil War to Civil Rights* (2000); Laura F. Edwards, *Scarlett Doesn't*

Live Here Anymore: Southern Women in the Civil War Era (2004), *Gendered Strife and Confusion: The Political Culture of Reconstruction* (1997); Drew Gilpin Faust, *Mothers of Invention: Women of the Slaveholding South in the American Civil War* (2004); Sharla Fett, *Working Cures: Healing, Health, and Power on Southern Slave Plantations* (2007); Elizabeth Fox-Genovese, *Within the Plantation Household: Black and White Women of the Old South* (1988); Craig Thompson Friend and Lorri Glover, eds., *Southern Manhood: Perspectives on Masculinity in the Old South* (2004); Glenda Gilmore, *Gender and Jim Crow: Women and the Politics of White Supremacy in North Carolina, 1896–1920* (1996); Kenneth S. Greenberg, *Honor and Slavery: Lies, Duels, Noses, Masks, Dressing as a Woman, Gifts, Strangers, Humanitarianism, Death, Slave Rebellions, the Proslavery Argument, Baseball, Hunting, and Gambling in the Old South* (1997); Jacquelyn Dowd Hall, *Revolt against Chivalry: Jessie Daniel Ames and the Women's Campaign against Lynching* (1979); Evelyn Brooks Higginbotham, *Righteous Discontent: The Women's Movement in the Black Baptist Church, 1880–1920* (1993); Martha Hodes, *White Women, Black Men: Illicit Sex in the Nineteenth-Century South* (1999); Pippa Holloway, *Sexuality, Politics, and Social Control in Virginia, 1920–1945* (2006); John Howard, *Men Like That: A Southern Queer History* (1999); Tera W. Hunter, *To 'Joy My Freedom: Southern Black Women's Lives and Labors after the Civil War* (1998); Anne Goodwyn Jones and Susan V. Donaldson, eds., *Haunted Bodies: Gender and Southern Texts* (1997); Stephanie McCurry, *Masters of Small Worlds: Yeoman Households, Gender Relations, and the Political Culture of the Antebellum South Carolina Low Country* (1997); Tara McPherson, *Reconstructing Dixie: Race, Gender, and Nostalgia in the Imagined South* (2003); Michele Mitchell, "Silence Broken, Silences Kept: Gender and Sexuality in African-American History," *Gender and History* (November 1999); Ted Ownby, *Subduing Satan: Religion, Recreation, and Manhood in the Rural South, 1865–1920* (1990); Nell Irvin Painter, *Southern History across the Color Line* (2001); Riché Richardson, *Black Masculinity and the U.S. South: From Uncle Tom to Gangsta Rap* (2007); Anne Firor Scott, *Making the Invisible Woman Visible* (1984), *The Southern Lady: From Pedestal to Politics, 1830–1930* (1970); Stephanie J. Shaw, *What a Woman Ought to Be and to Do: Black Professional Women Workers during the Jim Crow Era* (1996); LeeAnn Whites, *Gender Matters: Civil War, Reconstruction, and the Making of the New South* (2005); Bertram Wyatt-Brown, *Southern Honor: Ethics and Behavior in the Old South* (1983); Patricia Yaeger, *Dirt and Desire: Reconstructing Southern Women's Writing, 1930–1990* (2000).

Abortion

Humans look away or deny the evidence of their actual behaviors, and southerners are no exception to this tendency. Southern behavior belies many dominant images of the region. Although the South is described as the belt buckle of the Bible Belt, that belt is often, in fact, unbuckled. Abortion rates in the South provide one indicator of the complexities of southern reproductive behavior.

Denial about sexual behavior is rampant in the South. For instance, one entire southern state, South Carolina, lived in official denial about the late senator J. Strom Thurmond. Even though many people whispered for decades that Thurmond had an African American daughter, it was only in 2003 that the "open secret" was revealed when Essie Mae Washington made her heritage officially public. What southerners proclaim they abide by and what sexual behaviors they actually exhibit are often two different things. Thurmond's story is one illustration.

Given the solid conservative hegemony in southern states currently, it is interesting to recall that many southern state legislatures were among the first to modernize or liberalize their contraceptive and abortion laws in the 1960s and early 1970s. Although abortion was not the central concern of medical professionals during these decades, according to Gene Burns, in *The Moral Decade*, "the argument that physicians should decide when abortion was appropriate was entirely convincing to a number of state legislatures, especially in the part of the country we would least expect, that is, the South." One puzzle is how the quiet, elite movement to liberalize state abortion laws between 1966 an 1973 remained particularly uncontroversial in the South. Women's rights language was not used when liberalizing the abortion laws before the *Roe v. Wade* Supreme Court decision in 1973. Rather than appeal to morality or rights, advocates relied on medical legitimation, permitting medical doctors to be the gatekeepers for legal abortion. Scholars argue that reform laws, especially when based on humanitarian or medical grounds, were particularly successful in the South during the 1966–73 reform period because no feminist or Catholic groups emerged to polarize the issue.

Abortion is a common experience for many women within the United States. Half of all pregnancies in America are unintended, and out of this half that are unintended, nearly half end in abortion (4 in 10). Approximately 33 percent of American women will have an abortion by the time they are 45. But abortion rates have recently declined in the United States. After the *Roe v. Wade* decision, abortion numbers continued to rise until 1990, when they reached an all-time high of 1,608,600 abortions in that year. Since 1991, abortion numbers have declined slowly, to 1.21 million in 2005.

Since the *Roe* decision, from 1991 to 2000, abortion rates in the southern states of Alabama, Arkansas, Georgia, Kentucky, Louisiana, Mississippi, South Carolina, Tennessee, Texas, and Virginia have followed the national declining trends, and North Carolina and Florida have shown increased abortion rates. The reasons for these differences are not understood, but one reason may be that women are seeking abortions in states where clinics are more accessible than in their own states.

There are many possible explanations as to why abortion rates have declined in the United States. Some experts maintain that contraception use is more widespread; others contend that women are becoming less fertile. And certainly some decline in abortion rates has been caused by state restrictions placed on abortions. Although the Supreme Court, in *Roe v. Wade*, ruled that a woman has a constitutionally guaranteed right to abort in the early stages of pregnancy, state restrictions have eroded a woman's right to choose. Conservative southern legislators have been particularly instrumental in limiting abortion since the *Roe* decision. In fact, abortion rights in the South seem to be in jeopardy.

As can be seen in Table 1, state funding for abortions in Alabama, Arkansas, Florida, Georgia, Kentucky, Louisiana, Mississippi, North Carolina, South Carolina, Tennessee, Texas, and Virginia is only given in cases of rape or incest or when the life of the mother is in danger. In nine southern states, women must receive state counseling and then fulfill a waiting period before having an abortion. Eleven states require that a minor must receive consent from a parent to have an abortion.

Besides state restrictions within the South, partial birth or late-term abortion laws are being created to further reduce the number of abortions. In *Stenburg v. Carhart* (2000), the Supreme Court struck down a Nebraska late-term abortion ban, ruling it was unconstitutional because it did not include any exceptions for the health of the mother. In addition, the Court ruled that the Nebraska ban was overly broad. Almost all of the southern states have enacted similar bans on late-term or partial birth abortions. Most southern policies on late-term abortion are unenforceable because they do not include exceptions for the health of the mother, as required by the *Stenberg* decision.

Although southern states have officially continued to allow women to have abortions, fewer and fewer clinics exist that can perform the procedure, as can be seen in Table 2. Access to legal abortion throughout the South is dramatically declining. Arkansas, Kentucky, and Louisiana have two abortion clinics each. South Carolina has three abortion clinics. Mississippi has two abortion clinics for the entire state, down from six in 1996 and four in 2000. North Carolina had

TABLE 1. *Abortion Laws in Southern States*

State	Parental Consent If Minor[a]	Mandatory Counseling and Waiting Period[b]	No Public Funding Unless Emergency[c]	Not Covered by Insurance[d]	Covered by Private Insurance in Emergency[e]	Public Employees Have Insurance in Emergency[f]	Ban on Partial Birth Abortion
Alabama	★	★	★				★
Arkansas	★	★	★				★
Florida	★		★				★
Georgia	★	★	★				★
Kentucky	★	★	★	★	★		★
Louisiana	★	★	★				★
Mississippi	★	★	★			★	★
North Carolina	★		★				
South Carolina	★	★	★				★
Tennessee	★	★	★				
Texas	★	★	★				
Virginia	★	★	★			★	★

Source: Alan Guttmacher Institute State Center, 2006

a. The parent of a minor must consent before an abortion is provided.

b. A woman must receive mandatory state-directed counseling and then fulfill a waiting period before an abortion is provided. Alabama, Georgia, Kentucky, Louisiana, Mississippi, Texas, and Virginia have a 24-hour waiting period. Arkansas and South Carolina have a one-hour waiting period.

c. Public funding is available for abortion only in cases of life endangerment, rape, or incest.

d. Abortion is not covered in insurance policies for public employees.

e. Abortion is covered in private insurance policies only in cases of life endangerment, unless an optional rider is purchased at an additional cost.

f. Abortion is covered in insurance policies for public employees only in cases of life endangerment, rape, incest, or fetal abnormality.

TABLE 2. *Number of Abortion Clinics in Southern States*

State	1996	2000	2004
Alabama	14	14	5
Arkansas	6	7	2
Florida	114	108	26
Georgia	41	26	5
Kentucky	8	3	2
Louisiana	15	13	2
Mississippi	6	4	2
North Carolina	59	55	5
South Carolina	14	10	3
Tennessee	20	16	4
Texas	64	65	22
Virginia	57	46	8

Source: Alan Guttmacher Institute State Center, 2005; National Abortion Federation, 2004.

55 abortion clinics in 2000, and now has five. The numbers of abortion clinics in 2004 continued to decrease.

This means that in the South a woman must often travel long distances to obtain an abortion, necessitating taking time off work and having the funds to travel. In addition to the expense of the procedure itself, mandatory counseling, 24-hour waiting periods, and other regulations increase the costs of legal abortion for providers and patients. Help from significant others or family members with transportation, accommodations, or other expenses may be problematic for a woman who might fear the consequences of seeking such assistance.

Given that the South is the poorest region in the country, lack of funds for southern women adds further hardships to already poor and beleaguered populations. Even before *Roe*, women with money and connections had access to safe abortions. Abortion restrictions in the South will have a huge social class impact, given the large numbers of southern women without money or safe options. Poor women, having fewer options, will inevitably have more children, thus increasing their level of poverty.

The future of legal abortion now rests with the Supreme Court, which currently has a majority of justices who were nominated by Republican presidents and confirmed by a Republican-dominated U.S. Senate. Southern voters were vital components of those Republican presidential and Senate victories, and, ironically, if legal abortion is further restricted by federal courts, poor southern citizens will pay a disproportionately higher cost in health and safety because of the region's poverty. Southern policies based on inaccurate assessments of what southern people need, rather than on their actual, documented, complex behaviors, overlook the need for affordable, accessible, and safe reproductive health care.

CHRISTINE M. SIXTA
LAURA R. WOLIVER
University of South Carolina

Gene Burns, *The Moral Veto: Framing Contraception, Abortion, and Cultural Pluralism in the United States* (2005); Barbara Hinkson Craig and David M. O'Brien, *Abortion and American Politics* (1993); Donald T. Critchlow, *Phyllis Schlafly and Grassroots Conservatism: A Woman's Crusade* (2005); Karen O'Connor, *No Neutral Ground? Abortion Politics in the Age of Absolutes* (1996); Jean Reith Schroedel, *Is the Fetus a Person? A Comparison of Policies across the Fifty States* (2000); Mary C. Segers and Timothy A. Byrnes, eds., *Abortion Politics in American States* (1995); Rickie Solinger, *Pregnancy and Power: A Short History of Reproductive Politics in America* (2005); Raymond Tatalovich, *The Politics of Abortion in the United States and Canada: A Comparative Study* (1997); Laura R. Woliver, *The Political Geographies of Pregnancy* (2003).

Agriculture, Women and

Since the beginning of recorded history, women in the South have played a significant role in agriculture. The native women of the Southeast grew the crops that, along with intensive gathering and the men's hunting, sustained their families. Early in the 17th century, observers from the Jamestown colony reported Powhatan women working in groups to cultivate small fields of corn and beans, which they relocated every three years. Further south, Creek women cultivated communal cornfields and kept family-sized vegetable patches.

The Cherokee maintained a fairly rigid division of labor wherein men helped clear fields, planted, and hunted. Women cultivated the food crops, mostly large quantities of corn and beans along with peas, squash, and potatoes. Elderly women watched for predators. After the Cherokee acquired livestock in the 18th century, women had to exert diligence to keep the animals from the unfenced fields. Agriculture was a significant part of Cherokee women's social and sexual identity, with commemorations such as the Green Corn Ceremony connecting corn to the community and women to rebirth and reconciliation. After Europeans came to Georgia, the Cherokee added peach orchards, hogs, and sweet potatoes and began to sell their products to the new arrivals. When Americans began to exert power over the Cherokee, they transferred responsibility for farming to men, stripping women of much of the source of their power and social standing.

From the early 17th century, women from Africa came to the South. As slaves, they grew rice and tobacco and later sugar cane and cotton for the world markets. By the 19th century, more than 90 percent of slave women in rural areas worked in the fields, and in some places the majority of field workers were women. Women's work varied by crop and location. In some places, overseers or owners made work assignments by ability, not sex, and they expected women to perform the same tasks in the same quantity as men. At other times, work was divided by sex, and men and women might work in segregated gangs. The cash crops of the slave South depended on the labor of women. Despite their long hours in the fields, some slave women also gardened for their own families, raising peas, beans, onions, cabbages, turnips, melons, and pumpkins to augment their meager rations.

In the antebellum South, the wives of yeomen worked outside, gardening, milking, and caring for chickens, providing for their families and participating in the cash economy only rarely. The poorer their families, the more likely the women were to do field work. Slave owning women were least likely to work outside, but as families moved from the Atlantic Seaboard westward, at least some wealthy women found themselves slaughtering hogs and performing other outside chores.

After emancipation, many black women remained with their former owners, with the Freedmen's Bureau aiding landowners in forcing freed slaves to sign labor contracts. Many labored much as they had before the Civil War, even continuing to work in gangs: plowing, cutting wheat, splitting cord wood, planting potatoes and rice, and, of course, performing every step involved with cotton and tobacco cultivation, which dominated the postbellum agricultural economy. Rather than being under the employ of one farmer for an extended period of time, some freed women hired out to do specific agricultural chores. Although whites interpreted such behavior as indolence, black women chose to work on schedules dictated by the growing season, working particularly at times of heaviest labor: planting, cultivating, harvesting.

With a shortage of cash and an abundance of workers, southern landowners turned to the crop-lien system to finance their farm enterprises. The failure of the government to reapportion acreage ensured that most former slaves would remain landless, and the instability of the southern economy forced poor white farmers into dependence. As more southern farmers, both black and white, became sharecroppers or tenant farmers, they moved away from subsistence farming to growing staple crops. Poor white women began to spend less time on domestic production and more in the fields. The decline in food crops made feeding their families more and more difficult. The forced reliance of their men on the landowners for everything from coffee to doctors' services affected the power structure in many farm families. Most workers received a family wage, according to which they were paid as a unit rather than as individuals. Men usually controlled the family wage, and women had few funds to call their own.

Protests over the abuses of the crop-lien system began shortly after the close of the Civil War, and women became deeply involved with the Grange and the Southern Farmers' Alliance and with Populist and other cooperative movements. One of the reforms that focused on women aimed to increase their production of food products. By World War I, the Cooperative Extension Service of the U.S. Department of Agriculture was sending female home demonstration agents to work with farm women on such topics as canning and other types of food preservation. Women who grew enough food to feed their families saved precious cash for other purposes. As transportation improved, those who grew more than their families could eat and lived near an urban area could sell their eggs, butter, vegetables, and dressed poultry to urban women. Selling farm-raised goods brought needed money into perpetually cash-poor farm families.

The Depression that gripped southern agriculture in the 1920s and 1930s hurt farm families, and women worked harder than ever for little return. Mechanization pushed sharecroppers and tenant farmers off the land, as owners could farm more land with fewer hands. Farm wives became town wives, with dramatically altered situations, although many continued keeping chickens, gardens, and even cows at their homes in town. For those who stayed on the farm, New Deal reforms such as the Rural Electrification Administration and crop subsidies eased difficult living situations. World War II brought high commodity prices and opportunities for off-farm employment for women.

After the end of World War II, farm families changed dramatically. Many people who had moved to town for wartime jobs elected to remain in urbanized areas. Those who continued to live in rural areas could commute into town for a waged job and return to the farm at night. Expensive equipment required farmers to "get big" or get out, and many left agriculture. The minority of women who remained on the farm changed their work significantly. Some took an increasing role in bookkeeping and other farm management tasks. Many accepted off-farm employment, the proceeds of which subsidized the farming operation. Other women began performing more of the farm work as men took

Two children with a cantaloupe, Mississippi Delta, 1936
(Marion Post Wolcott, photographer, Library of Congress [LC-USF-34-9610C], Washington, D.C.)

off-farm employment and as technology began to substitute for physical labor. Farming remained challenging, however, and women actively participated in the farm protest movements of the 1980s. By the early 21st century, the number of women farming on their own was rising. Women have increasingly moved into niche and specialty farming such as organic vegetable production and into specialty livestock production such as goats, llamas, and alpacas. They continue to be an integral part of agriculture in the South, their roles changing as farming itself changes.

REBECCA SHARPLESS
Texas Christian University

Joan E. Cashin, *A Family Venture: Men and Women on the Southern Frontier* (1991); Laura F. Edwards, *Scarlett Doesn't Live Here Anymore: Southern Women in the Civil War Era* (2000); Margaret Jarman Hagood, *Mothers of the South: Portraiture of the White Tenant Farm Woman* (1939); Lu Ann Jones, *Mama Learned Us to Work: Farm*

Women in the New South (2002); Stephanie McCurry, *Masters of Small Worlds: Yeo-man Households, Gender Relations, and the Political Culture of the Antebellum South Carolina Low Country* (1995); Theda Perdue, *Cherokee Women: Gender and Culture Change, 1700–1835* (1998); Rebecca Sharpless, *Fertile Ground, Narrow Choices: Women on Texas Cotton Farms, 1900–1940* (1999); Melissa Walker, *All We Knew Was to Farm: Rural Women in the Upcountry South, 1919–1941* (2000); Melissa Walker and Rebecca Sharpless, eds., *Work, Family, and Faith: Rural Southern Women in the Twentieth Century* (2006); Marli F. Weiner, *Mistresses and Slaves: Plantation Women in South Carolina, 1830–80* (1998); Betty Wood, *Women's Work, Men's Work: The Informal Slave Economies of Lowcountry Georgia* (1995).

Antimiscegenation Laws

Antimiscegenation laws were statutes that banned interracial marriage and intimate relationships between whites and certain ethnic groups, particularly African Americans. The term derives from two Latin terms, *miscere*, "to mix," and *genus*, "race," and was created by Democrats opposed to Abraham Lincoln's reelection. Although the term did not appear until the 1860s, the laws that it referenced had their origins in colonial times. In 1662, Virginia became the first colony to authorize a special penalty for interracial fornication. Two years later, Maryland became the first colony to outlaw interracial marriage. In both cases, the colonial assemblies prohibited whites and people of African ancestry from having the proscribed relationships. By the end of the colonial period, 8 of the 13 colonies had similar regulations. On the eve of the Civil War, the number of states with antimiscegenation laws had grown to 21.

Prior to the Civil War, antimiscegenation laws served two purposes. First, they ensured the spread of slavery. By interdicting interracial relationships, local governments ensured that the children of such unions had no legal connection to their white fathers and, therefore, no right to freedom. These biracial children would remain slaves. Second, the edicts gave white men a measure of control of the actions of white women. Although, technically, both white men and white women could be punished for intimate relationships across the color line, slave ownership served to hide such relationships and shield white men from enforcement. Fewer white women owned slaves, making their interracial liaisons more conspicuous and punishable.

Reconstruction brought the first legal challenges to antimiscegenation laws. The Fourteenth Amendment, with its federal protections of citizens, caused some interracial couples to challenge the rights of states to prohibit their relationships. Yet the Alabama Supreme Court, in the case of *Burns v. State* (1872), was the only state high court to declare antimiscegenation laws unconstitutional. In 1881 the U.S. Supreme Court upheld the compatibility of antimiscegenation laws with the Fourteenth Amendment in the case of *Pace v. Alabama*.

Antimiscegenation laws survived the Reconstruction experiment and became part of the foundation for Jim Crow laws. With slavery over, the laws served as vehicles to reinforce the inferior status of blacks and other ethnic groups. State officials usually enforced the statutes in such a way as to give white men the right to use the bodies of black women sexually with impunity as long as white men did not formalize the relationships. However, authorities tended to more closely regulate and punish black male–white female couples. Furthermore, the edicts continued circumscribing the rights of biracial children in inheritance cases. According to W. E. B. Du Bois, one of the preeminent black scholars of the 20th century, antimiscegenation laws were "wicked devices designed to make the seduction of black women easier," and they denigrated African Americans by suggesting that "black blood was a physical taint."

The civil rights movement brought international attention to the poor treatment of African Americans and the laws that supported the caste system. Many segregation measures came under attack, antimiscegenation laws among them. After being convicted of running afoul of the Virginia statute, Mildred and Richard Loving, an interracial couple, took their case to the Supreme Court. In *Loving v. Virginia* (1967), the High Court ruled that antimiscegenation laws violated the Fourteenth Amendment's equal protection clause and were, therefore, unconstitutional.

CHARLES ROBINSON
University of Arkansas

Martha Hodes, *White Women, Black Men: Illicit Love in the Nineteenth Century South* (1997); James H. Johnson, *Race Relations in Virginia and Miscegenation in the South* (1970); Rachel F. Moran, *Interracial Intimacy: The Regulation of Race and Romance* (2001); Charles F. Robinson II, *Dangerous Liaisons: Sex and Love in the Segregated South* (2003); Peter Wallenstein, *Tell the Court I Love My Wife: Race, Marriage, and Law* (2002).

Appalachian Men and Women

The South has long been seen as the most patriarchal region of the United States, and southern Appalachia is no exception. In 1913 southern Appalachian observer Horace Kephart described the mountain household as one in which "the man of the house is lord and master." Yet gender roles in any society are permeable and shifting, and the behavior of real men and women frequently violates prevailing gender ideology. Household power relations and the gender division of labor in southern Appalachia often proved dynamic, particularly as the region's economy and culture were transformed by industrialization, beginning in the last quarter of the 19th century.

In the early days of settlement, a few southern Appalachian citizens (most of whom were white) lived in the region's towns and cities. Middle-class town men earned their livings as merchants, professionals, and government officials, and their wives most often engaged in the voluntary and household work that occupied middle-class women in towns all over America. Their working-class neighbors were employed as artisans, laborers, and domestics. But most whites and almost all black Appalachians resided in the region's mountains and rural valleys, where they secured the family's economic well-being through a combination of subsistence agricultural activities, small-scale lumbering, farming for the marketplace, artisanal work, hunting, and trapping. The majority of southern Appalachian farmers owned the land they worked, giving them considerable control over their economic choices. Even tenants were likely to exercise a fair amount of economic autonomy.

Rural men, women, and children shared the labor that provided for families, dividing their tasks by gender. Mountain people assumed that heavy labor such as field clearing, cutting wood, plowing, and construction were appropriate tasks for men and that food preparation and preservation, sewing, nursing, and child care were "naturally" within the female realm. Both sexes shared the work of planting, cultivating, and harvesting crops and caring for livestock. In actual practice, however, the type of work that a woman did depended on her class status. Elite and middle-class women were less likely to do field work or tend cows and chickens than their less prosperous sisters. Poorer mountain women—especially those few who headed households—often performed traditional "men's work," at least occasionally. Oral history accounts and memoirs are filled with anecdotes about women who hunted, chopped firewood, split fence rails, and even broke new ground.

Very few women lived outside the context of a nuclear or extended family. Appalachian missionary John C. Campbell observed that marriage provided the only viable means of support for most mountain women. Women found few off-farm jobs. The better educated—often migrants from outside the region or the daughters of town people—worked as teachers. Others ran mercantile businesses of one kind or another. Yet unless she had access to land, difficult to do when families passed land down to sons and women had few ways to earn enough money to purchase acreage, a single woman could not support herself by selling garden and livestock products. As a result, most mountain women found marriage more appealing than the prospect of life as a dependent spinster in a parent's or sibling's household.

In this world, men associated independence with control over their own decision making and with the power to control the labor of their dependents. In the words of historian Robert S. Weise, southern mountain households "represented a fundamental site for the exercise of power." The laws of most southern states awarded men considerable control over household business affairs and over the labor of wives and children. Yet the way men exercised this power varied from household to household. As in all households, the nature of the relationship between husband and wife and the personalities of the individuals determined the degree to which men exercised authoritarian control over family members. Often men and women made decisions jointly, and women frequently challenged men's power—sometimes using kin networks to circumvent the control of husbands.

In the last quarter of the 19th century, lumber and mining companies began to purchase resource rights and land in the southern Appalachians. Railroads laid miles of track to remove the timber and coal these companies extracted. As a result, men and women found their gender roles slowly but surely transformed. Mountain men often took jobs with the railroads, lumber companies, and mines, sometimes on a seasonal basis. At first many Appalachian men combined their wage work with farming. They seized on this wage work as a means of maintaining their independence, a task that was becoming more difficult as rising land prices drove up property values and increased the pressure to sell farms to the big companies. Cash wages also enabled mountain people to participate in the consumer economy to a greater extent than ever before. Men with some education found new and lucrative opportunities working for the administrative arms of the corporations, but many Appalachian men gradually lost their independence as they sold (or were cheated out of) their land and became dependent on their jobs as miners, timber cutters, and railroad workers.

The new extractive industries also created new opportunities for southern Appalachia's women. Some, particularly those who lived in or near lumber camps and mining towns, made extra money selling livestock products to other workers or taking in laundry. Appalachia's small population of black women (whose numbers grew as the mines brought in large numbers of black workers) were most likely to hold domestic jobs, but white women, too, used domestic work to supplement family incomes. A few enterprising women started boardinghouses and restaurants to serve the mining and logging communities. Women whose families moved to mining towns and permanent lumber communities also persisted with their subsistence activities, growing gardens and keeping livestock near their company-owned houses. The corporations often built schools, as did the northern social workers and missionaries who came to the region in droves at the turn of the century. In addition to elementary and high schools, Alice Lloyd College in Kentucky, Lees-McRae College in North Carolina, and a dozen similar institutions provided higher educational opportunities for mountain young people. Appalachian women proved particularly likely to seize the chance to obtain a college education, and they often parlayed this education into jobs as teachers and nurses.

During the first half of the 20th century, many areas of southern Appalachia became tourist attractions. Railroads and roads provided city folk from inside and outside the South with access to cool mountain air and spectacular scenery. The development of national and state parks attracted visitors, as did privately owned hotels and resorts. Like the lumber and mining companies, tourism created new jobs and challenged old assumptions about the appropriate gender division of labor. Mountain men and women developed entrepreneurial ventures that catered to tourists. Hotels, filling stations, and restaurants sprang up in picturesque mountain valleys and around mineral springs in places like Flat Rock and Asheville, N.C., Gatlinburg, Tenn., and the mountains of north Georgia. Mountaineers of both sexes participated in the revival of Appalachian handicrafts, producing traditional weavings and wood carvings for the tourist market. But tourism and handicraft production provided relatively meager incomes, particularly for women, who were often confined to the lowest-paying tourism jobs. The demand for land for tourist development also drove up local land prices, pushing the most marginal landowners off the land.

Wage labor did not always provide families with economic security. Men had often taken off-farm jobs in a calculated effort to maintain household independence and male authority. As timber stands were depleted, however, the lumber companies moved on, forcing families to move in search of work or eke out a living on environmentally damaged land. The fortunes of coal companies fluctuated with the demand for coal, resulting in a decades-long boom-bust cycle. When miners attempted to unionize in order to improve their wages and working conditions, companies evicted families from company housing and hired private mine guards to combat union activities. Many Appalachian women found that an increasing amount of the burden for the family's economic well-being was falling on their shoulders. In the years before and after World War II, millions of southern Appalachia's citizens left the region for midwestern cities in search of work.

New industries entered the region in the last half of the 20th century, creating new jobs in manufacturing and the service sector for men and women.

Federal and state funds also poured into economic development and educational activities. At the same time, mechanization enabled mines to reduce their workforces dramatically. Even as towns and cities grew and prospered in some areas of southern Appalachia—creating new opportunities for workers of both sexes—unemployment and poverty continued to plague other areas.

Some women seized on their increased earning power to claim new independence and authority in the household—a trend reinforced in the late 20th century by economic and legal changes in the status of women nationally. Nonetheless, new opportunities outside the home did not always translate into additional female authority within the household. Traumatized by the loss of economic independence, men sometimes redoubled their efforts to control wives and children, resulting in household strife and a rising divorce rate. In the early the 21st century, gender roles in southern Appalachia remain in a state of flux.

MELISSA WALKER
Converse College

Chad Berry, *Southern Migrants, Northern Exiles* (2000); John C. Campbell, *The Southern Highlander and His Homeland* (1921); David A. Corbin, *Life, Work, and Rebellion in the Coal Fields: The Southern West Virginia Mines, 1880-1922* (1981); Ronald Eller Jr., *Miners, Millhands, and Mountaineers: Industrialization in the Appalachian South, 1880-1930* (1982); Janet W. Greene, *West Virginia History*, vol. 49 (1990); Barbara J. Howe, in *Neither Lady nor Slave: Working Women in the Old South*, ed. Susanna Delfino and Michele Gillespie (2002); Horace Kephart, *Our Southern Highlanders: A Narrative of Adventure in the Southern Appalachians and a Study of Life among the Mountaineers* (1913); Mary Beth Pudup, *West Virginia History*, vol. 49 (1990); Melissa Walker, *All We Knew Was to Farm: Rural Women in the Upcountry South, 1919-1941* (2000); Robert S. Weise, *Grasping at Independence: Debt, Male Authority, and Mineral Rights in Appalachian Kentucky* (2001); Stephen Paul Whitaker, *Journal of Appalachian Studies* (2000).

Autobiography

With a seminal essay by Georges Gusdorf in 1956, scholarly commentators began to explore autobiography as a literary genre, calling attention to the autobiographer's need to understand and textualize a self in the process of its becoming, a need that seemed central to the development of major American texts by Benjamin Franklin, Henry David Thoreau, Mark Twain, Henry Adams, and others. Early commentators agreed that the inner life cannot be easily or directly rendered, that there is no single autobiographical style or form, and that the larger significance of any piece of self-writing lies beyond those things that can be proven through a verification of facts. Paul de Man went one step further and asked if perhaps autobiography itself does not "produce and determine the life." Alfred Kazin said, simply, that autobiography "is what a gifted writer makes of it."

Despite its openness in form, the genre was, with few exceptions, defined as primarily the preserve of men. Women's life stories, often focusing on private rather than public experience, were rarely subjected to sustained analysis. This pattern changed in the mid-1970s when feminism found a foothold in the nation's universities and feminist critics began to explore the contrasting ways in which women and men have defined themselves. Critics such as Patricia Meyer Spacks and, later, Sidonie Smith called attention to the woman autobiographer's double bind—her need to authenticate a self while reconciling self-assertion with the cultural expectation that she remain silent. Some feminist assumptions about the form of women's autobiography have been challenged, such as the notion that women favor nonlinear self-narratives while defining themselves in relation to an "other," but few would challenge the feminist argument that autobiographies cannot be written—nor should they be written about—without an awareness of gender as a major component in self-revelation.

In the South the processes of gender have played out most often to the benefit of the southern white male. Even such a regional enthusiast as Mary Chesnut, in her massive diary of the Civil War, did not whitewash the double standard determining the manner in which southern white men might satisfy their sexual needs. Chesnut's attention to the role of gender would become more pronounced in the 20th century as writers such as Katherine Du Pre Lumpkin, with *The Making of a Southerner* (1946), and Lillian Smith, with *Killers of the Dream* (1949), turned from diaries and journals to more forceful autobiographical critiques of southern culture.

Perhaps no southerner has given more attention to the interplay of gender and autobiography than Lillian Smith, whose lectures and notes on the subject prefigure more recent feminist considerations. Arguing that autobiography necessitates "a power struggle" in which "would-be selves" compete for dominance in a process complicated by both the inadequacies of language and the engendered restrictions on one's self-expression, Smith underscored women's fear of challenging and ultimately changing male psychology, and she empathized with their decision to maintain silence in the face of a public ideal that seemingly anchored the autobiographical project. Smith admitted that *Killers of the Dream* did not focus enough on her own self-development to qualify as formal autobiography—only in letters did she provide a more complete account of her sexuality and her most intimate relationships. Smith, therefore, did not exempt herself in concluding that women's evasions had prevented them from producing autobiographies "that deserve the word 'great.'"

Had she lived beyond the mid-1960s Smith might have revised this assessment. In 1969, playwright Lillian Hellman published *An Unfinished Woman*, the first of four memoirs that demonstrated many of the possibilities of self-writing. Through portraits of friends, acquaintances, and enemies, Hellman delineated what she perceived to be the larger meanings of both her intimate and her public experiences. A woman who was candid about her sexual life and who represented a clear departure from the submissive southern model, Hellman used the term "unfinished" to imply that she had never attended a finishing school in the genteel southern tradition and to further suggest that neither she nor anyone else could provide a fully coherent or finalized account of her life. Hellman presented herself as a woman open to the mutability of experience—the title of her final memoir is *Maybe* (1982). Hellman's self-writing was widely praised but also criticized for indulging in too much invention, too much falsification. Indeed, Hellman presented one of the key perils of autobiography—the lack of a policing force to verify or contest the truth of one's experience. As the Irish writer Elizabeth Bowen remarked, the autobiographer "addresses the potential biographer in us all."

Bowen's assertion is especially pertinent to an understanding of autobiography and gender. Eudora Welty's *One Writer's Beginnings* is a case in point. Welty's 1984 memoir, in which she traced the sources of her fiction, became a best seller and received unusually appreciative notices—with one very important exception. Feminist critic Carolyn Heilbrun could not accept "the bittersweet quality" of Welty's memoir and even claimed that the Mississippi author had "camouflaged herself" and that "to have written a truthful autobiography would have defied every one of her instincts for loyalty and privacy." For Heilbrun, a truthful autobiography would have to acknowledge a woman's anger at being the inevitable victim of patriarchy. Such an assessment, however, misses the larger way in which Welty's memoir speaks to engendered assumptions about women's creativity. Welty does not define herself as a wife, a mother, or a martyr to women's anger but as an artist whose inner life merits the reading public's attention. Perhaps anticipating a response such as Heilbrun's, Welty rejects the assumption that her "sheltered" southern upbringing has made her anything other than a "daring" writer of fiction and, by extension, of her own life.

The anger that is missing from *One Writer's Beginnings* is everywhere apparent in Georgia writer Rosemary Daniell's *Fatal Flowers: On Sin, Sex, and*

Suicide in the Deep South (1980). A poet who uses self-writing as therapy (and who through her Zona Rosa workshops has taught others to do the same), Daniell explores her upbringing in a region that expected her to remain a "girl-woman"—ladylike yet coy and manipulative, passionate and yet frigid, a woman who would be defined by the man she married. Although she married three times (once to a northerner) and produced one son and two daughters, Daniell could never live up to the ideal embraced by her mother, a woman who had also wanted to become a writer and yet who omitted the "I's" from her letters because she found them too self-assertive. Writing in order to understand her own sexual compulsions and what she had for years envisioned as her embedded penis, Daniell provides an unrelentingly explicit exposé of southern codes and restrictions that are reinforced through food, clothes, manners, and rituals. Daniell's self-exploration—her willingness to become "a kamikaze pilot of southern feminine experience"—convinces her that "the condition of being female" is in fact the condition of being "female and southern" and that she, her mother, her grandmothers, her sister, and her daughters "were trapped in a morass of southern moss, Bible Belt guilt, and the pressures of a patriarchy stronger than in any other part of the country." By the end of her narrative, Daniell embraces her bisexuality, which enables her to understand and forgive her mother's suicide, and she affirms her love-hate relationship with southern white men and the region that produces them.

Although denounced by readers who could not accept her sometimes lacerating probe, *Fatal Flowers* received the 1999 Palimpsest Prize as the most-requested out-of-print book and has achieved something close to a cult following. Daniell did not, however, initiate a trend of confessional autobiography with the goal of deconstructing southern gender norms, a subgenre such as the one illuminated by Fred Hobson in *But Now I See: The White Southern Racial Conversion Narrative* (1999). White southerners are routinely expected to find their way through to the other side of racism and white supremacy, but the open and unapologetic exploration of gender and sexuality still carries risks, and these risks are not confined to women. Southern playwright Tennessee Williams discovered as much through the generally hostile reaction to his 1975 *Memoirs*, in which he treats, without evasion, his alcoholism, his ongoing depression, and his homosexuality.

The official conservative ideologies of the South do not always speak to the reality of southern lives. The popularity of authors such as lesbian novelist Dorothy Allison—writers who just decades ago might not have found publishers—suggests a willingness to hear life stories that have been silenced in the past, such as the one Allison provides in *Two or Three Things I Know for Sure*

(1995), a memoir that confronts engendered spousal and child abuse through the lens of its author's childhood stigmatization as southern "white trash." The popularity of John Berendt's nonfictional *Midnight in the Garden of Good and Evil* (1994) ensured that readers would also turn to *Hiding My Candy* (1996), the autobiography by one of Berendt's most colorful informants, Savannah drag performer Lady Chablis. This carefully crafted memoir suggests that the gender norms that often reduce southern white women to caricature may also function as a means of empowerment for those who self-identify as transgendered.

Evelyn Scott, Ellen Glasgow, Zora Neale Hurston, Pauli Murray, Maya Angelou, Shirley Abbott, Florence King, Mab Segrest, bell hooks, Elizabeth Spencer, and Mary Lee Settle, among many others, have addressed gender issues in their autobiographies and memoirs, each providing evidence for Elizabeth Fox-Genovese's contention that gender is socially and historically constructed by the determining forces of race, class, and region. For all its changes, the South remains a place where high school males repeat grades in order to play football, where high school and college females compete in beauty pageants that have not lost their popularity, and where drag shows flourish in both large and small cities. Gender is not likely to disappear as a key component in the discourse of southern autobiography.

WILL BRANTLEY
Middle Tennessee State University

Elizabeth Bowen, *Saturday Review of Literature* (17 March 1951); Will Brantley, *Feminine Sense in Southern Memoir: Smith, Glasgow, Welty, Hellman, Porter, and Hurston* (1993); Paul de Man, *Modern Language Notes* 94 (1979); Elizabeth Fox-Genovese, in *Located Lives: Place and Idea in Southern Autobiography*, ed. J. Bill Berry (1990); Georges Gusdorf, in *Autobiography: Essays Theoretical and Critical*, ed. James Olney (1980); Carolyn G. Heilbrun, *Writing a Woman's Life* (1988); Alfred Kazin, *Michigan Quarterly Review* 3 (1964); Lillian Smith, *The Winner Names the Age: A Collection of Writings by Lillian Smith*, ed. Michelle Cliff (1978); Sidonie Smith, *A Poetics of Women's Autobiography: Marginality and the Fictions of Self-Representation* (1987); Patricia Meyer Spacks, *Hudson Review* 30 (1977), *Yale Review* 63 (1973); Elizabeth Spencer, *Landscapes of the Heart* (1998).

Beauty, Cult of

"The modern Southern belle has, of course, long been the Pageant ideal," writes Frank Deford of the Miss America contest, "so that—even in those years when a Southerner does not win—the likely winner is still probably patterned after that type." The "fundamental Southern-belle personality" that has become the nation's beauty ideal is "vivacious, sparkle-eyed, full of fun, capable of laughing at herself, and incapable of speaking either (a) briefly, or (b) without using the hands to illustrate all points." She has poise and personality beneath the outward physical attractiveness.

Beauty pageants such as the Miss America competition suggest the influence of southern ideas in shaping national ideals of beauty. Within the specifically southern context, beauty pageants are part of a cult of beauty, with certain definite ideas on what beauty is and why it is significant to be beautiful. The South's cult of beauty reflects southern attitudes on race, social class, and especially gender and sexuality, and these attitudes have changed significantly over time.

Beauty has long been related in the South to color. English colonists in North America brought European concepts of beauty, which became a factor justifying the enslavement of black Africans. Historian Winthrop D. Jordan has noted that "the English discovery of black Africa came at a time when the accepted standard of ideal beauty was a fair complexion of rose and white. Negroes not only failed to fit this ideal but seemed the very picture of perverse negation." Judged on this standard, blacks were seen as "pronouncedly less beautiful than whites." In his age, Thomas Jefferson asked whether skin color is not "the foundation of a greater or less share of beauty in the two races." He insisted that "the fine mixtures of red and white" were "preferable to that eternal monotony" of black skin. Jefferson's concept of beauty included "flowing hair" and an "elegant symmetry of form," both of which he attributed to whites more than to other races. "The circumstance of superior beauty," he wrote, "is thought worthy of attention in the propagation of our horses, dogs, and other domestic animals; why not in that of man?" The idea of beauty was associated, for southern whites, with ideas of sexuality and morality. Southern whites used the dark skin color of slaves as an outward indicator of the immorality of blacks, attributing to them impurities, lasciviousness, and evil.

The myth of the Old South included a prominent role for the beautiful white lady. Indeed, as W. J. Cash noted in *The Mind of the South* (1941), she became identified "with the very notion of the South itself." Physical beauty was a part of the definition of southern womanhood. The 19th-century conception of woman's appearance emphasized her fragility, purity, and spirituality, rather than her physical nature. The southern lady, according to Anne Firor Scott, was to be "timid and modest, beautiful and graceful." Anne Goodwyn Jones has pointed out that white women in the Old South "became not only the perfect embodiments of beauty" but also "the appropriate vehicles for the expression of beauty in language." Beauty itself, like the lovely woman who best represented that quality, "was fragile and ethereal, or sensuous and pleasurable, but it was finally irrelevant to the serious business of life." Beauty was a culturally admired trait, but it was also a limiting one for women.

The identification of whiteness and women with beauty survived into the 20th century. Cash wrote that the southern woman was "the South's Palladium," "the shield-bearing Athena gleaming whitely in the clouds," "the lily-pure maid of Astolat." Carl Carmer wrote in *Stars Fell on Alabama* (1934) of a University of Alabama fraternity dance that included a toast: "To Woman, lovely woman of the Southland, as pure and chaste as this sparkling water, as cold as this gleaming ice, we lift this cup, and we pledge our hearts and our lives to the protection of her virtue and chastity."

The southern ideal of the beautiful woman has evolved, though. The Scarlett O'Hara type, who is associated with the Old South, is beautiful but somewhat artificial. Sexuality is much more openly associated with beautiful women in the modern South. Victoria O'Donnell's typology of images of southern women in film points out that one dominant type is the "Sexual Woman": "She is beautiful, voluptuous, only partially clothed, and openly erotic. She is able to give sexual fulfillment, but she does so in order to impart strength to her man." Sometimes the beautiful southern woman becomes the "Rich, Spoiled Woman," who has "beauty, money, men, and friends" but is "spoiled and wild." Another film image of the modern southern woman portrays her as "earthier, gaudier" than women of the past, embodying open "carnal qualities, for she has lost her purity and chastity and is glad of it." The "Unfulfilled Sexual Woman" wants to be sexually appealing, but she is frustrated because "she has little to offer in terms of physical beauty." For all of these social types in the southern imagination, beauty remains an important ingredient of culturally determined happiness, which now includes sexual satisfaction.

Changing attitudes toward the sun have affected the southern ideal of beauty. In western civilization, white, pallid skin was traditionally a sign of upper-class status, and such makeup as face powder and rouge highlighted whiteness. With industrialization, upper-class Europeans and white Americans, including eventually southerners, developed an interest in outdoor life. Since the laboring class now worked indoors, the upper class sought suntans and outdoor recreation as an indicator of social-class status. "The lithe, sun-tanned, tennis-playing, outdoor woman," writes Marvin Harris, "became a respectable alternative to the cloistered, snow-and-alabaster ideal of the old regimes." Soon the middle class adopted this ideal of a physically healthy, athletic, suntanned woman.

This cultural change had special significance in the South, where the sun is intensely felt and "whiteness" has its most deeply rooted racial-cultural meaning. The sun has long helped determine southern social status—rednecks were laborers, and their women were said to be less beautiful because they were less pallidly white than the plantation wife. By the 1920s the South, according to historians Francis Butler Simkins and Charles Roland, had "learned to regard its very hot and very bright sun as a beneficent friend instead of as a cruel tyrant." Sunbonnets and long, tight-fitting clothes were abandoned for lighter garments, and the sun was soon regarded as a source of health. Sunbathing gradually became common, and "the acme of Southern comeliness became blue eyes, blond hair, and brown skin."

Black attitudes toward beauty have gone through their own changes. Illustrations of African Americans up to the 1880s show a predominance of natural hair and little cosmetic beautification of the face. By the turn of the 20th century, though, black males were beginning to use hot combs to straighten hair, while black women used oils and pomades. Evidence suggests that many blacks internalized white ideals of beauty. They used cosmetics to lighten the skin color and hair straighteners to "conk" the hair in attempting to approach the white ideal. This probably reached a peak during the 1940s. Beauty parlors became important institutions of the black community, and cosmetic manufacturers were among the wealthiest of black Americans.

Skin color has been a symbol of class status within the black community. John Dollard noted in *Caste and Class in a Southern Town*, his 1937 study of Indianola, Miss., that "consciousness of color and accurate discrimination between shades is a well-developed caste mark in Southerntown; whites, of course, are not nearly so skilful [*sic*] in distinguishing and naming various shades." Toni Morrison's *The Bluest Eye* (1970) portrays the tragic results of a black family's self-hatred because of a "white skin" ideal of beauty. Lawrence Levine cautions, however, against overemphasizing the effect of a cultural ideal of white beauty on blacks. For many blacks, a light skin did not suggest social status within the black community but rather a corruption of the race. If some black people have admired white skin, others have viewed black skin as natural, and many cosmetics have existed not to cloak that color but to highlight it. Moreover, when color preference has been seen in black cultural expressions such as blues lyrics, it has most often been brown, rather than either black or white-yellow. Paul Oliver's study of blues lyrics, *Blues Fell This Morning: The Meaning of the Blues* (1960), found that rural folk expressed an ideal of beauty somewhat different from the urban black-and-white ideal of "the streamlined woman." Bluesmen admired the "big, fat woman with the meat shaking on her bone." They also celebrated certain physical features, such as teeth that "shine like pearls" as a natural and attractive contrast with dark skin.

The civil rights movement of the 1950s and 1960s surely strengthened pride in a black ideal of beauty. "Black Is Beautiful" reflected a new appreciation of dark skin specifically, as well as a more general pride in black culture. Magazines such as *Beauty Trade* and *Essence* are now published by blacks outside of the South, but their ideas influence the southern beauty industry and black ideals of beauty. Black beauty pageants have become a fixture on black campuses and in black communities across the South.

The beauty pageant is the ritual event that best displays modern national and regional attitudes about beauty. Predecessors of American beauty pageants were European festivals that crowned queens. European May Day activities have included the selection of beautiful women as symbols of fertility. In the colonial era, this custom took root more in the South than among the Puritans. Schools for young southern white women throughout the 19th century included contests for the choosing of attractive, popular queens. Southern romanticism expressed itself in antebellum tournaments, re-creating medieval pageants, and these festive occasions included queens selected for their beauty. Postbellum festivals also included these contests. The Mardi Gras festival chose its first queen in 1871, despite the protest of some moralists who objected to any public display of women. These May Day, tournament, and festival queens were upper-class figures, and these contests reinforced, as historian Lois Banner has written, "the centrality of physical beauty in women's lives and made of beauty a matter of competition and elitism and not of democratic cooperation among women."

Commercial beauty pageants appeared first in the late 19th century. P. T. Barnum sponsored a female beauty pageant in 1854, but it involved only the display of daguerreotypes of women, with observers voting on winners. Carnivals in the South, often attached to agricultural fairs, helped pave the way for beauty contests displaying beautiful women in native costumes from around the world. The Atlanta International Cotton Exposition of 1895 had a beauty show on its midway, and this part of the exposition was described as "the Mecca of the show." By 1900 chambers of commerce and fraternal groups in the South were sponsoring carnival beauty shows at fairs, but it was still not considered appropriate for middle-class women to be on display in competitive contests. The first true competitive beauty contest was the Miss United States contest at Rehoboth Beach, Del., in 1880, but the South's beach resorts did not follow suit generally until after the turn of the century.

The Miss America pageant began in 1921, but the judges did not select a southerner until Texan Jo-Carrol Dennison was chosen in 1942. With the Americanization of the South — and the southernization of the United States —

Leigh Lucas, 1992 Mississippi Miss
Hospitality (1993 University of
Mississippi Yearbook, Vol. 99)

in recent decades, southerners have become identified with love of beauty pageants. The 17 September 1984 issue of *Newsweek* magazine estimated that 750,000 beauty contests were held each year at that time in the United States, ranging from pageants for school homecoming queens, to county fair and state fair queens, to festival representatives to the Miss America contest. "The phenomenon is strongly regional," said *Newsweek*. "The 'Pageant belt' stretches from Texas (where there are men who will date only titleholders) throughout the South, overlapping the Bible belt with odd precision."

Beauty pageants in the South are part of a regional cult of beauty. Young southern white women have long been encouraged in the feminine arts, and aspects of beauty have been taught in female academies, charm schools, and modern modeling salons. Cosmetologists, beauticians, and hairdressers are well-known figures in small and large southern towns, where concern for "looks" is endemic. Eudora Welty reproduced the ambience and conversational sound of the southern beauty parlor in her short story "Petrified Man."

Cosmetics were slow to take root in the poor rural South of the early 20th century. Even today, some Pentecostal-Holiness groups stress an ascetic ideal of outward plainness and inner beauty. Nevertheless, most women in small southern towns and cities have long accepted national views on cosmetics. Mary Kay Ash, founder of the successful Mary Kay Cosmetics, is from Texas; a key figure in the black cosmetics industry in this century, Madame C. J. Walker, came from Louisiana. Changes in contemporary southern religion's attitudes toward beauty are evinced by Tammy Faye Bakker, the television celebrity formerly on the Pentecostal-oriented show the PTL Club. Bakker flaunted her makeup by using a great deal of it. She even launched her own line of cosmetics.

Beauty pageants are central to small-town, middle-class life in the South and the nation. In 1970, for example, only 8 of 50 contestants in the Miss America pageant were from the nation's 25 largest cities. Few large urban areas sponsor contests, and even statewide beauty pageants tend to take place in smaller cities and towns. James Rucker, a former executive director of the Miss Mississippi contest, notes that whereas big-city northern girls enter the contest for the scholarship money or a chance at show-business success, "in Mississippi, it's tradition for the best girls to come out for the Pageant. In Mississippi, the best girls just want to be Miss America."

Beauty contests are community events in towns and small cities. The Universal/Southern Charm children's beauty pageant illustrates the pageant appeal. Arkansan Darlene Burgess founded Southern Charm in 1980 to provide an honest and professionally run pageant structure, holding contests in small towns throughout the region. Susan Orlean studies the pageants sponsored by Southern Charm and noted the appeal for participants. "They were ordinary people," she writes, "dazzled by glamour, and they believed truly and uncynically in beauty and staked their faith on its power to lift you and carry you away." For a child to win a beauty crown "might be the chance for your beautiful baby to get a start on a different life, so that someday she might get ahead and get away."

Beauty-contest winners are contemporary regional celebrities—the female equivalents of football stars. Beauty queens, whether Miss America or Miss Gum Spirits (representing the southern timber industry), make personal appearances, travel extensively, earn scholarship money, and have their photos on calendars. Meridian, Miss., rewarded Susan Akin, Miss America in 1985, with an enthusiastic hometown parade. She rode through town before a cheering crowd that included young girls who had won their own honors as Deep South Beauty Queen, Cameo Girl, Mini Queen, and Miss Cinderella Queen. This ritual event showed an intense American middle-class patriotism. The band played "This Is My Country" and "God Bless America." State representative Sonny Meredith was there to praise her, and Meridian's mayor named the day in her honor. Religion was a central feature. The pastor of the First Baptist Church gave an invocation, thanking God for "letting us live in a country where a neighborhood girl could be selected Miss America." The Baptist kindergarten students had penned portraits of the queen. A friend from childhood told the crowd that Susan Akin was "the one of us who earned immortality."

The culture of the modern South includes important religious roots, and evangelical attitudes toward beauty rooted in the middle and working classes are important ones in understanding its significance. The evangelical ideal of woman traditionally centered on her special moral and spiritual nature. She was an idealized symbol of region but at the same time a specific symbol of home and family. She represented the restraint, zealous morality, refinement, and self-discipline valued by evangelical culture. Samuel Hill has written of this idealized role model as the ideal of sainthood in the South, and "'she' is not likely to be perceived in corporeal terms."

Modern southern evangelicals have redefined their culture, though, so that the beauty queen seems a quite acceptable role for a moral southern woman. One can see the process through the example of Cheryl Prewitt, Miss America of 1980. Prewitt grew up in Choctaw County, Miss., the daughter of pious evangelicals. She attended church every time the church doors opened and sang gospel music with her performing family, the Prewitts. She was severely injured at age eleven in an automobile accident, which left one leg two inches shorter than the other. Overcoming the physical injury became the focus of Prewitt's testimony to God's power. At a revival she realized the need to be born again and to "discover for what reason God had put me into the world." She realized she would never be alone because she "would always have Jesus as my very real friend and guide." A Pentecostal preacher soon healed her through the laying on of hands at a prayer meeting. She was transported "to some faraway bright-shining place—a private place inhabited only by myself and Jesus." Afterward, her crippled left leg extended by two inches, until her heels met, "like two perfectly matched bookends."

The healing miracle set the stage for the transformation of the evangelical woman into the beauty queen, which represented the final stage of the miracle. Against her father's wishes, she enrolled in the Miss Choctaw County beauty contest in the hope of winning scholarship money for college. The economic meaning of beauty pageants to modern southern plain folk families is of paramount importance, even overcoming stern fathers' anxieties. Prewitt went on to win the Miss America pageant. Her father relented in his opposition and attended the pageant, telling her afterward, "I believe it's God's will that you won tonight. . . . Now you just be sure you live up to the big job He's given you, hear?" The beauty queen can thus witness for the faith.

Participants in the Miss America pageant and those who have studied it believe that southerners who compete have an advantage. After Tennessee's Kellye Cash won in 1986, another contestant claimed that Cash had won because judges desired a "sweet kind of non-aggressive Southern belle." Cash revealed her regional consciousness, when she said she was "basically a conservative Southern gal." The contestant representing Mississippi that year insisted that southerners had no special advantage, except that "they just work harder." Eight of the ten finalists, in any event, were from former Confederate states. Miss Montana, Kamala Compton, gave no evidence of knowing about John C. Calhoun's concept of the concurrent majority, which proposed having presidents from the North and from the South, but she suggested a variation of it. Southerners were "just a lot more prepared than us Western girls who try once for a title," she told a reporter. "I mean, they should have a Southern Miss America and a Western Miss America."

Southerners clearly devote considerable time and resources to doing well in the Miss America pageant. University of Southern Mississippi sociologists Don Smith, Jim Trent, and Gary Hansen have theorized in unpublished research reported in the 15 October 1986 issue of the *Clarion-Ledger* (Jackson, Miss.) that southern contestants are likely to do better in the national contest because of three factors: Pageant officials, judges, and contestants assume, based on past experience, that southerners will do well; the southern states encourage beauty contestants; and southern states have strong pageant systems. Twenty-five states have never won the contest, whereas Arkansas has won twice (1964, 1982), Texas has won three times (1942, 1971, 1975), Alabama has won three times (1951, 1995, 2005), and Mississippi has won four times (1958, 1961, 1980, 1985). In the 2005 Miss America pageant, four of the top five finalists were from the South.

Texas spends on contestants' clothes more than twice as much as Vermont spends for its entire pageant. Vermont has never placed a contestant in the top ten, but Texas obviously values its success. From 1945 to 1970, California led the nation in scholarship prize money ($47,300) awarded to contestants. Mississippi was second ($43,000), a state with a tenth of California's population. Four of the top seven states in amount of scholarship money won up to 1970 were Arkansas, Alabama, South Carolina, and Mississippi.

African Americans were barred by pageant rules from participating in the

Miss America pageant until the late 1960s. The first African American to win a state contest was in 1970, in Iowa, and the first black Miss America was Vanessa Williams from New York state in 1983. In 1994, Kimberly Aiken became the first black Miss America from a former Confederate state (South Carolina). Since 1990, African American contestants have won the pageant five times (1990, 1991, 1994, 2003, and 2004).

The Miss America contest and beauty pageants in general earn the condemnation of many men and women. "The whole gimmick is one commercial shell game to sell the sponsors' products," said critic Robin Morgan in 1968. "Where else could one find such a perfect combination of American values? Racism, militarism, and capitalism—all packaged in one 'ideal' symbol: a woman." Spokesmen for the Miss America pageant defend it, noting that it is the largest provider of scholarships for women in the United States. Women themselves are, of course, actively involved as participants and, behind the scenes, as trainers and managers, but men run the Miss America contest and other beauty contests. In September 1986, for example, no women were serving on the 12-member commission that represented the state pageants. The Jaycees are sponsors of most local Miss America contests, and men's service clubs are involved in other beauty contests. Pageants are hobbies for many men, a time for having fun and for theatrical displays. The head of the Miss Arkansas contest wears a hog suit, reflecting that state's razorback icon, and cheers for his choice each year; the state chairman in Mississippi dresses in a tuxedo made from Confederate flags. Beauty pageants, like other rituals of the South's culture of beauty, such as sorority rush, have often been rituals for the performance of what Elizabeth Boyd calls a "fairly specific, regional understanding of gender." Through speech, gestures, and adornment, "as well as codes of conduct and choreography, a regional, racialized definition of gender gets performed, again and again." The changes in the contemporary South show an evolution of such performances. The India Association of Mississippi staged its first Miss India–Mississippi beauty pageant, for example, in 2004. Contestants competed in the chapel at Millsaps College, performing Indian dance, music, martial arts, and theater for the talent segment. Contestants dressed in Punjabi costumes— golden turbans and embroidered vests—and some adapted rap dance moves to songs from India's Bollywood movies. India Association president Hitesh Desai reminded the audience of the association's many activities but noted that the "pageant is a step for us and it's big y'all."

CHARLES REAGAN WILSON
University of Mississippi

Lois Banner, *American Beauty* (1983); Julie Kirk Blackwelder, *Styling Jim Crow: African American Beauty Training during Segregation* (2003); Elizabeth Bronwyn Boyd, "Southern Beauty: Performing Femininity in an American Region" (Ph.D. dissertation, University of Texas, 2000), *Southern Cultures* (Fall 1999); Frank Deford, *There She Is: The Life and Times of Miss America* (1971); Lisa DePaulo, *TV Guide* (6 September 1986); *Ebony* (May 1983); Marvin Harris, *Natural History* (August–September 1973); Shelby Hearon, *Texas Monthly* (October 1974); Anne Goodwyn Jones, *Tomorrow Is Another Day: The Woman Writer in the South, 1859–1936* (1981); Winthrop D. Jordan, *White over Black: American Attitudes toward the Negro, 1550–1812* (1968); Robin T. Lakoff and Raquel L. Scherr, *Face Value: The Politics of Beauty* (1984); Lawrence W. Levine, *Black Culture and Black Consciousness: Afro-American Folk Thought from Slavery to Freedom* (1977); Tara McPherson, *Reconstructing Dixie: Race, Gender, and Nostalgia in the Imagined South* (2003); *Mobile (Ala.) Register*, 10 June 2004; Victoria O'Donnell, in *The South and Film*, ed. Warren French (1981); Susan Orlean, *New Yorker* (4 August 1997); Dawn Perlmutter, in *Beauty Matters*, ed. Peg Zelin Brand (2000); Kathrin Perutz, *Beyond the Looking Glass: America's Beauty Culture* (1970); Cheryl Prewitt, *A Bright-Shining Place* (1981); Julia Reed, *Queen of the Turtle Derby and Other Southern Phenomena* (2004); Anne Firor Scott, *The Southern Lady: From Pedestal to Politics, 1830–1930* (1970); Francis Butler Simkins and Charles P. Roland, *A History of the South* (1972); Elwood Watson and Darcy Martin, eds., *"There She Is, Miss America": The Politics of Sex, Beauty, and Race in America's Most Famous Pageant* (2004).

Beauty Shops and Barbershops

Women and men in all regions of America frequent beauty shops and barbershops. In the South the shops exhibit the gendered aspects evident throughout the rest of the country and also represent the racial divisions unique to the South. Far from being businesses that simply catered to the beauty and grooming needs of southerners, beauty shops and barbershops became important cultural institutions where people of different classes and occupations interacted. In a region where beauty is valued, both white and black women valued hair appointments so that they could look their best and perhaps share friendly conversation with friends and neighbors. For African Americans, the barbershop was one of the public spaces outside of church where blacks escaped the glare of white eyes and could share news, conduct business, and discuss any number of subjects. Beauty shops and barbershops developed along separate racial lines.

For southerners eager to improve their status by owning a business, barbering and hair styling became one of the most accessible avenues to entrepreneurship because of the small capital investment. Men and women of both races sought upward mobility by entering the beauty business. In the antebellum South, in particular, a rare path to prosperity for an African American man was barbering. In addition to the low cost of starting the business, barbering fit neatly into the concept of servility and deference that whites expected in the racial hierarchy. William Johnson, of Mississippi, known as the "Barber of Natchez," owned three barbershops and a plantation. At his death, in 1851, his estate was valued at $25,000. After the Civil War, other avenues opened for African Americans, and the percentage of black business owners that were barbers dropped from 10 percent to less than 2 percent. By the early 20th century, the black barbershop began to resemble the modern institution—that is, a rare black public space where men could openly discuss issues and share information that would perhaps be dangerous to discuss outside the protective wall of the racially segregated barbershop. For instance, the black barbershop would have been the only place to discuss, read, or purchase the *Chicago Defender*, a biweekly newspaper that promoted civil rights for blacks.

It was through the beauty industry that Madame C. J. Walker and Annie Malone became the first black women millionaires. Walker employed 20,000 agents to sell her products; Malone created a popular product called "Wonderful Hair Grower" and had 60,000 agents. The black beauty culture stressed greater opportunities through self-help and personal hygiene, placing emphasis on clean scalps and bodies and stressing greater societal opportunities through self-improvement and beauty. Successful beauty entrepreneurs were often community leaders and participated in civil rights activities—antilynching efforts, benefits for World War I veterans, and equality. The 1920 census listed 12,660 black barbers and hairdressers. Probably many more moonlighted and worked unofficially in their homes earning extra money.

White women also found career opportunities as beauticians. Before World War I, primarily elite women frequented beauty shops. The new popularity of bobbed hair, however, changed the beauty culture. Instead of simply having their hair shampooed and styled, women of all classes wanted their hair cut in a style that needed regular maintenance. Many white women also operated informally in their kitchens, fixing hair for friends and neighbors. By the early 20th century, beauty organizations began to professionalize hairstyling by instituting training requirements and requiring licenses and state agencies to inspect and regulate. During the New Deal, the National Recovery Act set codes, hours, and wages and targeted kitchen beauticians, who worked cheaper and often mixed their own products. The trade journals for white and black beauticians reveal the different attitudes toward the beauty culture. White trade publications stressed technical developments. African American journals also covered new technologies, but they also featured articles on female entrepreneurs, neighborhood shops, and political struggle.

Southern beauty shops and barbershops occupy an enduring place in southern society and culture. Eudora Welty set "Petrified Man" in a beauty shop. William Faulkner used a barbershop as a backdrop in "Dry September." Generations of Americans watched Floyd the barber on *The Andy Griffith Show*, and millions enjoyed the star-studded film *Steel Magnolias*. More recently, though not explicitly southern, the popular movie *Barber Shop* explored divergent aspects of black culture.

MINOA D. UFFELMAN
Austin Peay State University

Melissa Victoria Harris-Lacewell, *Barbershops, Bibles, and BET: Everyday Talk and Black Political Thought* (2004); Craig Marbery, *Cuttin' Up: Wit and Wisdom from Black Barbershops* (2005); Julie A. Willett, *Permanent Waves: The Making of the American Beauty Shop* (2000).

Belles and Ladies

Southern lore has it that the belle is a privileged white girl who is at the glamorous and exciting period between being a daughter and becoming a wife. She is the fragile, dewy, just-opened bloom of the southern female: flirtatious but sexually innocent, bright but not deep, beautiful as a statue or painting or porcelain but risky to touch. A form of popular art, she entertains but does not challenge her audience. Instead, she attracts them—the more gentlemen callers the better—and finally allows herself to be chosen by one.

Then she becomes a lady, and a lady she will remain until she dies—unless, of course, she does something beyond the pale. As a lady she drops the flirtatiousness of the belle and stops chattering; she has won her man. Now she has a different job: satisfying her husband, raising his children, meeting the demands of the family's social position, and sustaining the ideals of the South. Her strength in manners and morals is contingent, however, upon her submission to their sources—God, the patriarchal church, her husband—and upon her staying out of public life, where she might interfere in their formulation. But in her domestic realm she can achieve great if sometimes grotesque power. As a slave mistress, for example, she was capable of enormous cruelty as well as deeply felt kindness; she was a premier manager yet also a slave to the patriarch. Melanie Wilkes was a great, good lady; Marie St. Clare was a cruel and narcissistic one; and Scarlett O'Hara, that perpetual adolescent, never made it much past the belle.

Such a description can never satisfy, of course, for it is wrenched out of history, where the attributes of southern womanhood change over time, and it reflects only one out of the immense variety of attitudes about the southern woman. What has changed less than the southern woman's attributes and her reception, however, is her ontology. As the allusion to the fictional ideal suggests, southern womanhood exists as more than a historical prescription, job, role, or even source of identity. In fact, to see it as an actual identity is to literalize southern womanhood's function as a symbolic construct within southern ideology and thus to perpetuate that ideology. Southern girls who assume the roles of belle and lady take on an entire history of the meaning of the South—its class, race, and gender systems and its past and future. As belle and lady, a woman "becomes" the traditional South; as gentleman and scholar, a man enters into a complex relation to the South. He may be idolatrous worshipper, lord and master, or dashed and demoralized failure. In any case, he acts as subject to her object, as knower to her known. The gender roles thus work together to prevent change and to obscure reality both between human beings and within the South's conception of itself. Where they fail to work, as is increasingly the case in our time, where southerners of both sexes rebel against the belle (or worse, ignore her), the chance for change finds its place.

Southern men have toasted and celebrated southern womanhood since the South began to think of itself as a region, probably before the American Revolution. The lady, with her grace and hospitality, seemed the flower of a uniquely southern civilization, the embodiment of all that the South prized most deeply. In truth, southern womanhood has much in common with the ideas of the British Victorian lady and of American true womanhood. All deny to women authentic selfhood; all enjoin that women suffer and be still; all portray women as sexually pure, pious, deferent to external authority, and content with their place in the home. Yet southern womanhood differs in several ways from other 19th-century images of womanhood. First, the southern lady has been from the start at the center of a patriotic impulse—the identity of the South is contingent in part upon the persistence of its tradition of the lady. Second, the ideal of southern womanhood seems to have lasted longer than the other ideals, even to the present. Third, southern womanhood has from the beginning been inextricably linked to racial attitudes. Its very beginnings, some say, lay in the minds of guilty slaveholders who sought an image they could revere without sacrificing the gains of racial slavery. And finally, the class—aristocratic—that

A belle of the South (Ann Rayburn
Paper Americana Collection, Archives
and Special Collections, University of
Mississippi Library, Oxford)

the image of the lady represents has deeper ideological roots in the South than
elsewhere in the United States.

Thus, when Lucian Lamar Knight once again, in 1920, toasted the southern woman's "silent influence," "eternal vigil," and "gentle spirit," and when he
claimed that the "blood royal of the ancient line" still lives in her daughters, his
language suggested her primary ideological functions: to unify the South in its
difference, to sustain the desire for British class structure, to protect the racial
purity of legitimate white patriarchal inheritance, to provide a container for the
conscience that would perpetuate ideals without danger of contact with reality,
and thus to keep actual women elevated into perpetual silence and passivity.

Historians speculate variously about the origins and historical functions
of the concept of southern womanhood in southern ideology. In the knot of
region, race, sex, and class, historians find one thread clearer than others. In
general, they agree that the function of southern womanhood has been to justify the perpetuation of the hegemony of the male sex, the upper and middle
classes, and the white race.

Southern ideology placed women on a symbolic pedestal, as idealized figures. Anne Firor Scott sees the base of the pedestal in racial slavery: "Because
they owned slaves and thus maintained a traditional landowning aristocracy,
southerners tenaciously held on to the patriarchal family structure. . . . Any
tendency on the part of any of the members of the system to assert themselves
against the master threatened the whole, and therefore slavery itself." Thus, Scott
continues, it was "no accident that the most articulate spokesmen for slavery
were also eloquent exponents of the subordinate role of women." The threat of

violence takes a surprisingly strong role in even the most sophisticated pro-slavery arguments for women's subordination, as Kent Leslie's work on George Fitzhugh, Chancellor Harper, and Thomas R. Dew shows. Thus, when Louisa McCord argued against women's emancipation, she claimed that, without the protection of the pedestal, women would be intolerably vulnerable to male physical superiority. The argument can still be heard in the South today. W. J. Cash, also, found racial supremacy at the origins of the image. Woman alone could perpetuate white superiority, because of what Cash calls her "remoteness from the males of the inferior group," a remoteness not paralleled in the relationships between white men and black women. "The [white] woman must be compensated, the revolting suspicion in the male that he might be slipping into bestiality got rid of, by glorifying her," argues Cash. Lillian Smith, too, in *Killers of the Dream* (1949), sees the origin of southern womanhood in this "race-sex-sin spiral": "The more trails the white man made to backyard cabins, the higher he raised his white wife on her pedestal, when he returned to the big house. The higher the pedestal, the less he enjoyed her whom he put there, for statues are after all only nice things to look at."

Insecurities of a more class-related sort led southerners to create the "lady," according to William R. Taylor. Despairing at southern social and economic decline and fearing "social dissolution" (particularly in the forms of an open society and a dismembered family), southerners "grasped for symbols of stability and order to stem their feelings of drift and uncertainty and to quiet their uneasiness about the inequities within Southern society." But southern men, Taylor argues, could not associate feeling, introspection, or moral awareness with masculinity. The popular plantation novels solved this problem "without robbing the Southern gentleman of his manhood. The Southern answer to this question lay in the cult of chivalry—in having the Cavalier kneel down before the altar of femininity and familial benevolence."

Yet ultimately, as Sara Evans points out, "it made no sense to place women in charge of piety and morality and then deny them access to the public sphere where immorality held sway." Certain pre–Civil War southern men, Taylor says, "began regretting the moral autonomy which they had assigned to women" and returned full circle, to insist upon a rigid gender, race, and class hierarchy that made woman, slave, and yeoman subject to the Cavalier.

A suggestion that class takes precedence over race and gender in grounding southern womanhood can be found in examples of the "lady" in literature by black women. Harriet Jacobs's slave master, in her autobiography *Incidents in the Life of a Slave Girl* (1861), for example, promises her he will make her into a "lady" in exchange for sex; clearly the idea was not, even then, limited to white women. And in Zora Neale Hurston's novel *Their Eyes Were Watching God* (1937), Janie becomes a lady, ornamental and silent, within an all-black community, as a sign of class elevation. If a black woman can become a southern lady, then something other than racial exclusion is going on. But can a white lower-class woman climb into ladyhood? Eudora Welty seems to see the lady as a construct that preserves class immobility when she makes it clear in *The Optimist's Daughter* (1972) that Fay's lower-class origins prevent her from attaining the sort of consciousness that makes a "real" lady, that is, a lady in mind and in spirit.

Yet another argument finds the origin of southern womanhood in Western civilization's patriarchal tradition, antedating and then reinforcing racial slavery and class structure. Bertram Wyatt-Brown locates the source of southern womanhood in the South's retention of the ancient code of honor, the system of "patriarchy and womanly subordination." Public reputation, not private guilt, motivates behavior in this system; hence the "enforcement of gender and family conventions [is] community business" rather than personal choice. Men of all classes agreed upon female subordination and docility as a norm. And women participated willingly in their subordination, Wyatt-Brown argues, because southern womanhood meant not simply self-sacrifice and silence, but sacrifice for family honor, in which women took pride—and courage—in accepting fate without complaint. Thus did the patriarchal system of honor simultaneously subordinate its women and reward them for their acquiescence. John Ruoff also argues for the primacy of patriarchy over slavery as the source for southern womanhood. Southern settlers brought with them from England a belief in patriarchal values, says Ruoff. These values made the man the source of family authority, the family the source of societal order and stability, and the planter class the source of authority within society. Then, as early as the 17th century, a native southern aristocracy developed an "ethos of leisure and consumption" that "stipulated that women should perform an essentially ornamental function in society." The development of the master-slave relationship thus reinforced and was reinforced by the prior notion that the husband held absolute authority in the home.

Sara Evans also points to Europe for the myths about women that southern colonists brought along with their patriarchal social and familial assumptions. Those basic myths polarized women into the "virgin, pure and untouchable, and the prostitute, dangerously sexual." The clustering of images—goodness and light with virginity, evil and darkness with sexuality—seemed to be reified and therefore confirmed when white planters owned black slave women.

Race and sex thus fused to create in the "white lady" the southern version of the 19th-century's cult of true womanhood.

Whatever the relative importance of class, race, and patriarchy, it is the peculiar relation of patriarchal attitudes toward women with the development of a hierarchical slave society that produced, in the early 19th century, both the South's most intense period of self-definition and the refinement of the images of the lady as the slaveholder's ideal—and the dominant ideal of the South.

How have women fared through all this construction of ideology? Most have, of course, literalized the symbol; it would be nearly impossible not to. Thus, for most southern women "southern womanhood" has become a very practical and personal concern, a way to be—to reject, to revise, or to adopt.

Rarely, women have abandoned the necessity even to pretend to conform, have radically criticized their society, and have often left the South, in body if not in mind. The Charleston Grimké sisters moved North—Sarah in 1821 and Angelina in 1820—and, from that "refuge," at times addressing the southern white woman at home, directly attacked the "assumptions upon which southern society based its image of women," including, of course, slavery. In fact, Sarah's *Letters on the Equality of the Sexes* were, according to Anne Firor Scott, the "earliest systematic expression in America of the whole set of ideas constituting the ideology of 'women's rights.'" Sara Evans has shown that the 1960s feminist revival found its roots, too, in the South. Once again, southern white women—this time in the civil rights movement—saw the connection between racial and sexual oppression, thus providing the initial impulse toward contemporary feminism. Shirley Abbott, in *Womenfolks* (1983), offers herself as a contemporary explanation of why southern girls leave home.

At the opposite extreme from outright rebellion, some women have determined to shape themselves entirely into the ideal. "We owe it to our husbands, children, and friends," wrote Caroline Merrick to a friend in 1859, "to represent as nearly as possible the ideal which they hold so dear." At the extreme, such women blanked out their perceptions and repressed their feelings until they lost, almost entirely, a sense of self. Educated, on the other hand, into the belief that they were perfection itself, some real southern women found it hard to admit and harder to rectify such "besetting sins [as] a roving mind and an impetuous spirit."

More typically, though, southern women neither left home nor attained perfection. Instead, they made for themselves a public persona, a mask of sorts that coexisted with but did not always correspond to an inner self. Such self-division produced guilt both about what they felt was the wolf within and about the inevitable hypocrisy involved in concealing it. In the South, the conflict between image and reality took its purest form in the years before the Civil War. Although the ideology depicted them as passive, submissive, and dependent symbols of leisure, these women found that actual experience involved long days of hard active work making administrative decisions that determined how the household ran.

Whereas the image had her needing the economic protection of her husband, reality found her chafing, as did Mary Boykin Chesnut, at her economic dependence. Whereas the ideal southern woman was as chaste as a block of ice, many women felt a natural physical attraction to their husbands and even possessed a "humor so earthy as to contradict the romantic tradition of universal refinement among Southern ladies," says Bell Wiley. Whereas the woman presumably lived in ignorance of it, miscegenation aroused anguish in many. Whereas the ideal woman was a repository of culture and the arts, her actual ignorance of worldly reality (which the image called innocence) was maintained by the low quality of education available for women in the South. The ideal woman, however, remained a pious Protestant, and, in fact, evidence of any widespread (if private) religious skepticism is rare. Thus each element of the image—leisure, passivity, dependence, sexual purity, submission, ignorance (with the possible exception of piety)—failed to correspond to the reality of women's lives, and for women to undertake to match the ideal must have required creativity and persistence.

The history of women's specific accommodations to and revisions of the belle and the lady is complicated, fascinating, and ongoing. Anne Firor Scott, Jacquelyn Dowd Hall, and Suzanne Lebsock have notably pieced out parts of that story, a story too long to tell here except in the most generalized way. It seems that most southern women have in their daily lives worked around these conflicts with the ideology of southern womanhood. They have done so in the interests of values and desires that can be called "women's culture" and that subvert, at times, the values of the dominant culture. On the other hand, the fate of the belle in literature, as Kathryn L. Seidel untangles it, has been less hopeful. The belle has moved from the "madonna" of the antebellum period to the narcissistic and masochistic "Magdalen" of, for instance, Faulkner's Temple Drake. These are, for Seidel, two sides of the same person; they represent the psychosexual distortions inherent in the image itself.

Has southern womanhood died—co-opted by television and trashy passion novels—or has it metamorphosed into some sort of Sunbelt Total Woman? Long-held images of southern womanhood have not disappeared, any more than have the systems that produced them. Perhaps in a place like Sunbelt

Atlanta, though, the southern woman has finally found a suitable arena for her skills at manipulating the images.

ANNE GOODWYN JONES

Allegheny College

Irving H. Bartlett and Glenn Cambor, *Women's Studies*, vol. 2 (1974); Linda Brent, *Incidents in the Life of a Slave Girl* (1973); W. J. Cash, *The Mind of the South* (1941); Phyllis Fraley, *Atlanta Magazine* (October 1984); Jacquelyn Dowd Hall, *Revolt against Chivalry: Jesse Daniel Ames and the Women's Campaign against Lynching* (1979); Anne Goodwyn Jones, *Tomorrow Is Another Day: The Woman Writer in the South, 1859–1936* (1981); Suzanne Lebsock, *The Free Women of Petersburg* (1983); Tara McPherson, *Reconstructing Dixie: Race, Gender, and Nostalgia in the Imagined South* (2003); Michael O'Brien, *All Clever Men Who Make Their Way* (1982); Julia Reed, *Queen of the Turtle Derby and Other Southern Phenomena* (2004); John C. Ruoff, "Southern Womanhood, 1865–1920: An Intellectual and Cultural Study" (Ph.D. dissertation, University of Illinois at Urbana-Champaign, 1976); Anne Firor Scott, *The Southern Lady: From Pedestal to Politics, 1830–1930* (1970); Kathryn L. Seidel, *The Southern Belle in the American Novel* (1986); William R. Taylor, *Cavalier and Yankee: The Old South and American National Character* (1961); Bertram Wyatt-Brown, *Southern Honor: Ethics and Behavior in the Old South* (1982).

Blues

When a woman gets the blues she hangs her head and cries,
When a woman gets the blues she hangs her head and cries,
But when a man gets the blues, he grabs a train and flies.
— Traditional blues song

Although the word "gender" has rarely, if ever, appeared in a blues song, the blues tradition intersects richly with that analytic category. It is hard to think about the blues without hearing some brassy (or mournful) female singer's complaint about her "no-good man" or her male counterpart's answering diatribe against "these evil women who just won't let me be." *A Bad Woman Feeling Good: Blues and the Women Who Sing Them*, the title of a 2005 study by scholar Buzzy Jackson, succinctly frames the question: What exactly *is* a "bad woman," in a blues context? Or a "good woman"? Is either of them the same thing as the wild women evoked by Georgia native Ida Cox's 1924 recording "Wild Women Don't Have the Blues"?

I hear these women raving 'bout their . . . monkey men
About their fighting husbands and his . . . no-good friends

These poor women sit around . . . all day and moan
Wondering why their wandering papas . . . don't come home
But wild women don't worry . . . wild women don't have the blues

When contemporary Memphis barrelhouse pianist Di Anne Price sings those lines, edged with prideful defiance, she helps us understand what should already be clear: bad, good, or wild, blueswomen are women who refuse to be silenced by or subservient to the men in their lives. When in doubt, they opt for feeling good, whether that involves bragging about the "new man" who is pleasuring them, bewailing faithless love in a way that enables individual and collective catharsis, or dumping (or killing) the chump and moving on.

Bluesmen have their own ideas about who is in charge, of course, and how his behavior should be judged. One woman's "wandering papa" may be another man's heroic exemplar—that is, a trickster with a great rap who follows his bliss rather than letting himself be tied down to a plow, a woman, or a boss man. To speak about blues and gender in a southern context is necessarily to speak about the diverse ways in which black male performers use their voices, bodies, and instruments to evoke masculine personhood, often laced with sexual braggadocio and violence. It is no accident that such expressive art emerged during the Jim Crow years, when "boy," "uncle," and "nigger" were terms within which the white South strove to confine black masculinity. When 1,300 striking sanitation workers carried signs reading "I AM A MAN" during Martin Luther King Jr.'s Poor People's Campaign in Memphis in 1968, they were reiterating what Bo Diddley had asserted in considerably racier terms more than a decade earlier in "I'm a Man" (1955): "All you pretty women, / Stand in line, / I can make love to you baby, / In an hour's time. / I'm a man." Like Diddley, Muddy Waters and Willie Dixon were black Mississippi bluesmen who migrated north to Chicago and articulated a swaggering masculinity—as in Dixon's "I'm Your Hoochie-Coochie Man," recorded by Waters in 1954, which finds its assertiveness in the language of both southern folk religion and trafficked female flesh:

I got a black cat bone
I got a mojo too
I got the Johnny Conqueroo
I'm gonna mess with you
I'm gonna make you girls
Lead me by my hand
Then the world will know
The hoochie coochie man

"A hoochie-coochie dancer is a stripper," writes Debra DeSalvo in *The Language of the Blues*, "and a hoochie-coochie man is a pimp — or at least someone with strong powers of persuasion over women."

When masculine power in the blues turns violent, it acknowledges its origins on the frontier that much of the South once was, a region rife with codes of honor and vengeance that black southern men embraced, even as they suffered at the hands of white lynch mobs upholding such codes. The blues tradition is filled with men who beat, cut, or shoot their women — and other men — to keep them in line, from Skip James's "22-20 Blues" to Robert Johnson's "Me and the Devil." In Zora Neale Hurston's novel *Their Eyes Were Watching God* (1937), the playful and mercurial Florida bluesman, Tea Cake, beats his lover Janie Starks to "reassure himself [that he is] in possession" after his honor has been impugned by a light-skinned female acquaintance of Janie's who has dismissed him as "trashy." In "I'm Bad Like Jesse James" (1966), John Lee Hooker warns a man who claims to have cuckolded him that he's "the big boss" who does "the payin' off." "I've got three boys [to] do my dirty work," Hooker growls with exaggerated, almost cartoonish, menace. "They may shoot you / They may cut you / They may drown you / I just don't know." Chicago blues scion Lurrie Bell (son of Mississippi-born harpist Carrie Bell) promises in "I'll Be Your .44" (1982) to defend his lover's honor by gracing her with his deadly presence, using the striking metaphor of boyfriend-as-phallic-firearm: "You don't need no pistol, don't need to run / Don't look behind you, girl, cause I'll be your gun / I'm your .44, and I'll be your bullets too / Cause I love you baby, I swear I'll kill for you." In "Black Mountain Blues," Bessie Smith makes clear that she's capable of defending her own honor after the "sweetest man in town" has rejected her. "I'm bound for Black Mountain," she sings, "me and my razor and my gun / I'm gonna shoot him if he stands still, and cut him if he run." Southern belle not spoken here!

At the far extreme from bluesy badmen and badwomen stand artists such as B. B. King — a "clean" and "mellow" bluesman, to use the terms favored by his black Chicago audience, according to Charles Keil. King's stage persona is one of resolute gentility, a quality he enacts through his embrace of Lucille, his electric guitar. "I like seeing my guitar as a lady," he confesses in his autobiography, *Blues All Around Me* (1996), registering disapproval at the way in which white rockers such as Pete Townsend destroy their instruments. "I get cold chills just thinking of hurting Lucille. The idea of smashing her to bits against a wall or an amplifier makes me sick."

What male and female blues performers share, above all, is the signifying idiomatic language, at once risqué and inventive, through which they conduct their dance of desire and disillusionment. Here sexuality engenders person-hood—black manhood and black womanhood—with the help of metaphors drawn from the animal, vegetable, and mineral world. In a Broadway revue entitled *It Ain't Nothin' but the Blues* (1999), actor Gregory Porter shimmy-wobbles his way through a languid, smoldering version of John Lee Hooker's "Crawlin' King Snake," each word rippling with phallic signification, at once menacing and playful. "I'm gonna crawl up to your window," he croons, shifting his gaze between his black female and white female counterparts on stage. "I'm gonna crawl up to your door." Blueswomen have no trouble articulating responses to *that* particular call, and when the dance goes wrong they are doubly inventive: "If you don't like my peaches, don't you shake my tree," runs a traditional line. "If you don't like my ocean, don't fish in my sea," sings Georgia-born Ma Rainey in one variation. "Stay out of my valley and let my mountains be." In "Steppin' Out, Steppin' In" (1985), Belzoni, Miss., native Denise LaSalle imagines herself as a sort of vengeful chastity belt, personalized and freshly installed: "You came home this morning, and oooh what a shock / When you found out your key no longer fit my lock."

Although the blues lyric tradition is overwhelmingly heteronormative—a pas de deux of pistol-packing papas and jellyroll-flaunting mamas—homosexuality is an infrequent but continuing theme. The juke-joint demimonde within which urban blues performers and their audiences encountered each other during the 1920s was a bohemia of sorts, moderately more receptive to same-sex affection than the workaday world, and blues lyrics trafficked in slang figurations, according to scholar Paul Oliver: "freakish man," "sissy," "B. D. women." "B. D. women, they all done learnt their plan," sings Lucille Bogan. "They can lay their jive just like a nach'l man." Singer Gladys Bentley, who sported a white tuxedo and called herself "The Bulldagger Who Sang the Blues," was the most overtly lesbian blues performer of the era; a number of others, including Ma Rainey, Bessie Smith, Ethel Waters, and Alberta Hunter, lived their bisexuality or lesbianism more circumspectly. With the possible exception of rock and roller Little Richard, who spoke of his bisexuality candidly in his 1994 autobiography, openly gay male blues performers are a rare commodity indeed.

ADAM GUSSOW
University of Mississippi

Angela Y. Davis, *Blues Legacies and Black Feminism: Gertrude "Ma" Rainey, Bessie Smith, and Billie Holiday* (1998); Debra DeSalvo, *The Language of the Blues: From Alcorub to Zuzu* (2006); Daphne Duval Harrison, *Black Pearls: Blues Queens of the*

1920s (1988); Buzzy Jackson, *A Bad Woman Feeling Good: Blues and the Women Who Sing Them* (2005); Charles Keil, *Urban Blues* (1991); B. B. King, with David Ritz, *Blues All Around Me: The Autobiography of B. B. King* (1996); Paul Oliver, *Blues Fell This Morning: Meaning in the Blues* (1990).

Bubba, Image of

The word "Bubba" is used commonly in the American South as a man's nickname; most sources suggest the word is a familiar or diminutive form of the word "brother" or an imitation of a younger sibling's attempt to pronounce "brother," although the nickname is as often applied to friends or peers as it is to blood kin. The term is also used—often affectionately but sometimes critically—throughout the region and the rest of the United States to refer to southern working-class white men, their culture, and those who share or admire it.

As a nickname, Bubba has been used widely by both black and white southerners. Indeed, some sources suggest that Bubba was more commonly used by African Americans than by whites in the 19th-century South—the form Bubbuh is derived from the South Atlantic Gullah language. Applied to individual southern men, then, the word seems to have carried no particular history of racial exclusivity or overt stereotyping. Black and white athletes such as Charles Smith of the Baltimore Colts, William Paris of the San Francisco 49ers, Richard Crosby of the Cincinnati Reds, and John Phillips of the Detroit Tigers are all better known by the first name of Bubba. Other famous Bubbas include Benjamin Buford "Bubba" Blue from the novel and movie *Forrest Gump*, rapper Bubba Sparxxx, and Bubba, a beloved 154-pound Queensland grouper that lived until his death in 2006 at Chicago's Shedd Aquarium.

In recent decades, Bubba increasingly has been used to refer broadly to white southern men with working-class outlook and values. According to many definitions, Bubba is not necessarily low income or rural, but stereotypes rarely conform to logic or easy definition. Even if the nickname historically has been color-blind, the stereotype is freighted with powerful and contested assertions about race and social and cultural values. An offended Lewis Grizzard wrote that some observers hold that "men named Bubba are nothing more than ignorant swine who wear caps with the names of heavy equipment dealers on the front, shoot anything that moves, listen to music about doing bodily harm to hippies and put beer on their grits." The *Random House Historical Dictionary of American Slang* sweepingly and problematically defines the nickname as referring to "an uneducated white southern male," and, in offering synonyms, conflates Bubba with "'good ol' boy'" and "redneck." Like many stereotypes, the term "Bubba" signals broader arguments about southern masculinity and southern culture generally. White southerners who embrace their Bubbaness identify themselves with what they consider a normative, healthy masculine identity. Self-identified Bubbas typically value home and tradition, consider themselves patriotic and hardworking, and are skeptical of pretense and meddlesome outsiders. There does seem, however, to be less class resentment and judgmental feeling—whether toward blacks or other whites—in "Bubba" than in "redneck," for instance.

Indeed, most southerners likely would draw distinctions among the terms "Bubba," "good old boy," and "redneck." Although the good old boy is certainly a close kin of Bubba, the former term typically highlights the gregariousness, the clannishness, and the gender exclusivity of the type, while Bubba embraces a larger set of cultural values. Some southern women proudly claim Bubba status. Both Bubba and the good old boy, however, do bear resemblance to W. J. Cash's often-cited description of the southern frontiersman as a man who tended toward "a kind of mounting exultancy, which issued in a tendency to frisk and cavort, to posture, to play the slashing hell of a fellow." And the Bubba stereotype typically suggests a fondness for family and the domestic that those of the good old boy and redneck do not, even though redneck no longer carries quite the same automatic association with racism and violence that it did a generation or two ago.

In the last two decades, the national media has begun to see Bubba in political terms, that is, as the quarry that Ronald Reagan helped to flush out from the Democratic Party over to the Republican Party. Political observers typically define Bubba as culturally conservative (they disagree on how much residual racism Bubba carries) and generally hawkish on defense and national security matters; some argue that Bubba retains enough independence and sensitivity to economic matters to make his vote up for grabs in some parts of the South. Two recent students of southern politics argued confidently, if perhaps not definitively, about the distinction between Bubba and the Redneck: "In the world of campaigning, the most important [difference] is that Bubba is registered to vote. On the other hand, rednecks can't or don't vote . . . for any number of reasons—domestic violence, auto theft, every kind of auto part theft, breaking and entering, entering and breaking . . . and of course, another several thousand or so alcohol-related crimes." Another key distinction, they note, is that while "Bubba throws his own beer cans in the back of his pickup, a redneck throws his out the window." President Bill Clinton was frequently dubbed "Bubba" by the press, certainly because of his southern background, his gregarious, his unpretentious personality, and his comfortable familiarity with rural southern culture; by some accounts, Clinton detests the nickname. Journalists looking for a label for rural and working-class white southern voters began to write of the "Bubba vote." That use of the term has spread; grassroots defenses of southern land and waterways are increasingly termed "Bubba environmentalism."

To many people outside the South, the term still carries unflattering assumptions about racism, ignorance, and the old-fashioned ways of southerners and the South. But in other contexts, the name has moved beyond traditional stereotypes of southern backwardness and is well established and even embraced as a descriptive type of culturally conservative and socially unassuming white southern manhood.

TRENT WATTS
Missouri University of Science and Technology

W. J. Cash, *The Mind of the South* (1941); Lewis Grizzard, *It Wasn't Always Easy, but I Sure Had Fun: The Best of Lewis Grizzard* (1994); Steve Jarding and Dave "Mudcat" Saunders, *Foxes in the Henhouse: How the Republicans Stole the South and the Heartland and What the Democrats Must Do to Run 'Em Out* (2006).

Childbirth, Antebellum

Childbearing was the central life experience for nearly all southern women during the colonial and antebellum periods. Since most women married or lived with a male partner and since birth control devices were unknown or of limited effectiveness, a woman in good health could anticipate a pregnancy every two to three years during her fertile years. Society glorified motherhood as woman's sacred occupation.

Few details are known about childbirth during the colonial period. Research on the 17th-century Chesapeake region reveals that women there tended to bear children later than the norm, since a significant number of young women immigrated to this country as indentured servants. Having to fulfill their indenture meant that they usually married late and did not bear their first child until their mid- to late 20s. The unhealthy southern environment created an uncertain situation for newcomers but especially for childbearing women; miscarriages and infant and maternal deaths were common.

Through the end of the 18th century, most black and white southern women depended on midwives or female kin to assist with delivery. Giving birth was usually an all-female experience, with several women assisting a parturient woman with what could be a prolonged delivery. Nearly all women delivered their babies at home. Midwives and female attendants let nature take its course. Other than administering herbal concoctions and keeping up a woman's spirits, they did little to interfere with what was regarded as a normal process. Women had few effective means to limit their number of pregnancies, though in the early years of colonial settlement miscarriages and high infant mortality kept a check on large families. As the number of indentured servants decreased, families stabilized, and settlers grew more accustomed to the southern environment, women began to bear more children. As the first federal census of 1790 showed, the new nation was surprisingly fertile. Women of childbearing age averaged about seven live children.

A woman's primary caretaker during childbirth was her mother, and some southern women made every effort to return home to their parents for their deliveries. Female attendants continued to be important in the birthing room. Husbands rarely played a major role other than to deliver news of the newborn. Few women went to a hospital to have a baby—hospitals were few in number and generally regarded as unsafe places where doctors practiced their skills on the urban poor, who constituted the majority of patients.

Changes in childbearing occurred in the antebellum period. The process became more professional as male physicians became involved in the birthing process, most regarding it as a pathological rather than a natural condition. More men entered the medical profession and gained requisite skills by being apprenticed to an older doctor or attending one of the many proprietary medical schools established in the North and in the South. Though medical education proved of limited value because of the poor understanding of science and medicine at the time, obstetrics became a popular field. To enhance their reputations, physicians denigrated midwives as old-fashioned and unskilled. Several wrote advice manuals to provide information on pregnancy and childbirth. Doctors who were seeking respectability and greater income found their role as birth attendant an effective means to gain an entire family as patients. More physicians began to consider themselves experts in this field, whether that reputation was deserved or not. Because status surrounded the use of a male doctor in childbirth, more privileged southern white women began to depend on a doctor to deliver their babies.

Despite education and training, doctors had limited medical understanding of the birth process. They did not yet have a clear idea of the process of conception and believed a woman was most likely to get pregnant immediately before or after menstruation. Education on childbirth in medical school was done by lecture rather than live demonstration in order to preserve a woman's delicacy. Physicians who engaged in the birthing process did so with curtains and bedclothes drawn in order not to embarrass the parturient woman. In contrast to midwives, doctors were more likely to intervene, using their hands, drugs, bloodletting, and instruments to ease or hasten delivery. Taking a lead from Europe, some physicians used instruments such as forceps, tongs, and hooks for difficult births to help dislodge the fetus in order to save the mother's life. Many southern doctors believed in heroic medicine and often administered drugs and bled a parturient woman, believing that dramatic means would reduce pressure and ease the baby's birth. The sense among physicians was that the unhealthy southern environment demanded heroic techniques. These could produce negative results, for sepsis and the harmful effects of many drugs were not yet understood. A doctor's unwashed hands, clothing, and instruments could foster infection. Although outbreaks of puerperal fever usually occurred in hospitals, even rural southern women fell victim to this deadly, infectious disease.

Surgery began to play a minor role in childbirth. Physician James Marion Sims in Alabama made a medical breakthrough in 1849 by discovering a surgical cure for vesico vaginal fistula. A tear in a woman's birth canal during childbirth could lead to a lifetime of discomfort, seepage, and embarrassment. Without using anesthesia, Sims performed repeated surgeries on slave women to refine this surgical technique. Until the Civil War, no southern doctor had found a successful means to perform a Caesarean, although a few experimented with it in emergency situations.

More women began to depend on doctors, but there is little indication that childbirth became safer—although in a few cases, it became less painful. A few doctors began to administer ether or chloroform to the parturient woman, with varied results. Women found that anesthesia lessened or eliminated pain, and personal accounts by a few women who used it were positive. Many doctors, however, remained unconvinced of its usefulness. For one thing, they could no longer determine the depth or location of a woman's pain to help guide them through the process. Others believed in the biblical dictate, "In sorrow thou shalt bring forth children." If a woman did not experience pain, so the thinking went, she might not adequately love her child. Moreover, many doctors were not trained to know how to use the proper amount of anesthesia, and an overdose could have dire results.

Few antebellum women publicly announced their pregnancies, but if they did so it was in a circumspect manner. Medical advice books now offered women information on how to conduct themselves during pregnancy, including what to eat and how to exercise. Traditional tales shared among women cautioned them to monitor their behavior, since many believed that any action or "maternal impression" during pregnancy could have a lifetime impact on a child. Few antebellum women sought prenatal care from a doctor unless they were truly ill. Although pregnancy could be an uncomfortable and often unhealthy experience, most women tried to carry on as normal, tending to their myriad domestic activities, attending church, visiting family and friends, and raising their children. Most had little choice. Only the most privileged could indulge by luxuriating in an experience that was viewed as an illness rather than as a normal event.

Most women spent time during each pregnancy in a state of fear over what lay ahead. They had good reason, since many women died during or right after childbirth. The 1850 federal census shows that nearly twice as many southern women died in childbirth as women in the Northeast. A number of reasons help explain this difference. Bearing so many children in the unhealthy southern disease environment took its toll on women's health. Malaria, endemic to the South, had an even more negative effect on women during pregnancy—fostering miscarriages and debilitation and increasing women's susceptibility to anemia and other diseases. The high fever accompanying malaria could prove fatal to the fetus.

A few couples in the urban Northeast were beginning to practice some form of birth control, but there is little evidence that southern couples consciously tried to limit the number of babies a woman bore. Southern families tended to be large, and it was not unusual for a woman to bear a dozen children. Breastfeeding could delay menstruation for up to a year, and abstinence or absence proved effective in postponing conception. Rural couples valued large families, for each child born meant another potential laborer and higher farm productivity. Southern men generally felt pride in a large family, seeing their many children as a reflection of masculinity and honor, perhaps with little regard for how bearing so many children affected their wife's health.

Despite the growing importance of male doctors in childbirth, many southern women still relied on black or white female attendants. They also depended on their deep sense of faith to get them through each delivery, and they invariably thanked God for a successful outcome.

Slave women were valued not only for the work they performed but also for their childbearing ability, because each slave child born increased a plantation owner's wealth. Slave women usually depended on a midwife in the slave community, although a slave owner might call in a physician if the parturient woman was in distress. Most white southerners, including many doctors, assumed that hardworking slave women had an easier time in childbirth than did white women. Owners encouraged the birth of many slave children and often rewarded the mother with time off from work, lighter duties before and after delivery, or perhaps a small gift. Unlike white women, who were taught to shun sex before marriage, it was not unusual for a slave woman to bear a child before she married. The slave community attached no stigma to premarital sex. There is some evidence of greater spacing of babies born to slave women, who gave birth every two and a half to three years. This may have reflected delayed weaning, a poor diet, bad health, or the absence of a husband or male partner. Evident to all observers was the lightening of the slave population, especially in the Upper South. Some white men engaged in interracial sex with slave women, either forced or consensual. Infant mortality was high in slave quarters, because of limited time for infant care, poor diet, filthy living conditions, and infections and diseases such as neonatal tetanus. Yet, despite the risks involved and the possibility of ill health or even death, southern women most often embraced what they saw as their sacred occupation with amazing fortitude and commitment.

SALLY G. MCMILLEN
Davidson College

Lois G. Carr and Lorena Walsh, *William and Mary Quarterly* (October 1977); Judith Walzer Leavitt, *Brought to Bed: Childbearing in America, 1750–1950* (1986); Sally G. McMillen, *Motherhood in the Old South: Pregnancy, Childbirth, and Infant Rearing* (1990); John Harley Warner, in *Sickness and Health*, ed. Judith Walzer Leavitt and Ronald L. Numbers (1985); Deborah Gray White, *Ar'n't I a Woman? Female Slaves in the Plantation South* (1986).

Child-Rearing Customs

Child-rearing customs in the American South have been shaped by distinctive regional traits, particularly rural life and a biracial population, and by national and transatlantic trends in the "modernization" of child rearing. Thus, southern children's early years, from infancy through adolescence, evince characteristics widespread throughout the Anglo-American world, but with regional accents.

Details about southern child rearing are sketchy prior to the mid-18th century, when sex ratios evened out, life expectancies increased, and literacy rates rose, enabling more parents to read child-rearing literature and to record their own practices. It seems clear, however, that the relatively secular Anglicans who settled the southern colonies concerned themselves with "breaking the will" less than did their Puritan counterparts in New England. The relaxed, affectionate relationships that white parents enjoyed with their children—in part by assigning routine child care to slave playmates and caretakers and adolescent discipline to northern tutors and governesses—translated easily into the "modern" child rearing, predicated on affection and reason, that was adopted by well-to-do parents on both sides of the Atlantic Ocean in the mid- to late 18th century. At the same time, the rise of evangelical Protestant Christianity reinforced many southerners' commitment to family ties, both in this life and in the one to come.

Although modern child rearing may have increased the importance of maternal love (as opposed to paternal authority) in the Northeast, in the American South, both fathers and mothers—and, at least on the eastern seaboard, an extended network of aunts, uncles, grandparents, and other kin—participated in child care and child rearing. This was particularly true for slave children, whose parents' onerous work responsibilities and owner-forced separations often strained or limited familial relationships. Well-to-do white parents and kin in the antebellum South sought to motivate their offspring to duty and obedience through a combination of love and guilt, although their less-privileged poor white and enslaved black neighbors may more often have resorted to the rod than to reason in order to teach life lessons early and thoroughly. For all southern children, life lessons included learning one's place in the world, oriented along the axes of race, class, gender, and—of special importance in slave society—legal status. Parents' correspondence and children's memoirs frequently comment upon the many small dramas that taught even very young children what it meant to be black or white, rich or poor, male or female, free or enslaved.

Except for the wealthiest members of the slaveholding population, most children in the antebellum South also quickly learned how to contribute to agricultural production, assuming responsibility for some chores at about the same time that boys and girls traded loose smocks for trousers and skirts, around age six or seven, and being fully integrated into crop cultivation (for all boys and enslaved girls) or household production (for white and free black girls) by age 10 or 12. Meanwhile, the sons and daughters of the South's planting, mercantile, and professional elite and middle class increasingly attended, at first, coeducational day schools and, later, sex-segregated academies and colleges, to prepare them to become the social, cultural, economic, and (for men) political leaders of southern society.

The demise of slavery eliminated one of the axes of children's identity and threatened planters' wealth, but child-rearing practices remained fairly constant throughout the 19th century. To shore up claims to racial and class privilege, wealthy white women in the postbellum South may have become somewhat more likely to use black nursemaids than they had been in previous eras, when virtually all mothers breast-fed their own children. At the same time, emancipated African American parents, now heading independent households, reduced the field labor of women, children, and the elderly and gave priority to the education of the young, first in northern missionary schools, next in private schools established by black educators and ministers, and finally, in the 20th century, in segregated public schools.

The incursions of industrialization reshaped many southern children's lives in the 20th century, particularly in the mill towns of the Piedmont and the Appalachians, which employed entire farm families displaced by timbering and mining. The move from farm to factory weakened kinship networks and put more emphasis on the nuclear family unit. Both generational and gender tensions increased as both children and their mothers, for the first time, earned paychecks rather than contributing to a male-directed, family-based economic enterprise. At the same time, the increasing intervention of outside forces such as child labor laws and compulsory education reduced parental control, and southern children and adolescents responded enthusiastically to the pull of national popular culture in the form of radio, automobiles, and television.

Regional patterns changed again in the mid-20th century in response to civil rights activism and the rise of suburbia. In the wake of the 1954 *Brown v. Board of Education* Supreme Court case, which called for the desegregation of public schools, and the civil rights movement of the 1960s, which demanded the desegregation of public parks, libraries, and swimming pools, racial segregation lost much of its regional specificity (although not its significance) as affluent white southerners imitated their northern counterparts in replacing de jure segregation with de facto segregation through "white flight" to suburban communities. Meanwhile, the urban centers left behind by affluent white southerners were populated not only by less-privileged whites and African Americans, but also by "new" immigrants from Asia and Latin America, changing the racial and ethnic character of southern families, neighborhoods, and schools.

By the opening of the 21st century, southern child-rearing customs, no longer reflecting rural life or biracial culture, more closely resembled prevailing patterns in the rest of the nation than they had in earlier eras, with regionalisms such as insisting that children address adults as "sir" and "ma'am" appearing as quaint anachronisms. Nonetheless, opinion polls of southern college students continue to reveal regionally distinct values across lines of race, class, and gender, including respect for adult authority, pride in family ancestry, and at least nominal affiliation with Protestant Christianity.

ANYA JABOUR
University of Montana

Jane Turner Censer, *North Carolina Planters and Their Children, 1800–1860* (1984); Christie Anne Farnham, *The Education of the Southern Belle: Higher Education and Student Socialization in the Antebellum South* (1994); Lorri Glover, *Southern Sons: Becoming Men in the New Nation* (2007); Herbert G. Gutman, *The Black Family in Slavery and Freedom, 1750–1925* (1976); Jacquelyn Dowd Hall, *Like a Family: The Making of a Southern Cotton Mill World* (1987); Anya Jabour, *Marriage in the Early Republic: Elizabeth and William Wirt and the Companionate Ideal* (1998); Jan Lewis, *The Pursuit of Happiness: Family and Values in Jefferson's Virginia* (1983); Sally G. McMillen, *Motherhood in the Old South: Pregnancy, Childbirth, and Infant Rearing* (1990); John Shelton Reed, *The Enduring South: Subcultural Persistence in Mass Society* (1986); Jennifer Ritterhouse, *Growing Up Jim Crow: How Black and White Southern Children Learned Race* (1996); Daniel Blake Smith, *Inside the Great House: Planter Family Life in Eighteenth-Century Chesapeake Society* (1980).

Citizenship

Over the past generation, historians of women and gender have constructed a more complicated history of citizenship in the American South, one that illuminates the way gender and sexuality became key arenas for waging battles over citizenship after emancipation. These scholars have also viewed the act of petitioning the federal government for protection and state-sponsored aid as another manifestation of citizenship in the postemancipation South.

When the Thirteenth Amendment abolished slavery in 1865, it shook the foundation of southern society to its core and led federal lawmakers to contemplate the meaning of citizenship anew. In the aftermath of war and emancipation, competing definitions of citizenship existed across the South. Marriage and citizenship were overlapping themes in the federal government's approach to African Americans' transition from slavery to freedom. Well before the war had ended, army chaplains stationed in freedmen's camps throughout the South promoted legal marriage to freedwomen and freedmen behind the Union lines. In this capacity, the federal government acted as the negotiator of the moral practices that qualified newly freed African Americans for citizenship.

Emancipation signaled the inauguration of a new relationship between newly freed African Americans and the state. Before freedmen won the right to vote, hundreds of men and women turned to the Freedmen's Bureau, which was established in 1865, to monitor the transition to a free labor system and to protect black rights. In the Mississippi Delta, newly freed African Americans demanded that the federal government represent their interests, and men and women took public political action, filed suits, and pressed charges against those who encroached upon their rights. Black women's prominence in local courts undermined the idea that women had no legal self. In an effort to preserve their former privileges and position in plantation society, planter men and women in the same region made efforts to redefine the basis of their own citizenship through property.

Freedmen's Bureau agents, however, held varying ideas of what freedom and citizenship ought to mean for newly freed African Americans. Bureau agents, many of whom were former Union officers, believed that freedmen and freedwomen should have a relationship to the state, but they were particularly interested in establishing this connection by making sure that freedmen and freedwomen remained active in the workforce. It was not until the ratification of the Fourteenth Amendment in 1868 that citizenship for African Americans became a constitutional fact.

Asserting their rights to marriage and property ownership, their rights as free laborers, and their rights to pursue leisure activities, African Americans remapped the boundaries of citizenship in urban centers across the South. In Memphis, Tenn., for example, freedmen and freedwomen socialized, danced, drank, and celebrated with black Union soldiers, well into the early morning hours. They built independent community institutions and sponsored picnics, fairs, and other public events to raise money for churches. Informal battles over citizenship were carried out in the streets—in New Bern and Wilmington, N.C., the white press reported that white women and young black women clashed on the streets.

To manage the barrage of demands and complaints initiated by newly freed African Americans in local courts, lawmakers across the South drafted so-called Black Codes, measures designed to restrict and set limits on African Americans' right to own property, make contracts, and access the legal system. Until the Civil Rights Act was passed in 1866, African American men and women were denied even the most nominal legal recognition as citizens. The pressure to avoid vagrancy, for example, weighed heavily on newly freed African American women in particular. Freedwomen were required to perform heavy labor in the streets of Houston, Tex., as a punishment reserved for the vagrant and disorderly. White and black men were also arrested for disorderly conduct and required to work in the streets, a punishment, however, that wage-working white women completely avoided. In Louisiana, agents of the Freedmen's Bureau requested permission to recruit black women to work when they could not find enough able-bodied black men. White women had a very different responsibility to work. Thus, freedwomen's relationship to the federal government was different in substantial and important ways from that of African American men and white women.

In the early years of emancipation, within the local courts and before a congressional committee, poor women vigorously protested the physical abuse and sexual violence that they experienced at the hands of men. In Granville, N.C., poor whites and African Americans pushed the issue of sexual violence in order to call into question the manifestations of power that justified the degradation of poor women, both black and white. Between 1865 and 1886, men and women filed 24 cases of sexual violence involving poor women. In the aftermath of the Memphis riots of 1866, in which a white mob burned black schools, churches, and many homes, black women spoke before a congressional committee about the rape and sexual violence they experienced. By testifying publicly about the abuse they suffered, poor women, both black and white, performed a radical political act in the context of southern state law and tradition.

In the aftermath of slavery, newly freed African Americans turned to the government for state-sponsored aid to promote their vision of citizenship as well. In 1866 the Military Pension Bureau recognized the sacrifice of formerly enslaved African American Union soldiers by creating policies that extended financial support to their families. When newly freed African American women filed petitions for Civil War widows' pensions, they lay claim to new legal rights, despite the social, economic, and political barriers they confronted at the local and state levels. By making what they understood to be legitimate claims on the government through the Military Pension Bureau, freedwomen articulated their own understanding of widowhood and, by extension, citizenship rights, although black women would not enjoy the privilege of full-scale voting rights in the region until the passage of the Voting Rights Act in 1965.

The right to enjoy state-sponsored aid from the U.S. Pension Bureau, however, was linked to a series of responsibilities outlined in the Pension Bureau's rules. Sexual morality was a central theme in the Pension Bureau's approach to allocating benefits to newly freed African American Civil War widows. If a Civil War widow remarried or was believed to be engaging in a sexual relationship with a man, she forfeited her right to collect benefits. Influenced by concerns with morality, which defined women's reform movements during the late 19th century, some federal lawmakers believed that there was enough room between remarriage and cohabitation in pension law for Civil War widows to engage in sexual relations without paying the consequences. The Act of 7 August 1882 barred widows who cohabited or otherwise engaged in sexual activity from the pension rolls. All Civil War widows were subject to this law, but the law had a particular impact on African American Civil War widows who resided in the South. In eastern North Carolina, African American Civil War widows were routinely investigated because of the lingering belief that southern African Americans had a higher tendency to file fraudulent claims. Bureau examiners discredited African American women's claims on the government by casting them as sexually immoral—and, as a consequence, these women lost their access to state-sponsored aid.

By analyzing how informal assertions of citizenship took shape in the daily lives of men and women, historians of gender and the American South have shown how, and at what moments, men and women attempted to shape or reject the federal government's construction of citizenship. The significance of this approach is important because it restores a sense of humanity and human agency to the unstable history of citizenship in the American South.

BRANDI C. BRIMMER
Vanderbilt University

Elsa Barkley Brown, *Public Culture* (Fall 1994); Nancy Bercaw, *Gendered Freedoms: Race, Rights, and the Politics of the Household in the Delta, 1861–1875* (2003); Brandi Brimmer, "All Her Rights and Privileges: African American Civil War Widows and the Politics of Widows' Pensions Claims" (Ph.D. dissertation, University of California, Los Angeles, 2006); Laura F. Edwards, *North Carolina Historical Review* (July 1991); Katherine Franke, *Yale Journal of Law and the Humanities* (Summer 1999); Linda Kerber, *No Constitutional Right to Be Ladies: Women and the Obligations of Citizenship* (1999); Elizabeth Ann Regosin, *Freedom's Promise: Ex-Slave Families and Citizenship in the Age of Emancipation* (2002); Hannah Rosen, in *Love, Sex, Race: Crossing Boundaries in North American History*, ed. Martha Hodes (1999).

Civil Rights

The struggle for full civil liberties for American citizens has been a volatile mixture of competing agendas and priorities. The goals of black men and women and white women sometimes coincided and at other times came into conflict. All wanted social justice, but each group defined justice differently, set different priorities, and disagreed on strategy. The divide was pronounced over passage of the Fifteenth Amendment. Some abolitionists, including Fredrick Douglass and Julia Ward Howe, thought giving African American men suffrage was more important than opposing the amendment until female suffrage would be included. Prominent women like Elizabeth Cady Stanton fought against ratification because the amendment included the word "male."

Twice in American history the fight for civil liberties for African Americans has led to women's organized reform activity. In the early 19th century, women working in the abolitionist movement saw parallels between their inferior legal status and slaves. Furthermore, they resented the societal constraints that pre-

Columbia is speaking, with her hand on the shoulder of a Civil War soldier who lost a leg in the war. The caption reads, "Franchise. And not this man?" Published in Harper's Weekly, 5 August 1865 (Thomas Nast, illustrator, Library of Congress [LC-USZ62-102257], Washington, D.C.)

vented them from full participation in the movement. At an 1840 antislavery convention in England, Stanton and Lucretia Mott were not permitted to be seated with their male counterparts. They vowed to hold a convention to address discrimination against women, and eight years later they organized the Woman's Rights Convention at Seneca Falls, N.Y. In the second half of the 20th century, white women working for racial equality also saw themselves marginalized in the civil rights movement because of their gender, and some went on to lead what was then called the women's liberation movement. Black women were oppressed because of both race and sex, yet they were vital to the civil rights movement.

In the late 19th and early 20th centuries, during the era of segregation, there were instances in which black women and white women worked together to improve African American communities. Church missionary societies from black churches and white churches sometimes collaborated on projects. There was a great deal of biracial antilynching activism during the early 20th century. The modern civil rights movement became recognizable after World War II when black veterans came home to a society legally divided by race. Some Americans drew parallels between Nazi concepts of racial superiority and southern attitudes toward African Americans. College ministries, particularly those of the Methodists, began to criticize the institutional church for failure to address segregation and discrimination. Blacks in the South began to organize to fight Jim Crow.

The Montgomery, Ala., bus boycott proved a watershed moment for the civil rights movement because it demonstrated that coordinated and sustained economic pressure could produce victory. The event also gave prominence to Martin Luther King Jr., who became a national leader and a symbol of the movement. Rosa Parks, in Montgomery, Ala., refused to move to the back of the bus and became a potent and beloved symbol. She worked as a seamstress and was active in the NAACP. The boycott was successful because information was widely distributed in a short time, accomplished in large part by women acting as community organizers in secretarial type roles. Many black women worked as domestics for white families, and white women often provided transportation for their employees, undermining the boycott.

Black women in the South were vital participants in the civil rights movement—in various forms of protest, including sit-ins, boycotts, picketing, mass demonstrations, the canvassing of neighborhoods, marches, and voter registration. They also provided activists with food and shelter. Traditional female labor such as cooking became acts of subversion against the white power structure, and some observers noted that women were the backbone of the movement—perhaps men were more vulnerable in regard to white employers. And the possibility of violence may have acted as a deterrent for some men in becoming involved, although females also suffered violence for challenging white authority. Fannie Lou Hamer poignantly described her brutal beating to national reporters at the 1964 National Democratic Convention. Demographers have noted that more men than women had migrated north, but even in communities where there was a gendered balance, women still participated more than men. Years later, in interviews about their civil rights activism, none of the women consistently listed kin, friendship, or community networks as the reason they risked their jobs and safety but, significantly, listed their religious beliefs as a primary reason they participated.

Women related the nonviolent message of the movement to their Christian beliefs, and they felt at home in the church buildings where meetings and rallies were held. Churches held a significant place in southern women's lives. Martin Luther King Jr. observed that Sunday at 11:00 A.M. was the most segregated hour in the South. It was also true that Sunday might be the only day a woman working as a domestic could take off her white uniform and wear a stylish dress and beautiful hat. In some black churches, women could hold official leadership positions, and in other churches they led singing and wielded unofficial leadership and influence. And black women felt comfortable with black ministers who led the protests—it was natural to transfer song leading in church to leading protest songs and to look to ministers for direction.

Civil rights organizations—the NAACP, the Congress of Racial Equality, and Martin Luther King Jr.'s Southern Christian Leadership Conference—followed traditional hierarchies of male leadership with women in supportive roles. When student demonstrators in Nashville wanted to organize, long-time activist Ella Baker advised them to form a separate group. The student leaders established the Student Nonviolent Coordinating Committee (SNCC), which was more radical and not based on church hierarchy. The leaders were primarily men—John Lewis, Stokely Carmichael, and Julian Bond—but some were women, including Diane Nash and Ruby Doris Smith.

During the summer of 1964—Freedom Summer—hundreds of young men and women, many of them Jewish, traveled south to register black voters, and volunteers opened Freedom Schools to provide educational opportunities for black children. Work divided along traditional gender lines—most of the teachers were women, and men conducted the more dangerous job of registering voters. White women working alongside black men challenged the South's concept of appropriate social behavior and infuriated locals. Indeed, interracial social activity did cause dissension between black women and white women. The northern volunteers were impressed by the older black women, whom they called "mamas." These women took workers into their homes and fed them home-cooked meals. Traditional female labor was vital to the success of the movement and often brought on the wrath of white employers.

Female SNCC members grew increasingly upset about the sexual discrimination they felt within the organization. Two women, Casey Hayden and Mary King, wrote a paper on the status of women in SNCC, comparing the way women were treated to how African Americans were treated. This led to Carmichael's infamous joke that the only position of women in SNCC is prone. Sexist treatment in SNCC did not in itself cause the women's liberation movement, but the organization's open leadership structure allowed these women to challenge authority. Hayden and King's paper has become an important document for the modern feminist movement. However, a biracial sisterhood failed to develop because white, middle-class leaders defined feminism in terms of access to the workplace. The feminist movement did not address the needs of black and poor women.

Fannie Lou Hamer, who became an important leader and a symbol of someone willing to risk danger to secure rights, worked as one of the field secretaries for SNCC, registering voters and helping poor black families obtain government benefits. The Democratic Party refused to accept blacks, and Hamer helped form the rival Mississippi Freedom Democratic Party (MFDP). At the 1964 Democratic Convention, Hamer testified before the credentials committee, describing the violent beatings she and other African Americans had suffered at the hands of white Mississippians. Network news showed her dramatic testimony to an appalled national audience. The MFDP was unsuccessful in replacing the white delegation at the convention, but Hamer continued fighting discrimination.

During these years of the civil rights movement, women, like Parks and Hamer, became respected leaders, and concepts and symbols of gender permeated the movement. Striking sanitation workers in Memphis wore placards proclaiming "I AM A MAN." White-supremacist groups, organized to resist school desegregation, such as the Citizens' Councils, used a similar rhetoric of manhood to encourage white southerners to maintain hegemony and employed feminized images to caricature whites, whom they viewed as traitors. The Nation of Islam espoused conservative attitudes within the movement about the proper role of women. The Black Panthers promoted a form of militant masculinity. Eventually, white northerners who spent summers in the South went back home, taking with them the organizing skills they had acquired in the civil rights movement. Many applied their experience to other reforming activities, including the women's movement and antiwar activities.

MINOA D. UFFELMAN
Austin Peay State University

Steve Estes, *I AM A MAN! Race, Manhood, and the Civil Rights Movement* (2005); Sara Evans, *Personal Politics: The Roots of Women's Liberation in the Civil Rights Movement and the New Left* (1969); Jacqueline Jones, *Labor of Love, Labor of Sorrow: Black Women, Work, and the Family, from Slavery to the Present* (1985); Charles M. Payne, *I've Got the Light of Freedom: The Organizing Tradition and the Mississippi Freedom Struggle* (1995).

Civil War

By the end of the Civil War, some 90 percent of the age-eligible white men of the South had served in the Confederate army. Of those 800,000 men, close to a third would be killed or wounded and countless more would return home shattered in heart and mind by the experience. At the same time, close to 200,000 black men would find their liberation from slavery through their service in the Union military, and countless more black women and children would escape behind Union lines, effectively emancipating themselves from the institution as well. Between the loss of most adult white men for the duration of the war and the permanent loss of much of the slave population, the southern slaveholding household structure, which had formed the core of the antebellum social, economic, and cultural order of the region, was fractured along the lines of race, class, and gender. It would never be restored to its prewar form but would emerge instead, albeit unevenly, into a free labor–based, more domestically grounded, familial structure.

Changes in the gender roles for men and women, as well as for the enslaved and the free, were critical in this wartime transformation. During the war, many white men lost their ability to protect and dominate their households as they had in the past; black men gained not only their freedom but also the position as heads of their own households in the war's aftermath. Confederate women lost economic position along with their men, but they also gained domestic position during the war and continued to hold it in the postwar era in the face of their men's defeat. Freedwomen arguably stood at the center of this reordering of gender relations. The wartime destruction of slavery enabled freedwomen to put their own households and familial relations first to a much greater extent than had been possible for them as slaves in the antebellum southern household structure. Their children were finally *their* children and their husbands were *their* husbands, not their masters' slaves or their former masters' sharecroppers.

This revolution in gender relations was not what white men had expected when they seceded from the Union or when they marched off to make war against the federal government. Historians have aptly described the secession of the South and the formation of the Confederacy as an attempt to create a more "patriarchal republic," a republic where the position of free white men would be legally and politically secured against the threat of changing relationships of race and gender being generated by modernization in the North. Northern critics of the southern household order argued that southern white men had too much structural power as a consequence of their ownership of slaves, what they termed "the slave power." Southern white men viewed this criticism of their position, and especially legislative attempts to curb it—for example, the political struggle over the right of slaveholding households to move to the frontier—as an intolerable violation of their rights as free men, a violation that required them to take a stand in defense of their social order and their place in it as heads of slaveholding households.

The Civil War was initially viewed then as a test between two competing forms of manhood. Many Confederate citizens were convinced that what they viewed as the pale, urban clerks of the modernizing North would be no match for the courageous, hard-riding, straight-shooting southern man. It was a commonplace to shrug off the clear superiority of the northern population in terms of manpower and military supplies with the assumption that "one of our men is worth ten of theirs." This initial framing of the war as a struggle over what constituted the appropriate rights of free men would come to grief in the context of fighting the war itself. The Civil War was, after all, the first modern, industrial war, and it quickly became apparent that winning battles was not so much about manly courage as it was about order and discipline. The cavalry charge was rendered obsolete in the face of the accuracy of the rifle. Men spent long hours in trenches instead, as the defensive was empowered over the offensive by the development of new military technology.

Thus, their assumptions about what made a man were being deconstructed on the battlefield, and Confederate men found that the social order of the home front was dissolving as well. Confederate women were faced with the absence of their men in the running of the household, and slaves increasingly abandoned those households in acts of self-emancipation. Ironies abound here, for while Confederate men went to war in order to protect what they saw as their position as free men, even the very demands of fighting the war itself served to undercut this position. By the end of the war, the wartime policies of the Confederacy itself—the drafting of men, the confiscation or impressments not only of slaves but of critical farm implements and animals as well, and restrictions on the types of crop production—although necessary to the continued support of the Confederate war, served to further destabilize the southern household and to alienate some southern men from the Confederate cause.

The demands of fighting the war clearly undercut the gender identity of free white men, both because of their defeat by northern men on the field of battle and because of their loss of control over their dependents, but the gendered meaning of the war for the household dependents, whether slaves or white women, has been much debated by historians. Did the war "open every door" for southern women? Did the expanded opportunity to run their homes and farms, not to mention organize public associations in support of the war or take up wage labor to support their households, constitute a watershed in the position of white southern women? Or did the war have the opposite impact, causing them to realize just how dependent they were on their men when faced with the war-born necessity of trying to replace them with their own efforts? Perhaps what they learned from the men's absence was not how much they wished to have the rights of men but rather just how difficult their lives would be if they were to be permanently stripped of the protective power—a protective power that entailed their own gender subordination to the head of household but also represented their race and class privilege in the southern household order.

The impact of the war on the position of white women will undoubtedly always be debated, if only because there was a range of response. Some women appear to have welcomed their increased autonomy; others quailed at the challenges they faced in even temporarily taking over responsibilities they saw as fundamentally male in character. What is clear is that the combined impact of the wartime absence of their men and the dissolution of slavery created a fundamental break in their experience. Southern white women became more autonomous during the war, if only out of sheer necessity. In the war's aftermath, the economic and political losses of their men required that many of them continue to shoulder more responsibility for the economic support and public representation of their households. Some of the most class-privileged southern women found themselves washing dishes for the first time, taking up the labor that their female slaves would have performed before the war. Other women continued to run their households or to work for wages in the face of the permanent loss of their men. Wartime organizations of Confederate women, particularly the soldiers' aid societies, persisted as well in the postwar Ladies Memorial Societies and later in the United Daughters of the Confederacy. The cultural politics of these organizations constitute one of the most tell-

ing statements we have of the long-run impact of the war on white gender relations. However much white women may have gained power in relation to their
men as a consequence of the war, this did not mean that they did not stand by
them. Indeed, the core intent of these organizations was to continue to uphold
their men, even in defeat, and perhaps particularly in defeat.

At the same time, the wartime collapse of slavery allowed freedmen and
freedwomen to move toward the creation of their own separate households,
and historians have debated the consequences of this newfound household autonomy for black gender relations. The war gave black men the opportunity to
serve in defense of their people. As emasculating as white southern defeat was
for white men, Union victory was empowering for black men. In the postwar
period, the legalization of marriage for freedpeople, the establishment of the
sharecropping system with the head of household representing the members of
his family, and the acquisition of the vote constituted a structural empowerment
of black men in relation to black women. Historians suggest that this gendering of the freedpeople was not experienced as subordination of black women
to black men as much as a shared empowerment of freedpeople as a whole.
Indeed, whether white or black, male or female, what southerners gained from
the changes in gender relations set in motion by the Civil War was an increased
domestic integrity of the southern household. For black women, now free, this
meant that their very standing as wives and as mothers was legally recognized,
and the newly emergent sharecropping system gave them at least a cabin, however humble, to call home. For white women, the domestic separation of the
white and black dependents of the antebellum southern household also gave an
increased private and public significance to their roles as wives, mothers, and
daughters of once Confederate men.

LEEANN WHITES
University of Missouri at Columbia

Nancy Bercaw, *Gendered Freedoms: Race, Rights, and the Politics of Household in
the Delta, 1861–1875* (2003); Stephen Berry, *All That Makes a Man: Love and Ambi-
tion in the Civil War South* (2003); Edward D. C. Campbell Jr. and Kym S. Rice, eds.,
A Woman's War: Southern Women, Civil War, and the Confederate Legacy (1996);
Catherine Clinton and Nina Silber, eds., *Battle Scars: Gender and Sexuality in the
American Civil War* (2006), *Divided Houses: Gender and the Civil War* (1992); Karen
Cox, *Dixie's Daughters: The United Daughters of the Confederacy and the Preservation
of Confederate Culture* (2003); Drew Faust, *Mothers of Invention: Women of the Slave-
holding South in the American Civil War* (1996); Gerald Linderman, *Embattled Courage: The Experience of Combat in the Civil War* (1987); Anne Firor Scott, *The Southern*

Lady: From Pedestal to Politics (1970); LeeAnn Whites, *Gender Matters: The Civil War, Reconstruction, and the Making of the New South* (2005), *The Civil War as a Crisis in Gender: Augusta, Georgia, 1860–1890* (1995).

Clubs and Voluntary Organizations

Somewhat slower than northern women to form clubs and associations, southern women did not participate in social and public affairs through organized groups until after the Civil War and Reconstruction. The loss of one-fourth of the region's males and the accompanying poverty of the late 19th century forced women into the workforce and brought increased independence. Release from the burdens of directing large plantation households and the supervision and physical care of slaves added to the leisure time of women of means at the same time that the wives of professional and middle-class townsmen also gained added freedom from domestic duties. Moreover, as public colleges stressing industrial and commercial curricula were founded, more southern daughters entered professional fields. Finally, the increasing urbanization of the South facilitated the organization of groups in which women could express their growing sense of social usefulness, self-reliance, and initiative.

Southern women first banded together to further the foreign and home mission work of their churches. Anne Firor Scott has concluded that "the public life of nearly every Southern woman leader for forty years began in a church society." Methodist women formed the Board of Home Missions in 1882, and Baptist women formed the Women's Missionary Union in 1888. The church "circle" was the most accessible and approved institution outside the home through which women were able both to initiate reform through city missions and settlement houses and to lay the foundation for the interracial cooperation that would come in the 20th century. Concurrently, the Woman's Christian Temperance Union (WCTU), organized in the South after Frances Willard visited the region in the 1880s, developed under state leaders such as Caroline Merrick in Louisiana, Belle Kearney in Mississippi, Julia Tutwiler in Alabama, and Rebecca Felton in Georgia. The puritanical foundations of the temperance movement provided a model for the work of the WCTU in its crusade for the abolition of the convict-lease system, the establishment of industrial schools for girls and homes for youthful offenders, and other reforms.

In the late 1880s and 1890s, southern women were drawn into the club movement. Between 1894 and 1907, federations of various cultural and self-improvement groups were formed in every southern state, and by 1910 all were members of the General Federation of Women's Clubs (GFWC). Although the initial goal was self-edification, the federated clubs became, in the words of Mrs. Percy Pennybacker, a Texas matron who headed the national GFWC in 1913–14, a "recruiting station in which the unaccustomed women shall be trained to find themselves . . . and [assume] widening responsibilities in the world's work." As a major tool of social change in the South, women's clubs promoted statewide library and adult education programs, guardianship laws for divorced women, marital blood tests, sanitary milk supplies, child labor laws, protective legislation for women, and a myriad of other reforms. In their "alternative universities," clubwomen kept abreast of current events, mobilized public opinion, and, most important, promoted the woman suffrage movement. In the 1920s and 1930s, club representatives formed Joint Legislative Councils in most southern states to lobby for their club agendas at the statehouses.

Excluded from the GFWC, black women formed their own Southern Association of Colored Women's Clubs after Margaret Murray Washington began the Tuskegee Woman's Club in 1895. Unlike white women, black clubwomen were especially concerned with issues of importance to poor women, working mothers, and tenant wives. Their work was best represented by the community betterment and social service programs of the Atlanta Neighborhood Union initiated by Lugenia Burns Hope in 1908. Also important to southern black women were the mutual aid societies created to provide medical care and burial assistance. Some persisted well into the 20th century.

Beginning in 1851, when Ann Pamela Cunningham of South Carolina began the first woman's patriotic society in the United States, the Mount Vernon Ladies' Association, southern white women have responded to organizations commemorating the past. The unique history of the South has fostered a high level of interest in genealogy and an attraction to the Colonial Dames of America, the Daughters of the American Revolution (DAR) (its first southern chapter was founded in North Carolina in 1898), and especially the United Daughters of the Confederacy (UDC), founded by Nashville women in 1894 from numerous existing cemetery memorial societies and soldier relief associations. The UDC, like the DAR, was socially glamorous, perpetuating social hierarchies as it strove to glorify the southern war effort, particularly through the creation of libraries on the Confederate past. In recent years, as it has declined in membership, the UDC has shifted its focus to historical preservation.

In the post–Civil War years, southern college women founded a number of Greek-letter sororities, and such collegiate groups and related literary societies have remained popular in southern universities. Many women have "graduated" to high-society organizations that flourish in southern towns and cities, best represented by the Junior League and other benefit groups, whose principal functions are to raise funds for community arts and social services. For other women, principally those in small towns, social activities center around the meeting halls of the Order of Eastern Star and other auxiliaries to male fraternal orders.

Academic and professional women in the South created associations patterned after northern organizations. In 1903 the Southern Association of College Women (SACW) was formed in Knoxville and, under the strong direction of Elizabeth Avery Colton, devoted its energies to raising the standards of institutions of higher education for the region's young women. In 1921 SACW merged with the American Association of University Women. Delta Kappa Gamma, founded in 1929 by Annie Webb Blanton and a charter group of Texas teachers, grew beyond its early southern chapters into an international society for women educators. Altrusa International, begun in Nashville in 1917 as a service club for business and professional women, is one of many such groups that serve to coordinate the leadership and community service of women professionals. Another is Pilot International, founded in 1919 by a Kentuckian, Lena Madesin Phillips.

Rural women in the South, both black and white, are still active in home demonstration clubs organized before World War I by the extension departments of land-grant colleges. They are unique among women's organizations in that from the outset they have had professional leadership paid for by federal and state funds. Organized rural women have devoted their attention almost exclusively to home improvement and rural community development, often working with the American Farm Bureau to stress citizenship, safety, and home and community beautification. Urban women, too, through ubiquitous garden clubs, promote memorial plantings, highway beautification, antebellum home tours, and the restoration of historic homes and buildings.

Both the difficult economic situations of southern state governments and the general political conservatism of the region's electorate have led women to form associations to institute social change. One of the earliest was the New Orleans Anti-Tuberculosis League, formed by Kate Gordon in 1906. Early 20th-century women created societies for village improvement, modern roads, public schoolhouse improvement, and child labor abolition. Reflecting southern emphasis upon maternal responsibilities, the National Congress of Mothers (later the PTA) was founded by a Georgia woman, Alice M. Birney, in 1897, and the National Congress of Colored Parents and Teachers was begun in Atlanta by Selena Sloan Butler in 1926. In 1930 Jessie Daniel Ames of Texas formed the Association of Southern Women for the Prevention of Lynching (ASWPL), which eventually united 40,000 churchwomen to confront the issues of race, lynching, and interracial sex before it met its goals and ceased to exist.

The ASWPL is the most distinctive women's voluntary association in southern history.

With the enfranchisement of women in 1920, the eligibility of women to hold public office, and the increasing access of southern women to professions once the exclusive enclave of men, the club and voluntary association work of southern women has declined as many women have turned from volunteer work to paid jobs. Moreover, greater access to higher education for women has lessened the need to pursue education through cultural and literary organizations. As other agencies have arisen to meet society's needs, the federated clubs and reformist associations are no longer major agents for social change. Nonetheless, there is scarcely any southern town or city where women of both races do not still join together in numerous social, professional, and civic organizations.

MARTHA H. SWAIN
Mississippi State University

Karen Cox, *Dixie's Daughters: The United Daughters of the Confederacy and the Preservation of Confederate Culture* (2003); Sharon Harley and Rosalyn Terborg-Penn, eds., *The Afro-American Woman: Struggles and Images* (1978); Gerda Lerner, *Journal of Negro History* (April 1974); John Patrick McDowell, *The Social Gospel in the South: The Woman's Home Mission Movement in the Methodist Episcopal Church, South, 1886–1939* (1982); Margaret Nell Price, "The Development of Leadership by Southern Women through Clubs and Organizations" (M.A. thesis, University of North Carolina, Chapel Hill, 1945); Anne Firor Scott, *The Southern Lady: From Pedestal to Politics, 1830–1930* (1970).

Country Music

A mountain mother. A honky-tonk man. A coal miner's daughter. A rhinestone cowboy. A Dixie chick. To some, these terms may be meaningless, but to the country and western music connoisseur, they are the familiar characters that have been the most popular (albeit at different times) on southern commercial music stages since the genre emerged in the 1930s. Because the music has always been about people and stories, characters have mattered in ways different from other genres. And a character's gender has not only helped determine the form and content of country and western music, but it has been wielded to mark important changes in it over time. In turn, history has affected performers who, in turn, have used musical repertoires, costuming, and new technology in order to keep characters current.

What eventually became country and western music emerged out of an eclectic mix of radio programs (called "barn dances") in the 1920s and 1930s, some of which came from vaudeville, that supplied its initial stock characters. Barn dance radio programs typically appeared in large cities to which southerners had migrated by the mid-1920s but catered to all listeners within a given region. By the early 1930s, Chicago's *National Barn Dance* (by then, the genre's flagship program) found that using southern female images, like the mountain mother, allowed the program to attract substantial endorsement deals, to develop a national following, and to serve as a standard for the genre as a whole (western images like the cowboy and cowgirl also were popular). Listeners responded to the mountain woman's motherly qualities, which she had supposedly learned in her isolated Appalachian mountain community, qualities that had existed, pure and unsullied, since the area had been settled in the colonial era. The music, sung by performers such as Lulu Belle Wiseman, the "Hayloft Sweetheart," was the social glue that kept southern communities together in difficult times, and listeners, frightened by the Great Depression and World War II, saw these musical performances as an antidote to that chaos. Male performers were less successful since they represented pioneering men who had forged a civilization from "savages" (Native Americans) and dense forests (although no one could sing sentimental favorites that bemoaned the death of Mother or a beloved dog like Kentuckian Red Foley). Listeners preferred the mountain mother's stability, and Wiseman and the *National Barn Dance* were stunningly successful. Wiseman was named the most popular female radio performer in the country in 1936, and the *National Barn Dance* was usually ranked in the Top 10 nationwide.

By World War II, shows that imitated the *National Barn Dance* numbered more than 500 nationwide, but stock characters had shifted by then. They had begun featuring southern and western characters, and the eclectic mix that had dominated the *National Barn Dance* would no longer be at the forefront. The show had begun catering to new audiences created by another Great Migration from the South to urban centers, where munitions were being produced for the war effort. Jukeboxes and the Armed Forces Radio Network were new arenas to hear shows and stars such as sentimental singer Roy Acuff and spinster/gossip Minnie Pearl. Acuff mimicked Foley's sentimental sounds, singing, as one historian wrote, in "an utterly sincere and believable vocal style" and rendering songs in "an emotionally earnest and plaintive manner." Minnie Pearl greeted her audiences with an exuberant "Howdee!" before settling down to gossip about friends and family from the fictitious Grinder's Switch, a bucolic southern homestead.

A new commercial musical form called country and western music emerged in the postwar era, a form that required new characters and, eventually, new ways to hear to them. War mobilization caused working-class communities to form in areas such as southern California, communities that had money to spend and a desire to hear southern sounds. Record producers catered to their musical taste by promoting singers such as Hank Williams, the Maddox Brothers and Rose, and Kitty Wells, who sang about the heartaches caused by drinking and dancing (typically with someone other than a spouse) in new working-class bars called honky-tonks. Williams represented the new honky-tonk character especially well, singing songs that emphasized the lonesomeness of being southern and in love with a hard-hearted woman, so much so that a grown man could cry. The queen of gingham and modest virtue, Kitty Wells, challenged Williams's view of tantalizing women in 1952, singing that it was not God who turned good women into honky-tonk angels but wicked men who lured them to the dark side (or corner bar).

By the end of the 1950s, barn dance radio had disappeared, mostly because of television's popularity, and radio stations embraced a new phenomenon—the disc jockey—and used the reemerging record industry to sell country and western music to regional audiences. In Nashville, the only barn dance program, the *Grand Ole Opry*, drew the record industry to the area, and producers, publishing companies, and booking agents all relocated to the city, establishing it as the new center of the country and western universe. But that shift was accomplished, too, by a new kind of music, called the Nashville Sound, which promoted modern, more suburban-looking characters like the Southern Chanteuse (ably portrayed by Patsy Cline) and the "countrypolitan" Marty Robbins, both of whom depended as much on orchestras and ball gowns as they did on banjos and cowboy hats. Indeed, men like Robbins became what historian Diane Pecknold called "the man in the gray flannel Nudie suit," a reference to both Nudie Cohen, the flamboyant stylist to country music stars, and to the era's modern corporate ethic. Others in the 1960s continued to modernize the look, sound, and feel of country and western music, this time in response to youth movements. Singer Jeannie C. Riley, for example, socked it to the "Harper Valley PTA" in fashionable miniskirts in 1967. But others resisted this modern image, using an earthy demeanor that exposed an entrenched southern poverty while simultaneously challenging the smooth suburban aura of Cline, Robbins, and Riley. The Coal Miner's Daughter (Loretta Lynn) sang songs that demanded her husband not come home a-drinkin' with lovin' on his mind, and Tammy Wynette promised to stand by her man, even when it was hard to be a woman. Male stars like Buck Owens and George Jones also challenged that modern image, assuming a more retro look and sound reminiscent of Hank Williams. Still others made it a spectacle: Dolly Parton's first partner, singer Porter Waggoner, wore expensive western outfits designed by costumer Nudie and studded with flashy rhinestones. Others questioned the artificiality of country and western characters, like guitar impresario Glen Campbell, who made his name playing the Rhinestone Cowboy, his hit song by the same title, an ironic comment on the music's commercialism and its willingness to rely on flashy rhinestones as much as good music. Hippie antiauthoritarianism also appeared with the Outlaw Movement (singers Johnny Cash, Willie Nelson, Merle Haggard, and Waylon Jennings) in the 1970s, as the four men, dressed exclusively in black, promised to sing to suburban families, renegades, and prisoners alike and to shake up what they considered the staid, conservative country and western mainstream.

In the 1970s and 1980s, "crossover" characters like pop prince and princess Kenny Rogers and Barbara Mandrell appealed once more to mainstream, middle-class musical audiences rather than to strictly rural or working-class urban audiences. Mandrell, in particular, responded to the burgeoning Christian movement in the United States as well as to working women. According to her website, Mandrell was a woman of faith, a working mom and wife, and someone with whom you would be comfortable sitting at your kitchen table. But the star of the era was the bewigged, buxom, brilliant businesswoman and musician Dolly Parton, who became a superstar by being multiple women to multiple audiences. For traditionalists, she sang songs from the 1930s like "The Rosewood Casket"; for the working woman, she sang "9 to 5," which asserted women's independence; and for men who liked her "trashy" appearance, she appeared in movies like *The Best Little Whorehouse in Texas* (1982).

The affluent 1990s gave rise to the resurgence of a more traditional sound, especially in megastar Garth Brooks's embrace of Buck Owens's and George Jones's style, albeit rendered in remarkably modern ways (his stage shows were legendary in their ability to use techniques more common in heavy metal shows than in country and western shows), which became the standard for male characters. Shania Twain became Brooks's female equal, daring to show her belly button in music videos and using heavy metal producer (and husband) John "Mutt" Lange to record a pop version of country and western. Her popularity made the 1990s the "Year of the Woman" for many in the genre, as multiple female artists (Mary Chapin Carpenter, Tricia Yearwood, Patty Loveless, for example) scored commercial hit after commercial hit.

The events of 11 September 2001 remasculinized country and western music, as themes like heroism, rescue, and patriotism—perceived to be male traits—resounded in the music of performers such as Toby Keith and Darrel Worley.

Though female stars like the neotraditionalist Dixie Chicks have been popular, the Chicks' unwillingness to maintain a polite stage presence, as well as their criticism of President George W. Bush's Iraq policy, has caused the industry to rally around stars like Keith and Worley, who represent that more conservative, patriotic mold. Much of this has been driven by new radio conglomerates, especially Clear Channel and Cumulus Broadcasting, which own many of America's once-independent radio stations. Characters once again represent the South's regional identity but have been molded to support the president's conservative policies and the economic practices of corporate America in ways that the original barn dance characters could never have imagined.

KRISTINE M. MCCUSKER
Middle Tennessee State University

Kristine M. McCusker and Diane Pecknold, eds., *A Boy Named Sue: Gender and Country Music* (2004).

Dissemblance, Culture of

In her essay "Rape and the Inner Lives of Black Women in the Middle West: Preliminary Thoughts on the Culture of Dissemblance," historian Darlene Clark Hine was the first to posit the concept of a "cult of secrecy" among African American women, according to which they shrouded their private lives, sexual experiences, and desire in silence. Black women did this, Hine argued, in order to protect themselves from offensive and exploitative associations with immorality and degeneracy that might lead to rape, other forms of sexual violence and exploitation, or the general disparagement of their character. In popular cultural representations, from blackface minstrelsy to 20th-century film, black women were rendered as bestial and savage in their proclivities and desires, with their sexuality warped beyond human recognition. In response, they individually and collectively countered the "pervasive stereotypes and negative estimations of the sexuality of Black women" by creating "alternative self-images." Hine's theory of the existence of this habit or code of silence among African American women quickly became a guiding tenet of African American women's history and black feminist studies. Thus, Hine defined and explained a phenomenon, dissemblance, that scholars had continuously confronted throughout their investigations of African American history and culture and that continued to shape African American women's public personas and engagement with the sexual aspects of race politics.

The culture of dissemblance was intimately linked to "uplift" ideologies of racial advancement, which presumed the superiority of Victorian modes of self-representation, decorum, and sexual conduct. Whatever African American women did in their private lives, in public they endeavored to present an unassailable image of ladylike chastity, Christian devotion, and moral rectitude. African American women formed the National Association of Colored Women (NACW) in 1896 as a means to establish their respectability and to uplift the mass of African American women, whom leaders considered ignorant of these ideas. Thus, African American women institutionalized the culture of dissemblance and made it a central tenet of African American racial advancement strategies. Through the activities, publications, and public appearances of its adherents in the NACW and other institutions, such as churches and schools, the culture of dissemblance became a well-established political strategy, according to which black women of all classes sought to obscure their sexual selves in order to embody chaste morality and respectability and exhorted all black women to do the same.

Although the culture of dissemblance was the best weapon oppressed women developed to counteract the damaging stereotypes that not only humiliated them but also made them easy targets for rape and other forms of racist terror, this strategy for self-preservation was one of constraint rather than liberation. Hine lauded black women's ability, through the culture of dissemblance, to create "positive alternative images of their sexual selves" that "facilitated Black women's mental and physical survival in a hostile world." Yet, in adhering to the tenets of dissemblance, black women allowed themselves no public acknowledgment of lust or sexual fulfillment, or even sexiness, as aspects of their identities, because to do so was personally and politically dangerous. The demands of dissemblance rendered public sexual expression taboo in African American discourse and muted, even silenced, autonomous women's voices around sexuality and desire. Such a defensive mechanism resulted in both the stigmatization of women who did acknowledge the need for sexual expression and an inability to incorporate a self-generated idea of African American women's sexual self-determination into racial advancement ideologies, precluding the full incorporation of feminist tenets into the mainstream of African American politics.

Furthermore, the "cult of secrecy" around black women's sexuality and sexual oppression buttressed masculinist understandings of racism as an oppression predominantly affecting black men. The full reality of the oppression black women suffered—a fusion of racial and sexual, physical and discursive dehumanizations that stalked them through their bodies, reproductive capacities, and sexuality as well as through their economic and political freedoms—remained obscure and was relentlessly compounded by this enforced silence.

Originally developed as a defense mechanism, the "culture of dissemblance" became ingrained as a tenet of African American respectability and solidarity and ultimately contributed to the difficulty black women experienced in endeavoring to claim their sexuality, desire, and sexual expression and to incorporate these aspects of sexual self-determination into African American racial advancement politics.

ERIN D. CHAPMAN
University of Mississippi

Darlene Clark Hine, *Signs* (Summer 1989).

Education

Education brought progress and economic development to the South, but it also preserved patriarchy, southern identity, social custom, and caste. Like Puritans and pioneers had done in other regions, southerners used education for the teaching and learning of appropriate gender characteristics, behaviors, and roles. Yet southerners elevated the differences between males and females to mythological proportions and used the force of law and custom fiercely and over time to maintain social structure and order. As a result, a gender-differentiated hierarchy pervaded nearly every aspect of southern formal and informal "schooling." The kind and overall quality of education experienced by southerners varied by locale and vastly improved over time, but it remained rigid and slow to change relative to gender, race, and social class.

Although Thomas Jefferson first advocated public support for a state system of education, southerners favored a laissez-faire approach to education whereby individual ingenuity, family support, and philanthropy made possible sometimes impressive efforts to teach and to learn. As common schools spread literacy and Christianity in other regions through the early to mid-19th century, the South relied upon private academies for the teaching of middle- and upper-class children and charity schools evolved for the teaching of the poor. These early schools, led by male ministers or "schoolmasters," varied in curriculum and quality, although a few academies earned a reputation as college preparatory or became a university such as Washington and Lee. The perceived need to train military leaders and promote law and order led to the establishment of some of these schools, including the Virginia Military Institute (1839), the nation's first state military college, and the South Carolina Military Academy (the Citadel), which took on an educational mission in 1841. Early on, a small number of schools offered coeducation, and a few, such as the Georgia Female College, established in 1836, opened doors solely to young women.

Between 1800 and 1830 most southern states outlawed the learning of basic literacy skills among enslaved Americans, and cultural attitudes limited literacy for a large portion of whites. Frederick Douglass nonetheless covertly educated fellow enslaved men, and Sarah and Angelina Grimké, the privileged white daughters of a South Carolina Supreme Court judge, taught their black playmates to read at their plantation home. These examples exemplify the individual risks and efforts undertaken to enhance literacy behind the veil of slavery. Early Sunday schools, the Union army, and missionaries working in the Sea Island Schools—or later the "Yankee schoolmarms" of the Freedmen's Bureau, who labored along with legions of eager blacks to spread literacy—further illustrate the effort required to establish formal schooling in the region. High illiteracy rates among southerners, particularly for women and African Americans, lingered well into the 20th century as a lasting consequence of this miserly approach to public education.

The idea that males should be educated for leadership or "public" work and females for domestic work and reproduction marked educational philosophy and practice during the 19th and 20th centuries. In the South, religious conviction further sanctioned this order, and education varied most obviously by gender, with further nuance for race and class. For example, in the 1800s, elite, white males learned the family business or studied a classical curriculum while pursuing leisure sports such as hunting and horse riding. Elite white females attended finishing schools and learned the feminine arts of elocution, music, studio art, and needlework—though a surprising number of southern women studied Latin and the classics too. Select enslaved or indentured Americans apprenticed to learn gender-specific occupational skills that supported plantation enterprises, with black males learning skills such as blacksmithing, barrel making, carpentry, or tailoring, and black women learning cooking, sewing, or midwifery. In the late 1900s, before baccalaureate degrees became more common, these possibilities extended to females being educated for hairdressing, nursing, or clerical positions, and to males being taught woodworking or automobile mechanics.

Former slaves, assisted by the Republican Party and northern philanthropists, began to establish free schools during Reconstruction, but white southerners defiantly resisted modernization, democratization, and universal schooling—often against their own best interests. Confronting the possibility of increasing black literacy and liberation, whites began to paint a romantic picture of the planter regime, a picture suffused with patriotic dedication to Confederate heroes and war dead. Gender became a pillar of this new social construction, exemplified in the 1865 founding of the social fraternity Kappa Alpha Order. This fraternity honored Confederate general Robert E. Lee and eulogized the virtues of the southern gentlemen who, along with their beautiful belles, decorous and chaste, became the new touchstones of southern white masculinity and femininity. Though only a mirage for most whites who where uneducated, browbeaten, and exploited, the notion of superiority contributed to white solidarity against Reconstruction-era black advancement and to a growing sense of southern identity.

In this era, the teaching of children in the South's growing number of common schools became viewed as an extension of the home or "women's work." Unmarried women, recruited expressly for their conservative impulses and willingness to work for low wages, moved in increasing numbers into the teaching roles held by schoolmasters in earlier times. Normal schools, such as the Mississippi Industrial Institute and College for the Education of White Girls of the State of Mississippi (founded in 1884 and later the Mississippi University for Women) and the State Normal and Industrial School of North Carolina (founded in 1892 and later the University of North Carolina at Greensboro), were developed expressly for the role of preparing teachers. Though these institutions at first offered little more than the common school curriculum, normal schools became the primary institutions whereby females sought and gained advanced education in the region. Most of the region's normal schools evolved to comprehensive degree-granting institutions, many of them thriving coeducational state universities.

As Reconstruction-era gains began to erode, former slaves, with the assistance of the federal government and foundation philanthropists from the Northeast, sought to establish their own institutions whereby the race could be "uplifted" and the humanity and dignity that was denied the race during slavery could be achieved. Yet former slaves, such as Booker T. Washington, and their seemingly well-meaning benefactors took their cues from the past too, and these new institutions promoted familiar patriarchal and class-based strictures, using the perceived deficiencies of blacks for curricular inspiration. Thus, these new institutions, such as the Hampton Normal and Agricultural Institute, founded in 1868, and the Tuskegee Institute, established in 1881, educated for accommodation by responding to gender, sexual, and racial stereotypes — including the widely accepted idea that blacks needed education for industry along gendered lines and moral improvement. Though black institutions tended to be coeducational, single-gender institutions, such as the Daytona Normal and Industrial Institute for Girls, established in 1904 (later Bethune-Cookman College), also emphasized black women's respectability, for example, by enforcing very strict dress codes and curfews that lasted long after women at predominantly white institutions were free from such strictures.

The long-standing myths or stereotypes about the physicality and animalistic nature of blacks generated fear among whites and justified violence against the establishment of racially integrated schools. During slavery, the power of planter men had reached even into the homes of slaves, who were often denied their own family bonds. Even as blacks and whites lived and worked closely together in the service of powerful patrons, various myths and laws prohibited the voluntary association of persons of different races and castes. For example, myths about the exotic sexuality and promiscuity of black women legally excused the rape of black women by white men, and the "rape myth" that black men secretly desired to rape white women justified the lynching of black males for gestures of presumed familiarity. This was the situation in the murder of Emmett Till in Money, Miss., much later, during the 1950s. And, in reaction to the landmark 1954 Supreme Court ruling in *Brown v. Board of Education*, the fear of interracial dating and mating in Louisiana gave added impetus for the implementation of single-gender public high schools through 1980 and various "two prom" traditions, with separate proms held for blacks and whites as late as 2003. In sum, these social conceptions and fears ensured that the improvements made in education in the South happened primarily along racial lines in state systems made up of a mixture of public and private institutions that provided education for an apartheid social structure.

Private universities in the Northeast had a historical legacy of training clergy and clerics for religious and public service, but southern state universities attracted the sons of landed gentry, who were sometimes not interested in intellectual pursuits but rather sought to uphold southern social customs and fill future congressional or state legislative posts. The University of Virginia fully admitted women on an equal basis with men in 1969, but other southern state flagship universities have perpetuated male-dominated cultures of exclusivity marked by de-emphasis of intellectual pursuits and a strong adherence to campus traditions, including intercollegiate football, Greek life, and beauty pageants, to name a few.

Often presented as romantic, traditional, or distinctly southern, the patriarchal, racial, and class-based strictures of plantation life continue to influence opportunity, eligibility, and preparation for study and vocation for southern males and females. Many females choose female-dominant, lower-wage occupations of nursing or teaching, and many black males struggle to be a part of the educational enterprise at all—today more black males are in prison than

Teacher at Bethune-Cookman College, Daytona Beach, Fla., 1940s (Gordon Parks, photographer, Library of Congress [LC-USW-3-17125C], Washington, D.C.)

are enrolled in postsecondary education institutions. All too often, southerners use these traditional gender expectations to instill fear, mark outsiders, and punish nonconformity, as when a male who is identified as passive is called a "momma's boy" or when a female lacking "femininity" is labeled as a lesbian.

Though more southerners are seeking education at advanced levels than ever before, southern school systems continue to be at a disadvantage in promoting student learning because of patronage political systems that reward social networking over achievement in hiring and promotion. The slow progress and the need for taking legal action on the part of individuals, as well as the controversy around females seeking admission to the Citadel, which became coeducational in 1993, and the Virginia Military Institute, which became coeducational in 1997, or for that matter, around a male seeking admission to the Mississippi University for Women to its nursing program (1982), attest to the lasting hold of gender patterns on education in the South.

AMY E. WELLS
University of Mississippi

James D. Anderson, *The Education of Blacks in the South, 1860–1935* (1988); Dorothy C. Holland and Margaret A. Eisenhart, *Educated in Romance: Women, Achievement, and College Culture* (1990); Amy Thompson McCandless, *The Past in the Present: Women's Higher Education in the Twentieth Century American South* (1999); John R. Thelin, *A History of American Higher Education* (2004); Wayne J. Urban and Jennings L. Wagoner Jr., *American Education: A History* (2004).

Emancipation

In the mid-1990s, historians began exploring the connections between gender and emancipation. In this body of work, newly freed African American men and women have shown up as central political actors taking advantage of changing postwar economic and political conditions and engaging directly in the political struggles of the era—framing new definitions of freedom, manhood, and womanhood. Bringing gender into the history of emancipation has meant more than simply writing women into the dominant narrative of the Civil War/Reconstruction years. A new way to look at the meaning of freedom for newly freed African Americans and southern society as a whole has been formed.

At the heart of slave society lay a hierarchal gender system exemplified in the household, which functioned as the basis of domestic and political authority. White men assumed responsibility for their domestic dependents, slaves as well as white women and children, and their private authority extended into the political and economic rights in the public realm. In this system of racial and gender subordination, throughout the antebellum period slaves had no legal right to marry and no right to the custody of their children. White women were positioned above African American slaves in this social hierarchy, but their status and access to rights was narrowly defined in relationship to white men.

During the Civil War, slave men and women challenged the configuration of the antebellum household and all of the assumptions embedded in the southern gender system. In the Mississippi Delta, slave men and women took aim at white male patriarchy well before the Union army took control of the region by fleeing their plantations. In the rice planting region of Lowcountry South Carolina, slave women made their way to the Union-occupied Sea Islands. Slaves poured into federally occupied areas in eastern North Carolina, which held one of the largest concentrations of former slaves, to the point of being called by one observer a "Mecca of a thousand aspirations." In claiming their freedom, newly freed African Americans asserted their rights to claim and define manhood and womanhood on their own terms.

African American men and women occupied a distinctive position in post-emancipation society, a social status that contrasted sharply with the position of white women and white men. Race prevented African American women from achieving the social privileges associated with white womanhood. African American men lay claim to their independence by asserting control over their families and rallying for the right to vote. Gender barred black and white women from full citizenship. White men violently tried to preserve their positions of status and privilege and black men fought vigilantly for these rights.

With the passage of the Fourteenth and Fifteenth Amendments, all African Americans were formally granted citizenship and black men gained the right to vote, sit on juries, and hold public office.

After overturning their dependent status, newly freed African Americans rallied for legal recognition of their marriages. As one former slave declared in 1866, "The Marriage Covenant is at the Foundation of our rights." This observer understood that marriage cleared the path for black men and women to legally protect their children. As married women, free African American women could now position themselves as dependent wives and assure local courts of male supervision and economic support, a status that allowed them to lay claim to custody of their children. Legal marriage also connected African American Civil War widows to governmental institutions. In 1866 the U.S. Military Pension Bureau recognized the sacrifice of formerly enslaved African American Union soldiers by creating policies that extended financial support to their families. Legal marriage connected the woman to the male soldier and translated into an important body of rights and concrete economic resources from the Pension Bureau. This new policy opened up a new arena for newly freed African American women to lay claim to important economic benefits. Their access to these benefits hinged on their ability to legitimize their marriages to the federal government.

Freedmen's and freedwomen's decisions about marriage and family had a profound effect on the free labor system. Freedwomen who chose to withdraw from the labor force received harsh criticism from their white employers, who considered them to be "lazy" and "idle." Increasingly, African American women who remained in the labor force insisted on working on their own terms and in their own interests. In the rice-planting region of the South Carolina Lowcountry, African American women organized their labor according to their own community ideals, formed by their experiences in slavery. These women also worked to meet their obligations and responsibilities within their nuclear families as wives and mothers, as well as in their broader extended families as sisters, aunts, grandmothers, and neighbors. In urban areas like Atlanta, African American women were confined to domestic service, and these women had to struggle to define the terms of their labor on a regular basis. They labored with their own sense of right, with the guiding principle that wage labor should not emulate slavery nor should white employers infringe on their private lives.

Southern white employers often did not accept the rights African Americans now had to contract the terms of their labor. Apprenticeship enabled former masters, desperate for laborers, to counter some of the effects of emancipation by forcing the children of freedmen and freedwomen into extended labor contracts. In North Carolina, the Freedmen's Code of 1866 modified the antebellum law that specified that county courts could apprentice "the children of free negroes, where the parents with whom such children may live, do not habitually employ their time in some honest, industrious occupation," as well as all free children born out of wedlock. The new law instructed courts to apprentice former slave children and gave priority to former slaveholders in contracting the apprenticeship. African American women took bold steps to challenge the apprenticeship system directly, through the local courts. Apprenticeship, they argued, was a violation of their domestic relations. They turned to the Freedmen's Bureau, which was established in 1865, to monitor the transition to a free labor system and to protect black rights during and immediately after the Civil War. Though charged with the responsibility of protecting black civil rights in labor negotiations, the Freedmen's Bureau could not prevent widespread exploitation. Threatening leaflets were posted at the homes of freedmen and freedwomen by groups of whites in rural Tennessee in 1867.

Newly freed African American men and women took advantage of changing postwar social, economic, and political conditions by engaging directly in political struggles. Freedpeople's efforts to increase their political autonomy and economic resources were bound up with their desire to build, staff, and sustain educational and religious institutions. African American churches were important sites where women and men were able to articulate their ideas openly and freely. An important example of such an open expression occurred in Richmond, Va., where African American women of the community shared in decision making. African American women and children attended parades, rallies, and conventions. The Rising Daughters of Liberty Society, an organization of African American women, stood guard at meetings organized by men to allow them to meet without fear of reprisal. African American women were also at the forefront of organizing for benefits outside of formal governmental channels. In 1894, Callie House teamed with Isaiah Dickerson to organize the National Ex-Slave Mutual Relief, Bounty, and Pension Association, which held conventions, elected national officers, and worked for the passage of congressional legislation in support of slave reparations.

Newly freed African Americans creatively and persistently asserted their own definition of womanhood and manhood in the postemancipation South. Within their communities, African American women played a significant role in the reconstitution of their families, the negotiation of the terms for free labor, and the construction of the political process. Freedpeople continued to rely on the same legal and institutional frameworks that had justified their subordination before the Civil War. Unwilling to cede their position at the top of the social hierarchy, whites challenged freedmen and freedwomen at every turn, instituting new forms of economic subordination, racial supremacy, and gender oppression.

BRANDI C. BRIMMER
Vanderbilt University

Elsa Barkley Brown, in *The Black Public Sphere: A Public Culture Book*, ed. Black Public Sphere Collective (1995); Nancy Bercaw, *Gendered Freedoms: Race, Rights, and the Politics of Household in the Delta, 1861–1875* (2003); Brandi Brimmer, "All Her Rights and Privileges: African-American Women and the Politics of Civil War Widows' Pensions" (Ph.D. dissertation, UCLA, 2006); Catherine Clinton, in *Divided Houses: Gender and the Civil War*, ed. Catherine Clinton and Nina Silber (1992); Laura F. Edwards, *Gendered Strife and Confusion: The Political Culture of Reconstruction* (1997); Glenda Elizabeth Gilmore, *Gender and Jim Crow: Women and the Politics of White Supremacy in North Carolina, 1896–1920* (1996); Martha Hodes, *White Women, Black Men: Illicit Sex in the Nineteenth Century South* (1997); Tera Hunter, *To 'Joy My Freedom: Southern Black Women's Lives and Labors after the Civil War* (1997); Elizabeth Ann Regosin, *Freedom's Promise: Ex-Slave Families and Citizenship in the Age of Emancipation* (2002); Julie Saville, *The Work of Reconstruction: From Slave to Wage Laborer in South Carolina, 1860–1870* (1994); Leslie Schwalm, *A Hard Fight for We: Women's Transitions from Slavery to Freedom in South Carolina* (1997); Karen Zipf, *Journal of Women's History* (Spring 2000).

Family

People in the South sometimes like to claim that an attachment to family, or even a sense of family, is an important regional trait, but definitions of family vary so widely that it is clear that the concept has different meanings for different people. Perhaps the best generalization is that people in the South have often used the concept of the family to think, argue, and sometimes fight about who they are and who they want to be. To some southerners, family means a group of people one sees at family reunions or holiday dinners and honors in cemeteries or in pictures on mantles. To others, family means an expectation of sharing work and resources and the goal of living up to the family name. To still others, family has to do with frustrations about wrongs handed down through the generations. To many, but far from all, people in the South, family means a nearly permanent relationship, although the nature of that relationship has changed over southern history.

In the 1600s and 1700s, various groups of southerners faced new challenges to their understandings of family life, and many responded by adapting to dramatically new definitions of family. New groups of people, uneven gender ratios, new household and work situations, new insecurities about but also new hopes for the possibilities of frontier life, new health conditions, and the drastic changes involved in colonial slavery—all tested older definitions of family among Native Americans, Africans, or Europeans in the colonial South.

Most Native American tribes in the South practiced matrilineal kinship patterns, in which property and family name passed down through the female line. The demographic disasters of the colonial period, along with the new realities of intermingling with Europeans and, for some, the adoption of new notions of private property, challenged those traditional kinship patterns.

English colonists from Virginia to South Carolina faced new challenges as well. Poor health conditions complicated family relationships, and many children were raised by a series of stepparents and foster parents. Wealthier English colonists hoped that economic success in America might set them up to live as English gentlemen, with land and wealth for a long line of descendants. One reason wealthy Anglo-Caribbean planters moved to South Carolina was that disease made it difficult to build up family dynasties in the Caribbean. Many despaired of the unsettled nature of the colonial South, especially in the 1600s, but others such as William Byrd II of Virginia began to imagine his plantation as a setting in which family successfully extended to all of his dependents. Byrd wrote in 1726, "I have a large family of my own and my doors are open to every body. . . . Like one of the patriarchs, I have my flocks and my herds, my bondmen and bond-women, and every sort of trade amongst my own servants, so that I live in a kind of independence on every one, but Providence."

Ripped from their African homelands, slaves faced dramatic demographic challenges and the central reality that they could not organize their family lives as they wished. Learning new languages and confronting new health problems, always with the threat of being sold, meant reinventing some aspects of family life.

Issues of race became crucial to definitions of family early in southern history, when people used parentage to identify some people as white and deserving of certain privileges and to call other people nonwhite, with certain clear disadvantages. Colonial legislatures passed laws in the 1660s that made the racial identity of a child dependent on the identity of the mother. This had many consequences—most obvious, it relegated many children to slavery and created numerous tensions over the obligations of people related to each other by biology but not by family name, affection, or sense of responsibility.

In the antebellum period, some groups of southerners began to carve out distinctive regional definitions of the family. Political and intellectual leaders, in part in response to the abolitionist movement, claimed that the South had developed a form of paternalism that made fatherly kindness and control a key to organizing a humane society. In the 1830s, 1840s, and 1850s, with the rise of a British and northeastern middle class that idealized motherly affection, valued smaller families, and separated home from work, many British and northeastern abolitionists condemned slavery for separating slave families and allowing owners to have unchecked sexual control over slaves. Upper-class southerners responded that the antebellum South was based on paternalism, an old ideal with a newly professional and Christian face. Slave owners who wrote in their diaries about "my family, white and black" claimed that they considered all of their dependents to be part of their extended household, and that they loved them and punished them all to fit into their proper stations in life. Paternalism did not idealize motherly affection in the same way that the northeastern family ideals tended to do; paternalists claimed that fathers as well as mothers had roles in alternating affection with discipline.

The other family image developing into a southern ideal was the yeoman male, who valued independence from the control of anyone as a central goal. Yeomen shared with paternalists the goal of controlling dependent laborers, but most of those dependents were wives and children. Yeoman families remained large long after middle-class family size outside the South began to decline. The issues of the Civil War era—the question of slavery in the West, local control over laborers, and wartime issues of taxation, impressments, and the draft—all offered challenges to yeomen's notions that they controlled what took place inside their own homes.

African Americans used notions of families under pressure as part of their call for an end to slavery. In some of the most memorable early scenes of his autobiography, Frederick Douglass described living for only a short time with his mother, not knowing his father (or even who his father was), and living with continuing uncertainties about what constituted a household. Other narratives, such as Harriet Jacobs's *Incidents in the Life of a Slave Girl*, demonstrated intense commitments to keeping family members together, especially children, under extraordinary pressure. African Americans developed an understanding of family that was adaptable, with fictive kin, informal adoption, and special importance for the role of elders.

After the Civil War, discussions of family often included either creating families or preserving them. During and after the war, African Americans faced the exhilarating possibilities of creating and controlling their own households, and many traveled far and wide to find family members separated by slavery and war. Many African Americans built on the adaptable, multigenerational under-

Mother, family, and servant, in a needlework piece by Ethel Mohamed, Belzoni, Miss.,
photographed in 1978 (Jane Moseley, photographer, Center for Southern Folklore, Memphis)

standings of family they had developed under slavery. Sharecropping and tenancy tended to encourage large families working together, hoping to produce independence through large crops and shared thrift. But poverty and racial segregation often put heavy pressures on African American family life, and rates of divorce and abandonment were high in the late 1800s and early 1900s. Author Richard Wright dramatized the dual goals of celebrating family life while detailing its difficulties. In *Black Boy*, he created an image of family difficulty—he hardly knew his father, and his grandmother and depressed mother tried to teach him the rules of segregation. On the other hand, he celebrated the communal interest in children in his *12 Million Black Voices*: "Some people wag their heads in amusement when they see our long lines of ragged children, but we love them. . . . Like black buttercups, our children spring up on the red soil of the plantations. When a new one arrives, neighbors from miles around come and look at it, speculating upon which parent it resembles."

White evangelicals developed their own version of the Victorian family, with mothers as central figures in teaching religious morality but with the influences of male recreation and African Americans, rather than the northern and British Victorian fear of the harsh public worlds of work and politics, as the primary counterpoints.

Most of the ways evangelicals defined sin seemed a violation of home and family. Dancing seemed frivolous and too fashionable for solid church folk, and drinking alcohol, gambling, and fighting were primarily male activities that involved competition to the point of a loss of self-control, which violated family harmony. Surely one of the ugliest sides of southern conceptions of family life has been the recurring idea that African Americans posed threats to the home and family lives of whites, who in the late 1800s and early 1900s used family protection as justification for segregation, prohibition laws, and lynching. African American evangelicals developed their own versions of respectability, calling for particular emphases on dignity and self-control and rejecting accusations that black families did not teach those virtues.

White southerners' discussions of family also moved toward ancestor worship, with groups like the Daughters of the Revolution and then the Sons of Confederate Veterans taking central roles in defining how contemporary generations should venerate their ancestors. Along with this preoccupation with ancestors, southerners in the 20th century often engaged in troubled love/hate relationships with their older family members. The works of William Faulkner, Lillian Smith, W. J. Cash, Robert Penn Warren, and others showed people who imagined a great past, only to discover that greed, lies, and hypocrisy made a tragedy out of what scholar Richard King has called "the family romance." Some of the idealizing of southern family life came from people who witnessed or feared the decline of farm life. Country musicians and southern writers such as the Vanderbilt Agrarians sang and wrote about responsibilities that transcended lines of generation and gender, and they feared that those responsibilities and certainties were on the decline. Agrarianism balanced traditions of southern family life against modern movements toward individualism and argued that upholding family traditions held the only hope for the modern world.

Definitions of family again became objects of controversy during the civil rights movement. Supporters of civil rights, especially those inspired by religious commitments, frequently called on the concept of brotherhood, sometimes called the Brotherhood of Man under the Fatherhood of God, as the most important reason to oppose racial discrimination. Family thus seemed something flexible and useful in uniting people who faced similar challenges. On the other hand, opponents of the civil rights movement criticized "brotherhoodism" as naive and declared that families with clear parental authority were the key to an orderly society.

Some African Americans, after generations of defending African American families against charges of fragility or the absence of effective parents, began more than ever to celebrate a tradition of family flexibility. Many were offended by the 1965 report by Daniel Patrick Moynihan called *The Negro Family: The Case for National Action*, which blamed the persistence of African American poverty on a history of troubled family life, especially the absence of fathers as economic and personal contributors to family life. Beginning late in the 1960s and increasing in the 1970s, many African American writers and political figures began to praise African American family life for its adaptability, arguing that what had long seemed a weakness was in fact a strength—that is, an ability of the black community to take care of many people outside a nuclear family structure. The most dramatic and popular example was Alex Haley's book and television series *Roots*, which showed generations of African Americans respecting, negotiating, and redefining—but always valuing—family life. More recently, African American authors such as Joyce Ladner and Clifton Taulbert and child welfare leader Marian Wright Edelman have used traditions of adaptable family life to offer how-to books for raising children.

Opponents of the civil rights movement condemned school desegregation for its potential to encourage white children to reject the example of their parents. Some of the more vocal opponents of civil rights claimed that school desegregation was all about sexual integration and worried that it would produce more mixed-race families. The Citizens' Council, a white-supremacist group organized in the South to resist school desegregation, hailed the conclusions of the Moynihan Report as proof that African American families were in deep trouble and, therefore, that white children should stay away from black children.

Beginning in the late 1970s, the Religious Right made stern calls for a return to schools and homes with clear parental authority. The concept of family values, new in the decade, declared that certain household arrangements constituted families and others did not. Moral Majority leader Jerry Falwell rejected the conclusions of a 1979 White House Conference that, as he wrote in *The New American Family*, "finally decided that any persons living together constituted a family." Arguing that such a definition sanctioned homosexuality, encouraged government day care programs, and did nothing to combat abortion, Falwell sided instead with the definition of the National Pro-Family Coalition that "a family consists of persons who are related by blood, marriage, or adoption." The American Family Association, led by Methodist minister Donald Wildmon in Tupelo, Miss., developed in the 1980s to argue that a wide array of forces, especially in the media but also in the law and public education, were challenging parental control over what children believed about God, right and wrong, and the definition of the family.

People who claim that attachment to family is a distinctively southern attribute are most likely incorrect. Family has had too many connotations for a term such as "the southern family" to have much meaning. Perhaps the safest generalization one can make about contemporary southern family life is that problems and arguments over definition continue. Southern rates of single parenthood, poverty of female-headed households, and divorce are higher than the national average, and the South also seems to lead the nation in calls for returns to traditional family life.

TED OWNBY
University of Mississippi

Nancy Bercaw, *Gendered Freedoms: Race, Rights, and the Politics of Household in the Delta, 1861–1875* (2003); Kathleen Brown, *Good Wives, Nasty Wenches, and Anxious Patriarchs: Gender, Race, and Power in Colonial Virginia* (1996); Jerry Falwell, *The New American Family: The Rebirth of the American Dream* (1992); Elizabeth Fox-Genovese, *Within the Plantation Household: Black and White Women of the Old South* (1988); Eugene D. Genovese, *Roll, Jordan, Roll: The World the Slaves Made* (1974); Glenda Gilmore, *Gender and Jim Crow: Women and the Politics of White Supremacy in North Carolina, 1896–1920* (1996); Alex Haley, *Roots* (1976); Jacquelyn Dowd Hall et al., *Like a Family: The Making of a Southern Cotton Mill World* (1987); Richard King, *A Southern Renaissance: The Cultural Awakening of the American South, 1930–1955* (1980); Winthrop D. Jordan, *White over Black: American Attitudes toward the Negro, 1550–1812* (1968); Ann Patton Malone, *Sweet Chariot: Slave Family and Household Structure in Nineteenth-Century Louisiana* (1992); Bill Malone, *Don't Get Above Your Raisin': Country Music and the Southern Working Class* (2002); Stephanie Mc-Curry, *Masters of Small Worlds: Yeoman Households, Gender Relations, and the Political Culture of the Antebellum South Carolina Low Country* (1995); Daniel Patrick Moynihan, *The Negro Family: The Case for National Action* (1965); Ted Ownby, *Subduing Satan: Religion, Recreation, and Manhood in the Rural South, 1865–1920* (1990); Brenda E. Stevenson, *Life in Black and White: Family and Community in the Slave South* (1996); Stewart Tolnay, *The Bottom Rung: African American Family Life on Southern Farms* (1999); Richard Wright, *12 Million Black Voices* (1941).

Family, Black

In American culture, mention of "the family" suggests the ideal of a nuclear family household, which includes a legally married man and woman and their children. Many Americans might mention other family members, but seldom others beyond primary relatives with whom they have shared a household either as children (parents and siblings) or as adults (children and spouses). This family ideal has been popular in the United States for at least a century and is reflected in most of the family literature, in the media, in public policies regarding the family, and in the philosophy underlying human service programs oriented toward families.

But the southern black family includes more than a household of primary relatives. A history of economic and political marginality has made it necessary for southern blacks to depend on support systems beyond the household for their survival. Although friendship bonds and patron-client relationships with whites and other higher-status individuals contributed to southern black survival, rights and obligations within these relationships are not usually thought of as being as dependable as kinship bonds during times of need. Thus, early in their history, the concept of family for southern blacks began to extend beyond the residential unit to include not only parents, siblings, and children but also biologically related kinsmen such as parents' parents and siblings, siblings' children, and children's children, as well as people who are not related at all. Such extension has facilitated survival for blacks in the South by increasing the size and range (including people of different social, ethnic, and racial categories) of the "family."

Although protection, care, instruction, and discipline of children are the primary responsibilities of the parents in the nuclear ideal, southern blacks have used shifting residences, fosterage, and informal adoptions to spread these obligations among other "family" members. Children may grow up within a number of households within the family groupings, or they might grow up entirely in a household other than that of their parents. The relatives or friends with whom a child resides might become foster parents of the child, or they might informally adopt the child. In either case, the child's relationship with his biological parents is usually not severed.

As a way to extend the rights and privileges of the family relationship, southern blacks used kinship terms in addressing nonkinsmen. Thus, when someone is addressed with specific kinship terms such as "mother" or "brother," the user of the term is stating that he or she will behave like a son (or daughter) or brother (or sister) in his or her relationship to the person addressed, and that he or she is expecting a motherly or brotherly type of behavior in return. Southern blacks strengthened their links with distant relatives and nonkin relations by upgrading kinship terms, referring, for example, to a third cousin as an aunt or a wife's cousin as a brother-in-law.

In addition to the extended family relationship, the possession of land has given the southern black family a distinctive character. Landownership was a symbol of freedom for the free black during slavery and for the freedman following emancipation. Although land was always difficult for blacks to obtain, many did manage to do so. Among blacks in some southern communities, land was not a commodity to be sold but instead a resource to be used by kinsmen and to be passed down from generation to generation. In some families, the right to land and land use is controlled by one of the oldest and/or the dominant family members. Although black families are rapidly losing their land in the South, family land that resembles small villages with multiple households of related units is still visible in many places.

In an extended black family there is often a dominant dyad or individual, around whom many extended-family activities revolve. One of the family group's oldest couples or persons — often a widow — typically assumes this role. If there is family land, the dominant couple or individual usually lives on it, in many cases controlling its use. If multiple households live on the family land, the dominant person's household is the hub of local extended family activity, and nonlocal family members come first to that household when visiting. When the dominant family figure dies, another family member (usually an offspring) takes on this role.

Another key to understanding the southern black family is its relationship to the church. In many rural areas and small towns of the South, churches are made up of a number of extended families. The church also provides rules regarding marriage, male and female behavior, childhood socialization, and respect for the elders. The church provides a community that blacks control. Some churches have "missionary societies" whose primary function is to visit the sick and shut-ins. Churches respond to some of the economic needs of poorer black families through gifts during special times such as Christmas and through special collections of money during Sunday services. Close kinship terms such as "father" or "mother" are sometimes used to refer to all elderly people in the church.

Communal occasions reconfirm the extended social support systems of the southern black family. Sunday dinner is a weekly "small feast," which brings together local primary relatives who do not reside together. Large dinners on Thanksgiving and Christmas bring together primary relatives who live in the same area, as well as relatives who live elsewhere. Relatives also get together during other holidays such as Memorial Day, the Fourth of July, and Labor Day. Cookouts, picnics, and barbecues are main events at such occasions. Larger extended family groupings come together at annual family reunions, and even-larger groupings come together at church homecomings. Family reunions bring together the descendants of an ancestor or ancestral parents. A church homecoming brings together the present and past membership of a church. The overlapping between kinship and church memberships frequently results in church homecomings resembling large family reunions. Extended family and nonfamily friends also come together for weddings and funerals. These events bring people together and also serve to repay obligations, establish rights to new relationships, and reconfirm old links of rights and obligations.

Although blacks might have wanted to retain African family patterns in their pure form, the slave environment would not allow it. Unilineal descent as it was known in Africa was impossible to maintain because the slave masters would not allow the development of large corporate groups based on ties as strong as kinship. Slaves, in the meantime, needed social support wherever they could get it. Thus, not only did they most likely practice fosterage and adoption at that time, but they also attached kin terms to nonkinsmen and upgraded the kin terms of distant relatives.

By the end of slavery, black family life was becoming stabilized. But emancipation brought new pressures. Because freed slaves knew how to do little else but farm, the lack of opportunities to buy land and to obtain employment outside the plantation made it difficult for the vast majority of freed slaves to maintain a nuclear family, let alone an extended family. Southern postemancipation problems led to black migration in search of a better life, the emergence of a legal system that imprisoned a disproportionate number of black males, and a host of factors that contributed to the shortened life span of blacks, particularly males. All these factors caused an imbalance in local black sex ratios, which in turn affected the structure and function of the southern black family.

One pattern of migration, which accelerated during and after World War I, was to the urban North. For the first one or two generations, black migrants to northern cities maintained their southern kinship systems. They also developed support systems in the North similar to those that they knew in the South. These networks, though, had fewer kin involved than those in the South, and sometimes friends acted as kin. After two generations, some urban black families tended to form new extended families, but the lack of access to land in the urban North prevented black families from organizing themselves around landownership or from residing in multiple households of close proximity as in the South. As a consequence, land eventually lost some of its symbolic significance for northern blacks. And, when urban heirs sell family land in the South upon the deaths of their parents, the southern black extended family can be affected.

A growing reliance on social services, instead of on kin and friends, has taken place in the South, as well as among southern migrants to the North, particularly with the mechanization of southern farms and the displacement of farmworkers. Southern blacks, however, have managed to maintain to a considerable degree their attachment to the traditional kinship system, family land, and the church.

TONY L. WHITEHEAD
University of Maryland

Allison Davis, Burleigh B. Gardner, and Mary R. Gardner, *Deep South: A Social Anthropological Study of Caste and Class* (1941); K. Y. Day, in *Holding on to the Land: Kinship, Ritual, Land Tenure, and Social Policy in the Rural South*, ed. Robert L. Hall and Carol B. Stack (1982); John Hope Franklin, *From Slavery to Freedom: A History of Negro Americans* (1947; 5th ed., 1980); E. Franklin Frazier, *Negro Family in the United States* (1939); Herbert G. Gutman, *The Black Family in Slavery and Freedom, 1750–1925* (1977); Melville J. Herskovits, *The Myth of the Negro Past* (1941); Jacqueline Jones, *Labor of Love, Labor of Sorrow: Black Women, Work, and the Family from Slavery to the Present* (1985); E. P. Martin and J. M. Martin, *The Black Extended Family* (1978); D. B. Shimkin, E. M. Shimkin, and Dennis A. Frate, eds., *The Extended Family in Black Societies* (1978); Brenda E. Stephenson, *Life in Black and White: Family and Community in the Slave South* (1996); Stewart Tolnay, *The Bottom Rung: African American Family Life on Southern Farms* (1999).

Family Dynasties

When considering the ultimate expression of power in the American South, one thinks of the planter patriarch holding sway over a large plantation worked by gangs of slaves. With one hand the great planter marries off his children to other leading planters in order to augment his landed empire, and with the other hand he serves at the county court or the statehouse to reinforce his political power base.

This image, though not without historical foundation, is largely the product of a tendency to generalize from a particular moment in the life of the South. For, indeed, there was a golden age of planters in the middle decades of the 18th century, a time when significant parts of the plantation South—especially the Chesapeake and the Carolina Lowcountry—were governed by a few landed families. These elite members of the southern gentry sat atop the power structure (from the county courts and parish vestries to the lower houses of assembly), setting the tone for virtually all phases of social, economic, and political life. The influence of this elite group of planters was reinforced by ties of blood or marriage that had been first established in the last quarter of the 17th century. In the decades before the Revolution, for example, no less than 70 percent of the 110 leaders of the House of Burgesses were drawn from families resident in Virginia before 1690.

How did these few great planter families manage to extend their influence over the generations? Sons and daughters were carefully, strategically, placed on lands accumulated for them by the economic success and political power of their fathers. This small, homogeneous elite of perhaps no more than 100 wealthy families—English by descent, Anglican in faith, and linked to one another by ties of kinship and bonds of economic interest—monopolized political power in 18th-century Virginia. For example, seven members of the Carter family, the richest of all the Virginia clans in the 18th century, owned a total of 170,000 acres of land and 2,300 slaves scattered over seven counties.

The historical prominence of leading planter families such as the Carters, the Byrds, and the Lees should not obscure the relative brevity of their dominance of southern history. In fact, this golden age of great family dynasties flourished only between the early years of the unpredictable, dangerous settlement on the frontier and the 19th-century emergence of a much more diverse, middle-class society.

Younger sons of the English gentry arriving in Virginia in the early years of the 17th century fully expected to establish strong and prosperous family and kin groups. Their power base was to be grounded in the great fortunes they believed would be extracted from gold, precious metals, and (by the 1620s) tobacco. Although a few of these men became wealthy tobacco barons in the early years, most of them failed in finding fortunes and building family lines to perpetuate their status and power.

Most ambitions were stifled by the overwhelming odds against survival in the disease-ridden early South. An endemic malarial environment in the Chesapeake and parts of the Carolina Tidewater created a high mortality rate that stunted family size, produced a society of orphans and stepparents, and virtually precluded the development of an elderly generation. Perhaps most significant, the high death rates discouraged any tendency toward strong patriarchal authority. Few men who expected to build powerful, multigenerational family dynasties could hope to succeed in an environment where men generally did not live long enough even to see their grandchildren, let alone to nurture and direct their careers. Instead, most gentlemen in this Hobbesian world struggled simply to survive—abruptly finishing their lives with nothing accumulated, nothing permanent to pass on to their heirs. Not until the final decade of the 17th century, when life expectancies gradually lengthened and slave importations increased dramatically, did a few leading families begin to build the large tobacco plantations and powerful family dynasties that would prevail in the 18th-century South.

At the other end of this golden age of southern planters, essentially after

1790, the picture is more difficult to assess. Prominent southern family lines continued well into the 19th century; indeed, scholars consider the antebellum era as the flush time for self-consciously paternalistic planters, men such as George Fitzhugh, who intoned the virtues and obligations of the patriarch watching out for all his "people." Some historians, such as Eugene D. Genovese, believe that the paternalism of southern slaveholders reached something of a climax (both politically and ideologically) during the antebellum era. One can surely detect in the writings of these influential planter families an increasing self-consciousness about their patriarchal role—perhaps an indication itself of the minority position they held—as they laid great stress on family and kin loyalty, strategically planned marital alliances, a deep attachment to the land, and complete control in managing the slaves, servants, kin, and various hangers-on, who made up the great planters' "people."

By the 19th century, though, southern society had changed—perhaps not dramatically, for most of it was still based on a staple-crop economy—but clearly the practice of deference to a few leading planters had begun to decline and in some places to disappear altogether. Great wealth was no longer the only road to political power, as scores of middle-class lawyers, teachers, and middling planters found their way into the political arena of the antebellum South.

Clearly, the spread of slaveholding was instrumental in democratizing political leadership among whites in the antebellum South. Slave-based plantations, once the preserve of a relatively few wealthy tobacco and rice planters in the early South, became a much more widely diffused system of labor by the mid-19th century, as cotton spread throughout the Lower South. In some of the most heavily populated slave states (South Carolina, Mississippi, Alabama, and Georgia) between one-third and one-half of all white families held slaves in 1860. Most families owned a modest four to six slaves, but, more important, at least half the white families in the Deep South had a direct material interest in the protection and perpetuation of slavery. Hence, the number of legitimate spokesmen for slaveholding interests grew rapidly in the 19th century. Wealthy landed families continued to exert political influence, but that influence was increasingly outweighed by an expanding pool of slaveholding lawyers and merchants (particularly the former), who by mid-century controlled the county court in every southern state. By 1850 political power in the South carried a discernibly middle-class connotation.

In the postbellum South, the disintegration of family dynasties, especially in the political arena, was even more conspicuous. With the growth of urban centers in the New South, political life became an increasingly diverse affair.

Recent studies show that most urban officeholders in the South during the late 19th and early 20th centuries came from new families, not from heirs of old notable families.

More significant was the gradual deterioration of the planters' social and economic hegemony in the New South. According to C. Vann Woodward, the essential drama of the New South was "the story of the decay and decline of the aristocracy, the suffering and betrayal of the poor white, and the rise and transformation of a middle class." As hundreds of textile mills, railroads, and banking institutions emerged in the postwar South, economic power passed from the hands of landowners to manufacturers and merchants. Although some scholars see important family continuity between the elite planter class that prevailed in the antebellum South and the industrialists who dominated the New South, most historians detect an unmistakable fragmentation in planter hegemony during the postwar transformation of the southern economy.

DANIEL BLAKE SMITH
University of Kentucky

Eugene D. Genovese, *Roll, Jordan, Roll: The World the Slaves Made* (1976), *The World the Slaveholders Made* (1971); David Jordan, in *The Chesapeake in the Seventeenth Century: Essays on Anglo-American Society and Politics*, ed. Thad W. Tate and David L. Ammerman (1979); Aubrey Land, *Journal of Economic History* (November 1965); Daniel Blake Smith, *Inside the Great House: Planter Family Life in Eighteenth-Century Chesapeake Society* (1980); Charles S. Sydnor, *Gentlemen Freeholders: Political Practices in Washington's Virginia* (1952); C. Vann Woodward, *Origins of the New South, 1877–1913* (1951).

Family Reunions

"Next week be the fourth of July and us plan a big family reunion outdoors here at my house," says Celie, the main character in Alice Walker's *The Color Purple*. On the day of the reunion family members analyze the custom this way: "'Why us always have family reunion on July 4th,' say Henrietta, mouth poke out, full of complaint. 'It so hot.' . . . 'White people busy celebrating they independence from England July 4th,' say Harpo, 'so most black folks don't have to work. Us can spend the day celebrating each other.'" Among the other attendees are two women who sip lemonade and make potato salad, noting that barbecue was a favorite food for them even while they were in Africa. The reunion day is especially joyful for the two women, who had been thought lost until their appearance at the reunion, where they are joyfully reunited with Celie and the other family members.

Southern family reunions are characteristic of extended families, who plan the occasions around celebration, abundant good food, shared reunion responsibilities, simple recreational activities, and, above all, talk.

Although summer is the most popular season and the Fourth of July a popular date for family reunions for both black and white southern families, family reunions can happen at any time. Some families have them annually, others have them on a schedule best described as "every so often," and still others have them only once or twice in a generation's lifetime, depending on some member's initiative in getting the reunion organized.

Like the indefinite date for family reunions, there is an inexactness as to who constitutes "family" for each gathering. Some families invite only the descendants of a given couple and those descendants' spouses and children. Others invite the eldest couple's brothers and sisters and their children plus in-laws and some of the in-laws' relatives. Some gather households that have only a vague bond of kinship—those who are "like family" because of strong friendships. There is inevitably a logic of kinship and affection to each family reunion, and such a party is hard indeed to crash.

The impetus for a family reunion, if it is not an annually scheduled event, may be a late-decade birthday party for one family member, a holiday, a wedding anniversary, or the celebration of an achievement such as paying off a home mortgage. Sometimes a family holds a reunion for a homecoming of one of its members, as in the case of Eudora Welty's novel *Losing Battles*, which is a family reunion story focused around the day a son and husband return from a stay at Parchman, the Mississippi state prison.

Families often gather in someone's home, though summer picnic versions are commonly held in state or city parks. Motels, hotels, or restaurants host them, as do clubhouses or community centers, but by far the most popular settings after homes are churches. "Dinner on the grounds" in the churchyard, with food burdening tablecloth-covered makeshift tables set on sawhorses, is a happy memory of family reunions in the minds of many southerners.

The occasion for catching up on the relatives' news and gossip, perhaps for transacting a little family business, for settling or even stirring up family disputes, for generally getting in touch again, a family reunion in the South usually has no program. There might be an occasional game or swim or boat ride, but the main activities are conversation and eating. The time span may be overnight or even several days, but it is most frequently over only one meal.

The food might be barbecue with baked beans and coleslaw or fried fish with hush puppies, fried potatoes, and a salad. A restaurant meal might be ordered, but in a great many cases family reunion food is a large and generous potluck dinner in which each participating household brings versions of its best offerings of food and drink—fried chicken, ham, meat casseroles, rice dishes, cooked garden vegetables, fresh raw vegetables, potato salad, gelatin salad, seafood salad, homemade rolls and breads, cakes, pies, cookies, jams, preserves, pickles, watermelons, iced tea, and lemonade. A time for eating, conversing, and sharing each other's company, a southern family reunion is a special occasion for reaffirming family ties.

GAYLE GRAHAM YATES
University of Minnesota

Alice Walker, *The Color Purple* (1982); Eudora Welty, *Losing Battles* (1970).

Fatherhood

Historically, sharp divisions between males and females characterized family responsibilities in the South. The man was regarded as the unchallenged patriarch, the strong, respected provider, the mainstay of southern society. The traditional image of the chivalrous southerner, as opposed to the greedy Yankee, was centered in the southern father's devotion to family, tradition, and race; all these tempered the "natural man" that supposedly remained in the Yankee. At the same time the South has often been celebrated as a region that stressed the so-called masculine traits—a region characterized by violence, hard-nosed football, stock car racing, militarism, and hawkish attitudes about war and foreign affairs. Yet, in literature and sometimes in actuality, it is often a Scarlett O'Hara or her mother who ends up running the plantation and the mill.

The patriarchal nature of the southern family has been attributed to slavery. Dependent upon slaves as producers of income, the family head, the southern father, had to maintain control of the peculiar institution, and attempts by family members to assert themselves against the head of the family were thought to threaten slavery itself. As proslavery theorists attempted to justify the institution of slavery using every branch of knowledge, from the Bible to science, the rationale for the authority of the father in the household became increasingly the received wisdom of all southerners. Family, church, and community all reinforced patriarchy. Male dominance persisted in the political, cultural, religious, and economic spheres of the South.

Cotton ruled as King, not Queen, in the South. In the early 20th century, powerful U.S. senator Ben Tillman used a South Carolina law allowing him to deed his grandchildren to himself, thus thwarting their mother's claim to custody. Except for a brief period during Reconstruction, not until after World

War II was divorce legalized in South Carolina. Before child labor laws, southern children commonly worked in the textile mill for a family wage, which was paid directly to the father. In the South, the father was the family head, and considerable legal authority fortified his power.

Bertram Wyatt-Brown has shown that southerners venerated their male ancestors. Naming patterns in the South signified the importance of patriarchy. The tendency to name children after male family elders remains strong in the South, where phone books today still show many juniors and thirds after a name. Although individualistic impulses were in some ways influential, duty to family and one's forebears was paramount. The southerner's respect for history and tradition was reinforced by his obedience to his forefathers.

The legendary southern father was much like the myth of the southern gentleman: well-educated and genteel, with a firm and commanding personality, which demanded deference from all family members and from nonaristocratic whites. Thus, the myth of southern fatherhood has a distinct class bias. Eugene D. Genovese's brilliant work showing that slaves had room for cultural autonomy and arguing the patriarchal nature of slavery suggests that the hegemony of the planter class prevented lower-class whites and slaves from being patriarchs themselves. Other scholars, disagreeing, have demonstrated that the planters' status did not prevent less affluent white or slave males from reigning in their own families. The patriarchal values pervaded all levels of the society and culture.

Popular literature, however, has characterized the lower-class white family as a disorderly one led by irresponsible, lazy, drunken fathers. Thus, ironically, in the South, which supposedly contrasts with the North's emphasis on lucre, fatherly success was associated with financial success.

The father in the black family was generally believed to be absent or nonexistent. Studies of urban areas in the North have shown that racism in the occupational structure of modern society has made it difficult for African American men to get jobs in cities. Careful scrutiny of census and other demographic records shows that this is just as true of southern cities and even in small towns and villages. Whereas towns and cities offered both protection and domestic jobs for black women, black men there were excluded from jobs other than those associated with farming. Hence, when sociologists studied black families in the cities, they found males absent. In the rural South, however, where most blacks lived after slavery, landowning and tenant families were almost always headed by black men. White landowners were not willing to rent to female household heads unless they had older children to help in the fields.

Thus, in the sparsely settled rural areas, not in the cities where interviews and records were more easily available, the scholar found the black patriarch ruling his family very much as did his white counterpart.

Scholars have some records suggesting how planter-class fathers treated their children. Fathers had intense but ambivalent feelings about their children. They lavished affection on them during infancy but were torn between their love for their children and their desire to see the children—especially the males—become independent. They might be terribly affectionate with the children one day and then completely out of sight the next. One fatherly technique was to alternate providing and withdrawing intimacy in order to teach discipline and right behavior; this technique internalized guilt and shame in the children.

Parents were seen as exemplars. The children were expected to emulate their parents and other worthy relatives as much as possible, to respect adults, and to follow their basic moral precepts. Although fathers sought to teach their children independence, they also wanted the children to learn that they were not so much individuals as extensions of their parents. Their every move, therefore, was not only an indication of their own goodness but, just as important, also a reflection of parental worthiness.

One of the most important aspects of behavior that southern fathers could teach their children was aggressiveness. Even young girls were encouraged to be aggressive. But, of course, boys, and particularly the eldest boy, were the focus of this assertiveness training. Many southern fathers thought children should be given freedom to explore their surroundings, thus gaining the confidence needed to assert themselves fully. Sometimes, however, fathers went too far and merely spoiled their children. This mistake could end tragically, with the sons of prominent men often leading short and dissolute lives.

A variety of father images have appeared in southern literature and music, suggesting other dimensions to the role of the father in regional life. Sometimes fathers, like mothers, are sentimentalized, as in the Jimmie Rodgers country songs of the 1930s, "Daddy and Home" and "That Silver-Haired Daddy of Mine." This reflected the long Victorian influence in the South. Beverly Lowry's novel *Daddy's Girl* (1981) offers a humorous contemporary look at one of the most important southern family relationships—father and daughter, an excessively loving, manipulative, and demanding relationship. The nurturing father is an equally strong image and shows the father passing down folk skills and wisdom to sons and daughters.

Fathers have also been portrayed in harsh terms. Religion has contributed a powerful father image: the father as the Calvinist God's patriarch on earth, the person ruling the southern household and the plantation with an iron fist. The father, to Joe Christmas in William Faulkner's *Light in August*, is a stern figure, always judging, ready to mete out justice to wayward children. The poverty of the postbellum and modern eras and the humiliation for blacks in the racial caste system have also shaped cultural attitudes toward fatherhood. One country song says father was "a farmer but all he ever raised was us." The sharecropping father is seen as frustrated, unable to provide a good life for his family. Richard Wright's harsh portrait of his father in *Black Boy* is an extreme version of this, although Alex Haley's *Roots* gives images of warm, loving, and strong black fathers.

The sociological study of fatherhood is relatively new, and as yet there is little reliable information on regional differences in attitudes toward fathering, degree of involvement of fathers in child care, or parental authority patterns. In married-couple families with children present, southern fathers have already experienced marked changes in their sole responsibility as breadwinners during the last several decades, because today over half of their wives work outside the home. In the South, as elsewhere in the nation, the number of divorced fathers who have either sole or joint custody of their children is rising. Increasingly, fathers are emphasizing their nurturant roles, though social class differences, among others, still shape views about fathers as the authority figure in families.

Economic conditions dramatically affect the possibilities of the father's role in African American communities. By the mid-1990s, the growing economic divergence of black families became clear. About one-third were prospering, with married couples the most typical arrangement among the group. Only 7 percent of African American families of married couples lived in poverty in 1998. But a third of the nation's African American families were the working poor and members of an underclass found in northern cities and in the rural South. African American families headed by females had a poverty rate of 41 percent. The sheer unavailability of African American men became a notable social problem in the 1990s. High unemployment rates and relatively high incarceration rates, as well as higher mortality rates for black men compared to black women, have contributed to a weakened role of the father in underclass families.

Literary critic Richard King argues that the intellectuals and writers of the Southern Literary Renaissance in the 20th century were attempting symbolically to define their relationship with the region's "fathers." He notes the portraits of the "heroic generation" of ex-Confederates, the pictures of "stern, untroubled, and resolute" fathers that hung in southern parlors. Ironic sons and strong fathers have been predominant images in modern southern literature.

Allen Tate explored this theme in his novel, *The Fathers*. Jack Burden in Robert Penn Warren's *All the King's Men* searches for an understanding of his—and through him, the region's—past by defining a complex relationship to his father, both real and figuratively (in Willie Stark). William Faulkner seemed fascinated with the father, portraying ruthless, sometimes cruel patriarchs such as Thomas Sutpen, Carothers McCaslin, and the older Sartoris. These powerful figures succeed—yet eventually, through self-centered pride, are brought to earth. Sutpen's downfall, in particular, comes from his failure to acknowledge his son because the son has black blood; issues of race are bound up with fatherhood, as in other areas of southern life.

ORVILLE VERNON BURTON
University of Illinois

Andrew Billingsley, *Climbing Jacob's Ladder: The Enduring Legacy of African American Families* (1992); Orville Vernon Burton, *In My Father's House Are Many Mansions: Family and Community in Edgefield, South Carolina* (1985); Jane Turner Censer, *North Carolina Planters and Their Children, 1800–1860* (1984); Richard H. King, *A Southern Renaissance: The Cultural Awakening of the American South, 1930–1955* (1980); Daniel Blake Smith, *Inside the Great House: Planter Family Life in Eighteenth-Century Chesapeake Society* (1980); Bertram Wyatt-Brown, *Southern Honor: Ethics and Behavior in the Old South* (1982).

Feminism and Antifeminism

The South is historically the region of the United States most resistant to changes in the role of women. Of the 10 states that failed to ratify the Nineteenth Amendment by 1920, only one was north of the Mason-Dixon Line. More recently, southern legislatures were crucial to the defeat of the proposed Equal Rights Amendment—9 of the 15 states that did not ratify it were former Confederate states. Only Texas and Tennessee approved the amendment, and Tennessee later voted to rescind. Since the 1890s, however, southerners have also played an active role in the women's rights movement. The modern feminist movement, which began in the 1960s, has made its presence felt in the region but since the mid-1970s has encountered a powerful antifeminist challenge.

Both the more radical "women's liberation" branch of the feminist movement and the more moderate "women's rights" branch have been active in the South. In the late 1960s, women's liberation groups sprang up in many urban centers and university communities. By the early 1970s, both the National Organization for Women (NOW) and the National Women's Political

Caucus (NWPC) had chapters in every southern state, joining older established women's organizations, including the League of Women Voters, the Business and Professional Women's League, and the American Association of University Women, as advocates for women's rights. Several southern women rose to positions of prominence in feminist organizations: Liz Carpenter helped organize the NWPC and was a cochairperson of ERAmerica from 1976 to 1979; Frances Farenthold chaired the NWPC from 1973 to 1975; and Sarah Weddington successfully argued *Roe v. Wade* (1973), in which the Supreme Court liberalized abortion laws, and, as an aide to President Jimmy Carter, promoted feminist goals. As first lady, Rosalynn Carter was an enthusiastic advocate of the ERA.

Until 1972, in the South as in the rest of the nation, there seemed to be considerable support for feminist goals and little active opposition. Between 1971 and 1973 all southern states created commissions on the status of women. Both Texas (1972) and Virginia (1971) added equal rights amendments to their state constitutions. In the U.S. Senate, Sam Ervin of North Carolina fought to modify or defeat the ERA, but with little support from his fellow southerners. When Congress voted overwhelmingly in 1972 to submit the amendment to the states, only two southern senators (Ervin and Mississippi's John Stennis) and nine southern congressmen voted against it. Both Texas and Tennessee ratified within two weeks.

The decisive victory of the ERA in Congress and its warm reception in the states (14 states ratified within a month) awakened latent antifeminist sentiment, and opponents of ratification began to mobilize in the South and throughout the nation. In its 1972 platform, the American Party denounced "this insidious socialistic plan to destroy the home," as did other right-wing groups active in the South, including the National State's Rights Party, the Ku Klux Klan, and the John Birch Society. In the mid-1970s, "New Right" groups, including the Conservative Caucus and the National Conservative Political Action Committee, became involved in the ERA controversy in the South, and, through the use of sophisticated direct-mailing techniques, mobilized hundreds of thousands of southerners to write letters to their legislators opposing ratification.

Phyllis Schlafly of Illinois, working through the Eagle Forum and the National Committee to Stop ERA (founded in 1972), became the most visible leader of the opposition to the amendment. Along with her native Midwest, the South provided Schlafly her greatest following. She became a cult heroine to her supporters, political and religious conservatives who, sharing her conviction that women were most fulfilled through marriage and motherhood, opposed feminist reforms that they perceived as diminishing these roles and weakening the traditional American family. In the South, large numbers of ERA opponents were religious fundamentalists who rejected the whole concept of sexual equality as contrary to biblical teachings. The close cooperation between fundamentalist churches and Stop ERA and other opponents of ratification was a distinctive feature of the ERA controversy in the South.

The antiratification forces in the South faced off against state coalitions composed of state and local chapters of organizations that had endorsed ERA at the national level. In contrast to rank-and-file Stop ERA activists, these organizations were more often composed of professional women and upper middle-class housewives with greater experience in lobbying. However, the very diversity of the pro-ERA forces, together with the fact that most supporters were involved in other causes, meant that the state coalitions were often loosely coordinated and at a disadvantage against their opponents, who pursued with religious intensity the single goal of stopping the ERA.

A majority of southerners favored ratification of the ERA (Gallup poll, 1978), important regional newspapers endorsed the amendment, and prominent southern politicians—for example, James Hunt (N.C.), Reuben Askew (Fla.), James B. Edwards (S.C.), and President Jimmy Carter—actively supported ratification, but no other southern state ratified after 1972. The reactions of southern state legislators varied from Mississippi (a state eventually written off by ERA supporters), where the amendment never emerged from committee, to North Carolina and Florida, where the ERA succeeded in the House, only to be narrowly defeated in the Senate. There was also considerable support for ratification among state legislators in South Carolina and Virginia. As proponents searched for the last three states (of the 38 necessary for ratification), they felt frustrated by narrow losses and the skillful political maneuvering of their opponents; Liz Carpenter charged that "a handful of willful and mischievous men" in Florida, North Carolina, and South Carolina were blocking the ERA.

The most important reason, however, that additional states failed to ratify was that opponents were successful both in raising doubts about the potential effects of ratification and in linking the ERA to such controversial issues as abortion and gay rights. In the South, opponents appealed effectively to the southern penchant for chivalry and religious conservatism, as well as to the regional antipathy toward expansion of federal power. While proponents argued in vain that the ERA would protect women against discrimination in laws affecting domestic relations, employment, government benefits, and education, opponents insisted that American women would lose their right to be supported by their husbands, would be driven into the workforce, and would have to turn over their children to state-run child-care facilities. Fundamentalist ministers throughout the South testified that the amendment represented a direct rejection of God's will. Senator Ervin, whose minority report to the Senate was widely distributed by Stop ERA, lent his authority to the charges that the ERA would require sexual integration of prisons, dormitories, and restrooms and compel the military to draft women and use them in combat. This last point proved to be particularly damaging, as many southern legislators proved to be as passionate about the maintenance of a strong defense free of female encumbrances as about the protection of womanhood. The proponents' response, that Congress could draft women even without the ERA, was not particularly reassuring.

Some southern legislators saw the ERA, with its Section 2 providing for federal enforcement, as yet another infringement upon the rights of states and insisted that state governments could adequately guarantee equality for women. Still chafing over Supreme Court decisions on school prayer and integration, many southerners feared the outcome of the inevitable court battles over interpretation of the ERA. Others were upset by previous congressional action to protect the rights of blacks and women and, dismayed by what they perceived as a welter of changes forced upon the South from without, saw a vote against ratification of the ERA as an opportunity to register an objection to rapid social changes over which they seemed to have no control.

Having been stirred to action by the ERA controversy, antifeminists went on to form the "Pro-Family Movement" to promote and defend their concept of the family and to repeal feminist-inspired laws and court rulings. By 1977, the year of the United States Conference for International Women's Year (IWY), there were two strong social reform movements in the United States with conflicting ideological perspectives on women and the family. Feminists and antifeminists battled at state conferences leading up to the IWY convention over the election of delegates to the national convention and the right to speak for American women. Most successful in the South and in the heavily Mormon Southwest, the profamily forces elected all of the delegates from Mississippi and a few from Alabama, Georgia, Louisiana, and Texas. But these delegates, together with the delegates from southwestern states, accounted for a scant 20 percent of the total attending the Houston convention. At congressional hearings called by their champion, Senator Jesse Helms of North Carolina, profamily advocates testified that their point of view had been deliberately stifled. In Houston, feminists celebrated the unity of women of all ages, races, and regions in support of a broad platform of feminist demands, including passage of the ERA; a major federal role in developing child-care programs; gay rights; access to abortion, family planning, and sex education; and a host of issues that were anathema to the profamily movement. Across town, Schlafly led representatives of Stop ERA, the Eagle Forum, Conservative Caucus, National Right to Life, the Mormon Club, the DAR, and the John Birch Society in a counter-convention attended by 11,000 people. She denounced the IWY conference as a symbol of degeneracy financed by $5 million from the federal government.

Between 1977 and 1982 feminists gained an extension of the deadline for ratification of the ERA but no new states. Meanwhile, opposition to the amendment and to feminism in general was one of the key issues uniting an increasingly powerful political movement. The Pro-Family Movement helped solve the New Right's search for a constituency by drawing many previously nonpolitical conservatives into political activity. By 1980 the Pro-Family Movement had merged with the New Right to form an effective coalition that influenced the Republican Party to drop its support for the ERA and adopt an antiabortion plank. This coalition claimed credit for Reagan's decisive victory over Jimmy Carter, whose party platform endorsed federally funded abortions and the withholding of campaign funds from Democratic candidates who failed to support the ERA. Certainly, the resurgence of antifeminism and social conservatism was only one reason for Carter's defeat, but it helps to explain why Reagan carried the traditionally Democratic South, save only Carter's native Georgia.

When the deadline for ratification of the ERA passed in June 1982, the amendment was immediately reintroduced. Feminists vowed to change their tactics from the defensive to the offensive, to stop trying to persuade "negative politicians," and to elect legislators supportive of their goals. Taking lessons from the New Right, NOW formed its own political action committee (NOW-PAC) and claimed to have elected 61 percent of their candidates in the 1982 congressional elections. However, feminists still expend much of their energy defending previous accomplishments against antifeminist opponents who celebrate the defeat of the ERA as the beginning of their effort to restructure America in keeping with "Pro-Family" values.

MARJORIE J. SPRUILL
University of South Carolina

Janet K. Boles, *The Politics of the Equal Rights Amendment: Conflict and the Decision Process* (1979); David W. Brady and Kent L. Tedin, *Social Science Quarterly* (March 1976); Ann Fears Crawford and Crystal S. Ragsdale, *Women in Texas: Their Lives, Their Experiences, Their Accomplishments* (1982); Sara Evans, *Personal Politics: The Roots of Women's Liberation in the Civil Rights Movement and the New Left* (1979); Carol Felsenthal, *The Sweetheart of the Silent Majority: The Biography of Phyllis Schlafly* (1981); Marcia Fram, *National Catholic Reporter* (16 July 1982, 30 July 1982); Nancy Gager, ed., *Women's Rights Almanac* (1974); Susan Harding, *Feminist Studies* (Spring

1981); Jane DeHart Mathews and Donald Mathews, *Organization of American Historians Newsletter* (November 1982).

Food and Cooking

Men's and women's relationships to food have differed over the centuries and in many societies across the world, but working with food has fallen into surprisingly similar gendered patterns. For the most part, men have hunted while women have gathered and tended both small patches and large fields of food crops. In almost all cases, women have done much of the day-to-day meal preparation for their families. For several hundred years, most of the people in the American South followed this global pattern.

In the southeastern United States, Native Americans usually enjoyed abundant food in the woodlands. At the time of European contact, the Cherokee had a rigid division of labor. Men hunted, and women tended their large gardens, growing squash, gourds, sunflowers, watermelons, potatoes, pumpkins, peas, beans, and multiple varieties of corn. Women also foraged for nuts and wild fruits and berries, and they gathered honey and made sugar from maple sap. Cherokee women were solely responsible for cooking their bounty over open fires, usually one meal per day, and they made bread on clay or stone hearths. A significant part of the difficulties that the Cherokees experienced before the Trail of Tears was due to the pressure on men to become agriculturalists—to do women's work.

As Europeans and European Americans spread westward across the South, their diets varied widely according to their location and social status. In seaports, particularly Charleston, Savannah, and New Orleans, wealthy southerners could obtain almost any delicacy they desired. Many urban people kept gardens, chickens, and milk cows, purchasing other foods to supplement their homegrown supply. Fewer than half a million slaves lived in urban areas, and most Anglo town women likely cooked for their own families. Iron stoves slowly made their way into antebellum town kitchens, but much cooking was still done over the open hearth. Men participated in cooking primarily through such rituals as barbecues, cooking large pieces of meat—often whole pigs—out-of-doors.

In rural areas, the food of the common people was usually plain and often of poor quality. Most families in the backcountry raised their own corn and hogs and depended upon wild supplies for variety. Vegetable crops were often short-lived, but they were preserved by drying, and wild fruits could be made into jelly. Women tended their garden patches and did almost all of the cooking, while men raised field corn and livestock and hunted and fished. Men also did the dirtiest part of butchering at hog-killing time.

On large plantations, food for the master's family could be sumptuous or sparse, depending upon the season. In South Carolina, for example, pork and fowl were considered good, but beef, veal, and mutton were less palatable, and wild supplies from the woods and sea greatly augmented the tables of the big houses. In addition to locally grown produce, the wealthy could buy apples, white potatoes, and wheat from the North and all sorts of delicacies, such as almonds and anchovies, from the tropics and Europe.

The lavish fare of large plantations gave rise to numerous stereotypes of the antebellum South, one of the most prevailing being the slave cook. Postbellum paeans to these slave cooks created one of the most enduring images of that period. Slave cooks, according to the popular image, were large, dark-brown women in bandannas, cooking over open hearths and producing meals of extraordinary quality. Such women actually existed. As slaves, they spent years honing their craft and learning the tastes of individual family members. And some of them were fully capable of turning out significant feasts with limited technology and no ability to read recipes. They truly did cook by feel and instinct, and their results could strike awe in the people who ate their products. But the vast majority of slave women worked in the fields, not in the kitchen, and the fancy plantation cook was the exception rather than the rule.

The slaves themselves ate simply, in some places receiving weekly rations of one peck of cornmeal and three pounds of bacon apiece. If allowed, they supplemented their diets by growing gardens and hunting. Because slaves were often forbidden to have arms, African American men hunted animals that they could snare in simple traps, such as opossums. On some plantations a cook prepared food for all of the slaves and they ate communally; on others family units cooked and ate individually. Undoubtedly, some women, exhausted from a day's work in the fields, may have dreaded preparing meals; but others may have enjoyed fixing their families' limited viands as a means of showing love and care.

Following the lean times during the Civil War, southern diets began to evolve slowly, and for decades they remained rooted for many in corn and pork. On the farms, men grew corn in the fields along with cash crops, and women raised vegetable gardens and chickens. Under the developing crop-lien and sharecropping systems, food supplies suffered, as subsistence farming gave way to cash crops. Newly freed African Americans in particular often had scanty food supplies, with some landowners actually forbidding their planting gardens or keeping chickens. Genuine hunger existed among rural southern blacks, and women often had to scrounge to create meals for their families.

For common white people in the rural South, the greatest change in their diets after the Civil War came with the availability of canning technology. Although canning had been invented in Napoleonic France, it did not become commonplace in southern homes until the late 19th century. Women with access to canning equipment could preserve vegetables and even meat for use at a later time, greatly enhancing possibilities past the short growing seasons.

For affluent urban southerners, postbellum transportation developments brought significant changes to their diets. The expansion of the railroad and the invention of refrigerator cars made possible steady supplies of fresh milk, beef, and vegetables, as well as delicacies such as oysters. Greater availability of wheat flour made the biscuit ubiquitous in many southern homes. Grocers and meat markets sprang up in urban centers shortly after the Civil War, quickly becoming widespread. Often these stores offered a wide variety of foodstuffs, in addition to the usual cornmeal and pork products. Housewives, still maintaining chicken yards and vegetable gardens, learned new skills as consumers. Men's primary role in food production came to be supplying cash for its purchase.

Across the former Confederacy, freedwomen took paid positions as domestic servants, and in expanding southern urban areas perhaps a quarter to a third of white families had domestic help during the late 19th and early 20th centuries. The duties of these freedwomen often included cooking. With long hours and low pay, these African American women supplemented their own families' diets by taking leftovers home. This practice, known as "toting," meant that African American families often ate the same items as white families, except several hours later and almost surely in smaller quantities. As in antebellum days, some African American cooks developed significant culinary skills. The majority of cooks, like other types of domestic servants, changed positions frequently, however, and most did not have the time to hone their skills to suit their employers' tastes.

Almost all paid cooks in homes and boardinghouses were female, and for many years most paid cooks in restaurants were male. Indeed, the great chefs of the South, beginning with Antoine Alciatore of New Orleans in 1840, through Craig Claiborne (born in Sunflower, Miss., in 1920), were male. Not until the 1970s did female cooks such as Nathalie Dupree, Mildred Council, and Edna Lewis become known for their culinary artistry. Television made stars not only of Dupree but of men such as Paul Prudhomme and Emeril Lagasse, born in

Fall River, Mass., but carefully trained in New Orleans. For many Americans, these men represented the public face of southern cooking.

Throughout the 20th century, the southern diet increased in diversity. Chain grocery stores and national name brands made southern foodways begin to more closely resemble those of other parts of the United States. Commercial canned goods became more widely available, and produce could be brought in from across the United States. Following World War II, southerners became even more a part of the mainstream of American life. White housewives drove their cars to the grocery store and bought many of the same standardized brands purchased by their cousins in the North. In the postwar consumer boom, they bought shiny gas ranges for their new little houses. African American women entered the workforce in positions that did not include domestic service, and as their incomes rose, they, too, bought stoves and canned goods. By the beginning of the 21st century, women, black and white, were in the paid workforce in unprecedented numbers. Tired women coming home had many options—takeout, frozen dinners, or supper from scratch—and women still bore most of the responsibility for getting the family to the dinner table. For many, going out is an increasingly appealing option, and the food prepared in restaurants might be cooked by a male or a female.

REBECCA SHARPLESS
Texas Christian University

Esther Boserup, *Woman's Role in Economic Development* (1970); John Egerton, *Southern Food: At Home, on the Road, in History* (1987); Richard J. Hooker, ed., *A Colonial Plantation Cookbook: The Receipt Book of Harriott Pinckney Horry, 1770* (1984); Jacqueline Jones, *Labor of Love, Labor of Sorrow: Black Women, Work, and the Family from Slavery to the Present* (1986); David M. Katzman, *Seven Days a Week: Women and Domestic Service in Industrializing America* (1978); Martha McCulloch-Williams, *Dishes and Beverages of the Old South* (1913); Frederick Law Olmsted, *Journey in the Backcountry* (1860); Theda Perdue, *Cherokee Women: Gender and Culture Change, 1700–1935* (1998); Susan Strasser, *Never Done: A History of American Housework* (1982).

Food and Markets

Just as food has shaped southern cultures, so has food played a central role in the female economy of the rural South. Women's production for market both complemented cash-crop agriculture and shielded farms and families from the vagaries of prices for staple commodities such as cotton and tobacco. Memoirs of rural life, oral histories with rural elders, farm periodicals, and reports of home-demonstration agents who worked for the agricultural extension service reveal the intricacies and importance of women's commerce. Through their trade, women reduced indebtedness and reliance upon creditors, mitigated their own economic dependence upon men, and helped families to enjoy new consumer goods. They also found an outlet for entrepreneurial skills and talents.

In the early 20th century, southern farm women's production for market grew out of their production for home use. Although the spread of cash crops in the South had undermined diversified agriculture, rural families still tried to meet as many of their own dietary needs as possible. Women cultivated gardens and preserved vegetables and fruits. They raised chickens for meat and eggs and kept a cow for milk and butter. A family's ability to achieve self-provisioning varied by class, race, and its ability to determine the crop mix. In the early 1920s, rural sociologists who surveyed a cross section of North Carolina farmers found that both black and white landowners grew more of their own food than tenants and sharecroppers and that, in general, white families fared better than black. Although many poor farm families suffered dietary deficiencies, many rural elders who remembered the lean years of the 1920s and 1930s marveled that though cash was scarce they "didn't go hungry."

Through their marketing ingenuity, women turned a variety of goods into commodities for trade. Poorer women, in particular, gathered and sold what nature offered freely, foraging and selling berries that grew wild in the woods. For most farm women, poultry and dairy products formed the heart of their trade. A flock of chickens in the yard and a good milk cow or two provided a surplus for market as well as food for the family table. The fact that eggs and live chickens were available nearly year-round rather than seasonally enhanced their worth. Women stayed attuned to the market and calculated if eggs would be sold or would be eaten. When income earning took priority, sales of goods deprived some families of food or left them only with provisions of inferior quality.

The products of women's labor entered channels of commerce in a number of ways, ranging from casual exchanges to formal, state-sponsored markets. Modest transactions occurred so routinely that they might be taken for granted. In eastern North Carolina, for example, women traded eggs with men who peddled fish caught in the area's rivers from house to house. Storekeepers in country and town alike took butter, eggs, and live chickens in trade. Although the women might not have known it, they formed the first link in a supply chain as rural storekeepers joined scattered small producers and wholesale merchants located in cities. Itinerant merchants known as hucksters offered another marketing outlet. These traders traveled the South, paying cash for poultry and dairy products to the farm women who greeted them in their backyards and for eggs that storekeepers had accumulated when customers brought them in for swapping. Women also controlled their own retail operations, thus sidestepping intermediaries, as they sold butter, milk, eggs, and seasonal fruits and vegetables directly to individual customers.

One more mode of selling was state-sponsored cooperative markets. During the 1920s and 1930s, home demonstration agents who worked for the agricultural extension services organized curb markets in county seats across the region. Responding to the downturn in the farm economy and women's desire to control their sales, curb markets expanded at the same time that prices for cotton and tobacco declined. Women praised these markets for helping them obtain good prices for their commodities. In a close study of the curb market in Augusta County, Va., Ann E. McCleary concluded that the retail outlet reflected "a blend of the modern idea of the farm woman as business-person intertwined with a traditional perspective of farm woman as producer."

Curb markets served didactic as well as economic purposes. Home demonstration agents seized the opportunity to teach lessons about the standardization of products and the self-presentation of the sellers themselves. Women who sold at the curb markets had to honor regulations that determined all aspects of sales, from the prices they charged to the appearance of their assigned stalls and how they pitched their products. In this regard, they joined a long tradition of public markets the world over that established rules to govern vendors and to protect consumers. Home agents coached marketing women on how to approach potential buyers with poise and decorum. While customers surveyed the displays of dressed poultry, eggs, cakes, vegetables, and fruits, sellers had to remain in their designated places and to keep those spaces tidy. Market rules required women to wear washable white dresses whose uniform appearance suggested cleanliness and order.

In the era of Jim Crow, home demonstration markets practiced racial segregation. The bylaws that governed the market in at least one North Carolina county stated explicitly that only whites could sell under its auspices, and other markets followed the color line. Nonetheless, black home agents in the state acted as intermediaries between producers and buyers, encouraged club women to participate in city markets open to sellers of both races, and occasionally organized small curb markets of their own.

Many farm women enjoyed selling in a lively public venue where they mingled with friends and strangers, managed the transactions, and turned their private work into social labor. Sellers engaged in good-natured rivalries, and women reveled in the reputations their products and skills earned them. In addition, farm wives and mothers who could boast of market earnings might influence how the family allocated its labor, and husbands and children who helped them set up and sell also witnessed the value of their labors firsthand.

The income-earning strategies that Victoria Williams Cunningham pursued in the 1920s and 1930s combined sales at a home demonstration curb market in South Carolina with sales to individual customers. At the market, her son Tom recalled years later, Cunningham sold milk, butter, and eggs all year and offered other goods as the seasons changed. In the spring, she supplied tender greens and tangy onions. In the summer, watermelons, cantaloupes, and garden vegetables filled her market table. In the fall and winter, she sold cured hams, sausage, and peanuts. Victoria Cunningham also maintained a route of customers in Darlington. The family had a telephone, and townsfolk called the farm, about three miles away, to place their orders. On their morning trips to school, Tom and his siblings delivered milk, eggs, and butter to town doorsteps. "My mother," he said, "knew exactly who got milk what day and how much."

During the bleakest years of the Great Depression, the income that farm women generated made a crucial difference for many families. Tom Cunningham could not estimate what proportion of the family economy his mother's earnings represented because he was a child during the heyday of her sales. He did know, however, that his mother "helped to keep body and soul together back during those Depression years, when there just wasn't any money. I know that she worked at it diligently and that my father worked at the farm and between the two of them, they kept the bills paid and we were fed well; we had adequate clothing even though sometimes we had patches on our elbows and knees. But we fared well. We got along real good. And I know it took both of them to do it." The Cunningham family was not alone.

Proceeds from women's trade often made a substantial difference in a family's budget. The cash and credit that women earned met mortgage payments and allowed any profits to be reinvested in the farm enterprise, underwrote home improvements, put extra food on the table, and bought school clothes for their children. Women's income sometimes provided the few small luxuries that rural children enjoyed, and in oral history narratives southerner elders often remember the ways in which women's earnings were spent with a loving precision unmatched in stories about men's income. In the early 1920s when it came time for Jessie Felknor to graduate from high school in east Tennessee, sales of her mother's chickens paid for her class ring. Women used proceeds from the "butter and egg trade" to underwrite education and invest in their children's futures.

Farm women were crucial players in household and local economies, and their goods entered regional and national economic channels. Women's earnings kept families afloat during hard times and helped them enjoy some of the stock on store shelves during better times. Earnings might also shift the balance of power within farm families, giving women more influence over farm decisions and a measure of autonomy. In hindsight, it is clear that commodities like tobacco and cotton were the bricks of the southern farm economy, but the products of women's labor were often the mortar that held it together.

LU ANN JONES
University of South Florida

Lu Ann Jones, *Mama Learned Us to Work: Farm Women in the New South* (2002), in *Cornbread Nation 1: The Best of Southern Food Writing*, ed. John Egerton (2002); Ann E. McCleary, in *Women, Family, and Faith: Rural Southern Women in the Twentieth Century*, ed. Melissa Walker and Rebecca Sharpless (2006); Rebecca Sharpless, *Fertile Ground, Narrow Choices: Women on Texas Cotton Farms, 1900–1940* (1999); Melissa Walker, *All We Knew Was to Farm: Rural Women in the Upcountry South, 1919–1941* (2000).

Gays

Lesbian, gay, bisexual, and transgender (LGBT) people would seem to encounter more difficulties in the South than in other regions. In surveys, southerners are more likely to oppose gay rights and describe homosexuality as sinful than respondents from any other section of the United States. The nation's foremost antigay activist organizations often have been headquartered in the South, from Anita Bryant's Save Our Children in the 1970s to Donald Wildmon's American Family Association in the 1990s. And despite repeated retractions, televangelists such as Virginia's Jerry Falwell and Pat Robertson persist in denunciations of same-sex relations, which in turn help fuel gay bashings. As one of a growing number of antiviolence projects reported, in 1995 in the state of North Carolina two separate murders were attributed to antigay hate. And two occurred in Houston in 2002. With uneven police record keeping, however, such crimes are underreported and the criminals are frequently not apprehended.

Sodomy statutes remained on the books longer in the southern states, yielding the two most important Supreme Court rulings affecting LGBT Americans: 1986's *Bowers v. Hardwick*, from Georgia, upholding the constitutionality of sodomy laws, and 2003's *Lawrence v. Texas*, which finally overturned them and expanded the right to privacy. In both cases, gay male couples literally had been arrested in their own bedrooms. In many states, lesbian mothers had their children taken from their homes. Through the years, doctors have prescribed shock treatment; to this day, quacks concoct "coming-out-of-homosexuality" regimens. The South's religious, legal, and medical establishments—pastors, politicians, policemen, and physicians—often have been decidedly hostile to its LGBT citizens.

Nonetheless, LGBT southerners have demonstrated extraordinary daring and ingenuity in building networks and crafting relationships. The nominally conservative institutions of small-town and rural life—home, church, school, and workplace—have been the very sites where queer sexuality has flourished. For rural southerners, these mainstream community institutions have served as the key sites for meeting friends and sex partners: at house parties and church choir practice, in school gymnasiums and on the shop floors. Though usually clandestine, same-sex relations have been enabled by the distinctive qualities of rural landscapes and social structures. Though they may publicly denounce homosexuality, many southerners practice a day-to-day, quiet accommodation of difference.

Often made to feel "the only one," rural queers have used cars and roads, letters and the Internet, to overcome distances and avoid isolation. Unsurprisingly, with private homes—even bedrooms—under surveillance, they have re-appropriated public spaces such as roadside rest areas, parks, riversides, and beaches. Unlike residents of gay enclaves in major cities, they have relied on circulation more than congregation. They have set up households together or devised acceptable roles within their families of origin as spinster aunts or confirmed bachelor uncles.

Same-sex schools and colleges facilitate homosexual interaction and, for women in particular, they often instill feminist ideals. Other homosocial environments, such as the South's numerous military bases, likewise provide homosexual possibilities. Camps and other rural retreats have proven important. Laurel Falls summer camp for girls, on Old Screamer Mountain, Ga., run by partners Lillian Smith and Paula Snelling in the 1930s to 1940s, was a forerunner of Camp Sister Spirit, near Ovett, Miss., operated by Brenda and Wanda Hinson since the early 1990s. The gay men's spiritual/pagan collective Radical Faeries holds regular international gatherings and publishes its long-running magazine RFD on Short Mountain, Tenn.

In the more anonymous urban areas, ostensibly freed from small-town values, LGBT southerners have developed elaborate institutions and rituals. Much more than watering holes, queer bars are bedrock community centers and information clearinghouses. Whereas the sole gay bar in a small city becomes a remarkably democratic space, the large numbers in major metropolitan areas such as Atlanta or Dallas can mean a specialization of bars, not unlike mainstream culture, along lines of age, class, and race (black, white, Latino, Asian American), as well as gender (women, men, trans) and self-presentation or erotic proclivity (lipstick lesbian, bulldyke, s/m, leather, hustler, country/western, club kid, gym bunny, bear). Many LGBT clubs and organizations meet in bars before or in lieu of acquiring their own buildings.

Among these are sports teams, especially lesbian softball squads, gay men's choruses, reading groups, and religious organizations. In addition to local congregations of the Metropolitan Community Church, founded in Los Angeles in 1968 by southerner Troy Perry, there are active affiliates of mainline Christian denominations, including Catholic Dignity, Episcopal Integrity, Methodist Affirmation, and the More Light Presbyterians. Lesbian readers have supported cutting edge literary/political magazines such as *Feminary*, published in the 1970s, and they have constructed vibrant community hubs interconnected with lesbian-feminist bookstores such as Atlanta's Charis Books and More, one of the nation's oldest.

Annual LGBT pride parades and events are held in many localities, usually in the summer, in part to commemorate New York's Stonewall Riots of late June 1969. Vital in reaching young adults questioning their sexuality, university student groups are also alternative social institutions, and they often organize spring breaks at Daytona Beach and elsewhere. Many LGBT southerners spend Memorial Day weekend in Pensacola, Labor Day weekend in New Orleans. Sadly, a few organizations seem predicated less upon lesbian and gay communion and more upon race and class exclusion: certain "executive networks," LG business associations, "A-list" events, and circuit parties. Although some retail establishments, including video shops and bathhouses, live or die by the "gay dollar," some weekly newspapers, to secure advertising, overstate its power.

Indeed, employment discrimination based upon sexual orientation has left many in precarious economic circumstances and has led to the section's most visible and sustained LGBT political action. When Cracker Barrel Restaurants announced its antigay employment policy in 1991 and fired at least 16 workers, the multiracial Atlanta chapter of Queer Nation mounted protests and directed a national boycott that garnered the support of a variety of liberal organizations and leaders, including Coretta Scott King. Cracker Barrel, headquartered in Lebanon, Tenn., finally rescinded its policy and included sexual orientation in its equal opportunity statement a decade later.

Building upon mainstream folk traditions of womanless weddings and all-male beauty pageants, transgender people have engaged in intricate drag performances perceived as distinctively southern. As early as the 1940s, black drag troupes toured juke joints across the region, including among their ranks the notorious Princess Lavone, aka "Little Richard" Penniman. For over 30 years, the Miss Gay America pageant has been conducted by white Arkansan Norma Kristie. Today, performances range from the racist blackface drag of Mississippi's Shirley Q. Liquor to the inventive "Sunday services" of Georgia's biracial Gospel Girls, who sing hymns and pass the collection plate. North Carolina's Cuntry Kings are just what the name suggests: drag kings performing country music.

For transgender persons seeking sex reassignment surgery, an increasing number of hospitals offer the procedure. But with costs rarely covered by insurance, many go away—as far as Belgium—for affordable services. Perhaps more urgent than the repeal of sodomy laws, trans activists have fought for the right to change the sex designation on their legal and medical documents, such as driver's licenses and birth certificates.

In the South especially, race and sexuality are inextricably intertwined. Lesbians and gays of various levels of outness were among the leaders and the rank-and-file participants in the African American civil rights movement. And segregationists not only red-baited but also queer-baited the activists. Although some gay male organizations have expressly promoted interracial relationships—first Black and White Men Together (BWMT), then Men of All Colors Together (MACT)—racial fetishization remains a danger. The gay argot "dinge queen" and "dairy queen," referring to white men who mostly date nonwhite and vice versa, are sometimes as much derogatory as descriptive labels.

As elsewhere, AIDS has transformed LGBT life in the South. As lesbians rallied around gay men hit hard by the crisis—and simultaneously established new lesbian health initiatives—many early AIDS service organizations like AID Atlanta and Birmingham AIDS Outreach faced charges of racial bias. After Senator Jesse Helms's trademark homophobic response to a plea on behalf of their sons, two North Carolina women founded MAJIC, Mothers against Jesse in Congress. The direct action group ACT UP forced important changes in federal policy, in part by splashy demonstrations at the Centers for Disease Control in Atlanta. And generally in the 1990s, "sex-positive" groups such as Lesbian Avengers pushed a radical rather than reformist agenda.

Such radical sentiments may be on the wane in the South. With increased "visibility"—of an assimilationist sort—in the mainstream mass media, many may have become complacent. The backlash against lesbian and gay marriage, President Bill Clinton's backtracking on military service, and a continuing climate of violence and discrimination suggest that efforts may need to be re-doubled.

JOHN HOWARD
King's College, University of London

John Howard, *Men Like That: A Southern Queer History* (1999); John Howard, ed., *Carryin' On in the Lesbian and Gay South* (1997); Suzanne Pharr, *Homophobia: A Weapon of Sexism* (1988); Minnie Bruce Pratt, *Rebellion: Essays, 1980–1991* (1991); Mab Segrest, *My Mama's Dead Squirrel: Lesbian Essays on Southern Culture* (1985).

Good Old Boys and Girls

The terms "good old boy" and "good old girl" are of southern origin. The terms describe social types, persons with particular social characteristics that make them identifiable to others. Although there are similar social types in other regions of the United States, the southern label may make them more obvious in the South.

The good old boy and girl have been pictured most frequently in popular literature. Perhaps the first reference to the social type was in William Byrd's *Histories of the Dividing Line betwixt Virginia and North Carolina* (1728). W. J. Cash discussed the type in *The Mind of the South* (1941), but the first writer to use the term itself was Tom Wolfe in an *Esquire* essay on stock car racing hero Junior Johnson (October 1967). William Price Fox, in *Southern Fried* (1962), presented several portraits of the type, including the legendary Georgia politician Eugene Talmadge. Willie Morris's *Good Old Boy: A Delta Boyhood* (1971) was autobiographical, and Paul Hemphill in *The Good Old Boys* (1974) wrote lovingly of them, mainly because his father was one. Florence King's *Southern Ladies and Gentlemen* (1975) sees the good old boy as mean and nasty. Sharon McKern's *Redneck Mothers, Good Old Girls, and Other Southern Belles* (1979) was one of the first literary applications of the concept to women. In *Crackers* (1980), Roy Blount Jr. suggests that "'good old boy' means pretty much the same as 'mensch.'"

The good old boy frequently appears in such country music songs as "Bar Room Buddies," "If You've Got the Money, I've Got the Time," and "Dang Me," and the term itself was used in Ansley Fleetwood's "Just Good Ol' Boys" (1979). Sometimes the term is used synonymously with "cowboy" in country music. Burt Reynolds embodied the good old boy in a series of movies in the 1970s.

The good old boy is described as blue collar, an outdoorsman, a patriot, something of a populist, basically conservative—a "man's man." He is also somewhat self-centered and scheming, particularly toward out-groups. Yet, to his in-group, he is an affable comrade and a man of integrity. Billy Carter, the brother of President Jimmy Carter and himself the essence of the type, defined the good old boy as someone who rides around in a pickup truck, drinking beer and putting his empties in a sack. A redneck, by contrast, rides around in a pickup, drinking and tossing his empties out the window. The "redneck" as a concept describes a more menacing figure.

The good old girl has not been studied as systematically as the good old boy. She has traits of bluffness, camaraderie, and loyalty, which make her more comfortable with men than with women. She is usually not seen as a sex object and, in fact, is somewhat asexual in social interaction. She is likely to possess the same affability and integrity as the good old boy and the same ability to manipulate people.

INGRAM PARMLEY
Francis Marion College

Gail Gilchrist, *Bubbas and Beaus: From Good Old Boys to Southern Gentlemen, a Close Look at the Customs, Cuisine, and Culture of Southern Men* (1995); Ingram Parmley, *Perspectives on the American South*, vol. 1, ed. Merle Black and John Shelton Reed (1981); John Shelton Reed, *Southern Folk, Plain and Fancy: Native White Social Types* (1986); Edgar T. Thompson, *South Atlantic Quarterly* (Autumn 1984).

Healers, Women

Women in the South have a long tradition of helping family and friends maintain and restore health. Healing traditions were brought to the South with the early settlers, and they evolved as ideas and procedures were incorporated from European medical practice, African traditions, and American Indian traditions. The passing of remedies and techniques for care of the sick through generations of women is found in many cultures. Distinctive southern healing characteristics stem from the types of rural areas in which folk medicine practices have predominated and from the healers' use of indigenous plants and animals. Because modern techniques for controlling infectious diseases were adopted later in the South than in the North and because many rural southern areas have had shortages of medical personnel, folk healing practices have been particularly important throughout the region.

A mainstay of southern healing has been the use of readily available ingredients. Traditionally, many rural women raised herbs and medicinal plants such as comfrey, ginger, and catnip, along with their flowers and vegetables. They also made use of wild plants and trees, such as cottonwood leaves and fever grass. Household staples—eggs, baking soda, sugar, and whiskey—were also important to the care of the infirm. Teas and syrup were the vehicle for many medicines; other agents were directly applied as poultices to sores, sprains, and pains.

Knowledge and advice about health and healing came also from purveyors of patent medicines, who traveled from town to town attracting a following through shows and testimonials of cures. Mail-order almanacs and manuals were also sources of new information.

The role of women in healing and nursing was strongly supported by tradition. In years when infectious diseases like smallpox, typhoid, and malaria caused much illness and death, women spent long hours alleviating the sickness and suffering. Death was a commonplace occurrence, but religious beliefs and the belief in a joyous afterlife helped to ease the pain associated with death. Before the 20th century, medicine was not a well-established profession based on scientific principles. Until the reform of medical education around 1910 almost anyone could claim competence and practice medicine. Mistrust of and disdain for doctors were widespread, as were social movements to restore the art of healing to the domestic sphere. Health-reform movements flourished throughout the country in the mid-19th century because of the failure of medical professionals to cure and because women sought a way to improve the quality of life in a confusing world undergoing major transitions. They were especially prevalent in the South because faith in self-treatment and the home healing arts was in harmony with tradition.

Many health reform sects such as the Thomsonians, the homeopaths, and the hydropaths prescribed specific remedies and formulas. These prescriptions were added to the already-rich base of healing knowledge in the South. Magical cures, formulas for healthful living, and medicinal cures derived from local plants and animals, and professional health care coexisted with minimal conflict. Of the many remedies known in the South, some work well and some have proven to be useless or dangerous. Behind them are generations of women who grew and gathered plants, raised animals, treated injuries, prepared barks, herbs, and plants for treatments, applied poultices, and administered medicines. Many of these beliefs and practices, which point out the self-sufficiency and independence of southern women and their families, are preserved in the Foxfire books.

Midwifery was another special preserve of women. With the exception of such areas as Appalachia and the Ozarks, southern midwifery was an occupation dominated largely by black women who passed their skills and knowledge down to their mature daughters or nieces. Although the practices of midwives were allegedly a cause of childbed mortality rates higher than those of the North, more recent investigations suggest that other factors, especially nutrition, were responsible.

In the 1920s, programs to train midwives in obstetrics were supported in southern states by the federal government. Midwives met in the county health departments and under the supervision of public health officials nurses learned how to keep germs away during births, fill out birth certificates, and care for the equipment they used. By the 1970s nearly all traditional midwives were retired from practice, although nurse-midwifery training programs continue today.

Nurse-midwifery increased greatly in importance when Mary Breckinridge began the Frontier Nursing Service in the 1920s. By the 1960s teams of medically supervised nurse-midwives from the University of Mississippi worked in locations throughout the South where infant deaths were disproportionately high. These nurse-midwives demonstrated that they reduced infant deaths and provided high-quality care.

In recent years the number and availability of physicians and other health professionals have increased, but there is also a greater acceptance of women as healers in roles outside the family. Today, women are entering the medical profession at the same rate as men. These changes reflect an increasing involvement of women in healing roles beyond the home and an accompanying belief that women can share economic responsibility without neglecting their traditional roles in healing and caring for their own sick.

MOLLY C. DOUGHERTY
University of Florida

Amanda Carson Banks, *Birth Chairs, Midwives, and Medicine* (1999); Mary Breckinridge, *Wide Neighborhoods: A Story of the Frontier Nursing Service* (1952); Elisabeth Brooke, *Women Healers: Portraits of Herbalists, Physicians, and Midwives* (1995); Marie Campbell, *Folks Do Get Born* (1946); Alex Freeman, *Kentucky Folklore Record* (October 1974); Paul F. Gillespie, ed., *Foxfire 7* (1982); Guenter Risse, Ronald Numbers, and Judith Leavitt, eds., *Medicine without Doctors: Home Health Care in American History* (1977); Sharon A. Sharp, *Women's Studies International Forum* (October 1986); Karen Shelley and Raymond Evans, in *Appalachia/America: Proceedings of the 1980 Appalachian Studies Conference*, ed. Wilson Somerville (1981); Jack Solomon and Olivia Solomon, compilers, *Cracklin' Bread and Asfidity* (1979); Wilbur Watson, ed., *Black Folk Medicine: The Therapeutic Significance of Faith and Trust* (1984); Richard W. Wertz and Dorothy C. Wertz, *Lying-In: A History of Childbirth in America* (1989).

Health

Gender is a crucial factor in understanding the history of health status and health care in the American South. Gender studies examine the social construction of womanhood and manhood to explore how differences have been created and given meaning, thus illuminating the gendered, and racialized, nature of health and healing. Reproduction is central in the history of women's health, war is central in the history of men's health, and public health is central in the history of women's health work.

In 1809 Jane Crawford of Kentucky rode 60 miles on horseback to be operated on by Kentucky physician Dr. Ephraim McDowell. Jane, a 47-year-old white woman, suffered from a rapidly growing ovarian tumor. At the time there was no reliable treatment so she agreed to an ovariotomy, a risky type of abdominal surgery. Dr. McDowell operated on Jane to remove her ovaries and found a cyst or tumor, which turned out to weigh an astonishing 22 pounds.

Responses to the gendered nature of this surgery were mixed. Jane must have been pleased, for she apparently made a complete recovery. However, some physicians were appalled that the surgery had taken place. They thought that gynecological surgery in general, and this procedure in particular, was too dangerous and too painful for white women to undergo. They believed that women's physical frailty meant that they could not tolerate such pain. Furthermore, they thought that such procedures violated female modesty.

Southern physicians' views of women's bodies were shaped by racialized views of womanhood, as indicated by the history of surgical experimentation. Not all women were included in gendered social conventions regarding female modesty and frailty. For example, Dr. James Marion Sims, who helped to develop the field of gynecology, launched his career through experimentation on the bodies of enslaved women. Although scholars know a great deal about Dr. Sims, they know almost nothing about these slave women whose role was absolutely essential to his development of new surgical procedures.

Dr. Sims practiced medicine in South Carolina and Alabama with little success until he moved into the field of surgery and developed the first reliable technique to repair vesico-vaginal fistulas. Some women faced this dreaded condition because of lacerations following long or difficult labor or the misuse of forceps in childbirth. Tears then developed in the perineal tissues or in the walls of the vagina, bladder, or even rectum. Such fistulas permitted urine or sometimes feces to constantly leak through the vaginal opening. It was very distressing for the women who had to live with this condition. They faced severe skin irritations, emitted unpleasant odors, and usually found themselves ostracized by others.

Slavery and the racialized views of black women's bodies made possible Sims's experiments. Dr. Sims, like most white physicians, was not concerned about issues of sexual modesty and the pain tolerance of African American women when he performed a series of experiments from 1845 to 1849 on several enslaved women who suffered from fistulas. Evidently in one case he even had to purchase his patient in order to operate on her. At a time when anesthesia was only just starting to gain acceptance for pain relief, he conducted extremely painful experiments repeatedly on black women without anesthesia. Three slave women in particular, Anarcha, Betsy, and Lucy, served as his subjects. Although they may have hoped his efforts would provide a cure for their health problem, they endured years as his surgical subjects, during which he invited other doctors to witness his operations. At times, a dozen men stood around watching as Dr. Sims operated on the women, who were placed in humiliating positions on their hands and knees on a table in his front yard in Montgomery, Ala. He even trained the subjects of his experiments to assist him when other doctors lost interest. After at least 40 attempts, he finally succeeded in repairing the fistula by using pewter spoons to make an early type of speculum and using wire sutures to sew up the holes. Apparently, a few white women came to Sims for treatment of their vesico-vaginal fistulas after his success, but none of them were able to endure a single operation. It was simply too painful, raising more questions about what the development of this procedure must have been like for the enslaved African American women.

Even as 19th-century doctors debated the appropriateness of surgery to address women's reproductive health problems and issues of which women's bodies were to be used, the American Civil War presented surgical dilemmas regarding the best way to address men's health needs as soldiers. Wars have had profound effects on the development of gendered health professions and health care.

The Civil War led to an unprecedented level of private and governmental involvement in medical issues. In the South, several thousand doctors served with the Confederate forces, and the Confederate government built up a military medical establishment to cope with wartime health problems. Doctors provided some medical inspections of troops and tried to address camp sanitation issues, but they faced difficulties in obtaining medical supplies. Civilians organized medical relief organizations to furnish volunteer nurses. The government drew on nurses, doctors, and pharmacists to organize ambulance wagon teams, hospital trains, and hospitals to care for soldiers.

As battles raged across the South, improvements in weaponry made amputation the most frequently performed military medical operation during the war. Amputation became the standard treatment for fractures, broken bones, and severely injured limbs. Indeed, the term "sawbones" to describe a surgeon dates from the war.

However, amputations were not uniformly embraced as the appropriate solution to the needs of wounded men. Some physicians were appalled at the actions of overzealous doctors, many of whom gained their first surgical experiences on the bodies of young men during the war. Critics viewed these surgeons as simply butchers who mutilated bodies, hacking off limbs. They argued that doctors had other alternatives but could not be bothered to choose them.

Meanwhile, other physicians argued that amputations were the appropriate treatment for severe appendage wounds in order to save lives in the context of a war. At this time, doctors were unable to treat the men once infection developed so they had to act fast, and an immediate amputation gave the patient the greatest chance for survival. Doctors performed amputations immediately to lessen the men's suffering. Men who were still in shock from their wounds and who were under the influence of alcohol or opium pills did not groan and scream nearly as much as men whose wounds were probed two to three days later. In addition, doctors chose amputation as the treatment of choice because of the sheer number of cases they had to treat. Battlefields produced too many wounded men to attend to at once, and it was easier to saw off an arm or leg than to do delicate surgery in the midst of a war. Indeed, excess time with one patient might mean the death of another. Finally, in a wartime situation, doctors and patients might be required to relocate at a moment's notice, so the doctor's task was to act quickly to save as many lives as possible. Hence, medical decisions and military pressures contributed to the high rates of amputations on the bodies of men.

The devastation caused by the Civil War affected men's health for years to come. Indeed, soldiers experienced widespread postwar mental and physical health problems. Furthermore, the huge number of amputations during the war stimulated the refinement and manufacture of prosthetics or false limbs.

Gender also shaped the body politic through public health initiatives. Men acted to improve the health of communities and reduce preventable deaths as leaders of professional organizations and paid government health officials. Women's greatest contributions emerged in their volunteer health work. Two examples illustrate the significance of women's health work in the South— white women's reform efforts in Appalachia and black women's health activism in Mississippi.

From the late 19th century to the early 20th century, white women's health activism was central to efforts to improve the health and well-being of some of the South's poorest populations. Women promoted scientific medicine, the skills of public health nurses, and modern values in communities across Appalachia, including Kentucky, West Virginia, and Virginia. White, middle-class club women organized efforts to provide modern health care to mining camps, and elite settlement workers provided health services to isolated mountain communities. As part of their health work, women volunteers paved the way for the displacement of traditional healers and midwives and greater acceptance of the authority of physicians. However, during the 1920s in Appalachia, doctors in their medical associations and doctors' wives in female auxiliaries of state and county medical associations tried to shut women volunteers out of community health work by dismissing their claims to community health knowledge.

In a parallel fashion, black women's clubs launched community health work, including clean-up campaigns, as part of a black health movement from 1890 to 1950 across the South. In 1915 Booker T. Washington nationalized such efforts in launching an annual observance of National Negro Health Week, supported by African American teachers, ministers, club women, businessmen, midwives, nurses, dentists, and physicians. Female lay workers continued to play an important role in black health work even after the health care professionalization of the 1920s because segregation and racism severely limited the number of black health professionals.

One of the most impressive volunteer health projects for African Americans was the Alpha Kappa Alpha Mississippi Health Project from 1935 to 1942. The project was designed, financed, and carried out by Alpha Kappa Alpha, the oldest black sorority. For several weeks during the Great Depression, Dr. Dorothy Boulding Ferebee led a dozen middle-class sorority volunteers in a health campaign for poor black sharecroppers in the Mississippi Delta. Each summer 3,000 to 4,000 people attended the clinics, which provided medical examinations, vaccinations, and health education. The effect on the health of children was perhaps most significant. The volunteers provided well over 15,000 children with immunizations against such devastating diseases as smallpox and diphtheria.

These examples from the history of medicine, surgery, and public health in the 19th and 20th centuries reveal how ideas about gender, as well as racial politics, operated in southern culture and shaped the experiences of southern women and men.

SUSAN L. SMITH
University of Alberta, Canada

Sandra Lee Barney, *Authorized to Heal: Gender, Class, and the Transformation of Medicine in Appalachia, 1880–1930* (2000); Estelle Brodman and Elizabeth B. Carrick, *Bulletin of the History of Medicine* (Spring 1990); James H. Cassedy, *Medicine in America: A Short History* (1991); Eric Dean, *Shook Over Hell: Post-Traumatic Stress, Vietnam, and the Civil War* (1997); Kenneth M. Ludmerer, *Learning to Heal: The Development of American Medical Education* (1985; 1996); Deborah Kuhn McGregor, *Sexual Surgery and the Origins of Gynecology: J. Marion Sims, His Hospital, and His Patients* (1990); Judith M. Roy, in *Women, Health, and Medicine in America: A Historical Handbook*, ed. Rima D. Apple (1990); Susan L. Smith, *Sick and Tired of Being Sick and Tired: Black Women's Health Activism in America, 1890–1950* (1995).

Honor

Southerners of the antebellum era made it clear that they subscribed to an ethic of honor, but they never specified exactly what honor meant. In large part, this was because the meaning of honor depended on its immediate context, on who claimed and who acknowledged it. In fact, honor might be defined as a system of beliefs in which a person has exactly as much worth as others confer upon him. Antebellum northerners and most 21st-century Americans have some difficulty understanding the idea of honor, for it runs contrary to what has come to be a national article of faith: each person, regardless of race, class, sex, or religion, possesses equal intrinsic worth—regardless of what others think of him. Insult has little meaning to people who share such a faith, but if one takes honor seriously, insult from a respected person can cut to the quick. Accordingly, much of the violence in the South from the 18th century to the present appears to have been sparked by insult, by challenges to honor. Southerners believed a man had to guard his reputation and his honor, by good manners and, if necessary, by violence. Insult literally could not be tolerated.

Women, although traditionally venerated in the South, could have no honor—only virtue. The ultimate protection of honor lay in physical courage, an attribute not considered to be within a woman's sphere. White men also refused to concede that black men could possess honor, although black southerners recognized honor among one another. Further, the honor of wealthy white men could not be damaged by men of lesser rank. Honor came into play only among equals. Contrary to stereotype, though, honor was not restricted to the southern aristocracy. Men of every class felt themselves to be honorable and could not tolerate affront and still enjoy the respect of their peers. Only the elite dueled, of course, but the duel was only the most refined manifestation of honorable conflict, the tip of the iceberg. Fighting, shooting, stabbing, feuding, and shotgun weddings were considered legitimate and inevitable results of honor confronting honor.

An emphasis on honor, along with high homicide rates, prevailed in the 19th-century South, although the cult of honor became less formalized (and probably more dangerous) after the Civil War. Duels faded away; shooting scrapes became more common. The concept of honor also spanned the subregions of the South, lowland and upland, slaveholding and nonslaveholding. It even persisted in southern cities, where volatile rural folkways combined with urban poverty and crowding to make southern cities particularly dangerous places to live.

The South was not alone in this culture of honor. With variations, it has flourished for centuries in Mediterranean cultures such as those of Sicily and Greece. Cultures of honor also flourished among the aristocracy of 17th-century England and among the Scots-Irish, all of whom exerted decisive influences on southern culture in its formative states. The idea of honor did not take hold among the Puritans, Quakers, or Congregationalists and seems to be at odds with the impersonal relations of a predominantly commercial society. Honor never sank deep roots in the North.

The South, on the other hand, from its very beginnings seemed designed to nurture honor. Slavery and the society it spawned provided the conditions in which the notion of honor could flourish. Honor thrives in a rural society of face-to-face contact, of a limited number of relationships, of one system of values. Honor depends upon a hierarchical society, where one is defined by who is above or below. Honor takes hold in a society where the rationalizing power of the state is weak; an adherence to honor makes the state, at best, irrelevant in settling personal disputes.

Honor found itself increasingly on the defensive in the 19th century, not only from the North and England, but also from within the South. Honor, necessarily a secular system of values, clashed with the ideals of Christian virtue. Evangelical southerners deplored and denounced the violence and pride honor condoned. In their eyes, people who let their actions be dictated by honor allowed themselves to become mere slaves of public opinion. The vast majority of southerners, of course, whatever their religious inclination, killed or assaulted no one, and even those who did resort to violence did so only once or twice in a lifetime—still enough to send many more southerners than northerners to jail and the penitentiary for violent crimes, although southerners were notorious for not prosecuting crimes of violence.

Black southerners, once they were liberated from slavery, also adapted to southern codes of honor. White observers, particularly those from the North, were appalled that blacks fought and killed each other over the same apparently trivial provocations as white southerners. Indeed, the homicide rates of both races in the South exceeded those of both in the North. Southerners of both races, consciously or not, have held to their notions of honor far into the 20th century, even in northern cities. Those who find that high homicide rates today correlate with southern culture seem to be measuring the fallout of a culture of honor. Those who find a correlation with low literacy rates or poverty are describing the characteristics of a place in which honor can best survive in the present.

EDWARD L. AYERS
University of Richmond

Edward L. Ayers, *Vengeance and Justice: Crime and Punishment in the 19th-Century American South* (1983); Peter Berger, Brigitte Berger, and Hansfried Kellner, *The Homeless Mind: Modernization and Consciousness* (1973); Pierre Bordieu, in *Honor and Shame: The Values of Mediterranean Society*, ed. J. G. Peristiany (1965); Kenneth S. Greenberg, *Honor and Slavery* (1997); Bertram Wyatt-Brown, *The Shaping of Southern Culture: Honor, Grace, and War, 1760s–1880s* (2000), *Southern Honor: Ethics and Behavior in the Old South* (1982).

Humor

Literary humor in general has not received its deserved critical attention. In his 1993 study, *The Comic Imagination in American Literature*, Louis D. Rubin Jr. points out that "there is scarcely an important American writer who does not at one time or another see the problem before him comically," and yet there is still little written about this ubiquitous aspect of life. And neglect of humor is not limited to literary study. Freud noted that "jokes have not received nearly as much philosophical consideration as they deserve in view of the part they play in our mental life."

When it comes to women and humor, especially in the American South, even less has been offered. This lack originates from many cultural, social, political, and religious sources. Nancy A. Walker, author of *"A Very Serious Thing": Women's Humor and American Culture*, writes that "being a female humorist in America has been problematic in a number of ways that are tied closely to other issues in women's history: the tension between intellect and femininity, male and female 'separate spheres,' women's status as a minority group, and the transforming power of a feminist vision." Freud's ideas about humor in many ways exclude women. Freud basically theorized that women do not need a sense of humor, because humor, in his opinion, is used to repress uncomfortable and unacceptable feelings, feelings women apparently have fewer of. Contemporary theorists often disagree, of course, but most still see women as receivers of jokes and men as givers—at least in situations where both sexes are in attendance. When added to the cultural differences in the South, these issues of humor and gender multiply. Take, for example, Mary Johnston's 1910 quotation in the *Atlantic*: "In the South we are not used to woman's speaking." Clearly, it is quite difficult to be funny when talking is not an option.

One of the reasons humor is more often associated with males is that humor tests boundaries and pushes limits, and in a culture like the South, with very clearly marked territory for different sexes, the difficulties are often magnified. Humor—which requires making a joke and putting oneself in the spotlight— challenges expectations for "feminine" behavior, which is usually seen as more passive than that of the active male. But one kind of humor—"kitchen humor"—exists exclusively in the female domain. Humor among women in a safe environment (like the kitchen) has always been a part of women's experience. This kind of humor can be dangerous and disruptive from the male perspective, though, because men are completely excluded from it—and are often the target. Because men never hear the humor, it might seem completely harmless to them, but it is not. Kitchen humor—like a great deal of women's humor— is aimed at the powers that dominate women, particularly men and religion (which generally still see women as representatives of Eve, forever tainted by that First Sin). If the women are in the kitchen making Sunday dinner, there is bound to be much laughter, but if a man calls in from the other room, "What's so funny?," the answer is bound to be a unanimous, "Nothing!" As targets of the humor, men cannot be let in on the joke.

Men, on the other hand, since they are at the top of the sociological food chain, tend to make jokes about what they fear, partly in an attempt to make the object (person, institution) less intimidating. The target, as Freud explains, receives "the hostile or sexual aggressiveness" of the joke teller. This humor attempts "to exploit something ridiculous in our enemy which we could not, on account of obstacles in the way, bring forward openly or consciously." Freud's theory explains why the target of men's humor can be both women and the boss.

A woman, in contrast, rarely makes jokes about someone less powerful than herself or about an aspect of a person (or institution) that cannot change. This tendency has been termed the "humane humor rule" by Emily Toth, and it explains much about why men and women laugh at different things. Using this rule as a guide, it becomes clear why men laugh more often at physical humor—the slapstick humor in Faulkner's "Spotted Horses" (or in *The Three Stooges*)—and women prefer more subtle humor (especially verbal humor) found in pieces like Flannery O'Connor's "Revelation" (or in Woody Allen's movies).

Another difference in humor and gender results from cultural expectations. Traditionally, the man has been the one to tell the story and the woman to laugh. This active-versus-passive pattern has dominated Western culture and, more specifically, southern culture. Consider films about the pre–Civil War South, for example, with the image of the dashing young man entertaining the demure female, giggling shyly behind her fan. Anne Bealts, a contemporary comedy writer, noticed that in films of the 1960s the pattern is especially evident. Annette Funicello, the archetypal Good American Girl, never laughs at the antics of the boys. In such movies, it is only the Bad Girl who laughs, partly because laughing openly and with gusto suggests a slightly sensual, even sexual, nature for a woman. It suggests she is worldly enough to "get the joke," and that loss of perceived innocence in places like the South—where reputation is extremely important in some circles—can have significant repercussions. Some women would prefer to keep their humor in the kitchen—or, for writers, keep it in publications or venues where only females tread.

Because the women's movement of the 1970s was slower in coming to the South than to other regions, women's humor that openly challenges the traditions of southern culture has also been slower in appearing. And to use humor publicly, more women writers use their comic spirit subtly, relying on satire and parody. As Doris Betts describes it, humor is doled out with a "hand inside the velvet glove [that is] sometimes stainless steel." Satire, for example, has long been the weapon of choice for the powerless and oppressed, and women—especially southern women—have made good use of it. Addison's oft-quoted definition of satire, that it will "pass over a single foe to charge whole armies," serves southern women well. Women writers can speak the truth about southern culture without alienating individual listeners, as seen in Rita Mae Brown's searing look at southern intolerance and religion in *Rubyfruit Jungle* and other novels, or in Lee Smith's hilarious attack on contemporary southern culture in the final pages of *Oral History*.

Questioning traditions and stereotypes using satire is a valuable way to effect change, an important step in creating a culture that allows women to have more input in the governing of their lives. In traditional comedy of ancient Greece and medieval Europe, a comedy ended with the establishment or restoration of order, which, of course, means the established male hierarchical order. Female humor, in contrast, attacks the order already in place, questioning the validity and control over society and often suggesting new possibilities for a more positive social construct—which is why women's literature is thought to be more open ended than male literature. Women leave room for transformation and progression in a new direction.

BARBARA BENNETT
North Carolina State University

Regina Barreca, *They Used to Call Me Snow White . . . but I Drifted: Women's Strategic Use of Humor* (1991); Sigmund Freud, *Jokes and Their Relation to the Unconscious* (1960); Louis D. Rubin Jr., *The Comic Imagination in American Literature* (1973); Emily Toth, *Massachusetts Review* (Winter 1981); Nancy A. Walker, *"A Very Serious Thing": Women's Humor and American Culture* (1988).

Hunting

Ultimately, hunting is about killing. A host of meanings radiates outward from this single defining act. These meanings have varied considerably over time, but they have played a consistent role in the construction of southern conceptions of masculinity.

Every major group of Indians in the South relied upon hunting as an essential source of provisions, clothing, tools, and trade goods. This reliance continued, and in many cases intensified, after the arrival of Europeans and Africans. The growth of the deerskin trade made many southeastern tribes dependent upon exchanging the products of the hunt for manufactured goods, firearms, and alcohol.

In these societies, women often processed the animals men killed into usable products, but the elements of hunting that took place outside settlements and hunting camps were all completely identified as male activities. This gender division of labor was agreeable to Europeans, but many of them criticized Indian men for spending too much time hunting in the woods and not enough in the fields tending crops. Alarmingly for Europeans, women performed most of the daily agricultural labor. Many considered this evidence of degeneracy and backwardness.

These criticisms reveal important elements of the dominant understanding of hunting in the 17th century in Europe, where population density and aristocratic privilege made hunting a leisurely pursuit of the elite. These conceptions quickly altered as colonization continued. The abundant land and apparently inexhaustible supply of game in the New World transformed hunting from elite amusement to common endeavor—hunting became democratized.

In the colonial era, many southerners hunted, but most only occasionally.

Those who chose to hunt usually did so as part of their efforts to provide for their families, and success in the field helped confirm their status as heads of household. Some hunted and trapped to protect their farms from predators, rodents, and birds. Others sought meat and hides. Some households made use of other parts of the animals hunters killed. Fat provided material for shortening, candles, soap, and grease. Feathers stuffed pillows, and tripe made good food for hogs and dogs.

Colonial elites often encouraged white settlers to hunt because it provided them with a sort of paramilitary training, but this enthusiasm waned as favored game species like deer and bear became rare and other species like bison and elk were extirpated. In an effort to conserve these species, colonial legislatures began passing laws that set seasons, banned certain, especially destructive forms of hunting, and, in a few cases, attempted to limit hunting to members of the elite. Essentially unenforceable in the sparsely populated colonies, these laws moldered on the books.

The failure of these laws meant that colonial hunters possessed significantly more freedom to hunt than their counterparts in Europe, but because hunting required expertise and an investment of time and resources, few depended upon hunting as a primary source of income or subsistence. Those who did were market hunters like Daniel Boone; they were successful because they were specialists who hunted without restraint. Together with Indian hunters, they killed most of the large game east of the Appalachians.

After the American Revolution, hunting became increasingly popular because it became easier. State courts struck down colonial laws restricting hunting and trespassing, making it possible to hunt on unimproved private land at any time of the year. Technological changes in firearms further accelerated the growth of hunting. Guns became more plentiful, easier to use, and more accurate.

The economic importance of hunting declined in the antebellum South, but its cultural significance increased, especially among the maturing white elite. Wealthy men began using hunting as a venue to display their masculinity—hunting as "sport." The idea of sport was not limited to the South, but it became particularly popular there because it provided opportunities for hunters to display masculinity with distinctively southern notes of mastery and paternalism, qualities expected of a master class.

A good day's hunting still required a kill, but for a growing number of hunters, the physical products of the hunt became less important than the act of hunting itself. Instead of equating masculinity with the ability to provide a household with meat and hides, elites increasingly associated it with the ability

A young hunter gets 50 cents per rabbit, South Carolina, 1908 (Lewis Wickes Hine,
photographer, Library of Congress [LC-DIG-nclc-01498], Washington, D.C.)

to kill with restraint and self-control (wildfowl must be shot on the wing and
deer should not be shot by firelight, for example). Sportsmen also valued the
ability to manage the slaves, dogs, and horses that usually accompanied their
hunts. Sport became a popular symbol of class position and power.

In creating a vision of hunting divorced from the quotidian demands of
the market, these elites drew a line between themselves and their less wealthy
neighbors. Indeed, few nonslaveholding southerners cared much for the ideals
of sport. Yeoman farmers, slaves, and poor whites continued hunting for pro-
saic reasons—for food. Although lacking the rituals and ceremonies surrounding the sportsman's hunt, hunting still provided them with opportunities to
demonstrate less genteel images of masculine prowess and authority. The ability
to make a difficult kill might impress some elite audiences, but everyone else
expected a tangible benefit from the hours hunters spent in the woods.

Beginning with Reconstruction, the tension between sportsmen and other
hunters (previously limited to the lamentations of sportsmen and a few feeble
attempts to pass hunting laws) intensified as a result of social and technological
changes. The first important development was another improvement in firearms. Breech-loading repeaters enabled hunters to take multiple shots without
reloading. The second was the expansion of the railroads, which made remote

areas with plentiful game more accessible. Both of these innovations proved especially useful for the remaining market hunters, who became increasingly far-ranging, efficient, and deadly.

These developments were complemented by the efforts of landowners to regain control of agricultural labor by eliminating the ability of poor whites and blacks to supplement their incomes though subsistence hunting. State wildlife commissions and newly restrictive laws regarding trespass, hunting seasons, and licensing circumscribed the opportunities for hunting and closed the open range. These changes, all of which had been advocated by antebellum sportsmen, became politically possible because they became an extension of the larger struggle by the landowning elite to assert their power.

Despite these legal restrictions, poor men, white and black, continued to hunt to help provide for their families. This practice remained common until the 1930s when New Deal programs began taking marginal land out of agricultural production. Sharecroppers moved off these lands or were expelled, and much of the South began to be reforested. Game species began recovering, but both subsistence and market hunting essentially passed from the scene.

By the middle of the 20th century, recreational hunters had come to define hunting in the New South. The elite sportsman and the older notion of hunter as provider persisted, but they lacked much of their former power. A hunter returning from the woods with fresh meat remained an easily understandable demonstration of masculinity, but it became one with little grounding in actual household needs. Families continued to enjoy the material benefits of hunting, and these could be considerable, but by the middle of the 20th century they were easily surpassed by the fruits of wage labor. Although most hunters brought home what they killed, their absences in the woods no longer promised a benefit for the household economy. The growing cost of equipment, licenses, and transportation usually outweighed the material benefits of the hunt.

In this way hunting came to resemble other organized sports with their expensive and well-designed equipment, complex rules, and distant, specially designated arenas. Hunting remained an enjoyable, social, and often deeply meaningful activity for its participants in the modern South, but athletics, automobile racing, and electronic gaming crowded it out of its once preeminent place in southern culture.

Wildlife management and the growth of timberland resulted in a massive, late 20th-century increase in many game species, yet the number of hunters declined. A significant number of southerners continued to hunt, but it became difficult to ascribe much sectional distinctiveness to the practice. At the beginning of the 21st century, 6 percent of Americans hunted. Southerners in states along the eastern seaboard hunted at a rate slightly below the national average (5 percent), and although hunting was more common in other parts of the South (9 percent), these rates did not surpass those of the Plains states, where 12 percent hunted.

Despite these changes, hunting remained firmly associated with the display and development of masculinity. Few other areas of southern society remained as gender differentiated as the hunt. Although the overall number of women hunters had begun to increase slightly in the early 20th century, southern hunters remained overwhelmingly (99 percent) male. The absence of women from hunting may have contributed to the connection many hunters drew between themselves and hunters of the past. This, in itself, connected hunting to an earlier era, but hunters drew other connections as well. Hunting is about killing; hunting is in the woods; hunting helps boys learn what it is to be men. Despite the host of social, legal, and technological factors that altered hunting in the South over the centuries, these elements remained constant. Hunters in the modern South do not hunt to provide for their families or display their mastery; they hunt because it has become a southern tradition.

NICHOLAS PROCTOR
Simpson College

Kenneth S. Greenberg, *Honor and Slavery: Lies, Duels, Noses, Masks, Dressing as a Woman, Gifts, Strangers, Humanitarianism, Death, Slave Rebellions, the Pro-Slavery Argument, Baseball, Hunting, and Gambling in the Old South* (1996); Steven Hahn, *Radical History Review* (1982); Charles H. Hudson Jr., in *Indians, Animals, and the Fur Trade*, ed. Shephard Krech III (1981); Stuart A. Marks, *Southern Hunting in Black and White: Nature, History, and Ritual in a Carolina Community* (1991); Ted Ownby, *Subduing Satan: Religion, Recreation, and Manhood in the Rural South, 1865-1920* (1990); Wiley C. Prewitt, "The Best of All Breathing: Hunting and Environmental Change in Mississippi, 1900-1980" (M.A. thesis, University of Mississippi, 1991); Nicolas W. Proctor, *Bathed in Blood: Hunting and Mastery in the Old South* (2002); Jacob F. Rivers III, *Cultural Values in the Southern Sporting Narrative* (2002); Timothy Silver, *A New Face on the Countryside: Indians, Colonists, and Slaves in South Atlantic Forests, 1500-1800* (1990); Richard C. Stedman and Thomas A. Heberlein, *Rural Sociology* (December 2001); Nancy L. Struna, *People of Prowess: Sport, Leisure, and Labor in Early Anglo-America* (1996).

Independence, Manly

The concept of manly independence has been used by males in southern history to explain their rejection of activities that threaten to control them. Thinking broadly, the term means that men should work for themselves and take orders from no one. The topic has been especially important as a point of contrast—people who claim to have manly independence have seen themselves as essentially different from slaves or women or children or poor people or industrial workers.

The concept of independence resonated with many Americans in the Revolutionary War era, as supporters of the Revolution claimed that a republic was only possible in a society of independent farming men who would vote for individuals who would protect that independence. Revolutionary leaders condemned the tax policies of the British government and the credit policies of British lenders for, in their language, robbing them of their independence or making them more like slaves.

Manly independence became crucial as part of southern political language in the antebellum period. Antebellum men liked to contrast their positions to those of slaves and northern and European factory workers, whom some proslavery theorists consistently described as wage slaves. The manly part of manly independence concerned two things: the willingness to fight the forces that threatened to control them and the pride in and responsibility for controlling dependents. Politicians and ordinary men frequently used the language of sexual power—raped by their debts, stripped or unmanned by tax assessors— to describe how they hated threats to their independence. Running an independent household meant trying to stay largely free of market forces, relying instead on an agriculture based on corn and vegetables grown by women and children, hogs that ran free on the open range, and game men gathered through hunting and fishing.

Sectional divisions over slavery and its expansion often returned to the concept of manly independence. Southern political leaders claimed it was essential to have the freedom to take slavery west, not just because they supported the interests of planters but also because independent farmers would suffer if larger landowners, forced to restrict slavery to where it existed, started buying up all of the region's farmland. According to historian Stephanie McCurry, the language of independence and mastery helped unite small landowners, who usually described themselves as "self-working farmers" to wealthier planters.

The concept of manly independence is generally most meaningful when people use it in contrast to a position they fear or hate. For farmers, having large debts or paying taxes often forced people to have to work for cash for someone else. For Confederate soldiers, manly independence first meant opposing a distant government that wanted to keep them from preserving or securing their own independence through the opportunity to own slaves and take them west. As the Civil War continued, increasing numbers of men started to claim that it was the Confederate government itself, by instituting a draft and impressing the livestock and crops of ordinary farmers, that was actually working against their independence. During Reconstruction, manly independence meant standing against what many white southerners considered an oppressive government run through force and corruption.

African Americans faced the question of whether or not to adopt the language of manly independence in their search for land and economic control over their lives after emancipation. Many claimed that access to land would bolster their claims to be full citizens with the full political rights of free American males. But the notion of independence, which numerous white southerners either expected, assumed, or argued for as a natural right for males, tended to conflict so dramatically with the nature of African Americans' economic and political lives that, with many exceptions, discussions of manliness among African Americans have centered less around the question of landed independence and more around issues of respectability and self-defense.

For white southerners in the late 1800s and early 1900s, the factory stood as the clearest threat to manly independence. Industrial work was more common in the Northeast, it forced people to work indoors for bosses, and, especially in textile mills, it could blur distinctions between male and female work. In the postbellum South, some industrial leaders hoped the South could have industry without dependence, by hiring only young women while men retained their independence on the farms. The language of manly independence lived on when men who went to work in those factories expressed dissatisfaction with the experience of being controlled, and perhaps it lived on in a new way when some factory boosters claimed that the South was gaining independence from northern economic control by building industries separate from northern control.

The concept of manly independence has survived especially in aggressive forms of cultural expression. In 1930, Vanderbilt Agrarian Andrew Lytle, in an attempt to discourage farmers from getting involved in mechanized methods and from purchasing consumer goods, claimed that the best of the South, "the farming South, the yeoman South, that great body of free men, had hardly anything to do with the capitalists and their merchandise." Less certain of the virtues of independence but certainly envious of the experience, W. J. Cash wrote in 1941 that the southern environment and the institution of slavery made independence quite easy for the typical free man in the antebellum South. "In this world he was to have freedom from labor beyond the wildest dream of the European peasant and the New England farmer wrestling with a meager soil in a bitter, unfriendly climate." For Cash, leisure and independence produced a hedonism he partly despised but perhaps also admired. Country musicians have consistently looked to country life as the site of freedom from anyone's control, and in the 1970s, Charlie Daniels wrote a popular song demanding, "If you don't like the way I'm living / you just leave this long-haired country boy alone." Perhaps the clearest voices of manly independence today are in country music, where rowdy young men claim to be itchin' for a fight, or in extreme conservative political language, where no-tax and libertarian groups claim to uphold traditions of men who controlled their households through strong wills, the right to carry weapons, and opposition to most government programs.

TED OWNBY
University of Mississippi

W. J. Cash, *The Mind of the South* (1941); Lacy K. Ford, *Origins of Southern Radicalism: The South Carolina Upcountry, 1800–1860* (1988); Craig Thompson Friend and Lorri Glover, eds., *Southern Manhood: Perspectives on Masculinity in the Old South* (2004); Bill Malone, *Don't Get Above Your Raisin': Country Music and the Southern Working Class* (2002); Stephanie McCurry, *Masters of Small Worlds: Yeoman Households, Gender Relations, and the Political Culture of the Antebellum South Carolina Low Country* (1995); Grady McWhiney, *Cracker Culture: Celtic Ways in the Old South* (1988); Bertram Wyatt-Brown, *Southern Honor: Ethics and Behavior in the Old South* (1982).

Indian Men and Women

Prior to contact with Europeans, gender egalitarianism characterized relations between men and women throughout the Indian Southeast. Although it would be a mistake to idealize these cultures, it is fair to say that early non-Indian visitors, typically traders and missionaries, failed to find in the Indian South the male dominance that they were accustomed to in European societies. Instead, they encountered civilizations that gave priority to a balance among things that were seen as oppositional. Existence itself was contingent upon the maintenance of harmony, and reciprocal and nonconfrontational relations between genders was a priority. Therefore, in southeastern Indian societies, men and women filled distinct but interrelated roles, and survival depended upon each gender fulfilling its obligations to the other.

The cosmology of southeastern Indians demonstrated this concern with balance between men and women, and it provided models for them to follow. Most southeastern people subsisted on game, hunted by men, and corn, grown by women. The Cherokee explained the origin of this gendered subsistence cycle through the story of Kana'ti and Selu. Kana'ti, whose name means "lucky hunter," released game into the woods, and, for this reason, men left the village or town to hunt; and Selu, through her blood, provided corn, which women tended in fields near their homes. Like the first man and woman, both husband and wife, hunter and farmer, were essential to the subsistence of Indian families throughout the Southeast.

This balanced division of labor empowered each gender in its own sphere. Women worked collectively with their female relatives, and they controlled the fruits of their labor—corn, beans, squash, and other plants that they gathered. Probably providing the majority of food regularly consumed by their families, women presided over the internal affairs of their households, generally composed of a female elder, her husband, their adult daughters, and their spouses and children. Most southeastern Indian societies, in fact, were matrilocal, meaning that men moved into the households of their wives, but most men maintained close ties with their own families. Men were not totally peripheral to the daily activities of southeastern Indian domestic life, but their workplace was generally the forest and not the field. Notably, non-Indians tended to misinterpret this gendered division of labor. In particular, they considered women's agricultural labor to be a mark of native people's supposed savagery, and as a result, they assumed that Indian women had low status in their communities. On the contrary, Indian women's work accorded them power. It empowered them to claim rights to land when American leaders began pressuring for land sales. Likewise, because corn, their staple crop, was considered to be sacred, women's labor was celebrated no less than the hunt.

Further suggesting the importance of harmony, sophisticated matrilineal kinship systems ordered most southeastern Indian societies. Southern Indians identified with the clan of their mother, and this social identity gave them their place in the world. Although the number of clans varied widely from as few as four to as many as a hundred, these kin groups tended to serve particular functions. Within the household, clans set standards for behavior, dictated responsibilities, and protected the rights of their members. Beyond the household, they facilitated the redistribution of wealth, property, and marriage partners; provided political organization; and shaped ceremonial life. Notably, women, particularly elders, were the center of this system, which created distinct social groups tied to one another through reciprocal giving and intermarriage. The matrilineal clan system thus enabled gender egalitarianism.

Because this concern for harmony, particularly between genders, permeated southeastern society, contact with Europeans, whose worldview embraced hierarchy and male dominance, created distinct challenges for Indian men and women. This pressure intensified during the 18th century in response to the "civilization" program of the U.S. government and Christian missionaries. Across the South, tribal societies became divided, as some men and women embraced elements of Anglo-American culture while others steadfastly refused to assimilate. Some historians have demonstrated how the acceptance of non-Indian lifeways prompted a decrease in women's power. For example, as the Cherokees, Creeks, Choctaws, Chickasaws, and Seminoles, or the "Five Civilized Tribes" as they were commonly called by non-Indians, adopted plantation agriculture during the early Republic, the use of black slaves as agricultural laborers reduced the status of those who had always worked the fields—women. Economic pressures may have created profound tension and even violence between Indian men and women as they struggled to move from a subsistence economy to a market economy. Neither gender needed the other in the same way, and the balance between them proved precarious when the demand for trade goods and, eventually, cash undermined customary, reciprocal ties.

At the same time, gender egalitarianism permeated southeastern Indian society so deeply that old ways persisted. For example, in many southeastern Indian communities, women retained their customary right to divorce into modern times, when states guaranteed women's access to legal divorces. Furthermore, many Indians adapted to Anglo-American society without wholly adopting its patriarchal gender conventions. Southeastern Indians tended to embrace education, and from the earliest public school system, established by the Cherokees prior to the Civil War, to the oldest state-supported four-year college for Indians (what is now the University of North Carolina at Pembroke), founded by Lumbees in the 1880s, southeastern Indians adapted the Western educational system to their cultures by providing equal educational opportunities and, in some cases, coeducational schooling, to students of both genders. Women also tended to retain their ceremonial roles, particularly in communities that practiced traditional religions. Busk, or the Green Corn Ceremony, which some tribal communities continue to celebrate today, especially in northeastern Oklahoma, involves both men and women in the restoration of order and harmony.

Perhaps the prominent role of women in modern southeastern Indian societies most aptly demonstrates the persistence of gender egalitarianism. Throughout the 20th century, southeastern Indian women assumed leadership positions in tribal governments, including their highest offices, and this distinguished them from western tribal people, many of whom did not recognize women's formal political authority until relatively recently. Alice Brown Davis, a member of the Tiger clan of the Seminole Nation of Oklahoma, served as principal chief from 1922 to 1935. Although appointed by President Warren G. Harding, Davis gave high priority to strengthening relations with Florida Seminoles as well as to defending the integrity of the Seminole's resources and tribal institutions. In 1967, Florida Seminoles elected Betty Mae Jumper to their highest office, chair of the Tribal Council. Jumper was a strong defender of the rights of her people, and she drew national attention to the uniqueness of Seminole culture. The election of Wilma Mankiller to the office of principal chief of the Cherokee Nation in 1987 captured national attention. (Beginning in 1985, Mankiller had completed the term of the previous principal chief, Ross Swimmer.) An advocate of community revitalization in northeastern Oklahoma, Mankiller coauthored an autobiography (with Michael Wallis) that topped best-seller lists and explained Cherokee history and culture and demonstrated native resilience to readers the world over. In 1995 the Eastern Band of Cherokee Indians elected Joyce Dugan to be their chief. Dugan emphasized generating employment opportunities and increasing access to health care, but she also initiated the restructuring of the tribal government, essentially dispersing power among elected officials.

Recent scholarship on gender among southeastern Indians has emphasized the persistence of egalitarianism while not dismissing the negative impact of assimilation on women's customary power. It is notable, however, that many non-Indians now share the beliefs in women's rights that once were viewed in southeastern Indian societies as abnormal and inferior. In this way, aspects of traditional gender roles may have persisted long enough in the face of intense pressure to assimilate to ensure their future survival.

ROSE STREMLAU
University of North Carolina at Pembroke

Virginia Moore Carney, *Eastern Band Cherokee Women: Cultural Persistence in Their Letters and Speeches* (2005); James Taylor Carson, *Searching for the Bright Path: The Mississippi Choctaw from Prehistory to Removal* (1999); Carolyn Ross Johnston, *Cherokee Women in Crisis: Trail of Tears, Civil War, and Allotment, 1838-1907* (2003); Theda Perdue, *Cherokee Women: Gender and Culture Change, 1700-1835* (1998); Michelene E. Pesantubbee, *Choctaw Women in a Chaotic World: The Clash of Cultures in the Colonial Southeast* (2005); Claudio Saunt, *A New Order of Things: Prosperity, Power, and the Transformation of the Creek Indians, 1733-1816* (1999).

Industrial Work

From the colonial period to the 21st century the work performed by women in the American South has varied dramatically by race, class, and ethnicity.

Enslaved African American women worked for many generations as agricultural laborers and became the South's first industrial workers in the antebellum period. White women also worked on farms throughout the region, and after the Civil War they were the first members of their families to enter the weave rooms in New South factories. The patterns of women's work in the South changed as northern factories moved south in search of cheap, nonunion labor, southern agriculture declined, and urbanization increased. Southern women have a long history of working to support themselves and their families, and during the 1920s and 1930s many looked to trade unions as a way to gain fundamental rights in the workplace. The civil rights movement of the 1950s and 1960s brought substantial, albeit slow changes to the South in terms of women's work. Black women gained access to factory work for the first time since before the Civil War. Clerical work expanded dramatically for white women and gradually opened to black women. In the 1970s increasing numbers of southern women entered the paid workforce. During the following decade, they actively resisted occupational segregation and worked to obtain equal pay for equal work. By the 1990s, however, southern manufacturers began to move their operations out of the region in a search for fresh sources of cheap, nonunion labor, and immigrant women, particularly from Mexico, formed the newest and most rapidly growing sector of working women in the South.

In the 17th and 18th centuries, work throughout the southern colonies was performed by Indian women, enslaved Africans and their descendants, indentured servants, and free white women. The vast majority of women's work, like that done by men, was home-based and geared toward life in an economy dependent on agricultural production. In the early 17th century, most southern domestic workers were female white indentured servants. Later in the century, these workers were replaced by black slave women, who performed a myriad of skilled and unskilled jobs in antebellum southern society. Slave women worked as children's nurses, cooks, seamstresses, housekeepers, midwives, dairy maids, and agricultural laborers. Forced to spend most of their time working for others, slave women were only occasionally allowed to garden and raise poultry for consumption by their own families or for sale. During the period between 1775 and 1820, slave women were trained as skilled spinners and weavers, and their labor changed the South from a region that imported all manufactured goods to one in which home manufacturing was widespread.

By the early 19th century, the majority of enslaved black women spent their lives from dawn to dusk producing annual crops of rice, indigo, and cotton. Black, Indian, and white women performed agricultural work and also gave birth to and raised children, spun thread, wove cloth, prepared food, and sewed and laundered clothes and linens. Repetitive, labor-intensive, household labor, together with high rates of childbirth, defined the parameters of most southern women's lives. That said, the work performed by women in the southern colonies varied widely according to terms of condition of servitude, class, race, and place. In Virginia, for example, Indian women built houses, farmed, and provided the principal means of production. As white women came into the colonies in greater numbers, they managed households on plantations or smaller farms. White southern women with limited education and training worked as retail dealers, monopolized the millinery and dressmaking trades, and sold foodstuffs and liquor. Southern farms and plantations, as well as households and businesses in urban areas like New Orleans, Mobile, Savannah, and Charleston, were dependent on essential female labor, much of which remained slave-based and largely invisible. The labor of enslaved women, in particular, was not only economically essential when it came to agricultural and home production, but absolutely crucial in terms of child-bearing, or slave procreation, which after the close of the slave trade in 1807 became the region's sole source of new enslaved workers. The urban South supported the development of wealthy elites, a regional supraclass within which white and some mixed-race women performed distinctive cultural roles as household and/or farm managers who supervised enslaved workers or servants, educated and trained children, and entertained guests, including family political and financial contacts. Middle-class urban women, particularly widows, during the 19th century increasingly became small business owners, opened schools, and in rare cases supported themselves as writers or playwrights.

Work for women in the early 19th-century South continued to be defined by an agricultural, slave-based economy. Slave women worked in agriculture and domestic service. Wealthy white women, dependent on slave labor, administered large plantations or ran large homes in southern cities. Wives of yeoman farmers managed much smaller farms with the help of their children. The dominance of staple-crop agricultural production affected the lives of southern women, regardless of their social or economic status. But the Civil War changed the work lives of all southerners. Enslaved women gained their freedom and in the postwar period whenever possible chose to marry, raise a family, and work within their own homes, consciously refusing to work for white families. This domestic strategy was met with fierce resistance on the part of southern whites dependent on the domestic and agricultural labor of black women. Between 1865 and World War I, an increasing number of communities throughout the South adopted vagrancy laws and work requirements that put pressure on black women to leave their homes for paid labor as domestics or field hands. Racialized public policies, combined with the meager wages paid to black men, compelled large numbers of black women to return to domestic work in white homes, although they insisted that day work replace the live-in arrangement so reminiscent of slavery.

In the decades after the Civil War, increasing numbers of black and white southern farm families lost their land, mortgaged future cotton or tobacco crops to obtain money for supplies, and struggled for survival in a cashless, debt-dominated economy. By the end of Reconstruction, a new system of sharecropping and tenant farming kept former slaves and many poor white families in an entrenched cycle of debt and rural peonage that remained largely intact until the 1960s. The post–Civil War years did open some new opportunities for a slowly expanding white middle and working class in industrial and urban areas. As in New England a century earlier, white women from impoverished farms across the South, those who could most easily be spared from agricultural labor, migrated to newly built cotton and hosiery mills across the region, where they began to work as spinners and weavers. Enslaved black women had been the South's first textile workers in the few antebellum mills scattered across the Carolinas and Georgia, but manufacturers eager to create an industrialized workforce offered coveted positions in New South mills to white workers and their daughters, southerners who could no longer make a living in agriculture or hold onto their farms. Over the decades following Reconstruction, in New South mills and factories, female mill workers and their children and grandchildren became the region's first industrial workers and provided farm families with cash wages, which were increasingly necessary for survival. Urban and commercial development was slow in the South in the late 19th century, and only a few women from southern middle-class families had the opportunities to work in urban areas as teachers and clerical workers.

In the 20th century, the occupational distribution of women workers varied dramatically between the North and the South. In 1910, 83 percent of the southern female workforce was in agriculture and domestic service, compared to 33 percent in the North. As late as 1950, manufacturing employed fewer than 18 percent of the region's women workers, compared to 34 percent of those in the North. In the 1920s, with the onset of agricultural depression in the region, farm tenancy increased for both white and black women. White women had the option of industrial work more frequently than black women, who were usually denied manufacturing jobs, except for seasonal handwork in the tobacco industry. The large number of southern women in agriculture and domestic service constituted a reserve pool of workers waiting to "move up" to manufacturing work. This labor surplus reduced the job security of female industrial workers and increased the leverage manufacturers had over them.

The margin of survival for southern women workers was always much thinner than for their northern sisters. Before 1940 southern wages were substantially lower than the national average, although the cost of living in the South was only 5 percent lower than in other regions. In 1946 southerners made up 25 percent of the nation's population but had only 8 percent of the national income. Because wage rates were low for all workers, southern families often depended on the wages of two or more family members, and thus women's wages were more critical to the family economy than in the North. Southern women working in cotton textiles, for example, typically provided 30 to 40 percent of the family income.

The biracial composition of the female workforce in the South and rigid occupational segregation by race affected both black and white women workers. In 1910, 60 percent of the southern female workforce was black, and the figure was 40 percent as late as 1940. White women workers feared being replaced by black workers as managers repeatedly threatened to hire black workers in the place of white employees. Black women migrated north and west to obtain the industrial work denied them within the region or moved into urban areas within the South to toil as domestic workers for an increasingly prosperous white middle class. Only with the civil rights movement of the 1960s did black southern women gain access to work in the textile industry, the South's largest employer, and to clerical positions. This racial shift within southern industry was also important because of its impact on unions. Black women, many of whom had gained organizing experience in the civil rights movement, often proved to be more willing supporters of unions and more active union members than their white counterparts.

Black domestic workers were among the first southern women to participate in organized resistance to existing working conditions. Their locally organized and self-financed efforts were modest in scale, rarely involving an entire community or municipal area. In 1880, for example, black washerwomen in Atlanta organized an association in a black church, and a year later 3,000 washerwomen, cooks, servants, and child nurses struck for higher wages. For each publicized protest of this type there were no doubt hundreds of similar, even smaller efforts of which no record has survived. The history of southern women forming unions began with the response of black and white women workers, including homemakers and farmers' wives, to the Knights of Labor. Women who had been active in the Grange and Populist movements responded to the Knights and joined locals in communities across the South. In 1889 over

Student training in mechanics at Bethune-Cook College, Daytona Beach, Fla., 1940s
(Gordon Parks, photographer, Library of Congress [LC-USW-3-14883C], Washington, D.C.)

50 women's local assemblies were already in the region—10 of which had been organized by black women—and southern women's locals made up 30 percent of the Knights' women's assemblies in the United States. After the demise of the Knights in 1890, American Federation of Labor (AFL) craft unions concentrated on organizing male workers and ignored the needs and concerns of female workers, who turned to middle-class reform groups for support.

Throughout the 1920s the conditions faced by women workers in the South drew the attention of the YWCA, the National Women's Trade Union League, and the Southern Summer School. These groups emphasized the importance of organizing all the workers within a given industry, focused on the needs of the thousands of southern female workers, and offered direct assistance to striking southern workers. These efforts provided a crucial transitional form of organizing, which transcended the limited goals of the AFL and later encouraged the emergence of the Congress of Industrial Organizations (CIO) in the South. In 1937 the clothing unions joined with the Textile Workers' Organizing Committee to launch the CIO's first major campaign in the South. Female organizers, especially native southerners, were now hired to work throughout the region. After World War II the CIO launched "Operation Dixie," a far more intensive effort to organize southern workers than the union drives of the 1930s. Since the CIO focused on the textile industry, in which women made up over 50 percent of the workforce, organizers emphasized union benefits for women workers. The drive brought 400,000 new members into southern locals, over half of them women.

Southern women workers faced strike defeats and declining union membership during the 1950s and 1960s, followed by a resurgence of collective organization in the 1970s and 1980s. After the civil rights movement and the opening of industrial jobs to black southerners, new efforts in southern union-organizing drives came increasingly from black women. Long denied access to jobs in the industrial sector, black women held over 50 percent of the operative positions in many southern plants in the 1980s. By the mid-1980s the southern female workforce reflected national trends more than regional differences, with 48 percent of all southern women working outside the home, compared to 50 percent nationally. Among black women, 52 percent held paid jobs. The gains made in the 1980s began to erode in the following decade as southern working women faced the consequences of deep recessions in the region's basic industries — textiles, tobacco, furniture, and steel. At the beginning of the 21st century, southern women are still among the lowest paid workers in the United States, earning 89 percent of the average wage for women nationally. Racial and ethnic differentials continue to persist. For example, in the state of Louisiana in 2000, white women's average earnings ($24,377) were 37 percent higher than African American women's earnings ($17,779) and approximately 13 percent higher than Asian and Hispanic women's earnings.

By the 1990s southern manufacturers began to leave the region to establish new factories, or "maquiladores," across the southern U.S. border in Mexico and Central America. Between 2001 and 2005, the U.S. textile and apparel sector lost 375,000 jobs, the vast majority of which were in the South. As the industrial base of the southern region continued to erode, the jobs held by women manufacturing workers in the region moved to the "Global South," where new groups of women workers provide cheap, nonunion labor. Like southern women in the early years of the 20th century, however, women workers in this newest "South" are organizing to protect their workplace rights and fight for economic justice, working through independent organizations or in trade union federations, such as the Frente Auténtico del Trabajo. Between 1990 and 2005, immigrant women, particularly from Mexico, formed the most rapidly growing group of working women in the South. The regional economic importance of immigrant workers from Mexico and Central and South America continues to increase, particularly in low-paid jobs in the manufacturing, agricultural, and service industries.

MARY E. FREDERICKSON
Miami University of Ohio

Victoria Byerly, *Hard Times Cotton Mill Girls: Personal Histories of Womanhood and Poverty in the South* (1986); Laura Edwards, *Scarlett Doesn't Live Here Anymore* (2000); Leon Fink, *The Maya of Morgantown: Work and Community in the Nuevo New South* (2003); Mary E. Frederickson, *Journal of Developing Societies* (June 2007), in *Taking Off the White Gloves: Southern Women and Women Historians*, ed. Michelle Gillespie and Catherine Clinton (1998), in *Women, Work, and Protest: A Century of U.S. Women's Labor History*, ed. Ruth Milkman (1985); Margaret J. Hagood, *Mothers of the South: Portraiture of the White Tenant Farm Woman* (1939, reprint 1977); Jacquelyn Dowd Hall et al., *Like a Family: The Making of a Southern Cotton Mill World* (1987); Dale Hathaway, *Allies across the Border: Mexico's "Authentic Labor Front" and Global Solidarity* (2000); Tera Hunter, *To 'Joy My Freedom: Southern Black Women's Lives and Labors after the Civil War* (1998); Janet Irons, *Testing the New Deal: The General Textile Strike of 1934 in the American South* (2000); Dolores E. Janiewski, *Sisterhood Denied: Race, Gender, and Class in a New South Community* (1985); Jacqueline Jones, *Labor of Love, Labor of Sorrow: Black Women, Work, and the Family from Slavery to the Present* (1985); Lu Ann Jones, *Mama Learned Us to Work: Farm Women in the New South* (2002); Alice Kessler-Harris, *Out to Work: A History of Wage-Earning Women in the United States* (1982); Sally G. McMillen, *Southern Women: Black and White in the Old South* (2002); Julia Cherry Spruill, *Women's Life and Work in the Southern Colonies* (1972).

Ladies and Gentlemen

Anyone with exposure to American popular culture has a firm, though probably paradoxical, image of the southern lady and the southern gentleman, both in real life and in fiction. Dinner party arguments—or barroom fights—can ignite from deciding who qualifies and who does not. Melanie Hamilton, Coretta Scott King, and Rosalynn Carter easily make the ladyhood list, but does Dolly Parton? Robert E. Lee, Arthur Ashe, and Coach Bobby Bowden are surely southern gents, but is Lyndon Johnson?

Whether ladies and gentlemen are born or made is a quintessential southern philosophical debate. Scarlett O'Hara opines that you can't be a lady without money. For Caroline Compson, in Faulkner's *The Sound and the Fury*, ladyhood is an absolute: "I was taught that there is no halfway ground, that a woman is either a lady or not." As for the southern gentleman, he tends to come in two flavors, contemplative or active, Hamlet or Hotspur, or, to put it in regional terms, Quentin Compson or J. E. B. Stuart. His position is just as vexed as the southern lady's. Members of the Kappa Alpha Order, a fraternity founded in 1865 to (among other things) venerate the "parfit gentil knight" Robert E. Lee, call themselves "the last southern gentlemen." They wear Confederate uniforms and hold an annual party, Old South, to which they invite young women in hoopskirts, the tribal costume of the southern lady. Much alcohol is consumed, and, not infrequently, the ideal of the "chivalrous warrior of Christ" and the "purity of southern womanhood" comes under some strain.

Sex and violence are key elements in the making of the lady and gentleman. Southern ladies are supposed to be miraculously immune to desire, and southern gentlemen are to retain the potential for violence in the name of honor. These class-based behavioral roles descend from British and European models of the 18th century. Antebellum white women could be born ladies or have ladyhood thrust upon them through marriage or education. But if a woman transgressed sexually, she became, as Mary Chesnut says in her diary, "a thing we cannot name." Chastity for middle-class women was essential to property inheritance, but it became celebrated as a moral imperative, a mark of women's spiritual elevation.

Men were free to be as unchaste as they liked, even with (in some cases especially with) female slaves, though they were never to discuss their behavior in mixed company. There was a famous toast, reported in the 1930s by Carl Carmer in *Stars Fell on Alabama*: "To Woman . . . as pure and chaste as this sparkling water, as cold as this gleaming ice." In *Southern Ladies and Gentlemen* (1975), Florence King translates this as "To Woman, without whose purity and chastity we could never have justified slavery and segregation, without whose coldness we wouldn't have had the excuse we needed for messing around down in the slave cabins. . . . We pledge our hearts and our lives to the protection of her virtue and chastity because they are the best political leverage we ever did see."

Being a gentleman implied a certain amount of wealth (either in the present or in the past), behavior according to a complex code that included generosity, ferocious protection of his and his family's good name, and a measure of (apparent) Victorian respectability. Birth into a prominent family accorded an automatic assumption of gentlemanliness, but the antebellum South's class system was fluid, allowing a working-class white man to rise through ownership of land and slaves. In *The Mind of the South* (1941), Cash describes an Irish immigrant who starts off a small farmer with a log cabin and ends up a Carolina planter universally described at his death as "a gentleman of the old school." In Faulkner's *Absalom, Absalom!* (1936), however, Thomas Sutpen comes up from Appalachian poverty to found (or "tear violently," according to Miss Rosa Coldfield, the novel's arbiter of gentlefolks' ways) the greatest estate in Yoknapatawpha County, but he is never accepted as a gentleman of any school, old or new.

Black men and women have only recently gained access to the status of lady or gentleman. Under slavery, black men could not be self-determining and black women could not assume that white men would respect the integrity of their bodies. In *Incidents in the Life of a Slave Girl* (1861), Harriet Jacobs argues for a redefinition of ladyhood, taking into account the fact that black women did not always have the luxury of chastity. She exhorts white women, "whose purity has been sheltered from childhood, who have been free to choose the objects of your affection, whose homes are protected by law, do not judge the poor desolate slave girl too severely!" Until the 1970s, blacks were rarely accorded courtesy titles or called "sir" or "ma'am." Today, however, a rising southern black bourgeoisie has created its own ceremonies and trappings of ladyhood and gentlemanhood: sororities and fraternities, Jack and Jill debutante balls, golf and tennis clubs, and charity work.

Literature by white southerners did much to codify the iconic figures of the lady and the gentleman. Plantation novels such as John Pendleton Kennedy's *Swallow Barn* (1832), William Gilmore Simms's *Guy Rivers* (1834), and Mary H. Eastman's *Aunt Phillis's Cabin* (1852), to name but a few, reiterate the "natural superiority" of the lord and lady of the Big House as a justification for slavery. Lost Cause writing represented the lady especially (the gentlemen had often died at Manassas or Gettysburg) in quasi-religious terms. In "Social Life in Old Virginia before the War," Thomas Nelson Page says breathlessly of the plantation mistress, "What she really was was known only to God." In her 1904 memoirs, Virginia Clay likens the "brutalization" of upper-class white women during the Civil War to the trials of French aristocrats during the Reign of Terror. Still, she suffers with grace: "Take these flowers over to Dr. French and say Mrs. Clay sends them with her compliments." Clay says to tell him that blossoms "are like Southern ladies—the more they are bruised and oppressed the sweeter and stronger they grow!"

Even William Faulkner, who pitilessly deconstructs the moonlight and magnolias of plantation fiction, is susceptible to this white aristocratic myth. Col. John Sartoris, both Bayards, and Gavin Stevens are recognizable from literary antecedents of a century before, while Isaac McCaslin and Quentin Compson struggle to redefine what being a gentleman in the postslavery South might mean. Miss Jenny DuPre and Miss Habersham perfectly fulfill the role of Confederate lady as she was defined by the Lost Cause, and Faulkner's younger upper-class women—Temple Drake and Caddy Compson most notably—jump down from their pedestals straight into sex and "depravity," shattering the lady's statuelike perfection.

The lady and the gentleman have been under siege ever since the cocktail-drinking, bobbed-hair Zelda Sayre Fitzgerald (a Montgomery ex-debutante) became a more important role model than the doe-eyed Bride of the Confederacy, Varina Davis. Margaret Mitchell's *Gone with the Wind* (1936) is rightly castigated for its reactionary racial politics. But the novel is also a debate on the viability of traditional gender and class roles in the New South. Ashley Wilkes exemplifies the chivalrous southern gentleman, utterly unlike the cad of a blockade runner Rhett Butler, of whom one society maven says, "He is not *received*." The self-sacrificing, forgiving Melanie Hamilton is contrasted with the grasping, greedy Scarlett O'Hara, who knows—because her mother and her mammy told her—how to be a lady, but just can't help herself. Mitchell makes it clear that Ashley and Melanie belong to the ruined, outmoded Old South, while Rhett and Scarlett personify the future.

The lady and the gentleman still wield cultural power in the South, where gender roles have been slower to change than in the rest of the country. Etiquette classes, cotillions, and an obsession with manners still define the middle-class South. But the old ways are under siege. Instead of suffering in saintly silence, Maybelle, who still goes to the Junior League when she can fit it in around her interior design business, is demanding a divorce from Beauregard plus half the assets and the bass boat, too. Beauregard, raised, as Quentin Compson says, never to disappoint a lady, is in therapy trying to confront his feelings about his mother and the failure of his marriage to Maybelle. The rules are different. The gentleman still believes in chivalry—even if he's on Prozac. The lady still believes in the purity of southern womanhood—or at least its appearance. As always in the South, the negotiation between the ideal and the real continues.

DIANE ROBERTS
Florida State University

Virginia Foster Durr, *Outside the Magic Circle* (1987); Richard Dyer, *White* (1992); Jacquelyn Dowd Hall, *Revolt against Chivalry: Jessie Daniel Ames and the Women's*

Campaign against Lynching (1979); bell hooks, *Ain't I a Woman? Black Women and Feminism* (1981); Tara McPherson, *Reconstructing Dixie: Race, Gender, and Nostalgia in the Imagined South* (2003); Marlyn Schwarz, *The Southern Belle Primer* (1986); Bertram Wyatt-Brown, *Southern Honor: Ethics and Behavior in the Old South* (1982).

Latino Men and Women

How does gender impact Latino, or Hispanic, men and women in the South? How does it affect where Latino immigrants work, where they live, and how they understand their "place" in southern communities? How does gender influence the ways that long-term southern residents perceive their new Latino neighbors? How does gender shape workplace interactions among Hispanic, white, and African American workers and supervisors in the South? How does it impact Latino settlement patterns and local reactions to immigrant neighborhoods, and are these reactions the same in rural and urban locales? How does gender influence the South's changing racial and ethnic relations, categories, and politics? In brief, what difference does gender make in the emerging saga of Latino immigration to the increasingly diverse South?

The simple answer to these questions is that gender matters a great deal in how Hispanic men and women, as well as long-term residents, experience rapidly changing southern communities, large and small. On a basic level, gender affects Latino immigration patterns, particularly around the question of who migrates to southern communities first. Although Hispanic men and women have been in parts of the South for multiple generations, most southern states first experienced Latino immigration in the late 1980s and early 1990s, when young Mexican men arrived in search of higher wages, lower living expenses, and better social climates than were available in the southwestern United States at the time. Responding to triggers, including large-scale amnesty in immigration legislation in the late 1980s and the new geography of Sunbelt economic and population growth in the 1990s, Hispanic men headed to both rural and urban southern communities and, in the process, transformed immigration patterns traditionally centered on larger cities like Los Angeles and Chicago.

Although job availability and lower living costs made southern communities particularly attractive for many Hispanic migrants, Latino immigration to the South has not been a solely economic phenomenon. Other factors, ranging from political unrest in parts of Latin America to anti-immigrant sentiment in parts of the southwestern United States, also influenced this immigration. Some Hispanic migrants, for example, have framed their move to southern communities as a desire to start life anew, away from the urban frenzy of Los Angeles or the constricting ties of family and marriage in home countries. These factors have been particularly influential for some Latina women. Although few Hispanic women, or men, come to southern communities with no acquaintances, a surprising number of young Latina women have come alone, either to extricate themselves from uncomfortable home and family situations or to redirect a life that has not gone as they had hoped.

This last point highlights the difference that gender makes in the ways that Latino residents come to southern communities and subsequently experience life in them. In crucial ways, the gender composition of initial Hispanic immigration to southern communities, for example, affected where Latino men settled, what kinds of work they performed, and how long-term residents reacted to these new arrivals. In many southern locales, initial reactions to a growing Hispanic presence rested on the assumption that Latino residents were all male, single, Mexican, and likely undocumented. The visibility of young *mexicanos* who gathered after work in southern communities' public spaces amplified the sense among some local residents of an overwhelming Latino population whose racial, ethnic, linguistic, and cultural differences were perceived as threatening. The sense of exclusion that many Latinos initially felt from long-term residents, however, was at least somewhat deflected by the belief for many immigrants that their presence in southern locales was not permanent. In a desire to maximize savings and reduce their own household labor, many Latino men who first arrived in southern communities lived together in collective households whose cramped spaces and shared housework seemed bearable only because this arrangement was understood to be temporary.

When Latina women joined husbands, brothers, and other family members a few years into this immigration, local understandings of the permanence of Latino settlement in southern communities changed, as did the expectations for Latino migrants themselves. For many Latino men, the first step toward establishing a more permanent presence in southern locales was the arrival of Hispanic women and, later, children. Frequently coming directly from Latin America, Latina women changed the gender composition of the South's Hispanic communities, as well as the living arrangements for, and divisions of labor within, Hispanic households. In many cases, reunited Latino families began to seek single-family housing and home ownership in southern locales, often outside established Hispanic neighborhoods. Through these factors, as well as others, like the growing presence of U.S.-born Latino children, southern communities began to realize that Latino men and women had become permanent local residents and that the South neither looked nor sounded as it once did.

This realization has generated a variety of responses across southern communities. As the gender composition of the region's Latino population changes and more Latino families settle, the visibility of Hispanic women and children in health-care facilities, public schools, and elsewhere in southern communities has changed local reactions to new immigrants. Just as the visibility of young Hispanic men in southern communities' public spaces influenced local reactions to this growing population, the presence of Latino families within key community institutions has generated both new efforts to reach out to the South's newest arrivals and new initiatives to exclude immigrants from local communities altogether.

The arrival of Hispanic women, however, has changed more than just local reactions to a growing immigrant presence. Because many Hispanic women joined the formal workforce for the first time when they moved to the South, Latino households themselves have frequently experienced clashing expectations about family responsibilities and gender roles. Needing dual incomes to make ends meet in the low-wage labor market within which many Latino workers find employment, Hispanic households face the challenge of sorting out both new gender relations within the family and new gendered divisions of labor within households that now include at least two breadwinners.

A gendered division of labor may also be emerging for Hispanic men and women in the broader labor market. Whereas many Latino men work in construction, agriculture, and landscaping in southern locales, Hispanic women often work in the region's service economy and in light manufacturing. Although the public image of Hispanics in the South links "Latino" and low-wage labor, Hispanic men and women are also part of the region's professional workforce. The daily experiences of Latino professionals, many of whom are involved in providing services to Latino populations in their communities, are often quite different from those of Hispanics employed in lower-wage jobs. These differences highlight the need to examine class, as well as national, distinctions among the South's Hispanic population, which includes not only low-wage workers from rural Mexico, Guatemala, and elsewhere but also highly trained professionals from across Latin America.

Throughout the South, the arrival of Hispanic men and women is transforming local workplaces and work relations, creating new interactions, coalitions, and conflicts among workers and supervisors. Gender does matter in these changing relations, whether in the polite silence between white and Mexican women working in east Carolina's crab industry or in new possibilities of cross-cultural "border crossings" among white, black, and Mexican working-class women in rural Tennessee. Moreover, for Hispanic men and women, work itself is gendered. Latina women are typically responsible for most of the household labor, child care, and other aspects of social reproduction; and this double workday changes their experience of southern communities. With more household responsibilities, Hispanic women often have less leisure time and a constricted daily geography across southern locales, even as they experience more economic mobility through formal waged labor. Conversely, many Latino men are forced to stretch their labor geographies across the region, as they seek temporary work that takes them from state to state in serial employment.

The gendered effects of Latino immigration to southern communities are also felt beyond the South itself. Because many Hispanic migrants to southern locales maintain social, economic, political, and cultural connections across international borders, the gender-specific nature of early Latino immigration to the South affected households in Latin America as well. In both new destinations like Nashville, Tenn., and communities of origin across Latin America, household structures and economies, child-rearing practices and family dynamics, and other facets of immigrant lives have changed through Latino immigration to the South. In this way, throughout the *nuevo* New South and the Latin American communities to which it is increasingly linked, gender affects how Latino immigration has proceeded, how it has been understood by long-term residents, and what issues it has raised for local communities.

In many ways, gender is central to understanding how Hispanic men and women have come to, and made a place in, southern communities. Despite gender's saliency to the demographic, cultural, economic, and social transitions observable across southern communities, few studies have paid attention to its role in Latino immigration to the South. As Hispanic communities continue to grow in the South, scholars, advocates, and policymakers would do well to reflect on the differences that gender makes in the lives of Hispanic men and women in southern communities and the long-term community residents with whom they live. Until studies address this issue, understandings of Latino immigration to the South will remain limited, and the assumptions that Latino men and women are not only all the same, despite class and national distinctions, but that they experience immigration in the same way, despite key gender differences, will go unchallenged.

JAMIE WINDERS
Syracuse University

Fran Ansley and Susan Williams, in *Neither Separate nor Equal: Women, Race, and Class in the South*, ed. Barbara Ellen Smith (1999); Altha J. Cravey, *Antipode* (2003); Leon Fink, *The Maya of Morganton: Work and Community in the Nuevo New South* (2003); Martha W. Rees, in *Latino Workers in the Contemporary South*, ed. Arthur D.

Murphy, Colleen Blanchard, and Jennifer A. Hill (2001); Emily F. Selby, Deborah P. Dixon, and Holly M. Hapke, *Gender, Place, and Culture* (2001); Loida C. Velazquez, in *Neither Separate nor Equal: Women, Race, and Class in the South*, ed. Barbara Ellen Smith (1999); Jamie Winders, in *Progress in Human Geography* (2005).

Lynching

Lynching is part of the American, especially southern, tradition of vigilante terrorism. Vigilantism has taken several forms, depending on purpose: so-called whitecappers usually flogged, or made threatening night visits, to "regu-late" or intimidate their enemies; the charivari was usually a semifestive ritual (such as tar and feathering or merely serenading with "rough music") meant to humiliate transgressors of community standards; lynch mobs killed their victims. Thus lynching is the deadliest form of vigilantism.

Col. Charles Lynch of Virginia, whose extralegal "court" sentenced Tories to floggings during the American Revolution, apparently provided the origin of the term "lynch law." Until the 1850s, lynch law (lynching) was commonly as-sociated with corporal and extralegal punishment but not killing. Then, during the last decade before the Civil War, southern vigilantes, particularly in Louisi-ana and Texas, routinely inflicted death upon outlaws and on individuals sus-pected of plotting slave insurrections. That is when lynching took on its lethal connotation.

The Civil War and Reconstruction intensified southern lynching activity. Vigilantism in Texas alone during the war probably accounted for over 150 deaths. Lynching became more widespread in the Reconstruction years and was directed mostly at ex-slaves, because the free blacks, no longer valued as property, were often viewed as threatening the existence of white civilization. The example of Haiti and its bloody slave rebellion of the 1790s, white fear, and predictions of race war helped multiply acts of terrorism.

Not until 1882 were efforts made to gather data on lynching across the United States. During the 70 years from 1882 to the early 1950s, by which time lynch-ing had virtually ended, a total of 4,739 persons reportedly died at the hands of lynch mobs in the United States. (Since these figures were compiled solely from lynching stories printed in leading urban newspapers of each state, it is likely the actual total was higher, perhaps near 6,000.) Lynching statistics do not, of course, include those blacks or whites who died in race riots; nor would ordinary interracial homicides, where a person of one race killed someone of another race, be listed.

Reported lynchings for the entire United States averaged 150.4 per year dur-ing the last 19 years of the 19th century (1882 through 1900). The all-time peak lynch-law year was 1892, with 230. During the first decade of the 20th century (1901–10), lynchings nationally averaged 84.6 per year and dropped further for 1911–20 (to an average of 60.6 annually for the decade). After 1920 reported lynchings continued to decline, with the decade of 1921–30 averaging 27.5 per year. For 1931–40 there were 114 total lynchings (11.4 annual average). The decade of 1941–50 averaged 3 per year. Then lynching virtually ceased. From 1951 to 1985 only 10 lynching deaths were reported in the United States. Approximately 82 percent of all lynchings listed since 1882 took place in the South ("the South" defined here as being the 15 slave states of 1860). Western and midwestern states account for nearly all the remainder. Nationally, 72 percent of all lynch mob victims have been black; in the South, 84 percent were black. Over 95 percent of the victims, both nationally and regionally, were males. Among the states, Mississippi ranks first in lynching from 1882 to the present, with 581 deaths (539 of them black); Georgia is second with 530 (491 of them black); Texas is third with 493 (352 of them black); and Louisiana is fourth with 391 (335 of them black). Very few participants in lynch mobs were prosecuted in any state, and prior to World War II almost none ever served time in prison.

Lynch law was supposed to be, in the blunt words of one advocate of the practice, "the white woman's guarantee against rape by niggers." Ridding society of "black brutes" who violated Caucasian females was indeed the most often mentioned justification for lynching. "Whenever the Constitution comes between me and the virtue of the white women of South Carolina," exclaimed Gov. Cole Blease, "then I say 'to hell with the Constitution.'" Since an accused black rapist of Blease's time and place would almost certainly have faced quick legal execution, why was mob action deemed necessary? Because, according to the rationale of lynching, a ravished white woman must be spared the agony of testifying in court, and the accused presumably would enjoy and be flattered by "the pomp and ceremony of formal justice."

In fact only about one-third of all lynching victims were suspected of rape or attempted rape. Murder or attempted murder was more often the alleged crime. Others who died at the hands of lynch mobs were accused of transgressions such as arson, burglary, slapping a white person, stealing chickens, chronic impudence, or simply being "vagrant and lewd." Whatever the supposed crime, lynching was widely assumed by whites to be a significant deterrent to black criminality. Black males were thought to be more afraid of lynch mobs than anything else. And rape, despite its secondary place in lynch law statistics, was of prime importance in justifying the concept of vigilante action. Whenever lynching was discussed, rape became the central theme. Whites who objected to lynching ran the risk of being accused of sympathy for black rapists.

Most lynch mobs killed swiftly. The typical victim, after being hoisted with a rope tossed over a tree limb, trestle, or utility pole, would have his death throes ended by a fusillade of bullets. But some lynchings involved prolonged torture and fire. Mississippi, Georgia, and Texas were most likely to witness scenes of medieval horror during the 1890–1920 years. Nearly all torture-lynching victims were blacks accused of both raping and murdering whites. Most were burned at the stake, after preliminary tortures. One accused murderer in Louisiana, a white man, was slowly skinned alive.

Lynch mobs are not easily categorized. The larger throngs were probably made up of people who thought of themselves more as observers than as participants, such as the "hundreds of the best men in Atlanta" who, in 1899, boarded "excursion trains" bound for Newnan, Ga., to see accused rapist-murderer Sam Hose burn at the stake. Sometimes lynch mobs were racially integrated, as were most of the crowds who watched legal executions. Occasionally, black mobs lynched blacks accused of crimes against members of their race. There is one reported case of a white South Carolinian, in jail for molesting and murdering a black child, being handed over to an enraged black mob.

The stereotyped image of poor "redneck" whites making up the mobs who lynched blacks is only partially true. White vigilantes came from all strata of society. Middle- and upper-class participation in lynch mobs was especially common in Louisiana. True, most of the vocal opposition to lynchings came from prominent whites, notably religious leaders, lawyers, and judges. But without the tacit approval of most of the dominant elements in the white community, lynching could not have been so frequent. The South, after all, was essentially a hierarchical society.

Southern newspapers prior to 1920 usually hedged on the question of lynching and seldom condemned it if the mob victim was a black male accused of raping a white female. An outspoken defender of vigilante murder was Henry J. Hearsey (1840–1900), editor-publisher of the *New Orleans Daily States*, the official journal of that city's government. The question of actual guilt, Hearsey admitted, did not really concern him; he was sure that lynching deterred black crime, and that was the important thing. Other journalists, not as bloodthirsty, sometimes became so desensitized to lynching that they reported such events with sly humor. As one example, the Port Gibson (Miss.) *Reveille* in 1892 thus described the death of John Robinson, black, who had robbed and killed a white man: "He offered to lead the mob to a railroad trestle under which the money lay buried. John and the money have now exchanged locations."

Antilynching crusaders, both nationally and within the South, began to see public opinion drift in their favor after 1920. Women such as Jessie Daniel Ames and Ida Wells-Barnett and groups such as the Association of Southern Women for the Prevention of Lynching were especially significant. Also, growing fear of legal consequences probably discouraged many would-be lynchers. The last known lynching took place in Neshoba County, Miss., when three civil rights activists were murdered in 1964.

The public presentation of lynching photographs and postcards in the past decade has focused renewed attention on lynching, and a spate of academic studies reflects the growing interest in lynching and its role in southern culture. A Senate resolution in 2005 officially apologized for the Senate's repeated failure to pass antilynching legislation.

WILLIAM I. HAIR
Georgia College

James Allen, Hilton Als, John Lewis, and Leon F. Litwack, *Without Sanctuary: Lynching Photography in America* (2003); Edward L. Ayers, *Vengeance and Justice: Crime and Punishment in the 19th-Century American South* (1984); Ray Stannard Baker, *Following the Color Line* (1908, reprint 1969); Richard Maxwell Brown, *Strain of Violence: Historical Studies of American Violence and Vigilantism* (1975); W. Fitzhugh Brundage, *Lynching in the New South: Georgia and Virginia, 1880–1930* (1993); W. Fitzhugh Brundage, ed., *Under Sentence of Death: Lynching in the New South* (1997); James H. Chadbourn, *Lynching and the Law* (1933); James E. Cutler, *Lynch-Law: An Investigation into the History of Lynching in the United States* (1905); Phillip Dray, *At the Hands of the Unknown: Lynching of Black America* (2002); Jacquelyn Dowd Hall, *Revolt against Chivalry: Jessie Daniel Ames and the Women's Campaign against Lynching* (1979); George C. Rable, *But There Was No Peace: The Role of Violence in the Politics of Reconstruction* (1984); Arthur F. Raper, *The Tragedy of Lynching* (1933); Stewart Emory Tolnay and E. M. Beck, *A Festival of Violence: An Analysis of Southern Lynchings, 1882–1930* (1995); Walter White, *Rope and Faggot* (1929); George Wright, *Racial Violence in Kentucky, 1865–1940: Lynching, Mob Rule, and "Legal Lynchings"* (1990).

Maiden Aunt

She is a favorite character of fiction and stereotype and a person who, in fact, touched the lives of most southerners—the maiden aunt. The demand for marriageable women exceeded the supply during the colonial era, but by the time of the American Revolution the spinster (single women at home were often drafted to the female task of spinning, the origin of the term) was a folkloric figure in southern states. The never-wed woman in southern culture was not only dependent upon men, like her married counterpart, but she was denied the status accorded to matrons and mothers. She was forced to live out her life on the fringes of society, a perpetually lone figure in a culture of tightly knit couples and children. Within the home (usually that of a brother or sister), however, she was often a cherished and fond member of the family circle. Indeed, the maiden aunt became both influential and indispensable.

It was assumed, because of social pressures to marry, that most unmarried women had been rejected, passed over, or not had the opportunity to snare a husband. This promoted several unattractive images of old maids. One antebellum girl described them as "forlorn damsels who made the midnight air echo with their plaintive bewailings, for only bats and owls return their melancholy strains." In southern society the "old" maid ranged anywhere from age 18 to 80. A girl might feel spinsterish if younger sisters married before she did, if she was not married by age 21, or simply if all her friends had "deserted" her for husbands.

Southern women, as a rule, married very young—younger than their northern counterparts and much younger than men. Shortly after puberty, black women often selected a mate, whom they married by folk custom though not by law. Historians of the slave community have found teenaged brides common on the plantation. Studies of planters have confirmed that white women also commonly wed as schoolgirls. In the Old South the average age of marriage for white women was 20; that for black women was slightly lower. Thus, women who remained unmarried in the South were classified as spinsters at a much earlier age than elsewhere.

The Civil War, of course, greatly reduced the supply of young men to marry. Many southern daughters during the second half of the century were thus demographically deprived of husbands. Strikingly, the Reconstruction era was the first period since early colonial days when interracial sexual relations and even marriage were accepted to any notable extent. However, a large number of the single white women—and especially those of the upper and middle classes—remained unattached, many becoming leaders in shaping new educational and employment opportunities for women. Gradually, career opportunities for females expanded, and the stigma associated with women who lived alone lessened.

Nevertheless, throughout most of the 19th century and well into the 20th, southern society attempted to shelter and confine single women. Those who failed to marry were often forced by custom or circumstance to spend their time and energy with "other women's families." Spinsters clearly served surrogate roles with the family—single daughters or maiden aunts might be welcome as an extra pair of hands or as substitute mothers—but they were also social outcasts, denied the status a woman could achieve only through her role as matriarch. Few parents, even those of enormous wealth, would bequeath money to an unmarried daughter.

Only in modern times have single women in the South received any of the family resources. Traditionally, a woman was expected to inherit through her dowry. If she did not marry she could only rely on the charity of parents or siblings. Brothers and sisters eagerly provided these spinsters with homes in exchange for valuable domestic services. Maiden aunts were teachers and nurses, confidants and disciplinarians. Indeed, their whole lives were bound up with the strenuous chores of child rearing, but, like servants, the children they tended were not their own.

"Aunt adoption" was a particularly southern phenomenon. Women often singled out a niece for special affection and in many cases quite lavish consideration. This cultivation of a favorite by aunts was traditional and certainly not limited to unmarried or childless females. It was not uncommon for a southern mother to "donate" one of her several daughters to the family of a beloved brother or sister who had no children, or even merely no female offspring. This would reduce the burden of the natural parents (costs for living expenses and dower) while maintaining family ties and offering emotional, and sometimes financial, benefits for the adopted child.

Upon occasion, a pregnant mother would secure a promise from a favorite sister that if she did not survive the ordeal of childbirth the surviving sister would look after the orphaned children; in some cases women wanted their husbands to remarry these spinsters. With death in childbirth very high in the South until the 20th century (nearly double that of the North), unmarried women sometimes literally inherited an entire family through marriage to the spouse of a dead sibling. These cases were extreme, yet they reflect the pivotal importance to southern women of the maiden aunt, despite her never-married, childless status.

The stereotypes of these women were most often unflattering exaggerations. Many fictional portraits of maiden aunts painted them as dizzy and foolish, the "Aunt Pittypat" character of *Gone with the Wind*. A more sympathetic portrayal has been developed by several southern authors who have characterized sturdy, proud females channeling their energies and talents into their nephews and nieces and leading challenging and fulfilling lives: variants on the theme were established in one of Faulkner's early novels, *Sartoris*, with the spirited and understanding Miss Jenny. Many of these characters, especially those created by women novelists such as Ellen Glasgow, possess a feminist component: they chose not to enter the ranks of women trapped and trampled by husbands.

Another significant variant for the never-married woman was the portrait of a lady of questionable character. There were women in southern society and southern fiction who chose to lead lives unhampered by spouses but who refused to deny themselves sexual companionship. For some, reckless behavior at a younger age had supposedly robbed them of their reputation for virtue, leading to a devaluation on the marriage market. Others purportedly were predisposed to this character defect—loose and immoral without hope of redemption. In either case, perpetual spinsterhood was their fate. This semitragic figure was most poignantly embodied in Tennessee Williams's Blanche DuBois, the fading belle of *Streetcar Named Desire*.

The plays, films, and novels of the South depict lone women in their variety and complexity, but these myriad roles cannot match the mark these women have made in the great drama of real life. Their impact has been enormous and their contributions monumentally enriching to southern culture.

CATHERINE CLINTON
Queen's University, Belfast

Josephine Carson, *Silent Voices: The Southern Negro Woman Today* (1969); Catherine Clinton, *The Plantation Mistress: Woman's World in the Old South* (1982); Laura L. Doan, ed., *Old Maids to Radical Spinsters: Unmarried Women in the Twentieth-Century Novel* (1991); Maria Fletcher, "The Southern Heroine in the Fiction of Representative Southern Women Writers" (Ph.D. dissertation, Louisiana State University, 1963); Elizabeth Fox-Genovese, *Within the Plantation Household: Black and White Women of the Old South* (1988); Anne Goodwyn Jones, *Tomorrow Is Another Day: The Woman Writer in the South, 1859–1936* (1981); John C. Ruoff, "Southern Womanhood, 1865–1920: An Intellectual and Cultural Study" (Ph.D. dissertation, University of Illinois, 1976); Lillian Smith, *Killers of the Dream* (1949); Julia Cherry Spruill, *Women's Life and Work in the Southern Colonies* (1938); Alice Walker, *In Love and Trouble: Stories of Black Women* (1973).

Mammy

The Mammy image is a cultural image, based on myth, that was developed in the South by the privileged class during slavery, in which the physical and emotional makeup of enslaved women was used to justify the institution of slavery. This image is of an obese, dark, and middle-aged domestic servant, with shining white teeth visibly displayed in a grin. She often wears a drab calico dress with a handkerchief tied on her head. Because of her physical appearance, size, perpetual grin, and comportment she is viewed as humorous and comedic— as asexual and the antithesis of American standards of beauty and femininity.

Moreover, although fiercely independent and cantankerous, she is a faithful servant who is devoted to ensuring that all of the needs of the family for whom she works are continuously met, and she never demands anything for herself. She is docile in her relationship with whites but exhibits aggressiveness toward African Americans, a quality not defined as feminine. In effect, she accepts her subordinate position and never challenges the social system nor expects that she should be anything but long-suffering and satisfied with her station in life. She is not only self-sacrificing but also neglects the needs of her own family as she remains committed to providing comfort, advice, and compassion to meet the physical and emotional needs of the white family.

The mammy cultural image was developed to contradict the beliefs that were spread by abolitionists throughout the South and North that slavery was a harsh, cruel, and brutal system. Contrary to these beliefs, the mammy image and other similar cultural images suggested that the institution of slavery was benign, humane, and benevolent. Thus, the mythological cultural image of mammy served the social, political, and economic interests of the slaveholding community, which was determined to preserve this system.

The mammy image became a symbol of African American womanhood and a permanent feature of American culture as it spread from the South throughout the United States, in large measure through the mass media. The characteristics inherent in the image as well as in the domestic servant role was generalized to African American women, long after emancipation. Ultimately, the cultural perception and expectation were that African American women conformed to the congenial, subservient, infantile mammy image and were best suited for the kind of work that mammy performed, which was domestic service. Initially, the print media and later the electronic media, including film, radio, and television, were responsible for the mammy image becoming inextricably woven into American culture. The mass media have played a major role in perpetuating this image, making it an indelible feature in American popular culture. Historically, the media have captured the its evolution, depicting many variations in the mammy image; yet what has remained constant is her ability to be comedic and provide entertainment. The mammy image was also maintained and proliferated through cartoons, caricatures, and advertisements and through artifacts such as cookie jars, dolls, salt and pepper shakers, and numerous other collectibles and memorabilia.

Many literary works, especially novels, contain a mammy character, such as those in Carson McCullers's *The Member of the Wedding*, Fannie Hurst's *Imitation of Life*, and Margaret Mitchell's *Gone with the Wind*. The mythological cultural image of mammy as the very dark, overweight, masculinized woman was first prominent in films, beginning in 1914. Mammy as a cultural image appeared as characters in many popular films, debuting in *Coon Town Suffragettes* (1914), and made later appearances as Claudia McNeil in *A Raisin in the Sun* (1961) and Beah Richards in *Hurry Sundown* (1967). The image appeared in television, beginning in 1950 in *Beulah*, a television show, and later in the 1970s and 1980s in television sitcoms such as *Maude* and *Gimme a Break*. Although the mammy image evolved and appeared as different characters, it always retained the mythological physical and emotional makeup and performed household duties and domestic chores. In spite of the meager monetary compensation, mammy was always grateful for the intrinsic satisfaction she derived from catering to the needs of the family for whom she worked.

The most popular and legendary actresses to play mammy were Hattie McDaniel, Louise Beavers, and Ethel Waters. Playing the mammy in film or television, which was sometimes controversial, provided African American actresses with employment, afforded them an opportunity for individual artistic expression, and, occasionally, resulted in their successfully challenging various stereotypical aspects of the characters that they portrayed. However, mammy was usually required to be the maid that provided service and support to the lady of the house while displaying satisfaction, subservience, and intellectual inferiority.

Another mythological cultural image that evolved from the mammy image was Aunt Jemima, also a domestic, usually a cook, who was more jolly and agreeable than mammy. Nevertheless, the message was the same: the maid who was completely satisfied with slavery and servitude and who believed that it was her obligation to ensure the total well-being of the mistress and her entire family, in spite of any adversities that she encountered in life or as a result of her dedication.

The mythological cultural image of mammy was developed to reflect the enslaved woman's work in the slaveholder's house as a domestic. An informal stratification system was created for enslaved persons, placing house servants in the highest class, artisans or tradespeople in the middle class, and field workers in the lowest class. Slaveholders used this class division to separate the enslaved population for the purpose of assigning tasks on the plantation, to establish social distance and dissension among those who were enslaved, and to encourage loyalty from mammy and others working in the slaveholder's house. In so doing, slaveholders attempted to make it appear as though mammy and other enslaved house workers had an easier workload and a more satisfying life than those who worked outside the slaveholder's house. This was untrue, as mammies were required to work extremely long hours—cooking, cleaning, rearing children, and assuming the responsibility of being a personal servant to the mistress, which meant being at her beck and call. In reality, mammies were not always middle-aged, as they were depicted in popular images, but were often younger women who were required to serve as wet nurses, since they themselves had often recently given birth to babies themselves, who were nursed by other women in the slave quarters. Contrary to the mythological cultural image, the physical and emotional makeup of real life mammies was varied, and they represented all shapes, sizes, and hues. Mammies were also expected to accompany the slaveholder's family to church and social functions. The demands for their domestic services were of such a magnitude that they had little time to spend with their own children and families. The work of the mammy was arduous and painstaking, providing little reason for celebration or contentment, contrary to the image of mammy as presented in the mainstream media.

Artists, scholars, and activists during the 1960s and 1970s challenged the mammy image as representative of African American womanhood, an image that suggested that African American women were valued for their comedic qualities and were best suited for domestic service. The artwork of Murry De-Pillars uses images of an angry Aunt Jemima drawing back a pancake turner. Jon Lockhard painted an Aunt Jemima on a pancake box with a raised fist saying, "No More." These images, along with scholarly critiques and critical analyses of the mammy cultural image, contributed to the reconstruction and redefinition of African American womanhood.

K. SUE JEWELL
Ohio State University

Donald Bogel, *Toms, Coons, Mulattoes, Mammies, and Bucks: An Interpretive History of Blacks in American Films* (2001); Elizabeth Fox-Genovese, *Within the Plantation Household: Black and White Women of the Old South* (1988); K. Sue Jewell, *From Mammy to Miss America and Beyond: Cultural Images and the Shaping of U.S. Social Policy* (1993); Kim Marie Vaz, *Black Women in America* (1995).

Marriage and Courtship

Marriage reflected and shaped the core values of southerners—Indian, white, and black. Native peoples living in the precontact South belonged to numerous distinctive nations, but they generally shared in common a set of views about marriage that fundamentally differed from those of the English who sought to colonize their lands. The Cherokee provide a revealing example. From before the era of contact with whites through the mid-18th century, the focus in Cherokee marriages and Cherokee society in general centered on balance: men and women complemented each other. So although Cherokee husbands and wives performed very different functions (as they did in English culture), there was no rigid hierarchy to those roles (which was the case among colonists). Husbands did not control wives or children, and wives did not subordinate themselves to husbands. Indeed, the Cherokee, like many Indian societies, traced lineage and clan membership exclusively though women, who were the only permanent members of a household. When a man married, he left his mother's household to join his wife's household; children were not considered blood relatives of fathers. The Cherokee did not condemn couples who divorced: unhappy matches were easily dissolved without stigma. In cases of divorce, the husband returned to his mother's household, and family possessions and children remained with the mother and her kinfolk. Women could change husbands, but they did not practice polygamy. Men did, however, commonly take more than one wife. By the early 19th century, white influences contributed to the Cherokee nation's decisions to outlaw polygamy, alter property holding, and change inheritance practices to promote the authority of husbands—all of which made relationships between Cherokee husbands and wives more like those in hierarchical white households.

English colonists wanted to reproduce the strictly ordered, patriarchal households their culture valued, but social instability in the early 17th-century Chesapeake thwarted those desires. Marriage was an uncertain prospect for colonial newcomers. Male migrants to Virginia outnumbered females by as much as four to one, and most single women came to the region as indentured servants and were barred from marrying until they completed their terms. This delayed the age of first marriage for white men to the mid-to-late twenties, and it meant that some white men, particularly immigrants, did not marry at all. Native-born white women, lacking the legal restraints placed on servants and in short supply, married at younger ages (as early as the late teens) and usually to older husbands. The dangerous environment in the Chesapeake region fragmented families in much the same way that divorce does in contemporary America. While the statistical evidence is less than precise, historical demographers reasonably calculate that 17th-century Virginia colonists seldom lived into their fifties, which resulted in a society of widows and widowers, orphans, stepfamilies, and half siblings. Women, who married younger and lived longer, often buried several husbands, sometimes acquiring extensive property as a consequence. Colonial law granted a widow a one-third share in her husband's estate, and men could and often did bequeath their wives even more. Surviving several spouses could make a woman very rich and thus very desirable in Virginia's highly competitive and acquisitive culture. High mortality rates also contributed to the speed of remarriages after a spousal death and therefore truncated courtships—life was too fleeting and marriage too advantageous to delay weddings. Young men on the make and aware that Virginia law granted them access to and authority over much of their wives' property, aggressively courted older, rich widows, creating what one historian called a "widowarchy"—a social and economic power structure built around strategic marriages to wealthy women. Not until near the turn of the 18th century did sex ratios and mortality rates stabilize in the Chesapeake. These factors greatly transformed courtship rituals and marital relationships but not the connection between marriage and power among emerging southern elites.

By the mid-18th century, Virginia and Maryland proved far safer for colonists, who created stronger patriarchal families. The growing prosperity of these colonies also contributed to the rise of self-conscious gentility among Chesapeake elites, including in their courtship rituals. Planters' sons and daughters met at plays and balls, and they carried out romances in ways that etiquette writers defined as respectable and genteel. Wealthy colonists who populated the colony of South Carolina, particularly Charles Town, replicated this refined culture, but mortality rates in South Carolina remained high throughout the 18th century, and thus spousal death and remarriage continued to frustrate efforts to develop patriarchal, nuclear households in the Lowcountry. Throughout all of the 18th-century southern colonies, marriage was a powerful tool for amassing wealth and social power. Cousin marriages and exchange marriages, where siblings from one family married siblings from another, consolidated family holdings and so were popular among established elites. Marrying wealthy widows/ widowers and other strategic practices allowed ambitious men and women to join the gentry ranks.

The 18th-century South witnessed not only the creation of powerful elite kin groups but also significant emotional transformations within those families. What scholars have termed "the rise of the affectionate family" between the mid-18th and early 19th centuries infused an intense emotionalism into courtships, marriages, and parent-child relationships. Young people in particular increasingly touted romantic love—not property or power—as the proper basis for making matches. Elite parents came to value affection as well, and many accepted love as central to successful marriages. However, wealthy parents also understood the financial and social dangers of "marrying down," and they usually sought to guide their children toward romantic attachments that protected rather than imperiled family assets—that is, parents wanted children to marry for love but only to similarly circumstanced, wealthy, genteel partners.

By the mid-19th century, shifts in family values had made romantic love the legitimate basis for selecting a spouse, but this change did not undermine the social hierarchy that southern elites presided over. Gentry sons and daughters seldom married outside their class, and those who did risked ostracism and penury. Courtships among southern elites continued to be highly ritualized, despite youthful zeal for emotional expressiveness. Courtship letters conformed to a particular code, as did dances, visits, exchanges of gifts, and all the purportedly spontaneous but actually scripted signs of romantic love. Successful suitors learned to express their feelings according to precise rituals, displaying at once their love and their gentility. Elaborate weddings, increasingly popular in the 19th-century South, likewise symbolized the abiding love of the couple while publicly affirming their elite status. Further, these new values did not challenge the legal, political, and social subordination of white wives to husbands. Husbands continued to control wives' estates and in rare cases of divorce or separation retain custody of children. So while marriages were supposed to be (and often were) emotionally fulfilling to both husbands and wives, they were by no means egalitarian.

The southern gentry's quest for order also shaped the marital lives of African Americans, as did demographic instability. Enslaved African Americans faced a myriad of obstacles in creating and protecting marriages. Slave owners did not want their slaves' family bonds to threaten their economic ambitions, so white laws denied legal marriages to slaves. Thus, any husband or wife could be sold away at an owner's discretion. In the late 17th and early 18th centuries, imbalanced sex ratios, because of slave importation patterns that favored young men, compromised the ability of many slave men to marry. High death rates in the colonial period also sundered unions. By the early 19th century, sex ratios among slaves equalized and mortality rates stabilized, but the expansion of the American Republic into the West introduced a new kind of trauma: the internal trafficking of slave families. And throughout the slave era, owners sought to manipulate slaves' sexual lives to advance their own financial interests.

Despite all of these difficulties, enslaved men and women in the antebellum South did enter into devoted marriages, and they created family lives that, although never immune to owner interference, held great emotional meaning and formed the basis of African American communities and cultures. Making matches involved a complicated balancing of (and tensions between) the emotional connections of the young couple, the oversight of the larger slave com-

Catholic wedding, Louisville, Ky., c. 1950
(Photographic Archives, University of Louisville, Louisville, Ky.)

munity, and the economic interests of white owners. Slaveholders' influence was stronger when couples lived on different plantations. Owners could refuse passes and so end relationships, or they could purchase desired spouses. Members of the slave community also involved themselves in young peoples' courtships and marriages by organizing clandestine dances and, when they approved of matches, planning weddings and providing household goods for newlyweds. Weddings blended African traditions with Christian rituals, and they were extremely important to couples because they publicly affirmed unions that lacked legal standing.

Marital laws continued to be an important tool for the social order in the postbellum South. After emancipation, southern whites' fears about interracial relationships led some states to pass legislation criminalizing marriages between whites and blacks. Such prohibitions had existed in various forms since the early colonial era, but African Americans' new legal status in general and the Fourteenth Amendment in particular required additional statutes to police the South's color line. Southern states were not alone in passing such laws but were particularly resolved in defending them and strident in punishing violators. Not until 1967, in *Loving v. Virginia*, did the U.S. Supreme Court strike down that state's law making interracial marriage a felony, thereby ending white southerners' use of those sorts of marriage laws to promote racial segregation.

LORRI GLOVER
University of Tennessee

Jane Turner Censer, *North Carolina Planters and Their Children, 1800–1860* (1984); Nancy F. Cott, *Public Vows: A History of Marriage and the Nation* (2000); Lorri Glover, *All Our Relations: Blood Ties and Emotional Bonds among the Early South Carolina Gentry* (2000); Anya Jabour, *Marriage in the Early Republic: Elizabeth and William Wirt and the Companionate Ideal* (1998); Edmund S. Morgan, *American Slavery, American Freedom: The Ordeal of Colonial Virginia* (1975); Theda Perdue, *Cherokee Women: Gender and Culture Change, 1700–1835* (1998); Marie Jenkins Schwartz, *Born in Bondage: Growing Up Enslaved in the Antebellum South* (2000); Daniel Blake Smith, *Inside the Great House: Planter Family Life in Eighteenth-Century Chesapeake Society* (1980); Brenda Stevenson, *Life in Black and White: Family and Community in the Slave South* (1996); Steven M. Stowe, *Intimacy and Power in the Old South: Ritual in the Lives of the Planters* (1987).

Matriarchy, Myth of

In the 1920s, African American sociologist Edward Franklin Frazier began publishing articles outlining what would become his seminal analysis of racial oppression and the resulting "disorganization" of African American family life. While working at the Atlanta School of Social Work, Frazier focused on the experiences of the African American majority who remained mired in the rural South of the early 20th century, where poverty and Jim Crow mores dictated the status quo. Frazier theorized that the long history of slavery and ongoing racial and economic oppression had damaged African Americans' abilities to create and maintain stable, functional, "organized" families according to the traditional, patriarchal model valued by mainstream U.S. society. Instead, Frazier lamented, African Americans struggled even to maintain dysfunctional, "disorganized" families in which fathers were either absent or ineffectual and mothers provided the bulk of both livelihood and leadership.

Frazier was well aware of the circumstances that necessitated African American mothers' participation in the paid workforce, despite their responsibilities to their families. Since the onset of Reconstruction and throughout the first half of the 20th century, Jim Crow laws and their capricious, often violent enforcement combined with dire economic hardship to undermine African American familial stability. The growing numbers of black men in the nation's cities were chronically underemployed. Overwhelmingly, they worked seasonal, low-paying, often dangerous jobs. Black wives and mothers compensated by taking in laundry, working as domestic servants, or, in some cases, making brave forays into the world of industrial labor. Rural black families subsisting on agricultural labor or tenant farming required the participation of every family member to maximize meager profits. Furthermore, black women were often called upon to work double or triple duty—in the fields, in the landowners' homes, and, of course, in their own homes. Black people's bleak economic outlook made it almost impossible for black women to confine their work to unpaid service to their own families. Many African Americans, especially women, considered this fact a hardship, another unwelcome indication of the depth of their oppression.

Frazier came to focus on this aspect of African American life—the gender dynamics of the family—as the area both most ravaged by racial oppression and most easily addressed and repaired by African Americans themselves. Focusing on economic factors and sociological statistics, Frazier concluded that African American women were the primary and most reliable breadwinners in their homes. From this he extrapolated that they wielded inappropriate and damaging influence over other family members, particularly men. Furthermore, black men's particular hardships, especially their inability to serve their families as primary providers, compromised their sense of masculinity and encouraged their abandonment of their roles as husbands and fathers, leaving black wives and mothers to serve as heads of households as well as breadwinners. In this way, according to Frazier, the African American family had become "disorganized" and a tradition of "matriarchy" had emerged where an organized, respectable patriarchy ought to have been.

Yet, unlike the imposition of segregation and employment discrimination, the reorganization of their families was well within African Americans' control. Through his publications in scholarly and popular publications and through his work teaching African American social workers who would then serve poor African American families, Frazier sought to encourage the amelioration of this situation. He criticized African American family life and black mothers in particular in the hope that they would recognize their failings and improve upon them. Unfortunately, this criticism tended to imply that black women themselves were to blame for the "disorganization" of their families and their own apparent and supposedly inappropriate leadership roles within them. Frazier's focus on black men's perspectives and the effects on black children worked to confirm the impression of black mothers' culpability and empowerment through their roles as "matriarchs."

Frazier's flawed theory of black matriarchy proved to be one of the most

Woman washing clothes by hand, Vicksburg, Miss., 1968 (William R. Ferris Collection, Southern Folklife Collection, Wilson Library, University of North Carolina at Chapel Hill)

influential and insidious ideas of the late 20th century. Perhaps Senator Daniel Patrick Moynihan did the most to popularize and substantiate Frazier's theory of a matriarchy among African Americans by drawing upon it in his federal report, *The Negro Family: The Case for National Action* (1965) (the Moynihan Report). As assistant secretary of labor for policy in the Kennedy administration, Moynihan and his staff blamed slavery and white supremacy for the contemporary poverty and oppression of African Americans. Like Frazier before him, Moynihan sought to prove that racial equality was not merely a matter of equal rights but also of equal opportunity, equal access, and equal employment. However, the Moynihan Report precipitated a storm of controversy for its reliance on the theory of matriarchy. Through the Moynihan Report, the federal government seemed to endorse the view that African American men were wholly emasculated and that African American women were guilty of both transgressing gender mores and disempowering their husbands, brothers, and sons.

There were various and contradictory responses to the Moynihan Report. Some vehemently criticized it, even as their arguments seemed to confirm its findings. The burgeoning Black Power movement seized upon the report's discussion of black sexual politics to support its radical criticism of a socioeconomic system that "castrated" black men and utilized black women as tools in the furtherance of racial oppression. By this formulation, black women were not themselves the victims of racial oppression. As "matriarchs," or "Amazons," as Eldridge Cleaver termed black women in his hugely popular Black Power publication *Soul on Ice*, black women wielded inordinate, oppressive psychological and economic power over black men and black communities. Indeed, according to this formulation, African American women were so far from the placid, yielding, supportive feminine ideal as to be placed entirely outside the category of "woman." Black Power rhetoric exhorted them to "step back" into more feminine, helpmate roles, both within the movement and in their personal relationships. This re-creation of traditional, patriarchal sociopolitical structures within African American communities would allow black men to take their rightful leadership roles and right the racial and sexual imbalance of power. African American sociopolitical freedom was dependent on the establishment of traditional patriarchal gender roles in the context of social and political resistance to the racial status quo.

In this way, the theory that African American families and communities were organized around matriarchal power structures infused both the federal government's civil rights policies regarding the eradication of racial and economic disparities and the baby boom generation's popular notion of black liberation.

Not everyone was convinced, however. The theory of matriarchy and its codification in both popular culture and federal policy galvanized the era's black feminist movement. Writing under titles such as "Is the Black Male Castrated?" black feminists decried the notions that black men had been wholly denied access to patriarchal power and male privilege and that black female "matriarchs" were to blame for African Americans' lowly socioeconomic position. Far from wielding inordinate power in their society or among African Americans, black feminists argued, black women suffered multiple forms of oppression, including racism, class bias, and sexism. In 1977 black feminist activist Michele Wallace published her infamous treatise *Black Macho and the Myth of the Superwoman*, which ridiculed the excessive masculinity of Black Power rhetoric and challenged the theory of black matriarchy.

Wallace elucidated the oppressive nature of matriarchy theory. She pointed out that the masculinist reaction to Franklin's ideas as restated in the Moynihan Report encouraged an empty, irresponsible macho attitude among young black men. Rather than assuming the weighty responsibilities of benevolent patriarchs supporting families and leading communities, young black men assumed the accoutrements of power and prestige—a strutting attitude of defiance and belligerence draped in leather and armed with shotguns. Liberal social elements excused such behavior, citing the necessity for black men to assert their "manhood." At the same time, black women's particular oppression remained invisible, hidden behind the focus on black men's perspectives and black women's supposed power and strength.

Wallace observed that whether black women were celebrated as "strong," capable survivors or condemned as domineering matriarchs, their need for liberation from racism, economic exploitation, and sexism remained hidden. Seen as "superwomen," black women were inhuman and therefore oblivious to pain and impervious to attacks on their physical and psychological well-being. By unpacking the matriarchy theory and its implications, Wallace laid bare its dehumanizing implications. In defending black women and arguing for a black feminist "analysis," Wallace became the first to identify the theory of matriarchy and its view of African American gender relations as a fictional, racist, and sexist mythology.

In her seminal article, "Mama's Baby, Papa's Maybe: An American Grammar Book," literary critic and cultural theorist Hortense Spillers built upon black feminist insights like those of Michele Wallace. Spillers further documented the "myth" of matriarchy theory and the depth and breadth of its insidious effects in American culture and sociopolitical life. She focused on the inheritance of enslaved status from the enslaved mother, which supposedly left the father nearly irrelevant. Rather than being empowered by this anomalous lineage pattern under slavery, Spillers argued, black women were actually rendered socially and culturally invisible because their "power to name" excluded them from any sociopolitical or cultural understanding of the category of woman. The myth of matriarchy relied upon the idea of black women's empowerment through their motherhood and family leadership. Yet, as Wallace and Spillers help us understand, enslaved women's motherhood was a principal source of their oppression and dehumanization. Thus, the idea that black women rule over African American families and communities as matriarchs is an extension of this oppression, continuing their exclusion from society's concepts of womanhood and the invisibility of their true sociocultural status.

Today, there are two generations of scholarship that have identified the theory of matriarchy as an insidious and denigrating myth. In the 1970s and 1980s, historians such as Herbert Gutman, Eugene D. Genovese, John Blassingame, and Deborah Gray White investigated the enslaved black family and found that, although slavery certainly impeded the construction of stable, permanent black families, African Americans were by no means wholly stripped of gender identity. In general, black men understood and endeavored to assert their identities as men according to the standards of contemporary American society, and black women did the same. Furthermore, both black men and black women cared for and assumed responsibility for their children as well as for one another. Their enslavement and the ensuing racial oppression required African Americans to develop creative, pragmatic strategies for survival and sustenance, but their families could not be fairly described as "disorganized" or "pathological." Building on these insights, a new generation of historians writing in the 1990s and in the early 21st century, exemplified by Kathleen Brown and Jennifer Morgan, has refuted the notion that black women were somehow less oppressed under slavery than black men. These historians have also revealed the constant interplay of race and gender as factors in the function of slavery and the imposition of racial hierarchy, further illuminating black women's particular oppression and reconfirming the mythological nature of the theory of matriarchy.

ERIN D. CHAPMAN

University of Mississippi

John Blassingame, *The Slave Community: Plantation Life in the Antebellum South* (1972); Kathleen Brown, *Good Wives, Nasty Wenches, and Anxious Patriarchs: Gender, Race, and Power in Colonial Virginia* (1996); Eldridge Cleaver, *Soul on Ice* (1968, 1991); E. Franklin Frazier, *The Negro Family in the United States* (1939); Eugene D.

Genovese, *Roll, Jordan, Roll: The World the Slaves Made* (1974); Herbert G. Gutman, *The Black Family in Slavery and Freedom, 1750–1925* (1976); Jennifer Morgan, *Laboring Women: Reproduction and Gender in New World Slavery* (2004); Daniel Patrick Moynihan, *The Negro Family: The Case for National Action* (1965); Anthony M. Platt, *E. Franklin Frazier Reconsidered* (1991); Lee Rainwater and William L. Yancey, *The Moynihan Report and the Politics of Controversy* (1967); Hortense J. Spillers, *Black, White, and in Color: Essays on American Literature and Culture* (2003); Michele Wallace, *Black Macho and the Myth of the Superwoman* (1990); Deborah Gray White, *Ar'n't I a Woman? Female Slaves in the Plantation South* (1985).

Miscegenation

Late in 1863, between the Emancipation Proclamation in January 1863 and the November 1864 presidential election, the word "miscegenation" first appeared, authors unnamed, in a 72-page booklet: *The Theory of the Blending of the Races, Applied to the American White Man and Negro*. Instigated by Democratic Party congressman from Ohio, Samuel S. Cox, it was authored by two New York City newspapermen, David G. Croly, managing editor of the *New York World*, and one of his journalists, George Wakeman. From the Latin words *miscere*, to mix, and *genus*, race, these three Democrats created a political weapon to stigmatize the Republican Party, the Emancipation Proclamation, and the recruitment of black Union regiments as promoting the sexual mixing of races. From 1863 to the present, despite miscegenation's actual infrequency in the United States—especially in comparison with other multiracial societies in Latin America and South Africa—the word has served as a threat to continuing white supremacy and supposed racial purity. Throughout history, racial purity has been a social concept, not a historical reality. Africans who were brought to the New World, many from Portuguese colonies, already had mixed sexually with Europeans and Asians. Well before 1863, the phrase "racial amalgamation" had been commonly used to denote sexual intercourse between members of different races, but the term also could include the production of mulatto children (judged "hybrid") from this liaison. Although "racial amalgamation" and "mulatto" were less pejorative words than "miscegenation," they also reflected widespread negative white American attitudes about black-white sexual relations.

Demography, historical events, and geography, along with race, gender, and class, helped shape attitudes and actions concerning miscegenation. In the Chesapeake Bay area, during the 17th century, race mixing was stimulated by more male slaves than females being kidnapped and shipped to North America, just as indentured lower-class single white English women arrived in the colonies as household servants for a designated time. This shortage of same-race partners along with relatively little concern for racial purity among the poorer classes stimulated race mixing.

In the 17th and early 18th centuries, however, the growth of a freer and more privileged mulatto class was resisted more in the British colonies than in any other slave society in the Americas. North Carolina and Georgia passed laws opposing racial amalgamation in the 18th century. Pennsylvania and Massachusetts, despite relatively small black populations and very little slavery, banned intermarriage, fearing the decline of allegedly homogeneous white culture in cities like Philadelphia and Boston.

By the beginning of the 18th century, the female indentured white servant class diminished throughout the South, and the female-to-male ratio among black slaves became more equal. Although race mixing became less likely between white females and black males, the prohibition of racial amalgamation continued. Laws against racial amalgamation now served to enforce the notion that only blacks could be slaves and that white freedom depended upon this racial distinction. The Lower South, like Latin America, drew a distinction between the status of mulattoes and of blacks. In Charleston, Mobile, and New Orleans racial mixing was shielded by urban anonymity. On the other hand, the disappearance of a white indentured class on large South Carolina plantations, for example, where blacks were both field and house slaves, accounted for a relative decrease of racial amalgamation between whites and blacks.

From the 18th century to the Civil War, sexual intercourse occurred between white slave masters and black female slaves. The 1850 census indicated that the Upper South contained two-thirds of the mulattoes in the entire South, where there were some 246,000 mulattoes among 3.2 million slaves. In 1860 the number grew to 411,000 mulattoes among 3.9 million slaves. Fugitive slaves fleeing to freedom in the North and in Canada were mostly mulattoes from the Upper South.

Except for the period of the American Revolution, when a belief in freedom moved a few northern states to abolish slavery and partially modify their prohibition of racial amalgamation, antimiscegenation laws continued to proliferate in the North. Until the Civil War, both free and slave states entering the Union usually prohibited intermarriage by law, and some of the older states made interracial marriage both illegal and punishable. Not until 1843 did Massachusetts's antislavery sentiment stimulate the abolition of the state's laws opposing interracial marriage—laws that had not only banned intermarriage but had fined clergymen performing such marriages. A person was defined as black if he/she had a black or mulatto ancestor in the previous three generations.

The Emancipation Proclamation giving freedom to all slaves living in those states in rebellion, accompanied by the creation of the word "miscegenation," raised the specter of increased race mixing. The almost simultaneous recruitment of black regiments for the Union army further increased white trepidation of growing African American power. White supremacy under slavery had assumed the childlike, docile quality of male slaves and the aggressiveness of freed blacks; the end of slavery transformed this image of male slaves into one of sexually potent men desiring to seduce or rape the daughters of white men. Adding to these deep fears were Victorian images of white women as pure and vulnerable or, alternately, as creatures of their own uncontrolled sexual passions.

Criticism of post–Civil War Radical Reconstruction was replete with this imagery, and the end of Reconstruction brought more state laws against racial intermarriage than ever before. Even northern abolitionists needed to be assured in 1864 by the Republican's American Freedmen's Inquiry Commission that mulattoes were likely to "decrease and disappear in a few generations." Slavery's abolition, of course, ended the dominant institutional relationship of white masters over black female slaves, thus causing a sharp decline in interracial mixing. Racial segregation increased and less racial mixing occurred than under slavery—a common contrast between all slave and free societies. Yet the worst incidents of white mob rule and lynching of blacks occurred in the late 19th and early 20th centuries under the guise of preventing racial mixing.

By 1850 a mulatto elite had developed, and this group's importance was dramatically apparent in South Carolina during Radical Reconstruction (1868–76), where some 13 percent of the politicians were mulatto. Descended from New Orleans, Mobile, or Charleston mulatto society, from illicit plantation liaisons, or, as many were, from antebellum free African Americans, mulattoes provided a significant source of race leadership well into the 1920s. But the period from 1880 to 1920 was also the age of "passing," when many light-skinned African Americans chose to identify themselves as whites in order to avoid the disadvantages of being black in a racist society. Passing and its meaning for black identity remained major social and literary concerns in the 1920s for writers and leaders of the Harlem Renaissance. W. E. B. Du Bois, for example, supported the right of intermarriage but opposed its practice.

As recently as 1930, 20 states still outlawed intermarriage between whites and African Americans, and mixed marriages (because of social disapproval) were rare in other states. In 1965, Virginia trial court judge Leon Bazile sentenced an interracial couple to jail: "Almighty God created the races white, black, yellow, malay, and red, and he placed them on separate continents. The fact that he separated the races shows that he did not intend for the races to mix." In 1967, 16 states still had laws prohibiting racial intermarriage, when the Supreme Court decision, *Loving v. Virginia*, declared unconstitutional all laws against intermarriage. Marriages between whites and African Americans, however, remained very infrequent. Most mixing occurred between blacks and mulattoes.

From the 18th century to the mid-20th century, it is revealing that William Shakespeare's frequently performed *Othello* had stimulated actors and audiences in the United States to use the play as a forum for their attitudes about miscegenation and racial intermarriage. Not until 1942 was Othello played by a black actor (Paul Robeson) and Desdemona by a white woman (Uta Hagen) on the same stage. Subsequently, Robeson refused to perform the play in any theater that practiced racial discrimination—sharply reducing the frequency of *Othello* performances.

Since the 1960s African Americans have turned toward asserting their racial identity and sense of black pride while seeking equal rights with whites. African Americans, therefore, have viewed race mixing sometimes as a positive symbol of integration and assimilation into white society and yet sometimes as an event that undermines black identity and racial pride.

TILDEN G. EDELSTEIN
Wayne State University

Ira Berlin, *Slaves without Masters: The Free Negro in the Antebellum South* (1974); Carl N. Degler, *Neither Black nor White: Slavery and Race Relations in Brazil and the United States* (1971); Elizabeth Fox-Genovese, *Within the Plantation Household: Black and White Women of the Old South* (1988); George M. Fredrickson, *White Supremacy: A Comparative Study in American and South African History* (1981); Laurence J. Friedman, *The White Savage: Racial Fantasies in the Postbellum South* (1970); Martha Hodes, *White Women, Black Men: Illicit Sex in the Nineteenth-Century South* (1997); Thomas C. Holt, *Black over White: Negro Political Leadership in South Carolina during Reconstruction* (1977); Winthrop D. Jordan, *White over Black: American Attitudes toward the Negro, 1550–1812* (1968); Werner Sollors, ed., *Interracialism: Black-White Intermarriage in American History, Literature, and Law* (2000); Joel Williamson, *New People: Miscegenation and Mulattoes in the United States* (1980); Forrest G. Wood, *Black Scare: The Racist Response to Emancipation and Reconstruction* (1970).

Motherhood

Street slang and graffiti that commonly refer to one's mother in northern cities are less frequently found in the South, even in its urban areas. Call a southern boy a "son-of-a-bitch" and he might break both your legs. Not because you have insulted him; you have done far, far worse: you have insulted his mother. And to insult any southern mother is to insult Virtue, Piety, Honor, and the South.

Images and popular stereotypes of "southern mothers" have varied along ethnic, regional, economic, class, and racial lines, yet two particular stereotypes of southern motherhood abound in the popular literature and movies—the black mammy and the upper-class white lady, both portrayed to perfection in *Gone with the Wind*.

Although a remarkable group of gifted scholars has written on southern white women, at present less is known about the white southern mother than about the African American mother in the South. This is at least partly because reality is confused with an image central to the development of the southern white identity. Although David Potter argued that women have not participated in the formation of the national character of the United States, William R. Taylor claims that the South adopted essentially feminine characteristics because the region failed in the masculine world of the marketplace. Most recent studies demonstrate that the South did not fail in the chase after wealth but simply took a different and perhaps more lucrative path. After the Civil War, however, both adherents of the Old South legend and advocates of the industrial New South acquiesced in a sentimental portrayal of the plantation South, which kept the southern lady at center stage in order to justify the existing social order.

In its worst forms, the idealization of the southern mother, and, hence, the southern white woman, was used to justify the barbarism of lynching black men. Winthrop D. Jordan has shown how sexual fantasies of Europeans, especially the English, were projected onto Africans and combined with slavery to foster an intense racism. After slavery ended, protection of southern womanhood became a battle cry for the repression of southern blacks. Many whites portrayed the African American as a destroyer of the social order, and they saw the white family, the basis of social stability, as the most obvious point of defense against imagined or real attacks. According to this myth, white women symbolized the family and needed protection from rape or from intermarriage with black men. Thus, such fears expressed both sexual and social concerns.

W. J. Cash called the idolatry of southern white women "downright gyneolatry. . . . Hardly a sermon . . . did not begin and end with tributes in her honor, hardly a brave speech . . . did not open and close with the clashing of shields and the flourishing of swords for her glory. At the last, I verily believe, the ranks of the Confederacy went rolling into battle in the misty conviction that it was wholly for her that they fought."

Despite the romantic plantation literature, the aristocratic southern white

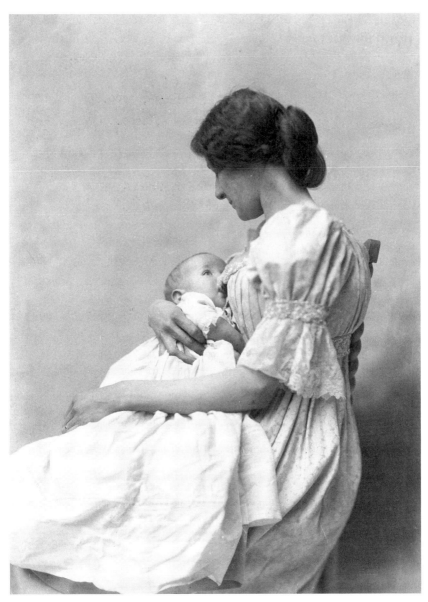

Mother and infant, c. 1900 (Photographer unknown, Library of
Congress [LC-USZ62-107553], Washington, D.C.)

wife was not the only figure idealized. All successful southern men owed their accomplishments to their mothers—whatever heights they obtained were attributed to their mother's love, teachings, sacrifices, and examples. Two southern leaders identified with the common man were Andrew Jackson of the antebellum South and Ben Tillman of the late 19th-century period of agrarian unrest. Both men's fathers died before the sons were born, and both leaders were reared by their mothers—women celebrated for teaching correct patriarchal values to their famous sons. President Jackson praised his mother: "She was as gentle as a dove and as brave as a lioness. . . . The memory of my mother and her teachings were after all the only capital I had to start life with." U.S. senator Tillman explained that his mother taught "habits of thrift and industry; to be ambitious; to despise shams, hypocrisy, and untruthfulness; to bear trouble and sorrow with resolution." As their nicknames "Old Hickory" and "Pitchfork Ben" imply, both Jackson and Tillman were celebrated for the so-called masculine traits one might expect from leaders in a patriarchal society.

Historically, the southern woman was the guardian of the family. She had children with remarkable frequency, rarely talking about the pain and suffering that accompanied almost constant childbearing. Usually she celebrated her childbearing role. When she was not confined to bed in pregnancy or childbirth, environmental, social, and economic conditions dictated her day-to-day routines: gardening, canning, preserving, cooking; spinning, weaving, sewing, knitting; washing, ironing, cleaning; nursing and caring for husband, children, friends, and animals.

Despite the differences between the North and the South, the role of the mother in the 19th century was very similar in both sections. She had primary responsibility for the rearing of the children and was the inculcator of domestic moral values. According to the prevailing view, the southern woman was the moral superior of her husband, and upon her fell the burden of making a decent and moral home, providing a good example for her young children and a refuge for the family patriarch from the turmoil of the workplace or the realm of politics.

Because few public schools were available, the southern white matriarch played a substantial role in educating her children. The early education of most southerners therefore depended upon the knowledge of their mothers and the degree to which they took this role seriously. Some southerners were extremely well taught, but others lacked the most rudimentary book learning. Most mothers taught their girls to sew, weave, and care for younger children; fathers taught their boys to handle responsibility.

As the upholder of key moral values, the woman was also expected to teach the children piety. She did this primarily by example. Although men were active in southern churches, the mother typically was the more constant churchgoer and usually inducted her children into the social order by taking them to church and by reading them the Bible. With religious values so closely allied to family solidarity, the woman's role in introducing the children to religious faith in the South was seen as an effective way for her to strengthen family ties. As keeper of the family's religious flame, the woman made sure her home was a refuge from the meanness of everyday life.

One of the reasons women increasingly took on teaching positions in the North in the 1840s and later in the South was that the female teacher was widely regarded as a sort of classroom surrogate mother who eased the transition of the young child from the home to the community and prepared the child to take his or her place in the rapidly emerging industrial society. Women assumed an important role in the classroom in the South, even though industrial changes occurred very slowly there. Once public schools took hold in the South, the female teacher rapidly became almost universal in elementary schools, carrying out her maternal function of imparting the correct values to the young.

The role of southern mother, nonetheless, sometimes conflicted with the southern ideal of womanhood. Whereas the mother was expected to be a preeminent moral guardian and a tower of strength, as well as efficient, protective, and self-reliant, the ideal woman was often seen as gentle, submissive, flighty, independent, and seemingly unfit to rear children. Certainly, southern women, like northern women, struggled under such contradictions and limitations. If there was a resolution to this dilemma for southern women, it emerged with age, the flighty behavior of the southern belle, desirable in young adulthood, changing suitably with the arrival of the first child.

As novelist Gail Godwin pointed out, the roles of wife and mother have traditionally given identity to the southern woman. Godwin's fictional composite southern lady responds to the question of identity: "Who am I? I am the wife of a wonderful husband and the mother of four adorable children, that's who I am." Modern writers have been much more unkind about the image and its impact on the South. Among others, Flannery O'Connor, Lillian Smith, and William Faulkner portray the damage done to women and to the South as they tried to live with the requirements of perfectionism that symbolized white southern motherhood. Women struggled to reconcile the expectations and realities of the modern world and the legend of southern motherhood. And southern white men have been accused by many pop psychologists of exhibiting a "madonna-whore" attitude toward women—the southern mother was worshipped and put upon a pedestal while other women, those of lower economic status, the daughters of white tenants and textile workers, African American or Indian women, were fair game for the South's young bloods.

The sentimentality of the Victorian era that helped shape the image of southern white motherhood has been preserved in modern regional popular culture. Early country singer Jimmie Rodgers sang "Mother, Queen of My Heart," and Hank Williams later wrote and recorded "Message to My Mother," one of a number of poignant country tunes dedicated to mourned dead mothers. Dolly Parton's "Coat of Many Colors" is a tale of the triumph of a mother's love over poverty. Southern popular culture, black and white, conveys images of endlessly toiling, long-suffering mothers. "Mama Tried" is Merle Haggard's tribute to a mother whose good influence was unable to keep her boy from trouble. "I'm the Only Hell My Mama Ever Raised" is Johnny Paycheck's lament of a boy hell-bent for trouble who rejected his mother for questionable friends and fast cars.

The image of the southern black mother has taken a different path. Although most black women worked in the fields and not in the planter's house, the most popular image of the black woman has been the mammy. The black mammy, like the southern lady, was also born in the white mind, a creation of slavery, as "the black mammy, that creature of impeccable virtue, administrative skill, power and nurturing ability, who yet inexplicably remained in bondage." Suckling a white baby at one breast and a black child at the other, mammy was simple, religious, strong, practical, and tough enough to knock about male slaves caught with a finger in the pie or scores of home-sacking Yankee "bluebellies" and poor white trash scalawags. Unlike the mythical southern aristocratic mother, mammies were not ladylike. White women were viewed as unladylike if they worked; black women were considered lazy and impudent if they resisted working long hours at hard labor. The black mammy sweated over boiling cauldrons, toiled with wash, scrubbed the kitchen, and minded the children. The black mother had to take care of herself and she had to teach her children to accept their inferior place in society. Mammy's religious strength was elevated to sainthood by William Faulkner's character Dilsey.

White mothers were stereotypically submissive to their patriarchal husbands, but the strength of the black mother led to the myth of the black matriarchy. The myth that black women were the dominant force within their families and that fathers were often absent originated with well-intentioned reformers and goes back at least to abolitionist literature. Early depictions of slave mothers pointed to the horrors of breaking up the family by selling children and spouses, the arbitrary beatings of slaves by whites, and the sexual exploitation of slave women by white men. Until the 1970s scholars and the public generally accepted the notion of the "weak"—fatherless—black home, and this in turn reinforced and influenced white society's attitudes toward black people in general. The concept of black matriarchy dominated scholarly literature and became a political issue in the wake of the controversial 1965 study by Daniel Moynihan, who held that the contemporary black matriarchal family had its principal origins in slavery.

In the mid-1980s, concerns about the black family gained new attention because of the increase in the percentage of black single-parent, female-headed families. For example, in six southern states in 1980, over 60 percent of all the single-parent, female-headed families were black. In 1980, nationally, 40 percent of African American families were headed by a female with no husband present, and that figure rose to 44 percent in 2000. The increase in female-headed households among African Americans has been attributed to such factors as racism, the economic vulnerability of blacks, the shorter life spans of African American men, the increasing rate of out-of-marriage parenthood, and changing gender roles accompanying the growth of female autonomy. The disparity in male and female populations among African Americans also contributes. In 2000 there were 86 males to every 100 females in the United States.

Many studies have corrected the grosser misconceptions about black family life, including that of the matriarchy. Herbert Gutman in particular proved the African American commitment to the family as an institution, in both slavery and freedom. He and other historians have confirmed for African Americans what is normally assumed for other groups: the two-parent nuclear family was the normal means for organizing primary experiences (sex relations, child rearing, and descent). As a result, scholars increasingly concentrate on other questions, such as illegitimacy, attitudes toward working wives, the influence of religion, and the division of authority in the family. Nevertheless, black leaders are also calling for more attention to the needs of poor, single-parent black families and to efforts for enhancing the stability of black families.

A certain irony in the study of the black matriarchy suggests, however, a symbiotic relationship between racism and sexism. For over 60 years, scholars, mostly male, pointed to the black family and called it matriarchal and therefore deficient. With the civil rights movement, young northern white women who came to the South began to see heroes in strong black women such as Rosa Parks and Fannie Lou Hamer. When the feminist movement needed heroes, it turned to the scholarly literature on the black matriarchy for role models. *Ms.* magazine devoted an issue to black women as historical heroes for modern women, at the same time that mostly white male scholars have been arguing that there was no black matriarchy.

One of the paradoxes within recent historical scholarship has concerned the place of black women and white women within American families. As scholars have "rehabilitated" the male role in the black family, feminist scholars have shown the power of the wife within white middle- and working-class families. Historians are just beginning to understand the images and the roles of black and white mothers in the American South.

ORVILLE VERNON BURTON
University of Illinois

Maxine Alexander, ed., *Speaking for Ourselves: Women of the South* (1984); Irving H. Bartlett and Glenn Cambor, *Women's Studies*, vol. 2 (1974); Orville Vernon Burton, *In My Father's House Are Many Mansions: Family and Community in Edgefield, South Carolina* (1985); Bette D. Dickerson, ed., *African American Single Mothers: Understanding Their Lives and Families* (1995); Walter J. Fraser Jr., R. Frank Saunders Jr., and Jon L. Wakelyn, eds., *The Web of Southern Social Relations: Women, Family, and Education* (1985); Herbert G. Gutman, *The Black Family in Slavery and Freedom, 1750–1925* (1977); Sally G. McMillen, *Motherhood in the Old South: Pregnancy, Childbirth, and Infant Rearing, 1800–1860* (1990); Stephanie J. Shaw, in *Mothers and Motherhood: Readings in American History*, ed. Rima D. Apple and Janet Golden (1997).

Movie Images and Stereotypes

Stereotypical notions of southern masculinity and femininity circulated in popular literature and drama before the invention of cinema. Hollywood film-makers, however, wasted little time in picking up these notions of gender and organizing them into southern "types" that proved to be impressively durable. This cinematic typology of southern gender was based on strict delineations of race and social class.

From American cinema's earliest days, three stereotypes were available to southern black male characters (characters who were, in fact, played by white men in blackface well into the 1920s): the tom, the coon, and the brutal black buck. The tom, first seen in Edwin S. Porter's *Uncle Tom's Cabin* (1903) and still working overtime in *Driving Miss Daisy* (1990) and *The Green Mile* (1999), was faithful, selfless, loving, and sexually unthreatening—a socially acceptable face of black masculinity and a perfect foil for white male power. The coon, best exemplified by the actor Stepin Fetchit (born Lincoln Theodore Monroe Andrew Perry) throughout the 1920s and 1930s but featured as late as 1994 in the character of Bubba Blue in *Forrest Gump* (1994), was lazy, bumbling, and hilariously (at least to white viewers) inept—another socially acceptable black masculine foil for white male intelligence (Bubba, for example, was even more mentally deficient than Forrest Gump). The brutal black buck was physically powerful, nearly savage, and certainly sexual—the opposite of the tom and the coon. Like Gus, the would-be rapist (played by a white man in blackface) in D. W. Griffith's *Birth of a Nation* (1915), the buck served the interests of segregationist propaganda, his image and its connotations reminders of the need to keep black men separated from white society and under surveillance.

The buck's durability in the movies through the era of 1970s blaxploitation and even into political advertising of the late 20th century (the notorious Willie Horton ad produced by the George Bush campaign in 1988 was a descendant of Griffith's black rapist scenario) has always depended upon the similar durability of another southern gender stereotype: the inviolate white woman. As described by Tom Brady in his 1954 anti-integration manifesto *Black Monday*, the "well-bred, cultured Southern white woman" is "the nearest thing to an angelic being that treads this terrestrial ball." She was, in short, "the loveliest and purest of God's creatures." The movies have agreed. From Flora Cameron in *Birth of a Nation*, who leaps to her death to avoid a fate worse than death at the hands of a black rapist, to Scarlett O'Hara in *Gone with the Wind* (1939) and Blanche DuBois in *A Streetcar Named Desire* (1951), to the gaggle of Louisiana chatterboxes in *Steel Magnolias* (1989), to the lawyers' wives in the many John Grisham movie adaptations of the 1990s and *Ghosts of Mississippi*, to the Ya-Ya Sisters in their 2002 film incarnation and Ada, the pale, perfect preacher's daughter in *Cold Mountain* (2003), "belles" have been a staple of American cinema. Despite the fact that almost no actor has mastered even the broader aspects of various southern accents, the stereotype persists—in pointed contrast to another equally durable white southern female type: the poor country girl.

If the belle's appeal stems primarily from her class positioning, so does the country girl's. Although poor whites live in swampland, Delta fields, and piney woods, Hollywood has preferred to focus upon rural women from the hills and mountains of the South. This is particularly true for the popular genre of musical biographies, or "biopics." The stories of Loretta Lynn (played by Sissy Spacek in *Coal Miner's Daughter* in 1980), Patsy Cline (played by Jessica Lange in *Sweet Dreams* in 1985), and June Carter (played by Reese Witherspoon in *Walk the Line* in 2005) have all been immensely popular at the box office, with Spacek and Witherspoon both winning an Oscar for Best Actress.

Hollywood has long been fascinated by southern mountain folk, especially the male stereotype of the "harmless hillbilly." The ignorant white buffoon was played by actors like Andy Griffith (in comedy records, numerous films, and *The Andy Griffith Show*, 1960–68), Tennessee Ernie Ford (as Lucille Ball's backwoods cousin on *I Love Lucy*, 1951–57), and Buddy Ebsen (in the television series *The Beverly Hillbillies*, 1962–71). The casts of *Hee-Haw* (1969–97) and *The Dukes of Hazzard* (1979–85) and even caricatures of Bill Clinton throughout his term as president used the stereotype.

The harmless hillbilly, though, has a "dark" side. As scholar Anthony Harkins has noted, the "growing national fascination with the Southern mountains" in the 1930s had much to do with what was seen as the region's "authentic folk culture" but also with the area's perceived "social degradation, political unrest, and economic desperation." Part of the comic hillbilly's appeal stemmed from his ignorance, backwardness, and laziness (which in some ways mirrored that of the coon), but also from his latent—almost prehistoric—savagery. Hillbilly violence was certainly present in silent films and found ironic representation in Howard Hawks's highly popular *Sergeant York* (1940), which starred Gary Cooper as the pacifist Tennessee mountain boy whose innate way with a rifle and bayonet erupted heroically in World War I. The most blatant depiction of Appalachian bestiality appeared in *Deliverance* (1970), a film whose violent hillbilly stereotype has not been surpassed by any Hollywood film to date.

A companion to the poor white hillbilly man is the redneck, a man of the lowlands. Equally as ignorant and as poor as the hillbilly, but not as geographically isolated nor as culturally backward, the redneck exhibits a similar tendency toward violence, with one difference: his aggression is racially motivated and directed. Since the Supreme Court's *Brown v. Board of Education* decision of 1954, the redneck has functioned in American films as a cautionary character. The "white trash" southern man who refuses to change or to learn new social attitudes meets a grim end (apocalyptic death or insanity) in films like *A Face in the Crowd* (1957), *Thunder Road* (1958), and the original *Cape Fear* (1962). Those who alter their behavior and attitudes meet social redemption (usually through marriage or education) in films like *Jailhouse Rock* (1957), *Sayonara* (1957), and *The Long Hot Summer* (1958).

Offsetting the social threat of male hillbillies and rednecks, upper-class white southern males have played an important political role in Hollywood films. If racism and rural ignorance are indelible characteristics of the region, they are not, according to the movies, characteristics of all people from the region. "Poor white trash," not the educated planter class, provides recurring villains in movies about the South. In fact, the scapegoating of working-class southern white males as inherent criminals became a narrative staple of mainstream films of the 1950s and 1960s, the climactic years of the civil rights movement (1962's *To Kill a Mockingbird* and 1967's *In the Heat of the Night* are explicit examples), and reappeared in the last decade of the century in films that revisited the movement's legacy in the region (1988's *Mississippi Burning*, 1996's *Ghosts of Mississippi*, and film adaptations of John Grisham novels like 1996's *A Time to Kill* and *The Chamber*). Such films reworked the commercially successful strategy of *To Kill a Mockingbird*: redeeming the middle- or upper-class white southern male by blaming poor white males for the outrages of racism. The primary dramatic tensions of southern films—white women and men threatened by black men, black men threatened by poor white men—ensured the secondary narrative status of black women. The "tragic mulattoes" (usually played by white actors like Jeanne Crain and Ava Gardner) and "Jezebels," which Donald Bogle called two of the major roles historically available to African American female performers, have faded from mainstream films, but one role has not: the mammy.

Definitively embodied by Hattie McDaniel in *Gone with the Wind* (1939), the "instinctively" maternal, asexual, and often comic black woman persisted into the 1990s as an American cinematic fantasy. Whoopie Goldberg's roles in the *Sister Act* films of 1992 and 1993 and her reprise of Hattie McDaniel's Mammy in the 1990 *Ghost*, while not southern, grew from the movie typology of the region. (Not surprisingly, given this lineage, Goldberg won an Oscar for Best Supporting Actress in the latter film, the same award won by McDaniel for *Gone with the Wind*.)

Exceptions to these gendered stereotypes have usually served to prove the rules. Sidney Poitier's pronounced dignity and intelligence in films like *The Defiant Ones* (1958) and *In the Heat of the Night*, for example, called attention to the typically demeaning roles of African American men in the 1950s. The critical acclaim for *Monster's Ball* (2001), the first film for which an African American woman, Halle Berry, won an Oscar for Best Actress, focused on Berry's relatively unstereotypical role, but the film itself was a reprise of the "reformed racist" formula of the 1950s and 1960s, with Billy Bob Thornton playing a sympathetic ex-racist in opposition to his unreformed southern racist father. Not surprisingly, the former is rewarded for his reformation with the love of a beautiful woman, while the latter is punished (banished against his will to a bitter old age in a nursing home).

Revisions and subversions of the century-long gender typology for black and white southern women and men, however, have appeared in independently produced films since the 1980s. Documentarian Ross McIlwee (*Sherman's March* [1986], *Time Indefinite* [1994], and *Bright Leaves* [2003]); nonsoutherner writer and director John Sayles (*Passion Fish* [1992], *Lone Star* [1996], and *Sunshine State* [2002]); Memphis screenwriter and director Craig Brewer (*The Poor and Hungry* [2000], *Hustle and Flow* [2005], and *Black Snake Moan* [2006]); Ira Sachs, another Memphis-reared writer and director (*40 Shades of Blue* [2005]);

and North Carolinians Angus MacLachlan and Phil Morrison (*Junebug* [2005]) have created male and female roles across race and social class that either blatantly challenge or ironically comment upon the southern cinematic gender stereotypes of the 20th century. In this, independent filmmaking functions as a parallel, and often critical, arena of southern representation.

ALLISON GRAHAM
University of Memphis

Donald Bogle, *Toms, Coons, Mulattoes, Mammies, and Bucks: An Interpretive History of Blacks in American Films* (1996); Thomas Cripps, *Making Movies Black: The Hollywood Message Movie from World War II to the Civil Rights Era* (1993), *Slow Fade to Black: The Negro in American Film, 1900–1942* (1977); Allison Graham, *Framing the South: Hollywood, Television, and Race during the Civil Rights Struggle* (2001); Anthony Harkins, *Hillbilly: A Cultural History of an American Icon* (2004); Linda Williams, *Playing the Race Card: Melodramas of Black and White from Uncle Tom to O. J. Simpson* (2001); J. W. Williamson, *Hillbillyland: What the Movies Did to the Mountains and What the Mountains Did to the Movies* (1995).

NASCAR and Masculinity

NASCAR (National Association for Stock Car Auto Racing) was founded in 1948 by Bill France in Daytona, Fla., and today claims to be the fastest-growing spectator sport in the United States, with 75 million fans and attendance of 200,000 people for certain races.

Although NASCAR sanctions several divisions of racing, the Nextel Cup (originally the Strictly Stock division, then the Grand National division, and most recently the Winston Cup) has been its flagship racing series since 1949. At the beginning, many rural and small-town white southerners embraced NASCAR by attending races or by helping friends and family race their own cars in NASCAR events. Some drivers learned their racing skills while transporting moonshine over southern back roads (depicted in the 1958 film *Thunder Road*, starring Robert Mitchum). Many of these folks attempted to win money by competing in the fast cars they used to outrun law enforcement officials. Southerners identified with these outlaw drivers—and stock car racing in general—like no other group of Americans, typically believing that the men piloting the stock cars were rugged good old boys—men much like themselves.

NASCAR races were originally held throughout the United States (including many sites in the Midwest and on the West Coast), with drivers coming from afar for sanctioned events. By 1960 race locations were clustered in the South, and the majority of drivers participating in NASCAR events were southerners. Although 1972 is considered to be the beginning of the modern era of NASCAR, national televised coverage of the sport began in the late 1970s. Today, approximately 50 percent of NASCAR tracks are located in the South, and nearly 50 percent of Nextel Cup drivers claim southern hometowns.

Historically, NASCAR has maintained a large fan base in part because of the emotional connection supporters make with colorful, personable, and accessible drivers. Of the approximately 3,000 people who have driven in Nextel Cup races, nearly all have been white males and about half have claimed southern hometowns. Throughout NASCAR's history, no female or minority driver has achieved consistent on-track success and long-term, widespread fan support.

In the early years of NASCAR, many drivers were fiercely competitive and driven men, as a result of their humble origins and lifelong economic struggles. Many of the pioneer drivers of NASCAR created larger-than-life personalities, driving recklessly during races and living on the edge with hard partying when off the track. Often they died young. Drivers Glenn "Fireball" Roberts, Curtis Turner, and Joe Weatherly were stars who died prematurely after on- and off-track accidents.

One of the first good old boys with mass appeal was Junior Johnson. While growing up in Ronda, N.C., Johnson was convicted of a felony and then incarcerated for working as a moonshiner. Once he began racing stock cars, Johnson developed a reputation as a courageous competitor and aggressive driver. He was at the end of a tremendously successful career in 1965 when author Tom Wolfe portrayed him as "The Last American Hero" in *Esquire* magazine. Wolfe characterized the racer as a chicken farmer, outdoorsman, former moonshine runner, and fearless stock car driver. Johnson was, according to Wolfe, a true representation of southern white male values. Because of the national circulation of *Esquire*, Wolfe's article no doubt furthered the widespread perception that NASCAR was the sport of testosterone-laden, rural, white redneck men.

Many other drivers followed in Johnson's footsteps by crafting a racing identity that appealed to blue-collar southern males, with each driver expressing unique personal characteristics. Richard Petty, son of NASCAR champion Lee Petty, began racing in the late 1950s. By the time his career was complete, he had won a record 200 races, a record-tying seven championships, and the simple nickname of "The King." Petty's primary contribution to NASCAR was not his record-setting career but his role as informal ambassador for the sport. Although he did not have the rugged appeal of an ex-moonshiner, Petty attracted fans because of his humble demeanor, small-town origins (Level Cross, N.C.), accessibility to fans, and regular victories. He maintained the image of a southern gentleman and has continued to be one of NASCAR's most popular and recognizable icons, even after his retirement in 1992.

One of the most memorable displays of NASCAR machismo occurred at the 1979 Daytona 500, the Super Bowl of stock car racing. In the first major race ever broadcast in its entirety on network television, a large national audience watched on CBS as leaders Donnie Allison and Cale Yarborough crashed on the last lap. While Richard Petty raced to victory, Bobby Allison stopped at the accident site to assist his brother. As pit crew members joined in, the ensuing brawl captivated the television audience and no doubt convinced millions of first-time viewers that NASCAR drivers were fearless men who were frequently fighting and wrecking when not racing. The next day, a *New York Times* story that described the race with an accompanying photograph of the fight introduced even more Americans to the unique culture of NASCAR.

More recently, Dale Earnhardt used his rough driving and frequent victories in his black Chevrolet to cultivate the image of a hardworking, rugged southerner who would not back down from challengers. He has built a business empire, with his steely stare and all-black clothing selling a variety of products to fans. After his death in 2001, most of his fans embraced his son, Dale Earnhardt Jr., as the new favorite of NASCAR traditionalists. The younger Earnhardt has been voted "Most Popular Driver" by NASCAR fans since 2003, owing to his outgoing personality, reputation for frequent partying, and Budweiser beer sponsorship. He is a new type of NASCAR hero—a combination of a traditional good old boy and modern hip-hop mogul overseeing a growing list of endorsements and business connections.

Many of the most loyal NASCAR fans have attempted to emulate their hard-driving, hard-living heroes, and the fan base has been regularly stereotyped by the national media as consisting of bigoted, beer-drinking, catcalling southern rednecks. The traditionally monolithic nature of NASCAR fans has caused some observers to argue that stock car racing is a white sport with little appeal to minority fans or potential minority drivers.

Although recent media coverage of the sport typically has focused on the geographic expansion of NASCAR to new markets, including Chicago, Kansas City, and Las Vegas, many fans continue to view NASCAR as a significant part of the unique regional identity of the South. To traditional followers, historic tracks such as North Wilkesboro (North Carolina), Darlington (South Carolina), and Rockingham (North Carolina) are unique and irreplaceable sites of white male southern sports history. They are locations where the regional identity of fans (the ubiquitous trackside Confederate battle flags are the most controversial example) can be freely expressed in an otherwise politically correct world.

Recently NASCAR has attracted new fans, many of whom are women, minorities, and high-income followers from outside the South. For example, estimates show that nearly 50 percent of fans attending races are women. As the sport reaches out to attract new markets, sponsors, and followers, change is inevitable. Long gone are the days when NASCAR races regularly featured scantily clad women carrying signs promoting sponsors while sashaying in front of stands mainly filled with males. The grandstands have become family-friendly places where the most overt displays of violence and intolerance are not allowed. In a world where the forces of homogeneity and globalization can overwhelm regional distinctiveness, NASCAR remains a unique sport where southern white male values are promoted and cherished by many fans.

DOUGLAS A. HURT
University of Central Oklahoma

Derek Alderman et al., *The Professional Geographer* (2003); Duane Falk, *The Winston Cup* (2001); Robert G. Hagstrom, *The NASCAR Way: The Business That Drives the Sport* (1998); Paul Hemphill, *Wheels: A Season on NASCAR's Winston Cup Circuit* (1997); Mark D. Howell, *From Moonshine to Madison Avenue* (1997); Douglas A. Hurt, *Southeastern Geographer* (May 2005); Jeff MacGregor, *Sunday Money: Speed! Lust! Madness! Death! A Hot Lap around America with NASCAR* (2005); Joe Menzer, *The Wildest Ride: A History of NASCAR* (2001); Richard Pillsbury, in *The Theatre of Sport*, ed. Karl Raitz (1995), *Journal of Geography*, vol. 73 (1974); Neal Thompson, *Driving with the Devil: Southern Moonshine, Detroit Wheels, and the Birth of NASCAR* (2006); Tom Wolfe, *Esquire* (March 1965).

Paternalism

In the past two decades, historians have advanced and enriched our understanding of the South by applying new paradigms to some old questions. Paternalism and gender, separately and in combination, have been two of the most insightful, offering historians new ways to understand a range of familiar problems. Most of all, paternalism has offered a framework for reexamining class relations and identity. Southern historians have produced some of the most influential, award-winning works of this generation by reexamining race, class, gender, and religion within the paradigm of paternalism. Beginning with historians of the Old South, paternalism has now been applied to much of the region's history in the 19th and early 20th centuries.

Briefly, paternalism describes a set of relationships between individuals that are based on mutual obligations and reciprocity. They resemble those between parents and children and suggest emotional attachment—although not necessarily affection—that helps bind the parties together. Paternalistic relationships are based on inequality and require varying amounts of deference on the part of "inferiors" toward their "superiors." They are hierarchical and often involve people of vastly different influence. But those below—no matter how disadvantaged—hold some degree of power, because through their loyalty or service they confirm status and help bring psychological completeness to those of greater rank. Finally, for many scholars, paternalism implies that the subordinate classes embrace the philosophy and culture of the ruling class. That acceptance of the dominant culture is frequently imperfect or very limited and often includes significant cultural variations generated from within the lower ranks.

Scholarly attention to paternalism began with some of the early 20th-century studies of slavery. White historians such as Ulrich B. Phillips argued that slavery was a benign institution that held masters and slaves together in a system that benefited everyone. Masters cared for slaves like members of the family, and slaves returned genuine affection. According to southern defenders of slavery, the institution was part of the Old South's social and cultural structure in which everyone knew his or her place. This was a paternalistic society defined by reciprocal, caring, and intentional relationships between men and women, slaves and masters, rich and poor. Freed of early 20th-century racism and sexism, a different sort of paternalistic interpretation of the Old South has been advanced by historians Eugene D. Genovese and Elizabeth Fox-Genovese. In a series of landmark publications, they argued that the region was defined by paternalism and reciprocity, resulting in an "organic," although far from harmonious, society. In their paternalistic South, masters were not kindly father figures who cared for their dependents; instead, they emphasized the implications of mutually binding expectations and obligations. Men and women carved out their own class- and race-dependent cultures within the dominant culture because paternalism accorded even the most disadvantaged people a certain amount of independence and power. As Genovese concluded in his 1974 classic, *Roll, Jordan, Roll*, "Paternalism's insistence upon mutual obligations—duties, responsibilities, and ultimately even rights—implicitly recognized the slaves' humanity." Slaves, in short, sustained their culture because paternalism forced masters to acknowledge that they were people. Yet the limited obligations that masters acknowledged, and that allowed slaves to express their humanity, also undermined slaves' solidarity and potential for more radical resistance.

Within that paradigm, then, poor white men and women drew on the paternalistic language of gender-specific obligations and rights to make their own place. The privileges of "manly independence" allowed even the poorest men to vote, own property, and exert legal and physical power over women, children, and slaves in exchange for—at least theoretically—protection and material well-being. But masculine rights and power also were tempered by men's obligation to treat "inferiors" with compassion, even indulgence. Particularly for the gentry, these expectations were laid out in the strictures of honor, an ethic that infused the reciprocal relationships of paternalism with ideals of masculinity and femininity. Feminine rights and duties similarly guided the behavior of white women. They forged a certain solidarity, although tempered greatly by class divisions, which allowed them to demand protection from certain abuses because it was "due" to them. In the paternalist paradigm, then, expectations of masculinity and femininity helped determine what "reciprocity" meant and how those relational ideals were translated into behavior.

Many historians conclude that whatever paternalistic notions existed in the Old South were wiped away by the Civil War and emancipation. But others have used the notion of paternalism effectively to examine and understand class and gender relationships in the late 19th and early 20th centuries. Studies using paternalism as a framework for southern history after the Civil War confront more explicitly (than histories of slavery) the question of elite manipulation. Was paternalism simply an idealistic cover for social control and upperclass manipulation of working-class men and women? Did paternalism simply undermine the potential solidarity and activism of those less powerful? Or was there truth to the idea that elites felt even some obligation to protect and nurture their employees? Much of this work has focused on southern mills and mill towns, sometimes portrayed as imperfect re-creations of the antebellum plantations. Much like Phillips's history of slavery, and at about the same time, Broadus Mitchell described white mill communities as big, extended families. Owners were benevolent father figures, and their employees were grateful for the material protection and uplifting care they provided. More critical, not surprisingly, was W. J. Cash, who decried the end result of mill paternalism: depressed and dependent men and women with no future, mired in poverty and ignorance.

Modern studies of postwar mills and mill towns revived paternalism as an analytical concept but reached conclusions much more subtle and complicated than earlier stereotypes of docile workers or benevolent owners. To the contrary, historians argued that workers and owners engaged in nearly constant tension, negotiation, and conflict. Wealthy owners did not treat workers like part of the family; workers expressed considerable solidarity, although tempered by gender and particularly racial divisions. Within the paternalistic model, many studies also find workers' ability to resist management undermined by persistent deference. More complicated was Douglass Flamming's *Creating a Modern South*, in which he argued that mill paternalism developed out of postwar conditions—rather than from a resurgence of antebellum ideals. Owners pledged to provide workers with real benefits; workers developed a culture of mutuality in the mill towns and then used it as the basis for labor activism in the 1930s. Finally, the groundbreaking study *Like a Family*, by Jacquelyn Dowd Hall and her associates, used oral history to trace life in southern cotton mills. They uncovered a world in which men and women forged relationships with each other (that made them "like a family") and with corporate leadership that was more complicated than one-dimensional models of paternalism suggested. Written from the perspective of mill workers, it demonstrated how men and women often recalled their experiences differently, although still within the framework of the paternalistic model espoused by mill owners. It reveals, in short, the relationship between paternalism and gender.

Paternalism continues to drive new work in southern history, with gender increasingly central to studies that examine class-based relationships. In the collection *Paternalism in a Southern City*, for instance, LeeAnn Whites considers the gender-based activism of white male mill workers who joined the Knights of Labor, as well as the "maternalistic" care offered to workers by owners' wives and daughters. That feminine sense of elite obligation, in turn, translated differently when directed toward male workers or toward female workers. Paternalistic reciprocity, in short, was clearly gender-dependent. These sorts of creative applications have breathed new life into the old reliable concept, and the examination of gender within paternalistic class relationships offers historians of the South still more new avenues of investigation.

CHRISTOPHER J. OLSEN
Indiana State University

Edward J. Cashin and Glenn T. Eskew, eds., *Paternalism in a Southern City* (2001); Douglass Flamming, *Creating a Modern South: Millhands and Managers in Dalton, Georgia, 1884–1984* (1992); Elizabeth Fox-Genovese, *Within the Plantation Household: Black and White Women of the Old South* (1988); Eugene D. Genovese, *Roll, Jordan, Roll: The World the Slaves Made* (1976); Jacquelyn Dowd Hall, *Like a Family: The Making of a Southern Cotton Mill World* (2000); U. B. Phillips, *Life and Labor in the Old South* (1929).

Photography

As Abigail Solomon-Godeau has argued, the relation of gender and photography should be considered in at least three ways: the gender of the photographer, the construction of gender within photographs, and the response of gendered spectators. In the South (as elsewhere), these considerations must be further complicated by cultural configurations of race, class, and geography, with particular histories of urban, rural, mountain, tidewater, and cross-cultural southern places. Invented in 1839, photography came to prominence at the same time as did the political entity known as "the South," and photography and the South have continued to shape each other over the course of their respective histories. Gender has been both a factor in and a product of this mutual shaping.

At first, as a new technology, photography was not considered an inherently masculine or feminine practice: as a result, women and men could make photographs as amateurs, or even professionally, with relatively few strictures. The first professional photographer in the South appears to have been Jules Lion, a free man of color who learned the art in France and set up a studio in New Orleans in 1840. His daguerreotypes were widely praised for their artistic and documentary merit. Frances Osborn Robb's research shows that even in a frontier state like Alabama, there were well over a hundred working photographers by 1861. As with all public (nondomestic) employments, the vast majority of photographers in the South were men.

However, untold numbers of women worked alongside these male photographers. Over time, as technology—and competition—proliferated, gender ideology influenced the assignment of proper tasks in photographic studios. Appropriate roles for women included posing female clients, darkroom work, and (because of their delicate hands and "eye for beauty") retouching and hand coloring images. Roles for white men included owning studios, directing studio and darkroom work, and hosting public showings. Economic necessity, racial segregation, and sheer artistic ambition sometimes challenged these gender divisions. Wives often assisted their husbands in running studios, taking over the business when the husband was unable to continue. Frances Benjamin Johnston, daughter of white Washington, D.C., gentry, opened her own photography studio in the 1890s and became one of the most prominent photographers in the nation, with commissions at the White House, on Admiral Dewey's flagship, and at the Hampton Institute. Ironically, the rise of Jim Crow segregation may have resulted in more economic opportunity for African American photographers, male and female, by creating a customer base that was not allowed to patronize white studios. For example, in 1922, Elise Forrest Harleston opened a successful photography studio in conjunction with her painter-husband, Edwin Harleston, to serve the portraiture needs of the black professional class in Charleston, S.C.

Questions of the effect of gender on the content of photographs (for example, is there such thing as a "woman's eye" or an inherently male gaze?) are inevitably challenged by what John Berger has called the fatally weak intentionality of photographs themselves. That is, although photographs reflect the desired framing of their makers, they also reflect accidents and ambiguities of content and context that open them to multiple readings. Although her status as a white woman almost certainly affected the type of photographs Eudora Welty was able to make as she traveled Mississippi working as a junior publicity agent in the Works Progress Administration in the 1930s, it is nearly impossible to establish only by looking at these photographs that they were made by a woman. Arguably, the documentary photographs made by Margaret Bourke-White for *You Have Seen Their Faces* (1937) are "harsher" and more exploitative than the quieter, more delicate compositions Walker Evans published in *Let Us Now Praise Famous Men* (1941). Laura Wexler has argued that gender conventions (Frances Benjamin Johnston's status as a "lady photographer," for example) enabled white women photographers (intentionally or not) to photograph imperial and racial domination with "innocent eyes," thus insidiously reinforcing dominant power relations. As Wexler's analysis demonstrates, questions of the gendered eye of the photographer most often come down to gendered readings by spectators. Knowing a photograph was made by a woman, or a man, adds layers of meaning to whatever the content in a photograph, because we as spectators have cultural expectations of what it means to see as a woman or a man. (Novelist David Madden has made a similar point about southernness in photographs: "Know a photograph is from the South, and meaning comes rushing in.")

One thing is certain: photography has played a crucial role in the construction of gender. Strongly associated with "the real" (William Henry Fox Talbot dubbed it "the pencil of nature"), photography has been used as evidence to assert that cultural notions of male and female are natural and essential. In the South, the gendering function of photography is inextricably bound to racial hierarchies. This mutually reinforcing dynamic is most obvious in pseudoscientific portraits made in support of the American School anthropological movement in the mid-19th century and the eugenics movement that lasted from the later 19th century until well past Hitler's disastrous "experiments." Seeking to prove the separate genesis of blacks and whites, Harvard anthropologist Louis Agassiz in 1850 commissioned J. T. Zealy to make a series of daguerreotypes

Famous photograph of Allie Mae Burroughs, by Walker Evans, published in Let Us
Now Praise Famous Men, taken in 1935 or 1936 (Library of Congress
[LC-USF342-T01-008139-A], Washington, D.C.)

of disrobed South Carolina plantation slaves. Such straightforward "scientific" portraits (part of a larger scientific project to justify colonial domination) were meant to demonstrate the inherent, inherited inferiority of their subjects. In the honor/shame culture of the antebellum South, the mere existence of such portraits would prove that those pictured were "Other," dishonored and dishonorable, and thus unworthy of proper gendered treatment as gentlemen or ladies. Paradoxically, the slaves are rendered both as visibly sexual objects in the daguerreotypes and as "unsexed" objects robbed of any conventional gender privileges. The supposedly neutral eye of the camera works to demonstrate that their racial and gender degradation is "natural."

Eugenicists similarly used photographs to demonstrate the need for careful racial breeding by invoking and essentializing gender norms and abnormalities. The case of Carrie Buck, a young white woman who was forcibly sterilized by the state of Virginia after she was raped and declared a "defective person," was heard by the U.S. Supreme Court in 1927. Photographs of the impoverished Buck, her mother, and her infant daughter influenced the majority to decide against Buck, with Chief Justice Oliver Wendell Holmes declaring, "Three generations of imbeciles is enough." Arguing for Virginia was noted eugenicist Arthur Estabrook, whose 1926 treatise, *Virginia Mongrels*, also used photographs to illustrate that "deficient" gender, race, and class characteristics of poor white and "mixed-blood" southerners were evidence of bad genetic stock.

Photography's greatest power for constructing and reinforcing gender roles, however, was in the everyday world of personal and popular culture images. Southerners of all races and classes sought out photographs as vehicles for memory and self-representation, first in the face of the very real possibility of early death, as in portraits of pregnant women facing the dangers of childbirth mortality or Civil War soldiers before heading off to battle. These photographs emphasized conventional gender attributes of southern womanhood (delicacy, beauty, feminism, strength, and dignity) and manhood (bravery, gallantry, honor, and stoicism). Although stereotypical images often denied these qualities to African Americans, black southern community photographers reasserted them in their commissioned works (South Carolinian Richard Samuel Roberts often retouched negatives to put a powerful gleam in the eye of a black patriarch, for example). The ability to commission such photographs, depicting middle-class gender and aesthetic conventions, was itself a sign of belonging—of being a citizen with a respectable, recognizable place in society. As technology advanced, cheaper and simpler cameras were affordable to more southerners. Family snapshots and photo albums became ubiquitous, home galleries of personal and familial identity. African American cultural critic bell hooks has explored the gender dynamics of these galleries: although her father was the family "picture-takin' man," her grandmother was keeper of the wall of photographs in the family home, thus asserting her own narrative of family identity. Regardless of who took the picture, family photographs were an important technology for *representing* desired gender and family relations, whether or not the family was able to practice them in reality.

As several photo historians have argued, family photography practice is crucially bound up with broader cultural representations, particularly in popular culture. Photography and film have been the chief conveyers of stereotypical southern gender roles, ranging from southern belles and mammies to Bubbas and "black beast rapists," to regional, national, and international audiences. Popular, art, and journalism photographs have supplied the "real life" imagery to make cultural images of southern woman and man visible and concrete. Southern women writers such as Rosemary Daniell, Robb Foreman Dew, and Jill McCorkle have described how hard southern white women worked to live up to the cultural images of the southern belle they saw in photographs. Popular postcards depicting African Americans and poor whites at the turn of the 20th century largely portrayed stereotypically southern scenes, such as watermelon eating and cotton or banjo picking; the sale, distribution, and appreciation of these images were by no means confined to the South. Nude or pornographic images of black women were common in Europe, but in the United States southern black women were more likely to be depicted at work as maids, servers, farmworkers, or washerwomen. Especially after Reconstruction, American popular imagery traded in the stereotypes that supported the reemergence of white southern power. With his controversial exhibit and book of early 20th-century lynching postcards and photographs, *Without Sanctuary* (2000), Atlanta collector James Allen focuses on the actual sexual and racial violence that undergirds such symbolic violence. One set of prints found in the attic of a prominent white Savannah, Ga., family, are mass-produced lynching souvenirs that evince the direct links between racial and gender terror that Grace Hale has discussed in *Making Whiteness*. On the back of one print is written, "Warning, The answer of the Anglo-Saxon race to black brutes who would attack the womanhood of the South." Thumbtack holes in the tops of some of the photographs indicate that they were displayed: others were incorporated into scrapbooks and family albums. Like Hale, Dora Apel, Shawn Michelle Smith, and Amy Louise Wood have argued that lynching photographs were important tools not only for putting a degraded black masculinity "in its place" but also for asserting and cementing a communal white southern masculine power. Bell hooks has described her grandmother's walls of family photographs as "essential to the process of decolonization" from such images. Certainly, Ernest Withers's famous photograph of Memphis sanitation workers on strike wearing signs asserting "I AM A MAN" constitutes a powerful response to visual as well as other forms of race and gender denigration.

These various images that present southern gender roles within the context of race and class constitute a vast visual legacy that leads to expectations on the part of viewers of southern photographs. The visual legacies of southern gender have remained an important topic in art photography in and of the South. Drawing on the iconography and myth of white southern womanhood and the grotesque, Clarence John Laughlin created elaborate scenes and collages of southern gender construction and decay. Sally Mann's controversial work featuring her children joins Ralph Eugene Meatyard's surrealist *Lucybelle Crater* series as a rumination on the mythic structures and sexual dynamics of southern family and childhood. By contrast, there is nothing grotesque or even "southern" about David Najjab's photograph, *Hanan and Nora, Lexington, Kentucky*. Here it is the interplay of image and caption that evokes visual and historical legacies, to assert the rightful and integral place of excluded Others in the southern landscape and to visually rewrite the story of southern culture. Southern photographers Fay Fairbrother (Oklahoma), Lynn Marshall-Linnemeier (North Carolina), and Clarissa Sligh (Virginia) approach the visual legacies of race and gender in the South more directly in their *Quilt Shroud Series* (1991–92), *The Annotated Topsy Series* (1993), and *Waiting for Daddy* (1987), respectively, to cite only a few examples.

With their various approaches, all of these photographs represent purposeful interventions into southern and, by extension, American representational politics. Photohistorians Deborah Willis and Carla Williams have asserted that "photography is the perfect medium for revisiting and reintroducing the black female body, for tracing a history coded in images bound by fear and desire," the contradictory emotions that Franz Fanon argues "lie at the heart of the psychic reality of racism." One could argue further that the visual traditions of the southern gender—especially as they are embodied in photographs—are the great source of these "contradictory emotions" in American culture, for both black bodies and white. In few places is America's doubled vision—its dialectic between fear and desire, tradition and change—more evident than in the complex and contradictory role of photography in both constructing and deconstructing raced and classed ideologies of gender in the South.

KATHERINE HENNINGER
Louisiana State University

Dora Apel, *Imagery of Lynching: Black Men, White Women, and the Mob* (2004); John Berger and Jean Mohr, *Another Way of Telling* (1982); Katherine Henninger, *Ordering the Facade: Photography and Contemporary Southern Women's Writing* (2007); bell hooks, *Art on My Mind: Visual Politics* (1995); Jeanne Moutoussamy-Ashe, *Viewfinders: Black Women Photographers* (1986); Frances Osborn Robb, *The Daguerrean Annual* (2004); Shawn Michelle Smith, *American Archives: Gender, Race, and Class in Visual Culture* (1999); Abigail Solomon-Godeau, *Photography at the Dock* (1991); Patricia Vettel-Becker, *Shooting from the Hip: Photography, Masculinity, and Postwar America* (2005); Laura Wexler, *Tender Violence: Domestic Visions in the Age of U.S. Imperialism* (2000); Deborah Willis and Carla Williams, *The Black Female Body: A Photographic History* (2002).

Politics, Women in, 1700s to 1920

In examining the historical interplay of gender and politics in the South, it must be stated at the outset that a great deal of black and white women's political power was indirectly exercised. In the face of male-dominated political, legal, and economic systems, which largely kept women intimidated, dependent, and vulnerable, southern women developed highly nuanced political styles and strategies. To address systemic problems and abuses, southern women developed various guises and subterfuges to create levers of power for themselves. Because they were eventually successful in rectifying some of the worst inequities, strong suspicion of women's true political intentions and a knee-jerk antagonistic attitude toward feminists remain fundamental characteristics of gender politics in the South.

Some of this antagonism seems to begin in early southern U.S. history with the predatory treatment of Native American women in the region. In the 1700s and 1800s native women such as Nan-ye-hi (Nancy Ward), the Beloved Woman of the Cherokee, played critical roles in making war and peace and forging political and diplomatic bonds, often by bearing children with influential white men to create blood alliances they believed would be respected. Colonial operatives used dishonest and brutal methods to deny traditional claims and take power and land from native women and matrilineal clans, methods that fostered peculiarly aggressive, self-serving, and possessive forms of paternalism and patriarchal politics in the South. The forced removal of southern native people in the 1830s was an early manifestation of states' rights doctrine that became a principal means of denying civil rights to women and people of color.

In colonial and early America, southern white women could and did formally petition individual officeholders and governing bodies to influence laws and public policies. More commonly, these women used informal powers of persuasion to influence policy decisions and elections and joined in solidarity with men, lending material, social, and moral support to family members and civic and religious leaders. In the 1820s Frances Wright challenged this indirect and inequitable system in west Tennessee, where she established a commune based on egalitarian and abolitionist principles. Wright's critics demonized her as dangerously immoral, ensuring her failure. Close relationships between abolitionists and women's rights activists in the mid-1800s deepened distrust of feminist movements in the South. Angelina and Sarah Grimké of Charleston left the region in the 1850s to agitate for both causes and were severely denounced as traitors to their slaveholding homeland. The publication of Harriet Beecher Stowe's *Uncle Tom's Cabin* further validated chauvinistic beliefs that independent-minded women who sought to exercise direct political influence constituted a threat to the status quo in the South.

The Civil War magnified the importance of women's allegiances as women took on responsibilities ordinarily shouldered by men. The female-majority gender imbalance in the South continued in the postwar years as men migrated west. Large numbers of southern white and newly freed black women supported themselves, even as chivalrous expectations, defining man as provider and protector of woman, remained woven into the South's social and legal fabric. Women depended more on each other and on female networks for survival, and sisterhoods became potential sites of political power and influence.

Southern "ladies" became a force to be reckoned with after the Fifteenth Amendment enfranchised African American men and opened the way for vigorous discussions about women's needs for similar political rights as a means of self-protection. Movements for white women's rights in the South devolved into skirmishes bordering on gender warfare. In 1872–73, debates raged in Memphis newspapers over female teachers' demands to be paid on an equal basis with male teachers. "Equal pay for equal work" simply stated the women's expectation of fair compensation for their labor. Male school board members rejected the request and fired two female teachers in the movement, using the women's economic vulnerability to undermine their labor movement and feminist activism. The incident politicized Memphis women. Sisters-in-law Elizabeth Avery Meriwether and Lide Meriwether directed this collective feminist outrage toward issues of women's property rights, divorce laws, temperance, and woman suffrage. Even though the Supreme Court ruled in 1874 that citizenship alone did not give women the right to vote, Elizabeth attempted to cast a ballot in the 1876 presidential election. She also introduced woman suffrage planks at the 1880 Republican and Democratic national conventions. Both Meriwether women had leadership positions in the National American Woman Suffrage Association in the 1880s.

At the same time, southern women began exerting their collective moral authority as Judeo-Christian mothers and teachers, advancing onto the fields of child protection and public welfare. Branches of the Woman's Christian Temperance Union (WCTU) formed and passed local ordinances limiting the sale of alcohol near schools, and state prohibition laws rapidly followed. The Meriwethers were also national WCTU leaders and worked closely with Mississippi's Belle Kearney, a formidable WCTU activist. Kearney, who publicly supported the Prohibitionist Party, drew sharp criticism from her Democratic brothers for breaking with their political faith. She and Nellie Nugent Somerville, another Mississippi WCTU activist, became leaders in state and national woman suffrage organizations and were the first women elected to the Mississippi legislature after women received the right to vote. By merging child and home protection issues with divine sanction and Bible Belt fervor, southern women found a key to political power and proceeded to challenge a host of inequities, injustices, abuses, and failures rooted in white male–dominated power structures.

Black and white southern women also poured their energies into highly politicized farm and labor insurgency movements during the 1880s and 1890s, demanding that politicians and public institutions not exclusively serve the interests of the economic elite. Women were active in the Grange, Southern Farmers Alliance, Colored Farmers Alliance, and Knights of Labor. Many also belonged to the WCTU, which encouraged women to agitate for a wide range of reforms. In Mississippi, a white WCTU/Grange coalition successfully pressured legislators to establish state colleges for nonelite white men and women. Soon the female faculty of the new women's college publicly demanded "equal pay for equal work." When male legislators rejected this, a core group of feminists emerged led by an extraordinary college professor, Pauline Orr, who later became president of Mississippi's Equal Suffrage Association. Following Mississippi's lead, other southern states established public white women's colleges, and many of these colleges became seedbeds of women's political and feminist activity for generations to come.

In response to victories scored by biracial "fusion" Populist and Republican tickets in the South, Democrats in the 1890s unleashed violent white supremacist campaigns to destroy these political alliances. With this, the history of gender politics in the South took a defining turn as large numbers of women of color moved north and west seeking better treatment and greater economic opportunity. It is perhaps ironic that thousands of black women who left the

South gained the right to vote sooner than their white sisters in Dixie. Two black women from Memphis, Ida B. Wells and Mary Church Terrell, organized in the North to fight white supremacist methods (especially the lynching of black men) in the South, working primarily through the National Association of Colored Women's Clubs (NACWC). Wells and Terrell, a loyal Republican who served on the school board in Washington, D.C., from 1895 through 1906, were both founding members of the NAACP and strong advocates of woman suffrage. Networks of black female southern expatriates prepared the ground for the modern civil rights movement that rocked the nation and the world.

Thousands of African American women who remained in or migrated to the South became mainstays of black educational, religious, and charitable initiatives that served as training grounds and centers of political activity. Public coed normal and agricultural institutes, such as Hampton Institute in Virginia, private black colleges, such as Fisk University in Nashville and Tuskegee Institute in Alabama, and prep schools, such as Palmer Memorial Institute in Sedalia, N.C., established by Charlotte Hawkins Brown in 1902, produced numbers of courageous "race women" who encouraged racial pride in the face of racial prejudice. Working with northern philanthropists and national organizations, a growing network of homegrown southern black female leaders cultivated relationships with non–African American professionals and government officials to direct more resources toward the improvement of conditions for blacks in the South. The respectability of such "race women" as Jennie Dee Booth Moton, wife of Tuskegee president Robert Moton, made her eviction from a whites-only Pullman car in 1916 seem all the more egregious. These women served as critical links between African American activists in the North and southern white liberals, and many became conduits for interracial cooperation in the development of public policies in the South.

As southern white men dismantled political powers granted to black men during Reconstruction, white women in the region obtained greater political influence. Their demonstrated interest in child welfare issues opened paths to public office for southern white women. In 1882, Julia Doak was appointed state superintendent of education in Tennessee to fill briefly a portion of her deceased father's unexpired term. The position of superintendent of Shelby County (Tennessee) schools was almost exclusively a woman's job from 1886 through the 1950s. Tennessee's example inspired white women in other southern states to demand similar recognition from their politicians. North Carolina's governor, Charles Aycock, honored the deathbed request of Claude Denson, secretary of the State Board of Public Charities, in 1903 and appointed Denson's daughter to succeed him. In 1904, Daisy Denson influenced state legislators to grant appropriations and pensions requested by the United Daughters of the Confederacy. Over her next 14 years in office, she insisted that women be placed on county boards of public welfare and worked to improve conditions in poorhouses, asylums, jails, and chain gangs, contributing to North Carolina's reputation as a progressive southern state, even as Jim Crow laws expanded government-sanctioned racism.

As southern white women exerted greater influence on public policies, they also made enemies. Secular white women's clubs joined forces through the General Federation of Women's Clubs (GFWC) and lobbied for prison reforms and juvenile courts and improvements in public health, safety, and education. Just as they used protective school zone laws to promote temperance, women's organizations strategically used literacy and education movements, specifically compulsory education laws, to combat the use of child labor in New South industries. To circumvent state legislators, many women's organizations supported the establishment of federal anti–child labor regulations. Industrialists fought back by insisting that a father's claim to a child's wages trumped child protection issues, invoking paternal prerogatives to protect corporate profits. Conservatives were dead set against extending the civil right of suffrage to these southern white women and charged that child labor reformers and woman suffragists who supported federal initiatives were in truth anti–states' rights traitors to the South. This adversarial corporatists-versus-feminists dynamic became entrenched as women's organizations increasingly focused on the root causes of poverty, especially the exploitation of women, children, and industrial and agrarian workers.

Even though many southern politicians argued that the federal woman suffrage amendment infringed on the states' rights to establish voting requirements, resistance to votes for women weakened in the South as woman suffrage organizations took the lead in home front volunteer programs and fund-raising during World War I. In 1917, Arkansas legislators granted women the right to vote in primaries, and Texas followed suit in 1918. That year, Dr. Annie Webb Blanton was elected Texas's state superintendent of public instruction (she ran unsuccessfully for U.S. Congress as a Democrat in 1922). In 1919, Arkansas ratified the Nineteenth Amendment and Tennessee women secured the right to vote in presidential elections. That same year, Lillian Exum Clement, a lawyer in Asheville, N.C., made history when she ran for a seat in the state's lower house and defeated male Democratic opponents in the primary, even though North Carolina women did not yet have the right to vote. She was elected in 1920 with new women voters strongly behind her. In early 1920, as ratification battles raged, Charl Ormond Williams, Tennessee's superintendent of Shelby

County schools, was named the first female vice chair of the National Democratic Committee. Williams deftly wielded her political influence during the fight over the ratification of the Nineteenth Amendment in Nashville that summer, and, after one of the hardest-fought legislative battles in U.S. history, Tennessee's ratification victory made woman suffrage the law of the land.

By 1920, women in the region had shaped political agendas and public policy, served in government, and established paths to power through gender-based organizations and family connections. As southern women exercised their power to staff the governments and determine the laws under which they lived, much of their post-1920 political activism continued along lines established prior to the passage of the Nineteenth Amendment. But the gender antagonism and racism that marked southern politics seemed to strengthen preemptively in anticipation of white and black southern women's heightened influence. Overcoming this resistance would require sharp political skills and greater access to and influence within the machinery of political parties, challenges that inspired the rise of superpolitical southern women in subsequent generations.

SARAH WILKERSON FREEMAN
Arkansas State University

Elizabeth Brooks Higginbotham, *Righteous Discontent: The Women's Movement in the Black Baptist Church, 1880–1920* (1993); Cynthia Neverdon-Morton, *Afro-American Women of the South and the Advancement of the Race, 1895–1925* (1989); Elizabeth Sanders, *Roots of Reform: Farmers, Workers, and the American State, 1877–1917* (1999); Marjorie Spruill Wheeler, *New Women of the New South: The Leaders of the Woman Suffrage Movement in the Southern States* (1993); Sarah Wilkerson-Freeman, in *Southern Women at the Millennium: A Historical Perspective*, ed. Melissa Walker, Jeanette Dunn, and Joe Dunn (2003).

Politics, Women in, 1920 to Present

After the ratification of Nineteenth Amendment, in the summer of 1920, black and white southern women became mainstays in politics as voters, campaigners, candidates, and policy makers. Their addition to the political process influenced the directions of the two major parties and played a critical part in determining the nation's future.

Except in Arkansas and Texas, where state laws enabled women to vote in the primaries, the first election in which most southern women could vote was the 1920 general election. To male-dominated election machines, generally engineered to produce Democratic victories in the South, newly enfranchised female voters represented an element of uncertainty. Anti–woman suffrage

Democratic candidates who were victorious in the primaries faced women with ballots in their hands in the fall. Fears of this unknown and untamed political force inspired Mississippi and Georgia legislators to use poll tax registration requirements to bar women from voting in 1920. Republicans, for their part, saw an unprecedented opportunity and worked to gain a foothold in the region by wooing the support of Dixie's new white female voters.

So began a fascinating moment in U.S. political history as the two major parties styled themselves to attract southern white women. The Republican Party pointed to its support of Prohibition and woman suffrage. Southern Democrats emphasized Wilson's vision of international peace while conjuring up images of "Negro domination" under Republican rule. To neutralize this tactic, some leading southern Republicans, such as North Carolina gubernatorial candidate Judge John Parker, deployed white supremacist rhetoric and denounced black male political participation. Southern black women learned that neither party would court their support nor protect their right to vote.

In this moment of uncertainty, white female candidates, who suggested that women might make a difference in government and public policy, stepped onto battlefields of southern politics. After her landslide victory in 1920, North Carolina state representative Lillian Exum Clement succeeded in passing legislation to reduce election-day intimidation of voters, establish homes for unwed mothers, and aid abandoned wives. Tennessee Democratic state senator Anna Lee Worley, who served the remainder of her deceased husband's term (1921–23), sponsored a bill to allow women to hold any public office in Tennessee. In 1925, Wilmington, N.C., mayor Katherine Cowan, who also replaced her deceased husband, unsuccessfully campaigned on her record of depoliticizing the police force. Mississippi's leading temperance activist and woman suffragist, Belle Kearney, was defeated in her 1922 U.S. Senate race, but she and fellow woman suffragist Nellie Nugent Somerville won seats the next year in the state Senate and House, respectively. In 1922, Georgia's governor appointed a formidable woman suffragist, Rebecca Latimer Felton, to the U.S. Senate seat vacated by the death of Tom Watson. Felton had led victorious fights for state prohibition and to end Georgia's convict lease system. She also notoriously promoted the lynching of black men. Felton was the first woman to serve in the U.S. Senate, but she was seated for only one day—signaling how little power Georgia's leading white men intended their women to have.

Soon after women began holding elective office in the South, it became evident that they neither necessarily represented a different agenda from their male predecessors nor ensured more honest government. Texas governor Miriam A. "Ma" Ferguson, wife of impeached former governor James Ferguson (who left office in 1917 because of charges of bribery and embezzlement), also faced allegations of corruption in her two administrations (1925–27, 1933–35).

In addition, rivalries among female candidates and factions revealed important divisions among women. After attorney Julia Alexander won a seat in the North Carolina House in 1925, she sought legislation to prohibit the teaching of evolution in public schools. Another attorney, Carrie MacLean, defender of free speech and big sister of Governor Angus MacLean, defeated Alexander in the 1927 Democratic primary and was elected. The feud pitted white female fundamentalist Christians against their more liberal sisters and exposed deep divisions over religious issues within the ranks of politically minded southern white women. A year later, protemperance, anti-immigrant, and anti-Catholic bigotry devastated the campaign of the Democratic presidential nominee, New York governor Al Smith. In the South, white "Hoovercrat" leaders of the WCTU bolted the Democratic Party and helped deliver much of the South to the Republican nominee, Herbert Hoover. The 1928 campaign drove a wedge between southern white women's organizations that had previously worked together for improvements in education, maternal and infant health care programs, and anti–child labor reforms.

Shut out of direct access to political power, African American women in the South increasingly sought to influence public policies through church, charitable, and civic organizations, such as the Commission on Interracial Cooperation (CIC), established in 1919 and headquartered in Atlanta. In CIC chapters, black and white women formed uneasy alliances dedicated to minimizing race-based violence, implicitly challenging the Ku Klux Klan. In the 1920s and 1930s, CIC women spotlighted the injustices of Jim Crow and the debilitating effects of racism. African American CIC leaders, such as North Carolina educator Charlotte Hawkins Brown and Atlanta's Lugenia Burns Hope, forged networks, established self-help initiatives, and prepared the way for civil rights activists.

As President Hoover demonstrated that the Republican Party had little to offer African Americans, a point made clear by his nomination of Judge John Parker to the U.S. Supreme Court, black voters in the North shifted their support to the 1932 Democratic presidential candidate, Franklin Roosevelt. The Great Depression exacerbated existing problems of poverty and underfunded public services in the South. After Roosevelt's election, black and white women, who for years worked as volunteers in social service organizations and held positions in public welfare agencies in the South, were absorbed into federal New Deal initiatives. This provided a critical entry point for southern women into political administrations, as networks of black and white social workers delivered government services and resources to African Americans and poor and working-class whites. Roosevelt's appointment of Mary McLeod Bethune, National Council of Negro Women founder and president of Bethune-Cookman College in Florida, to direct the Office of Negro Affairs of the National Youth Administration further indicated that black citizens could benefit from Democratic victories. Eleanor Roosevelt was especially influenced by Bethune, who advised the administration on minority issues.

In the volatile political climate of the 1930s, southern white women continued to make progress in gaining political office. In 1931, Gertrude Dills McKee became the first woman elected to the North Carolina Senate, holding the position for three terms. Hattie Caraway of Arkansas became the first woman elected to the U.S. Senate in a 1931 special election to complete her deceased husband's term. Caraway was reelected for a full term in 1932 against the opposition of Arkansas's Democratic leaders and with the help of Louisiana senator Huey Long. After Long's assassination in 1935, his wife, Rose, won a 1936 special election to serve the remainder of his term but declined to run for a subsequent term. In 1937, when Alabama's senator Hugo Black accepted a seat on the U.S. Supreme Court, Governor Bibb Graves appointed his wife, Dixie, to fill the six-month vacancy. Unlike Long and Graves, Hattie Caraway had strong political ambitions and was reelected in 1938 with the support of women, labor, and the biracial Southern Tenant Farmers Union. She fought for the Tennessee Valley Authority and federal aid for public education and generally supported New Deal initiatives.

Also during the 1930s, a contingent of North Carolina's female Democratic operatives succeeded in changing party rules to give women greater power to shape the national party platform. National Education Association lobbyist Charl Ormond Williams of Tennessee, who had been the Democratic Party's first female vice chair in 1920 and who had played a critical role in Tennessee's ratification of the Nineteenth Amendment, succeeded in adding support for federal aid for public education to the party platform. Williams, who was also national president of the Business and Professional Women's Clubs (BPW) and a close friend of Eleanor Roosevelt, pressured the administration to reverse federal policies that discriminated against married working women. Under Williams's watch, the BPW endorsed the Equal Rights Amendment (ERA), making it easier for Senator Hattie Caraway to introduce the ERA on the Senate floor in 1943 as women entered new fields in answer to wartime needs. Two other southern women, Mississippi's Earline White and Dallas physician Dr. Minnie Maffett, succeeded Williams as BPW president. Maffett, who served from 1939 to 1944, used her influence to include women's health and procreative issues in high-level government deliberations of postwar policies.

In the 1940s, white and black southern women became bolder in their efforts to secure political influence. Southern chapters of the BPW, the American Association of University Women, the League of Women Voters, and other white women's groups challenged poll tax requirements claiming that these disproportionately suppressed white women's voting power. Their efforts bore fruit in Tennessee and Alabama in the early 1950s. Women activists in the NAACP and the Southern Regional Council (formerly the CIC) also became more vocal in their demands for voting rights, antilynching reforms, and abolition of the white primary. A formidable black leader in South Carolina's NAACP, Modjeska Simpkins, pressured state Works Progress Administration leaders to provide jobs for black teachers and professionals and spearheaded successful NAACP-sponsored lawsuits in the 1940s to equalize the salaries of the state's black and white teachers. Although she was a delegate to the national Republican Party in 1944, Simpkins worked to establish the Progressive Democratic Party, a black organization that challenged the party's Jim Crow policies. After the defection of anti–civil rights Dixiecrats from the 1948 Democratic National Convention, Simpkins supported Henry Wallace's National Progressive Party. In 1952 she fully distanced herself from the Republican Party when she announced her support for Democratic presidential candidate Adlai Stevenson. Simpkins also played a key part in the NAACP's legal challenges to segregation that culminated in the 1954 *Brown v. Board of Education* decision.

When boycotts and sit-ins swept the South, southern black women across generations were at the front lines. Older veterans of the struggle, such as Montgomery's Rosa Parks and Joanne Robinson, Little Rock's Daisy Bates, and NAACP organizer Ella Baker, became powerful role models and enablers of college student civil rights activists, such as Fisk University's Diane Nash and Albany State University's Bernice Johnson Reagon. Some older white women, such as Alabama's Virginia Durr, joined forces with black civil rights activists. In the 1960s, black Freedom Riders and other civil rights activists, notably Mississippi sharecropper Fannie Lou Hamer, endured brutal beatings at the hands of law enforcement officials acting under the direction of white citizens' councils. Hamer's bravery and perseverance earned her tremendous respect, which she used to help form the Mississippi Freedom Democratic Party, an alternative to the white-controlled state party. Elected vice chair of the new party, Hamer challenged Mississippi's all-white delegation at the 1964 Democratic convention, making it increasingly difficult for national party leaders to resist African American demands for political and civil rights.

The civil rights movement inspired the second wave of feminism in the 1960s, and battles against gender discrimination took on new life with the infusion of activists from the biracial National Organization of Women (largely made up of professional women) and young veterans of civil rights and anti–Vietnam War protests. With the implementation of the Voting Rights Acts and the ratification of the anti–poll tax amendment, the voting power of southern black and white women increased substantially, and more women across the racial spectrum sought elective office. In 1966, Houston's Barbara Jordan became the first African American elected to the Texas state senate since 1883. A Democrat, Jordan won her 1972 bid for a seat in the U.S. House and made history during the Watergate hearings with her inspiring statements about the awesome power and responsibility that resided in her hands. Jordan's exhilarating keynote speech at the 1976 Democratic National Convention vindicated the efforts of Simpkins and Hamer to transform the Democratic Party.

Jordan was joined in the House in 1973 by Louisiana's Lindy Boggs, wife of white Democratic House Majority Leader Hale Boggs, who won a special election to complete the term of her husband (presumed dead after his plane disappeared). Both women played critical roles in drafting and fighting for women's rights legislation against extremely conservative antifeminist opposition. Boggs's success in passing legislation to grant women equal access to credit regardless of sex was a milestone in women's history. Jordan, a lesbian, kept her sexual orientation a private matter in order to minimize the harmful effects of homophobia on her work. She cosponsored legislation to extend the ERA's state ratification deadline and, after serving three terms, declined to run in 1978. Boggs continued to win resounding victories even after her district was redrawn as a black-majority district in 1980. She ran unopposed in her last four campaigns. Her congressional career (1973–91) began in the turmoil of Watergate and ended just before the dawning of the Clinton years.

Such hot-button liberal issues as the ERA, abortion rights, and the gay rights movement greatly complicated the political careers of southern female candidates, whose Bible Belt constituents often resented challenges to white patriarchal control. Ironically, veneration of patriarchy enabled many southern white widows to hold political office, presumably as their husbands' surrogates. Tennessee's Marilyn Lloyd took a seat in the U.S. House in 1974 after Democratic Party leaders chose her as the candidate to replace her husband (who died in a plane crash after his victory in the primary). Lloyd's moderate-to-conservative views (and Nixon's unpopularity) helped her win in a Republican district. Once in office, she kept the relatively liberal Congresswomen's Caucus at arm's length. But during her tenure, from 1975 to 1995, Lloyd reversed her opposition to legalized abortion and became a strong advocate on women's health issues, especially the treatment of breast cancer victims.

As the southern wing of the Democratic Party slowly accepted black influence, and as the national Democratic Party increasingly supported the expansion of rights and protections of women, children, gays, and people of color, more conservative southern white Democrats migrated into the Republican camp, especially during the Reagan years. Some southern white Republican female candidates, such as Texas's Kay Bailey Hutchison, began political careers as doors opened for women in the early 1970s. Hutchison won her first seat in the Texas House in 1972, served three terms, and temporarily left politics after losing a run for the U.S. House in 1982. She sat out the Reagan years and in 1990 was elected Texas state treasurer, succeeding Democrat Ann Richards. Hutchison narrowly won a 1993 bid to complete the last two years of Lloyd Bentsen's U.S. Senate term, but she was soon indicted on charges of using the treasurer office's resources to get elected. In spite of damaging evidence (deemed inadmissible) and the questionable circumstances of her acquittal, Hutchison, a supporter of big oil and George W. Bush, was reelected in 1994, 2000, and 2006. As senior senator from Texas, Hutchison is a powerful figure in the Republican Party, but the fact that she is on record as supporting *Roe v. Wade* complicates the possibility of her election to higher office.

Republican North Carolina senator Elizabeth "Liddy" Dole began her political career as a Democrat in the Johnson administration. She remained in the Nixon White House, and Nixon rewarded her with an appointment to the Federal Trade Commission in 1973. In 1975 she married Republican senator Robert Dole of Kansas and became a Republican. She served as U.S. secretary of transportation in the Reagan administration and as U.S. secretary of labor under George H. W. Bush. After serving as president of the American Red Cross and working on her husband's failed presidential campaigns, Dole ran unsuccessfully for the Republican presidential nomination in 2000. She succeeded in her 2002 bid for the U.S. Senate seat vacated by ultraconservative North Carolina senator Jesse Helms, but lost in the 2008 election.

Louisiana and Arkansas continue to produce high-level female politicians. Democratic Louisiana senator Mary Landrieu, a relatively conservative Democrat from a powerful political family, narrowly defeated her Republican rivals in 1996 and 2002. She was also reelected in 2008 despite complications by hurricane-recovery issues and displacement of Orleans Parrish supporters. Arkansas Democratic senator Blanche Lincoln was only 38 years old when elected in 1998 (the youngest woman elected to the Senate), and she became Arkansas's senior senator in 2003. As a moderate centrist southern Democrat, she has soundly defeated her more conservative Republican opponents.

Arkansas was also the political training ground for New York senator Hillary

Rodham Clinton, who as first lady of Arkansas championed improvements in public education and health care for the racially diverse constituents of Governor William Jefferson Clinton. Her work as the nation's first lady (1992–2000) and her own 2008 campaign, as the first viable female contender for the Democratic presidential nomination, further illustrate the transformative influence of southern women on American politics.

SARAH WILKERSON FREEMAN
Arkansas State University

Donald G. Mathews and Jane Sherron De Hart, *Sex, Gender, and the Politics of ERA: A State and the Nation* (1990); Charles Payne, *I've Got the Light of Freedom: The Community Organizing Tradition in the Mississippi Freedom Struggle* (1995); Jo Ann Robinson and David J. Garrow, *Montgomery Bus Boycott and the Women Who Started It: The Memoir of Jo Ann Gibson Robinson* (1987); Marjorie Spruill Wheeler, *New Women of the New South: The Leaders of the Woman Suffrage Movement in the Southern States* (1993); Sarah Wilkerson-Freeman, in *Southern Women at the Millennium: A Historical Perspective*, ed. Melissa Walker, Jeanette Dunn, and Joe Dunn (2003), *Journal of Southern History* (May 2002), *Journal of Women's History* (Winter 2002).

Poverty

Poverty is a characteristic of the social order of places. Associated with the dynamics of class, race, and gender inequalities and global shifts in political and economic structures, poverty is more prevalent in the South than in any other region of the United States. Historically, southern women, especially southern minority women, have been more likely to live in poverty than other women in the United States. But the gender and racial dynamics of poverty are changing. Now, economically vibrant southern communities receive new settlements of transnational migrants, primarily young, foreign-born, Hispanic males, to fill high demands for low-wage jobs. Consequently, poverty in southern communities is characterized by well-established historical patterns of class, race, and gender inequality, as well as newly emerging trends associated with transnational labor migrations.

From the New Deal era, when President Franklin Roosevelt described the South as the nation's number one economic problem, to 1964, when President Lyndon B. Johnson declared his "unconditional" War on Poverty, images of poverty in the South, and its underlying structure, changed very little. Today, despite recent growth in poverty in the Midwest, southern states (with the exception of Virginia) continue to be ranked lower than the national average for household income and higher than the national average for the poverty rate and for the percentage of people never completing high school. Southern women are overrepresented in poverty statistics, especially women living in the eight states of the south-central region—Alabama, Arkansas, Kentucky, Louisiana, Mississippi, Oklahoma, Tennessee, and Texas. These states consistently rank in the bottom third for the percentage of women living below the poverty line. Women of color in the region—both African Americans and Latinas—are more likely to live in poverty than white women. In Mississippi and Louisiana, states hit hardest by Hurricane Katrina in 2005, women were already the poorest in the nation, the least likely to have access to health insurance, and the most likely to find themselves trapped in low-wage jobs, despite high rates of workforce participation.

Historically, southern poverty among blacks and whites was rooted in the legacy of plantation slavery and sharecropping—a rigid political and economic system that perpetuated landlessness and dependency. For generations, underinvestment in educational and occupational opportunities benefited elite landowners, who wanted to secure a supply of low-wage labor, especially in rural communities and small towns. Subsequently, members of the working poor included black sharecroppers working in Delta cotton fields and living in weathered tenant houses, white drivers hauling black day laborers in pickup trucks to work seasonal jobs on tobacco and vegetable farms, white farmers feeding hogs on hardscrabble land, white men with blackened faces streaming from Appalachian coal mines, white women sewing textiles and finding housing for their families in company-owned towns, and emaciated white women standing on front porches of shotgun shanties holding barefooted children. A few images of southern urban poverty included black domestic workers riding buses to work in affluent white neighborhoods and black male workers walking alongside city garbage trucks to collect trash or reporting to industrial plants to fill low-paying, dirty jobs making tires and furniture.

Those images have not completely disappeared, but they have changed in the postindustrial, post–civil rights, post–North American Free Trade Agreement (NAFTA) South. A disproportionate share of the region's poor continues to be black and female. Many of the region's low-skilled and low-wage employees now work in catfish farming and processing plants. In Sunflower County, Miss., where the infant mortality rate is the highest in the United States and the poverty rate is greater than 40 percent, the catfish industry generates more than $300 million a year for the area economy. Critics claim that the pattern of land ownership, economic investment, and labor relations in the catfish industry reproduces the structure of the plantation economy and perpetuates race, class,

Bud Fields and his family, at home in Hale County, Ala., taken in 1936 or 1937
(Walker Evans, photographer, Library of Congress [LC-USF342-8147-A], Washington, D.C.)

and gender inequality. Similar criticisms have been made about the gaming industry in Tunica, Miss., and in the Gulf Coast region. Mississippi governmental and business leaders raised expectations that the gaming industry would improve the local standard of living, but, in fact, black unemployment rates increased in those communities.

The region's nonworking poor includes elderly and disabled persons trapped in disadvantaged communities, while the working poor struggle with underemployment, low wages, and limited educational and occupational opportunities. But the face of southern poverty changed because of economic growth and prosperity, especially the dramatic growth that occurred in six "New South" states in the 1990s, a time described as "the longest postwar expansion" in American history. The region's economic growth relied heavily on low-skilled, low-wage, foreign workers—both documented and undocumented. Subsequently, the South, described in the first half of the 20th century as a "sending" region for national migration to industrializing American cities, became a "receiving locality" for transnational migration. Six of the seven states with the fastest-growing Hispanic population from 1990 to 2000 are located in the South. Significantly, these states also have the fastest growth rates for Hispanics living in poverty.

These changes in the South's ethnicity have gender implications. Phenomenal economic growth, globalization processes, and unprecedented immigration from Latin American countries, mostly from Mexico, dramatically changed southern communities. Because of the region's high demand for low wage employees, the surge of young, male immigrants to southern states predates NAFTA. In the late 1980s, several southeastern states increased usage of the federal H-2A visa program to permit the hiring of temporary agricultural workers from Mexico and Central American countries. Many of these workers began as laborers in vegetable fields, then moved into low-wage, dirty, and dangerous jobs in poultry and pork processing plants. Some worked in carpet factories or filled jobs in construction and landscaping, often as day laborers (*jornaleros*), and many Hispanics moved to Atlanta in response to the city's high demand for construction workers to prepare for the 1996 Summer Olympics. Since Hurricane Katrina, Latino workers have immigrated to New Orleans and the Mississippi Gulf Coast to meet demands for construction workers. Latino settlements that began with a new immigration of young, Spanish-speaking, foreign-born males—most often from Mexico—have grown with the immigration of wives and the births of children. The continuing phases of migration, and high birth rates, have transformed small towns, cities, and suburbs. Many southern communities now have a Spanish-speaking majority student population in elementary schools.

These new settlements of Hispanics in southern states differ in many ways from older established settlement communities in California, New York, New Jersey, and Illinois. First, the rate of growth of Hispanic settlements in six New South states—Arkansas, Alabama, Georgia, North Carolina, South Carolina, and Tennessee—now outpaces the national average. Also, despite high rates of workforce participation, the poverty rate for Hispanics in these six states has *increased* since 1990—to more than 25 percent—while the overall poverty rate in those states *declined* for the same period. The poverty rate for Latinos *declined* in traditional settlement states. The increasing poverty rates for Hispanics in southern states, in contrast to declining poverty rates for Hispanics in traditional settlement states, is attributed to several factors. First, a lack of existing community preparedness to receive Spanish-speaking people exists throughout this region, which has received no large foreign immigration since the end of the slave trade. Subsequently, immigrants find fewer opportunities to learn English and become bilingual because of a lack of support from an existing ethnic community. Second, the region's wage differential pays lower wages to foreign-born Hispanic workers than to white workers, black workers, or native-born Hispanics. Discrimination on the basis of national origin limits educational and occupational opportunities. Third, as a result of language barriers and discrimination, both documented and undocumented Latinos/Latinas have low rates of high school graduation. They also have low rates of participation in assistance programs that provide food stamps and health services and low rates of participation in employer-provided health care coverage. Last, evidence from Georgia suggests that the teen pregnancy rate for Latinas in the South is double the national Hispanic average.

Unlike most poor white and black southerners, the poor Latino is more likely to be young and male. This, too, is a southern phenomenon, because the ratio of males to females in southern states also differs from traditional settlement communities. In traditional settlement states, the Hispanic sex ratio is nearly equal and the poverty rate is lower. In the six New South states, however, there are 173 Latino men for every 100 women, and the poverty rate is higher. In some counties, such as Mecklenburg County, N.C., and Cherokee County, Ga., the ratio of men to women is two to one. This imbalance is a result of the early phases of transnational labor migration. The ratio of men to women is expected to become more balanced as men are joined by spouses. Meanwhile, the face of poverty among Latinos in the Nuevo South is likely to be male, in contrast with the face of southern poverty, which historically has been black and female.

WANDA RUSHING
University of Memphis

Dana Harman, *Christian Science Monitor*, 26 November 2003; Avis A. Jones-Deweever and Heidi Hartmann, in *There Is No Such Thing as a Natural Disaster: Race, Class, and Hurricane Katrina*, ed. Chester Hartman and Gregory D. Squires (2006); Clyde Woods, *Development Arrested: The Blues and Plantation Power in the Mississippi Delta* (1998).

Rape

Any analysis of rape in the South must lead to a discussion about race and class. Sexual violence was part of the complex system of social control that maintained the racial, gender, and class hierarchies that structured the southern social order. Commonly held beliefs about rape mapped the contours of southern society and provide a shorthand description of power relations in the South. From the colonial period into the 1960s, African American women received little protection from the legal system, thus allowing rape to be an effective weapon used to colonize black women's bodies. The law did not recognize the rape of a slave woman as a crime, except insofar as it represented damage to her master's property, and slave owners could rape their female property with impunity. Black women fared little better in the 20th century.

In the same period, the rape of white women, theoretically at least, represented an assault on the honor of her husband or father and thus represented a serious crime—unless, of course, she was a woman of little social standing or dubious reputation. Rape convictions were often difficult to obtain because of persistent doubts about women's veracity regarding sexual matters. Although the contours of the law shifted over the course of southern history and the ideological underpinnings of rape evolved as part of the development of racial segregation, these broad outlines of rape remained constant. Black women were vulnerable to sexual assault, especially at the hands of white men. White women were theoretically placed on a pedestal, on which their protection from sexual violation came to represent protection of white supremacy. For poor white women, protection was considerably less absolute.

From the outset of the development of race-based slavery in the American colonies, the sexual exploitation of slave women worked to entrench a labor system of perpetual and inherited servitude. Bolstered by European assumptions that African women were inherently more libidinous than white women, the rape of slave women served to demonstrate white power. Slave men had little ability to defend African women, and the children produced through rape increased the capital of owners, once the law had determined that children inherited their slave status through their mothers.

That the legal system offered slave women little in the way of protection from sexual assault, however, does not mean that African American women meekly submitted to violence. Despite the odds against them, black women resisted their attackers through ingenuity and violence. Some even killed white predators rather than submit. Other black women used their master's sexual interest as leverage, gaining privileges and resources for themselves and their children. In other cases, there is evidence that the sexual relationships between slave women and white men grew out of affection. The law did not always dictate individual actions, despite the coding of racial hierarchy in rape law. Criminal statutes regarding forcible rape in the antebellum period were race specific, singling out white women for protection from black men and implicitly assuming that white men could only be charged with rape for crimes against white women. Statutes determining punishment for convicted rapists were also race specific, calling for prison terms for white men and castration or the death penalty for slaves. Despite the racial elements of the law, not all slaves were convicted when accused of rape by white women. Slaves represented valuable property and often received competent legal counsel provided by their owners. Some slave men were executed, but others were pardoned or transported and their owners compensated by the state. Unlike the postbellum period, white southerners in the antebellum period were not consumed by the fear of black men's assaults of white women.

Once the defeated states of the former Confederacy rewrote their state constitutions to comply with the Fourteenth Amendment during Reconstruction, explicit racial distinctions in the criminal code were no longer permissible. Black women now were able to bring charges of rape against white men, and formal discrepancies in punishments were removed. Maintaining rape as a tool of racial control nonetheless continued during segregation, however, as whites determined how to apply the law in individual cases. The legal system continued to ignore black women's charges of sexual violation and allowed judges or jury members to continue to inflict differential punishments on convicted defenders depending on race. For example, in Virginia, during Reconstruction, racial disparities in punishment were removed from the criminal code, allowing convicted rapists of either race to be imprisoned for anywhere from 5 to 20 years or sentenced to death. In practice, 54 men were executed for rape or attempted rape between 1908 and 1954, but not one of them was white. Well into the 20th century, rape remained a crime in which black men faced considerable legal jeopardy or even lynching for being accused of a sexual crime by a white woman. They faced almost certain conviction, they were punished more severely than white men, and they were far more likely to pay for their alleged crime with their lives, either through execution after trial or through extralegal violence.

White men, however, faced few consequences for their abuse of black women. For men accused of sexual assault by women of their own race, the results were more ambiguous. Few historians have systematically examined these cases at the county level. Anecdotal evidence suggests, however, that jurors routinely were suspicious of women's claims of rape. Charges that the victim was promiscuous, of poor character, or from a poor or marginalized family frequently implied that she was likely to consent to any sexual overtures, and the requirements that victims corroborate their allegations of nonconsent with evidence of violence usually confirmed those assumptions. As long as men were not accused of raping family members or particularly prominent women of unblemished reputation, punishments, in the unlikely event of convictions, were usually minor.

The adjudication of rape cases in southern courtrooms, however, did not always reflect the rhetoric about rape in the post-Reconstruction South. Discussions of rape in the South have usually meant invoking denunciations of "black beast rapists" and until recently have only appeared in historical scholarship as part of discussions of lynching. After Reconstruction, many white southerners believed that emancipation caused freed slaves to revert to their former state of savagery. Separated from the civilizing institution of slavery, African American men had developed an uncontrollable sexual desire for white women and a willingness to use violence to satisfy that desire. In response, white southerners felt themselves justified in inflicting immediate and severe punishment in an effort to deter future rapists, including the public torture and mutilation of accused black men without the benefit of trial. Analyzing the pervasive and heated rhetoric about "beasts in human form" who desecrated pure white womanhood, historians have concluded that white southerners conflated black men's desires for the political, economic, and civil rights of white men—indeed for manhood—with a desire for white women. Lynching, justified by the alleged propensity of black men to rape white women, thus became a critical tool of racial control during Jim Crow, and white women, assumed to be pure and virginal, came to represent the entire edifice of white supremacy. The convergence of racial and sexual violence became one important means by which historians analyzed racial terror in the South and African Americans' lack of basic rights. Although the rhetoric of black men's propensity to rape white women appeared frequently in cases of lynching, most extralegal violence against blacks did not involve charges of rape. The insistence that white southerners had a right and a duty to protect white women from black men, however, proved difficult for nonsoutherners to counter. It also placed considerable power in the hands of white women, who could falsely accuse black men to serve their own or their family's interests. Some white women, though certainly not all who made allegations of rape, seized this opportunity.

The myth of the black beast rapist, or what W. J. Cash termed the "rape complex," served as a tool to enforce white supremacy, but the fear of rape by black men on the part of white women also reified white men's patriarchal control over white women. White men's rhetorical promises of protection came only in return for white women's promise of obedience and adherence to the dictates of middle-class respectability. White men theoretically offered the cloak of chivalry to any woman with white skin, but protection, or, more accurately, retribution in response to charges of rape against a black man, in reality was not guaranteed. Women who failed to behave according to the mandates of ladyhood, or whose families did not abide by accepted standards of white behavior, might find their charges of rape treated with suspicion. Occasionally, juries acquitted the men such women accused. More often, although their accused assailant was convicted, he received a less severe punishment or was released early through a conditional pardon. Such actions placed qualifications on a white woman's claim to protection and served as a warning to other white women to uphold the values associated with pure white womanhood.

By the mid-20th century, many African Americans recognized that the prosecution of rape cases was part of the fight for civil rights. Notorious cases of allegations of rape, such as the Scottsboro case in 1931 and the Martinsville Seven case in 1951, became one vehicle through which civil rights organizations began to insist on legal protections for black men accused of rape. By the 1950s, in Virginia, civil rights lawyers not only defended black men who were accused of rape by white women but also represented black women who brought charges of rape against white men. Black women still faced an uphill struggle in holding white men to account for their sexual crimes, but white men increasingly faced trial and, occasionally, conviction, for their assaults of black women. At the same time, white women's charges against black men faced increasing scrutiny in the legal system. Despite the gains made by the civil rights movement in protecting the rights of black victims and accused assailants—and despite the gains made by the women's movement in demanding more reasonable standards of evidence at trial—race continues to matter in cases of rape. Many Americans continue to envision rapists as black men, and black women still face insinuations of promiscuity more than other groups of women. Nevertheless, lynching for charges of rape has virtually ended, and all women, white or black, have the possibility of a fair hearing in court.

LISA LINDQUIST DORR
University of Alabama

Peter Bardaglio, *Reconstructing the Household: Families, Sex, and the Law in the Nineteenth-Century South* (1995); Fitzhugh Brundage, *Lynching in the New South* (1993); Daniel Carter, *Scottsboro: A Tragedy of the American South* (1969); Lisa Lindquist Dorr, *White Women, Rape, and the Power of Race in Virginia, 1900–1960* (2004); Jacquelyn Dowd Hall, *Revolt against Chivalry: Jessie Daniel Ames and the Women's Campaign against Lynching* (1993); Eric W. Rise, *The Martinsville Seven: Race, Rape, and Capital Punishment* (1995); Diane Miller Sommerville, *Rape and Race in the Nineteenth-Century South* (2004).

Religious Organizations

Nineteenth-century religious organizations in the South followed a gender line that was almost as rigid as the color line. Women and men worshipped together in the same sanctuary in southern churches and synagogues, but their roles within these institutions were quite different and were confined mainly to male and female groups until well into the 20th century. In part this stemmed from the region's conservative traditions regarding the woman's place in the home, with its strong patriarchal family structure and system of paternalism. Women's roles expanded in the 19th and 20th centuries, resulting in gender accommodations in religious institutions across the South.

Independent female religious organizations in the antebellum South consisted mainly of Roman Catholic women organized into sisterhoods. In cities such as New Orleans, Galveston, San Antonio, Louisville, and Baltimore, the Ursuline Sisters dominated the educational sphere, creating schools for girls of Catholic families. The Ursuline Sisters came to New Orleans in 1727, where they established the first Ursuline Academy, today the oldest girls' school in the nation. The Ursulines also journeyed to Galveston in 1847, to San Antonio in 1851, and to Louisville in 1858. Usually within a year of arrival, the Sisters established an academy, which in most cities became the first academic institution for girls.

Other religious orders sent Sisters to many states across the South, including Sisters of Mercy to Alabama, Arkansas, Kentucky, Mississippi, South Carolina, and Texas. The Sisters of Charity of the Incarnate Word and the Sisters of St. Dominic went to Texas. Benedictine Sisters found their way to Arkansas, and Franciscan Sisters and the Sisters of Charity settled in Kentucky. By 1913 some 37 different Catholic sisterhoods and 70 convents existed in the South.

In 1828 the Oblate Sisters of Providence established the first African American Catholic sisterhood in the United States. The Sisters of the Holy Family, founded in New Orleans in 1842, established schools for free black children in various southern cities. Although Sisters were intent on teaching slaves and bringing free black and white children together in schools, some states forbade slave instruction, and hostile lay patrons objected to integration. In the postbellum era, Sisters of the Holy Ghost opened schools for African American children in Texas, Louisiana, and Mississippi. Women religious created universities, hospitals, schools, and orphanages, and they cared for the indigent in their communities. In an underinstitutionalized era in the South, Catholic Sisters not only offered missions to the poor and the dispossessed, but they also contributed important community services.

Among Protestants, women were the unacknowledged "mainstays of the churches," according to Suzanne Lebsock. In cities like Petersburg, Va., and Natchez, Miss., they worked in missionary societies and Sunday schools as early as 1817. By 1821, just after the nation's first economic "panic," women founded church benevolent societies to care for the needs of the poor. Before and after the Civil War, women made up two-thirds of the membership of southern Protestant churches, and most found both limits and opportunities for active organizing within them. Women were not able to vote, to hold governmental office, or to become ordained ministers. Men in black and white churches assumed visible leadership roles through the clergy, through voting, and by filling church governing boards as deacons (Baptist), stewards (Methodist), elders (Presbyterian), or vestrymen (Episcopal).

Women, mainly in urban areas, established their own societies, sodalities, prayer groups, missionary circles, altar guilds, and Sunday school classes. Among the first women's organizations in churches to emerge in the postbellum South were ladies' aid societies, which took up multiple tasks for their congregations, including founding mission churches, decorating and maintaining sanctuary and church interiors, and raising money for repairs. Women considered material culture as part of their domain and often introduced feminine artistic themes into church settings, choosing and donating stained glass windows, making cross-stitched kneeling pillows, and sewing altar cloths, wall hangings, and vestments for the clergy. They raised money for additional structures — for children's and adult Sunday schools, parlors, nurseries, libraries, choir rooms, offices, parsonages, meeting rooms, day care centers, and kitchens. They required parlors in which to meet and welcome visitors and kitchens to prepare banquets or church suppers. They brought aspects of their domestic lives to the church, thus transforming simple freestanding sanctuaries into complexes more welcoming to families and children. They created a women's world within an institution governed by men. The domestication of churches began under the direction of women's aid societies in the late 19th century, but today structural and interior changes continue, especially in large churches that include less gendered projects such as landscaping, sports facilities, gymnasiums, relief centers, and playgrounds.

As Protestant women extended their activism around the turn of the century, the male laity shifted to accept them, as well as children and families. Church programs reflected the change, giving laywomen opportunities for leadership within the realm of woman's perceived separate sphere. Although churchmen usually held supervisory positions in Sunday school administration, laywomen taught Sunday school classes and changed drab classrooms into colorful arenas with inviting Bible stories for children. Over time, some women created independent Bible study classes that developed a firm following. Southern congregations honored such women teachers by naming classes for them and by permitting the class a certain amount of autonomy. This affirmation of women's leadership changed them as well, exposing their moral authority and leading to public recognition.

Often Sunday school classes preceded the founding of mission churches in towns across the South. Sunday schools opened by women and funded by the church ladies' aid societies attracted unchurched children, youths, and adults. Only later did ministers follow and offer worship services, inviting the congregants to form a mission church. Thus women were instrumental in spearheading new churches. Toward the turn of the century, concern over the future of the younger generations increased, and church leaders responded with programs for adolescents. Every Protestant denomination of both races created youth programs or adopted nondenominational youth groups, among them Sunbeam Missionary Society, Baptist Young Peoples' Union, Methodist Epworth League, Juvenile Missionary Society, Young People's Society of Christian Endeavor, Luther League, Daughters of the King, and Daughters of Erin. Here women found another area for the expression of their leadership and teaching abilities, while men assumed supervisory roles.

In the postbellum years, the incidence of poverty was more visible in urban areas and was often the result of low industrial wages and discriminatory racial practices that kept many among the working poor. In a number of cases, church ladies' aid societies also functioned as female benevolent societies or as proto-welfare organizations. This was also true of Jewish synagogues, where women founded Ladies Hebrew Benevolent Societies or Ladies Auxiliary Societies, providing aid to indigent Jewish families, especially women. The members of these various societies helped the poor from a sense of religious conviction stemming from Old and New Testament readings that made helping the needy part of God's work. Most thought that aiding the poor was also decidedly a function of woman's nurturing role. Since women were considered "naturally" more tenderhearted, more caring, and more concerned with the well-being of dependents, they were better suited to serve those in poverty, especially widows and single women with children. The notion of woman's moral superiority complemented 19th-century concepts of ennobled womanhood, which both men and women believed, wrote about, and acted upon.

Benevolent societies functioned as sex-segregated entities within churches and synagogues, allowing laywomen the benefit of endorsement by clergy and male governing boards, but without intense oversight. Laywomen involved in benevolence usually met once a week; they raised money for their work by accepting donations (sometimes in the form of income-producing property), sewing garments, or making fancy work and food to sell at church bazaars and teas. Those who came to them as supplicants were sometimes judged by their need and their "worthiness," that is, whether they refrained from drugs and alcohol or illicit activities such as prostitution. The needy included stranded travelers, disabled working-class men and women, abandoned or sick women with children, widows without support, and unemployed working girls. In one New South city, over 80 percent of those aided were women. Religious female benevolent societies in the South served as safety nets for poor women and for the city's dependents in an era before government welfare. These societies prevailed until the 1920s when southern poverty reached such proportion in cities that municipal organizations such as the United Charities and Community Chest co-opted the role played by women's charitable organizations.

Providing aid for the poor in urban areas of the South was one way that women could step outside of their domestic boundaries. Support among women for home missions work through their denominations allowed them contact with the urban poor and an understanding of the ills of the industrial age. Their mission, although not usually considered part of the northern turn-of-the-century social gospel movement, indeed mirrored the work of northern Christian reformers. Methodist and Episcopal women in particular supported kindergartens, Wesley (settlement) houses, improved public education, and homes for "fallen" women. They voiced a critique of the social order when they joined movements to end child labor and the convict lease system, to improve the prison system, especially for delinquent youths, to improve race relations, to protect working women, and to legislate prohibition. The impulse to make the world more in tune with visions of God's kingdom spurred reforming Christian women toward religiously inspired activism. As Episcopalian Jean Scrimgeour Morgan of Texas noted, "Christian Social Service is the Church at work; it is Christ in action through us." In response to the needs of the urban South, in 1882 Southern Methodist Laura Askew Haygood established Trinity Home Mission in Atlanta to train women for outreach to the poor. Soon after 1900 both Methodists and Episcopalians approved the position of female deaconesses to further the work of home missions and as an extension of the social gospel.

Other means for worldly involvement developed when women became missionaries, created missionary unions for their support, and established theological seminaries to train women for the mission field. Members of the Southern Baptist Convention formed the Woman's Missionary Union (WMU) in 1888 with the express purpose of raising funds for foreign missions and disseminating information about missionaries' needs and activities. Thus the WMU offered to local churchwomen not only sisterhood but also a direct connection to a region-wide funding organization at a time when most Baptist churches gave no support to missions. The WMU, founded by Annie Armstrong and made up of laywomen, became the denomination's most effective fund-raising organization, revitalizing both foreign and home missions, creating such universally adopted methods as the tithing envelope (which originated in women's missionary societies), and raising $250,000 for missions in 1910. They were spurred on in their endeavors by such notable missionaries as Charlotte "Lottie" Moon, whose work in China began in 1872 and continued for 39 years. Through her influence, the Southern Baptist Theological Seminary admitted women for training in mission fields, thus opening to them avenues for further ministry. Women members of the Methodist Episcopal Church, South, formed the Woman's Foreign Missionary Society in 1870 in order to provide support for women serving in the field of foreign missions. Under the leadership of Belle Bennett Harris, the Woman's Foreign Mission Board also funded the establishment of Scarritt Bible and Training School for women missionaries in Nashville in 1892.

Among African American denominations, the Women's Home and Foreign Missionary Society of the AME Zion church was founded in 1880 to serve the needs of missionaries in Africa, and the church ordained women as deacons as early as 1894. The Colored Methodist Episcopal (CME) church also created positions for deaconesses in 1894 and founded the Women's Missionary Council in 1918.

The deaconess movement provided a small number of laywomen an arena in which to engage in practical ministry. Beginning with the Lutheran church but spreading to southern Methodist and Episcopal parishes after 1902, the role of deaconess was to provide service to individual congregations and foreign mission efforts or to establish Wesley houses, orphanages, hospitals, and homes for the elderly. Supported by their denominations, deaconesses were granted official status within the church and were consecrated to perform social service work in any area deemed necessary but without leading to ordination as clergy. Sometimes referred to as "Protestant nuns," they followed a calling to Christian service and were "set apart" for their work rather than ordained.

The logical extension of the movement to incorporate women into church life as missionaries and as deaconesses led to a general critique of laywomen's rights within southern churches. This movement paralleled the campaigns for woman suffrage in the South and the reevaluation of scripture that determined women's roles. In addition, the male-driven consolidation of denominational mission boards and seminaries in the 20th century led to the loss of women's autonomy on these boards and in female missionary training schools. Thus, the drive for women's laity rights, or the right to vote in church life and participate in denominational assembly, emerged among southern Methodist women in 1909 as a response to what they saw as sex discrimination; they won full rights in 1918. Southern Baptist women won theirs in 1917, and Episcopal women gained full voting and delegate rights only in 1970. It would be merely a matter of time before women sought entry to full ministerial status.

African American women in denominations that openly practiced the gifts of the Holy Spirit were among the first to preach the gospel in the South. Women who were able to win converts through their exhortations proved the power of the Spirit regardless of sex. The AME church accepted women preachers but refused to ordain them until the mid-20th century. Holiness and Pentecostal churches offered more opportunities for women evangelists in the late 19th century, and women of the Church of God, the Church of the Nazarene, and Pilgrim Holiness church had strong women preachers. Mainstream southern denominations were slower to respond to the calling felt by many women to preach and be ordained as pastors, ministers, or priests. By 1956, however, the United Methodist Church voted to ordain women as clergy; the Presbyterian Church U.S.A. (South) did the same in 1964. The Protestant Episcopal Church voted similarly in 1976 but two years later amended that sweeping change by allowing some bishops to refrain from ordaining women to the priesthood in their diocese. In 2007 there were three such dioceses, one in Fort Worth, Tex. The possibility for Reform Jewish women to be ordained as rabbis came in 1972, and in 1985 for Conservative Jewish women. Technically, Southern Baptist women may be ordained for ministry in some churches, but few serve as senior pastors. Most serve in education, chaplaincy, church music, or as associate pastors.

Modernization among Catholic churches in the South has allowed laywomen to obtain a more visible presence in church life and for Sisters to shed the traditional habit in favor of more practical clothing and more public roles. The fastest-growing segment within the southern branches of the Catholic church comes from Latino communities across the South. In 1970 Sisters Gloria Gallardo and Gregoria Ortega founded Las Hermanas, a Chicana activist religious group devoted to revolutionary change within the Catholic church and outside of it. Pushing the church toward greater acceptance of Latino and Latina leadership and demanding greater activism in Mexican American communities, they moved the church beyond its adherence to the separate spheres of sacred and social, combining the two in social activism in the areas of housing, immigration policy, voting rights, education, and employment. By 2007, however, despite activism on the part of many Sisters and laywomen, there has been no movement within the Catholic hierarchy to ordain women as priests.

Women's involvement in religious organizations changed the institutions, but it has changed them as well. Congregational life, missionary experiences at home and abroad, teaching, serving, and nurturing exposed them to values and behaviors that led to spiritual leadership, fund-raising, and sisterhood. Yet these did not bring women immediately to clergy status. In essence, women created parallel religious organizations that served the institutions' call to healing, caring, and religious instruction. At the same time, male clergy and laymen eventually shifted to recognize the immense importance of women's presence and to acknowledge their equality and claims to ordination as clergy. The movement of women into roles formerly occupied only by men has not resulted in the absolute decline of parallel institutions created by laywomen, especially among southern evangelical denominations, but it has brought a merging and a blending of roles formerly prescribed strictly along gender lines.

ELIZABETH HAYES TURNER
University of North Texas

Elinor Tong Dehey, comp., *Religious Orders of Women in the United States* (1913); Paul Harvey, *Redeeming the South: Religious Cultures and Racial Identities among Southern Baptists, 1865–1925* (2d ed., 2007); Evelyn Brooks Higginbotham, *Righteous Discontent: The Women's Movement in the Black Baptist Church, 1880–1920* (1993); Samuel S. Hill, ed., *Encyclopedia of Religion in the South* (2d ed., 2005); Suzanne Lebsock, *The Free Women of Petersburg: Status and Culture in a Southern Town, 1784–1860* (1984); Susan Hill Lindley, *"You Have Stept Out of Your Place": A History of Women and Religion in America* (1996); Donald G. Mathews, *Religion in the Old South* (1977); Sally G. McMillen, *To Raise up the South: Sunday Schools in Black and White Churches, 1865–1915* (2001); Roberto R. Trevino, *The Church in the Barrio: Mexican American Ethno-Catholicism in Houston* (2006); Elizabeth Hayes Turner, *Women, Community, and Culture: Religion and Reform in Galveston, 1880–1920* (1997).

Respectability, Politics of

Confronted with a racially defined middle-class status that restricted them occupationally and legally, black elites formulated a "moral economy" that stressed class distinctions, moral privilege, and patriarchal conventions within black communities.

Black middle-class and elite women, in particular, espoused a "politics of respectability," in which they sought to conform to the posture of a "lady." By demonstrating to whites that they were just as virtuous, nurturing, and genteel as white women, that they too merited protection from insult and assault, black women hoped to erase negative stereotypes ascribed to their morality and the race as a whole. Evelyn Brooks Higginbotham claimed that the practice of respectability "constituted a counter-discourse to the politics of prejudice" by its demand that every black, regardless of class background, assume responsibility for his/her own behavior and self-improvement. Individuals' successful policing of the self determined the image of the race as a whole. Though ineffective in eradicating all race discrimination, persistent displays of controlled and dignified behavior by blacks debunked racist portrayals of a childlike, immoral race and helped forge partnerships with sympathetic whites. Building bridges across race challenged skin color as the dominant marker of citizenship by debunking stereotypes that rationalized black's exclusion from democratic processes and protections.

Exhibition of "morals and manners" by the black community also validated the race's claim to self-definition and representation and to the power to shape and project its own identity separate from white constructions. Displays of race etiquette were motivated by the black community's evolving external and internal needs. Externally, it seemingly revealed a passive mode of resistance to prevailing Jim Crow practices in that blacks tended to hold their individual behavior, rather than governmental bodies, accountable for solving the race problem. The demand for respectable behavior across the race reinforced an assimilationist, conservative agenda antithetical to the cultural practices of the black masses. Viewed another way, however, self-regulated behavior by the black community helped shift emphasis away from fixed, scientific racial theories justifying race prejudice, allowing a wider interpretation of blacks' capacity for equal citizenship. Internally, displays of respectable behavior revealed the fluid debate among African Americans about community standards and values.

Although African Americans developed unique ideas about respectability in the 19th and 20th centuries, prior historical work on respectability focused on white society's use of this discourse. The first, used to differentiate between the "rough" working class and the "respectable" working class in the United States and Britain, encompassed the values of hard work, thrift, piety, and sexual restraint. A second discourse merged with the evolution of the middle class in the 19th century and stressed class status through appearance, manners, and institutional affiliation. These discourses' meanings were not static, fluctuating within distinct social contexts and over time.

Influenced to a degree by hegemonic cultural influences, the legacy of race segregation and discrimination produced unique expressions of respectability within African American communities. Restrained sexuality among black women rebutted debilitating characterizations of black female sexuality as naturally lascivious. With the black working class's support, the "politics of respectability," according to Higginbotham, sought to promote "temperance, industriousness, thrift, refined manners, and Victorian sexual morals." At the same time, it resulted in class tensions as black elites "disavowed and opposed the culture of the 'folk'—the expressive culture of many poor, uneducated, and 'unassimilated' black men and women." Building on Higginbotham's work, other historians of black women have stressed the role of respectability among middle-class and elite black clubwomen and professionals. In the late 19th and early 20th centuries, African American female reformers invested respectability with racial uplift ideology. As representative "race women," black female activists sought to distinguish themselves from their working-class counterparts while simultaneously endeavoring to uplift them and, by extension, the race.

The divergence in the meaning of respectability mirrored class tensions that became more acute during the Great Migration. Black female reformers, eager to reinforce an appearance of respectability, worked to stamp out behaviors they interpreted as undermining the race. Such behaviors included "ecstatic religious practices" and even menial occupations. Victoria Wolcott's recent study of interwar Detroit assesses the complexities of these class tensions. At the same time, she asserts the primary interpretation of respectability as a discourse primarily utilized by black middle-class female reformers. Charting the concept's evolution, she states that by the 1930s it had changed to encompass "the respect African American men demanded in order to protect and defend their homes and neighborhoods." In other words, a manly discourse of self-defense, as stressed through civil rights, unionization, and self-determination, had replaced female-based values of chastity, self-restraint, and domesticity as markers of respectability.

Increasingly, however, scholars have sought to expand gendered readings of respectability to embody notions of manhood and womanhood. Martin Summers, in *Manliness and Its Discontents*, stretches respectability's meaning by applying it to an array of rhetorical, performative, and institutional activity by middle-class black men, including the self-determinist elements of the Garvey movement. More broadly, scholars such as Elsa Barkley Brown and Andrea Hunter stress the necessity of placing black men and women within the same sphere of analysis. They support applying feminist methodology (women's role as "kin keepers," culture carriers, and stewards of morality)—which has broadened our understanding of black women's everyday lives—to black men.

Though historians' understanding of the politics of respectability continues to be remade, there remain noticeable gaps in the scholarship. The field of queer studies is increasingly seen as critical when considering issues of African

American conceptions of respectability. Roderick Ferguson notes that a race is made through "polymorphous gender and sexual formations," or a range of heterosexual and homosexual identities. He also observes a nexus between studies of middle-class respectability and queer sexuality as demonstrations of the former to solidify "middle-class status and embourgeoisement." Still largely unexplored are how notions of respectability manifested itself among the black working class, traditionally interpreted as the foil from which black respectability sprang. Having striven to achieve property ownership, educational attainment, and moral propriety, aspiring and elite blacks soon realized, with passage of Jim Crow legislation, that such signs of race progress did little to distinguish them from the black masses. Thus, at times, working-class and middle-class women's notions of respectability converged. Both stressed domesticity as central to race uplift, agreed that black women be protected from sexual assault, and worked to cultivate race pride. These mutual concerns have guided black women of all classes to utilize the trope of respectability to forward social mobility and craft positive images of community life. Respectability provided African American women's survival strategies and identities beyond class. The concept of respectability then, not unlike its gendered components, has proved flexible among African Americans regardless of their economic standing. Stephanie Shaw argues that, for black families, respectability proved essential to achieving social mobility. The goal of protecting and uplifting black women was a common one for all classes. Sharon Harley, too, has observed that "even among the poorest blacks, whose own standards of respectability were largely determined by the church and by the community in which they lived, their domestic ideology was not always diametrically opposed to middle-class norms of behavior." Given this, the time is ripe to explore anew the multiple understandings of respectability, including how the formulation intersects or diverges when viewed across classes and among black working-class men and women.

ANGELA HORNSBY-GUTTING
University of Mississippi

Elsa Barkley Brown and Gregg D. Kimball, *Journal of Urban History* (1993); Roderick Ferguson, *American Quarterly* (March 2006); Kevin Gaines, *Uplifting the Race: Black Leadership, Politics, and Culture in the Twentieth Century* (1996); Sharon Harley, *Signs* (Winter 1990); Paisley Jane Harris, *Journal of Women's History* (Spring 2003); Evelyn Brooks Higginbotham, *Righteous Discontent: The Women's Movement in the Black Baptist Church* (1993), *Signs* (Winter 1992); Andrea G. Hunter and James Earl Davis, *Gender and Society* (September 1992), *Journal of Black Studies* (September

1994); Anne Meis Knupfer, *Toward a Tenderer Humanity and a Nobler Womanhood: African American Women's Clubs in Turn-of-the-Century Chicago* (1997); Stephanie Shaw, *What a Woman Ought to Be and to Do: Black Professional Women Workers during the Jim Crow Era* (1996); Martin Summers, *Manliness and Its Discontents: The Black Middle Class and the Transformation of Masculinity, 1900–1930* (2004); E. Frances White, *Dark Continent of Our Bodies: Black Feminism and the Politics of Respectability* (2001); Victoria W. Wolcott, *Remaking Respectability: African American Women in Interwar Detroit* (2001).

Segregation and Desegregation

For more than three decades, the most salient historical question about segregation was a question of timing. One book title asks, *When Did Southern Segregation Begin?* Since the 1990s, however, gender analyses have helped to shift the ground of historical debate concerning both segregation and desegregation to focus on equally compelling and related questions of why and how: why, how, and by whom was segregation implemented and challenged over time?

Historians' fascination with the chronology of Jim Crow dates from 1955, when C. Vann Woodward disputed the conventional wisdom that segregation was a direct outgrowth of slavery and argued instead for discontinuities and "forgotten alternatives" in the history of southern race relations. Woodward's *The Strange Career of Jim Crow* became an instant classic, and a number of other historians wrestled with the "Woodward thesis," which described the period between 1865 and the passage of a number of segregation laws in the 1890s as a period of variety and experimentation in which segregation was not always the rule. Although several early studies lent support to Woodward's analysis, by the 1980s the preponderance of evidence showed that segregation, particularly informal or de facto segregation, was more deeply entrenched earlier and in more aspects of life than Woodward had considered. The work of many scholars, including Richard C. Wade, Joel Williamson, and Leon F. Litwack, argued for significant continuity in southern race relations. In *Race Relations in the Urban South, 1865–1890* (1980), Howard N. Rabinowitz concluded further that the legal segregation of the turn of the 20th century often replaced exclusion rather than openness toward blacks, making segregation something of an improvement in blacks' access to public facilities even as it perpetuated long-standing patterns of white racism.

Some gender analyses of segregation have emphasized continuity as well. In an examination of court decisions in railroad and steamboat segregation cases, Barbara Y. Welke argues that "any attempt to understand the postemancipation South must begin by acknowledging one point: The unwavering goal of white Southerners was to protect white womanhood." On trains, whites accomplished this goal by reworking a traditional distinction between the "ladies' car," which was reserved for women and their male traveling companions, and the "smoker," a less comfortable car for men traveling alone. In some post–Civil War cases, African American women denied access to the ladies' car were able to win damages from railroad companies by emphasizing their own claims to ladyhood. "State and federal courts interpreted the common law of common carriers to allow carriers to segregate passengers by race, but to require that they provide substantially equal accommodations to all paying the same fare," Welke explains. Because rail carriers had no financial incentive to create a black ladies' car, their preferred solution was often to allow respectable black women who could afford the fare to ride with whites. "By the late 1880s and early 1890s it had become clear that the wall guarding Southern white woman's sacred place—and hence white supremacy—was not secure in the hands of carriers and courts," Welke concludes, so state legislatures moved quickly to mandate racial segregation by statute. The ladies' car became whites-only first class, and all African Americans were relegated to the Jim Crow car, regardless of their gender or social standing.

Welke's emphasis on how black women demonstrated their respectability and exercised agency in bringing suit against the railroads reflects another recent trend in historical scholarship on segregation, a trend that is perhaps most notable in the work of Glenda Gilmore. Yet Gilmore and others who consciously put women and African Americans at the center of their accounts have tended to reach a different conclusion than Welke on the question of continuity versus change. "If one uses gender to analyze southern history, change overwhelms continuity," argues Gilmore in a retrospective on Woodward's *Origins of the New South*. Similarly, Gilmore and coeditors Jane Dailey and Bryant Simon assert in *Jumpin' Jim Crow: Southern Politics from Civil War to Civil Rights* (2000) that "shifting the focus from white to black southerners reveals a new definition of continuity and change. Black resistance, not white supremacy, was continuous, while white supremacy remodeled itself to meet any challenge."

Gilmore, Dailey, and Simon are wise to recognize a certain mutability in the very definition of what constitutes continuity and change. Woodward himself admitted that he argued for discontinuities in the southern past in part to give hope to civil rights activists of the 1950s who were trying to change the region's seemingly age-old and intransigent racial practices. Younger historians' emphasis on change is rooted in a similar sensibility, along with a recognition of generational differences between slaveholders and the white southern men who implemented segregation and disfranchised black voters. Thus, Gilmore's important *Gender and Jim Crow: Women and the Politics of White Supremacy in North Carolina, 1896–1920* (1996) not only highlights black women's involvement in southern politics, particularly through their club work and progressive reform, but also investigates the motives of the "New White Men" who, in North Carolina in 1898, manufactured a rape scare and rallied around a call to protect white women from black men in order to regain control over state politics. Unlike Welke, however, Gilmore describes the protection of white womanhood not as an "unwavering goal" rooted in tradition but as a political strategy adopted by relatively young men who were dissatisfied with their fathers' leadership and as anxious about white women's increasing participation in public life as they were about blacks' growing assertiveness.

White women's roles in the dramas of segregation and disfranchisement deserve further study. Recent books by Karen Cox on the United Daughters of the Confederacy and by Jennifer Ritterhouse on the racial socialization of children suggest ways in which white southern women could be very active collaborators in maintaining white supremacy. There is also a rich literature on southern women's activism, including their participation in the woman suffrage movement, at the turn of the 20th century. Yet much of the most widely read scholarship on segregation itself has had little to say about white women. Indeed, in Glenda Gilmore's essay "Gender and *Origins of the New South*" she offers the provocative suggestion that Woodward "deliberately excluded women" from his foundational scholarship "and that he did so with a motive." Committed to writing history that would make change seem possible, Woodward skipped over a major stumbling block to change by skipping over the white women whose very mention would raise the specter of interracial sex. "In the 1950s South, even white liberals feared interracial sex," Gilmore explains. "They did not think it was right, and they thought it would derail the movement for civil rights." Better not to mention sex, or even white women, at all. Unfortunately, even after Jacquelyn Dowd Hall's pioneering work in *Revolt against Chivalry: Jessie Daniel Ames and the Women's Campaign against Lynching* (1979, 1993) "recoupled race and sex" in the 1970s, many historians seem to have followed Woodward's cautious approach, remaining focused on men, laws, and the public sphere in their analyses.

Without question, the issue of interracial sex is central to the history of both segregation and desegregation and adds to the complexity of assessing continuity and change in southern race relations. As Jane Dailey has recently argued, segregationists of the 1950s and 1960s, like generations of white southerners before them, understood the separation of the races to be part of God's divine plan for the world. Interracial sex was therefore a sin of the greatest magnitude because it threatened to obliterate racial boundaries. "Turning to their Bibles, anti-integrationists found many narratives to support a segregated world," Dailey explains. Such narratives "had two key pedagogical aims: to make the case for segregation as divine law, and to warn that transgression of this law would inevitably be followed by divine punishment." Segregationists responded to the 1954 Supreme Court decision in *Brown v. Board of Education* in precisely these terms, despite the fact that "the *Brown* decision, limited as it was to desegregation of public schools, looked to be about anything *but* sex and marriage." Both the legal team for NAACP and the court itself had made sure this was the case, recognizing, as Gilmore suggests Woodward did, that interracial sex was a subject best avoided. "When the *Brown* decision was announced in May 1954, sex and marriage between those defined at law as white and those defined as nonwhite were prohibited in twenty-seven states—and had been, with a few brief exceptions during Reconstruction, for the previous three hundred years." Thus, in Dailey's view, "state antimiscegenation laws underpinned the edifice of racial segregation and discrimination in America."

If centuries-old prohibitions against interracial sex and marriage "lay at the heart of Jim Crow," as Dailey suggests, then what of Woodward and other historians' hopes for a changeable future based in a discontinuous past? As with Gilmore's generational focus in *Gender and Jim Crow*, a sensitivity to time and circumstance can make a seemingly continuous legacy of racism appear susceptible to change over time. Thus, an outpouring of recent scholarship on interracial sex both acknowledges official prohibitions and emphasizes that white southerners generally tolerated interracial relationships to a much greater extent than their rhetoric would lead one to suspect. Only during Reconstruction, when black men gained full citizenship rights, did fear of "Negro domination" translate into the figure of the black beast rapist and histrionic calls to protect white womanhood. "Expressions of white anxiety about sex between black men and white women reached an unprecedented intensity," Martha Hodes asserts. Meanwhile, recent work by Charles F. Robinson and Lisa Lindquist Dorr suggests that even in the postemancipation South, whites' enforcement of antimiscegenation laws and punishment of black men accused of raping white women were not always absolute but instead varied according to the class and character of the men and women involved in a particular case.

Such attention to nuance is a hallmark of the best recent scholarship on both the Jim Crow period and the civil rights era, some of which focuses on particular counties or states. Also prominent among studies that employ gender as a category of analysis are intellectual histories such as Kevin K. Gaines's *Uplifting the Race: Black Leadership, Politics, and Culture in the Twentieth Cen-*

tury (1996), biographies such as Patricia A. Schechter's *Ida B. Wells-Barnett and American Reform* and Barbara Ransby's *Ella Baker and the Black Freedom Movement*, and cultural histories focused on black manhood and womanhood such as Martin Summers's *Manliness and Its Discontents*, Steve Estes's *I Am a Man!*, and Stephanie J. Shaw's *What a Woman Ought to Be and to Do: Black Professional Women Workers during the Jim Crow Era* (1996). Together, such studies have broadened and deepened historians' understanding of a system of segregation that was both the product of a particular historical moment and the outgrowth of long-standing prejudices that involved gender as much as, and inseparably from, race.

JENNIFER RITTERHOUSE
Utah State University

Karen L. Cox, *Dixie's Daughters: The United Daughters of the Confederacy and the Preservation of Confederate Culture* (2003); Jane Dailey, *Journal of American History* (June 2004); Lisa Lindquist Dorr, *White Women, Rape, and the Power of Race in Virginia* (2004); Steve Estes, *I AM A MAN! Race, Manhood, and the Civil Rights Movement* (2005); Glenda E. Gilmore, *Journal of Southern History* (November 2001); Martha Hodes, *White Women, Black Men: Illicit Sex in the Nineteenth-Century South* (1997); Leon F. Litwack, *Been in the Storm So Long: The Aftermath of Slavery* (1979); Howard N. Rabinowitz, *Journal of American History* (December 1988); Barbara Ransby, *Ella Baker and the Black Freedom Movement* (2003); Jennifer Ritterhouse, *Growing Up Jim Crow: How Black and White Children Learned Race* (2006); Charles F. Robinson, *Dangerous Liaisons: Sex and Love in the Segregated South* (2003); John David Smith, ed., *When Did Southern Segregation Begin?* (2002); Martin Summers, *Manliness and Its Discontents: The Black Middle Class and the Transformation of Masculinity, 1900–1930* (2004); Richard C. Wade, *Slavery in the Cities: The South, 1820–1860* (1964); Barbara Y. Welke, *Law and History Review* (Fall 1995); Joel Williamson, *After Slavery* (1965); C. Vann Woodward, *Journal of American History* (December 1988), *The Strange Career of Jim Crow* (1955).

Servants and Housekeepers

Until the 1960s, the majority of employed African American women in the South worked as domestic servants, performing a variety of tasks, particularly cooking, cleaning, and child care. The hours were long, the pay was meager, and the fringe benefits (including Social Security) were nonexistent. A handful of African American women—most notably Idella Parker of Florida, Willie Mae Cartwright of Georgia, and Emma Jane Christian of Virginia—have given firsthand accounts through white amanuenses, but most of the depictions of African American servants are by white people. African American servants are among the best-known stock characters of 20th-century southern culture, with frequent nods to antebellum mammy figures.

In novels by white authors, African American servants are uniformly portrayed as devoted to their white employers. Their characters are always wise and giving, compensating for the brokenness of the white families who employ them. Their depictions are often condescending or amused.

In *The Sound and the Fury* (William Faulkner, 1929), *The Member of the Wedding* (Carson McCullers, 1946), and *To Kill a Mockingbird* (Harper Lee, 1960), African American women serve as mother figures to affection-hungry white children. Faulkner shows Dilsey Gibson as the island of sanity in the Compson family, all-wise and long-suffering, a strong contrast to the hypochondriac mother. McCullers portrays Bereniece Sadie Brown mainly through her care of the motherless girl Frankie. Brown spends most of her time in the kitchen, guiding Frankie through her mood swings accompanying her brother's marriage. Lee does not give Calpurnia a family name but shows her as a stabilizing force for Scout and Jem Finch during a time of racial upheaval in which their widowed father is defending an African American client.

The depth of these characters varies. Gibson has worked for the Compsons throughout her life, growing old and slow in their service. Gibson expects her children to care for the Compsons with solicitude equal to hers, and her grandson Luster bears her wrath for his carelessness with mentally handicapped Benjy Compson. A devout Christian, Gibson takes Benjy to church with her on Easter morning, providing an image of redemption and hope. Brown has no family of her own but has had four husbands, the last of whom beat her and damaged one of her eyes, and she still has an active social life. Empathizing with Frankie's frustrations, Brown makes candid statements about the limitations placed upon her by racism. Like Gibson, Calpurnia is devoutly religious and takes the Finch children to church, where they are surprised to learn that her son Zeebo, a garbageman by day, is a leader of the church choir.

Narciss, in *The Ponder Heart*, by Eudora Welty (1954), demonstrates some of the cracks appearing in Mississippi society after World War II. Narciss first appears driving the white Ponder family's old Studebaker, pushing the boundaries of independence for African American women. The close relationship between Narciss and Bonnie Dee Peacock Ponder tests the limits of acceptable behavior: when Bonnie Dee separates from Daniel Ponder, she leaves her good-bye note for Narciss and refers to her as her friend. In the end, the Ponder family tries

Mrs. Thomas, the wife of a wholesale grocer, in her kitchen with her maid, San Augustine, Tex., 1943 (John Vachon, photographer, Library of Congress [LC-USW3-025238-D], Washington, D.C.)

to downplay the social changes under way, as the narrator disparages Narciss's loss of ability as a cook: "But Narciss don't cook good any more. I hate to tell you—her rice won't stand apart."

The most controversial depiction of an African American servant was the self-sacrificing Delilah Johnston in Fannie Hurst's *Imitation of Life* (1933). A highly skilled cook, the widowed Johnston devotes herself completely to Bea Pullman, even massaging Pullman's feet and shoulders. Pullman makes a fortune making candy from Johnston's recipe and using Johnston's image on the packaging over her protests, then expanding with similar tactics into a string of waffle houses. Brokenhearted by her rejection by her light-skinned daughter, Peola, Johnston dies while kissing Pullman's ankles. Although African American literary figures originally praised the novel, Langston Hughes later produced a parody, *Limitations of Life*, in which a white woman waits on an African American family.

By the late 1980s, Anglo American authors turned directly to relationships between domestic workers and employers, most notably Ellen Douglas in *Can't Quit You Baby* (1988) and Christine Wiltz in *Glass House* (1994). Douglas explores the relationship between Julia "Tweet" Carrier and her longtime employer, Cornelia O'Kelley, during the 1960s. The women's long-term, complex relationship weaves in and out of tragedy and illness, concluding with a family-like fight that ends in laughter. Douglas indicates that friendship in such a relationship is difficult and takes a great deal of effort and time. In *Glass House*, Delzora Monroe helps rear the orphaned Thea Tamborella, who lives with her aunt. When the aunt dies, the adult Tamborella returns home to New Orleans into a tense racial atmosphere. Tamborella and Monroe negotiate a new relationship as adult to adult, giving hope for future generations.

Servants and housekeepers written by white authors are in the story only because of their relationships with white people, but they are actors in their own right in fiction by African American authors published after the civil rights movement. African American authors depict these women as more fully rounded human beings, with motivations that go far beyond pleasing their employers.

In *The Bluest Eye* (1970), Toni Morrison portrays Pauline Williams Breedlove as desperately unhappy with her life, finding escape in the movies, judgmental religion, and the fine home of her wealthy employers. She loves the Fisher family's elegant house and caring for their "pink-and-yellow" daughter, increasingly ignoring her own dreary rent house, abusive husband, Cholly, and two children. Her daughter Pecola (a direct reference to Hurst's Peola) suffers keenly from her mother's neglect and father's abuse, ultimately becoming insane after her father rapes her. While unveiling the tragedy of young Pecola, Morrison probes Breedlove's poverty-stricken southern childhood, unhappy marriage, and desires for a different life.

In Alice Walker's *The Color Purple* (1982), domestic work is forced on the high-spirited Sofia. The mayor's wife tries to hire her, she responds negatively, the mayor intervenes, and Sofia knocks him down, is sentenced to prison time for her deed, and is released into the employment of the mayor's family. In their service, she is forbidden to see her own family and gets to see her children for 15 minutes one Christmas. Many years later, she has a frank discussion with her employer's daughter about the supposed affection of African American women for their employers' children: "Sofia never wanted to be there in the first place. Never wanted to leave her own children. . . . I love children, say Sofia. But all the colored women that say they love yours is lying."

In *A Lesson before Dying* (1993), Ernest Gaines writes of a pair of elderly African American women who just happen to have been domestic workers but are far more than that in the novel. Miss Emma and Tante Louise were both cooks for the Pichot family, and the powerful Henri Pichot agrees to speak to Miss Emma about her nephew, Jefferson, because of all that she has done for his family over the years. It is Miss Emma who is determined that Jefferson will not die like a hog and persuades Grant Wiggins to work with him. Miss Emma and Tante Louise are wise old women first and former domestic servants second, although Miss Emma uses her relationship with her former employer to try to gain dignity for Jefferson.

Most of these novels were turned into movies, bringing the image of the African American servant to a popular audience. *Imitation of Life* was made into movies in 1934 and 1959, with Louise Beavers playing Johnston in the first production and Juanita Moore playing the character in the second. Ethel Waters had the role of Brown in the 1952 film version of *The Member of the Wedding*, Estelle Evans portrayed Calpurnia in the 1962 film version of *To Kill a Mockingbird*, and Oprah Winfrey played Sofia in the 1985 film version of *The Color Purple*.

African American housekeepers have appeared on television since its inception, but the shows are almost never set in the South. *The Beulah Show*, which ran from 1950 to 1953, was the only television show starring an African American woman until 1968. The character of Beulah, played by an Anglo male actress, first appeared in the early 1940s on the *Fibber McGee and Molly* radio series. In *1945* Beulah was spun off into her own show, eventually having the title of *The Beulah Show*. Hattie McDaniel played Beulah from 1947 to 1952 and was replaced sequentially by sisters Lillian and Amanda Randolph. The television production featured Ethel Waters, Hattie McDaniel, and Louise Beavers in the title role. The show was considered a comedy, with Beulah wisely helping her employers, the Hendersons, solve problems. The NAACP criticized *Beulah* for its stereotypical depictions of African American life.

The number of domestic workers dropped dramatically in the post–World War II period, and African Americans began appearing in other types of roles in the mass media. In the 1970s, however, three shows featuring housekeepers emerged as spin-offs of *All in the Family*, all produced by Norman Lear. The case of *Maude* (1972–78) included Esther Rolle as Florida Evans, the wise maid for Maude Findlay. Rolle starred in the spin-off *Good Times* (1974–79), which relocated the Evans family to the Chicago projects. Despite the fight by Rolle and costar John Amos for more meaningful roles, *Good Times* came to center on the buffoonish behavior of oldest son J. J. On *The Jeffersons* (1975–85), affluent New York African Americans Louise and George Jefferson employed Florence Johnston, portrayed by Marla Gibbs. Johnston and George Jefferson sparred constantly, with many verbal wisecracks.

From 1981 to 1987, on *Gimme a Break*, Nell Carter took the role of Nell Harper, the housekeeper of a California police chief and his three daughters, whose mother has died. Although Harper is not a career domestic, she draws her meaning in life from nurturing white children. And so the circle comes around in full: an African American housekeeper completes the broken white family.

REBECCA SHARPLESS
Texas Christian University

Trudier Harris, *From Mammies to Militants: Domestics in Black American Literature* (1982); Elizabeth Kytle, *Willie Mae* (1958; 1993); Blanche Elbert Moncure, *Emma Jane's Souvenir Cook Book* (1937); Idella Parker, *Idella: Marjorie Rawlings' "Perfect Maid"* (1992), with Bud and Liz Crussell, *Idella Parker: From Reddick to Cross Creek* (1999); Patricia A. Turner, *Ceramic Uncles and Celluloid Mammies: Black Images and Their Influence on Culture* (1994); Doris Witt, *Black Hunger: Food and the Politics of U.S. Identity* (1999).

Sex Roles in Literature

The heritage of a strong class and caste system in the South narrows the range of roles for men and women in southern literature. Within that range, the most prominent writers of the modern South—Ellen Glasgow, William Faulkner, Robert Penn Warren, and Eudora Welty—explore the depths of a variety of individual characters. In southern fiction, as in most American writing, a confused identity is often attributed to failure to deal with sexuality directly and responsibly, whereas healthy sexuality becomes the basis for self-awareness.

The southern white male appears in fiction most frequently as either the gentleman-father or his cavalier son. The prototype of the gentleman-father appears in John Pendleton Kennedy's *Swallow Barn* (1832). This character, Frank Meriwether, had dominion over all, white and black; his wife's control of daily plantation life frees him for leisure and contemplation. Meriwether's fictional descendants include the ineffectual Gerald O'Hara in Margaret Mitchell's *Gone with the Wind* (1936) and Battle Fairchild, continuing Meriwether's life into the 1920s in Welty's *Delta Wedding* (1946). Faulkner shows the deterioration of the southern aristocrat in alcoholic Mr. Compson in *The Sound and the Fury* (1929), portrays Sutpen ironically attempting to become a gentleman and found a dynasty in *Absalom, Absalom!* (1936), and further mocks the tradition in Flem Snopes's journey to his mansion-mausoleum. Warren satirizes the figure of the southern gentleman in Bogan Murdock, with his bogus sense of honor, in *At Heaven's Gate* (1943) and even has Jed Tewksbury, a redneck-scholar in *A Place to Come To* (1977), jokingly refuse to become an "S. G."

The fictional cavalier frequently dies young; if not, he may become a gentleman-father, a rake (like Rhett Butler), or a true southern bachelor. Thomas Nelson Page's hero in "Marse Chan" (1885), the ideal cavalier, dies in the war. Faulkner's cavaliers, often confused about sexual roles, are likely to destroy themselves early, like young Bayard in *Sartoris* (1929) and Quentin Compson in *The Sound and the Fury* (1929). In *All the King's Men* (1946), Warren details Jack Burden's rebellion against his aristocratic heritage in his long journey toward becoming a true gentleman. Will Barrett, Walker Percy's protagonist in *The Last Gentleman* (1966), is haunted by his past, particularly his gentleman-father's suicide. In *The Second Coming* (1980), Will finally frees himself from the past and achieves a sensitive relationship with a sexually free younger woman. Faulkner excels in his depictions of true southern bachelors, especially Ike McCaslin, whose obsession with the past destroys his marriage. Peter Taylor's *A Summons to Memphis* (1986) interrogates the dying breeds of the southern cavalier and gentleman-father when southerner Phillip Carver temporarily abandons his New York life to confront his father and his continuing patriarchal control. In contemporary fiction, like that of Barry Hannah, Harry Crews, and Larry Brown, the southern gentleman is often supplanted by lower-class southern heroes and troublemakers.

The most common roles in fiction for the southern white female are the lady-mother and the belle. Kennedy's Lucretia Meriwether, controlling domestic life in spite of her physical weakness, is followed by fictional lady-mothers like Ellen O'Hara and Ellen Fairchild. Augusta Jane Evans (Wilson) gives characters like Edna Earl in *St. Elmo* (1866) the education and opportunity to choose nontraditional roles, but they usually marry gentleman-fathers. In *The Awakening* (1900), Kate Chopin focuses on the unfolding sexual identity of Edna Pontellier, who marries and bears children, then realizes she is unsuited for the role of "mother-woman" in her Creole society. Glasgow's protagonist in *Virginia* (1913) rigidly follows the pattern of her lady-mother's life but loses her husband to an unconventional New York actress. Faulkner's Granny Millard in *The Unvanquished* (1938) is strong, but she relies on the conventions of society to the point of destruction; Mrs. Compson is lady-mother evolved into controlling matriarch. In recent southern fiction, white women grapple with balancing their creative talents and careers with the lady-mother role, for instance in Lee Smith's depictions of women like Ivy Rowe in *Fair and Tender Ladies* (1988) or Katie Cocker in *The Devil's Dream* (1992).

The life of a fictional belle is short, for she is most often portrayed as moving toward the goal of marrying a cavalier, as Kennedy's Bel Tracy does, and settling down as a lady-mother. The refusal to play the role of belle can have grave consequences, as seen in Faulkner's Drusilla Hawk and Caddy Compson. Katherine Anne Porter's Miranda, in "The Old Order" and other stories, must reject the legacy of the belle, with her destructive sexuality, before she can live as an independent woman. Glasgow's incisive portrait of Eva Birdsong in *The Sheltered Life* (1932) shows that marriage does not always offer the belle a new role; Scarlett O'Hara, rebelling at the prospect of becoming a lady-mother, finds new options in the chaos of the Reconstruction. However, in *The Moviegoer* (1961), Percy gives hope for stability in the comfortable role of the southern lady, while her cousin-husband Binx Bolling assumes the role of gentleman-father. The fictional South of the 1920s produces a variation on the role of belle, with the flapper, most notably Temple Drake in *Sanctuary* (1931) and Sue Murdock in *At Heaven's Gate* (1943), who both illustrate the dangers of irresponsible sexual freedom. Depictions of the belle often disappear as young southern women struggle with understanding their place in the postmodern world of malls and consumer culture. Characters like Bobbie Ann Mason's Sam Hughes in *In Country* (1985) or Josephine Humphreys's Lucille Odom in *Rich in Love* (1987) exemplify the independent woman of the contemporary South.

Although the fictional southern woman's sexuality may destroy her or imprison her in a prescribed role, it may also free her from tradition. Glasgow's lower-class rural protagonist in *Barren Ground* (1925) is saved from the entrapment of an illegitimate pregnancy by miscarrying. Faulkner's mythic Eula Varner Snopes is imprisoned by her sexuality, but Lena Grove in *Light in August* (1932) placidly bears her illegitimate child. In *The Reivers* (1962), Corrie rejects her life as a prostitute and is rewarded with an optimistic future with Boon Hogganbeck. Welty's Gloria in *Losing Battles* (1970) rejects the opportunity for freedom through education but gains a strong sexual identity in her relationship with Jack Renfro. Laurel McKelva Hand in *The Optimist's Daughter* (1972) finds hope for an independent future in understanding her parents' marriage and her own. Doris Betts portrays, in *The River to Pickle Beach* (1972), the healthy sexuality and strong marriage of Bebe and Jack Sellars, contrasted with the destructive perversion of Mickey McCane. Betts also confronts the complexity of woman's struggle for independence through librarian Nancy Finch in *Heading West* (1981). Percy's Allison is freed from a conventional role in society by mental illness, which allows her to find a positive relationship with Will Barrett.

Demeaning roles for black men and women, especially as the child and the brute, haunt the pages of southern fiction, from *Swallow Barn* through *Gone with the Wind* and after. Less demeaning but still lacking individuality and dignity are the tragic mulatto, male or female, and the faithful uncle or mammy. However, a few black characters, mostly in recent fiction, are freed from these roles and given autonomy as human beings. In *Clotel* (1853), William Wells Brown traces the suffering of three generations of mulatto women under the domination of insensitive southern gentlemen who perceive them as the lowest of human beings—black and female. George Washington Cable focuses on the Creole society of Louisiana for his moving story of Honoré Grandissime, a free man of color in *The Grandissimes* (1880). In *The House behind the Cedars* (1900), Charles W. Chesnutt allows Rena Walden to question her role in society as a black woman who appears white; her brother John can live with dignity only by assuming the identity of a southern cavalier. Faulkner portrays mulatto characters, especially Joe Christmas and Charles Bon, as individuals in their quests for identity; likewise, Warren's Amantha Starr in *Band of Angels* (1955) and Margaret Walker's Vyry in *Jubilee* (1966) transcend the limitations of stereotyping.

The stereotype of the black uncle, such as the narrator of "Marse Chan," has occasionally been displaced by the role of the autonomous black male. In spite of the ending of *The Adventures of Huckleberry Finn* (1885), Mark Twain gives the character of Jim dignity and wisdom in his quest for identity as a free man. Tea Cake, in Zora Neale Hurston's *Their Eyes Were Watching God* (1937), is an independent man who is strong enough to think of Janie's happiness as well as his own. Faulkner gives Rider, in "Pantaloon in Black" (1940), the sensitivity to be destroyed by the real human emotion of grief. Through the struggles of Bigger Thomas, in *Native Son* (1940), Richard Wright emphasizes the significance of race and sex in attaining self-identity, even in defeat. Black leaders Ned and Jimmy, although destroyed by white society in Ernest J. Gaines's *The Autobiography of Miss Jane Pittman* (1971), are autonomous. Gaines's *A Lesson before Dying* (1993) extends depictions of the independent black male in the characters of Grant Wiggins and his jail-bound protégé Jefferson.

The fictional black mammy, often seen in contrast to the aloof white lady, may have originated in the local color fiction of Sherwood Bonner; Mitchell and others strengthened the stereotype. Occasional black women characters are more complex, like Twain's Roxy in *Pudd'nhead Wilson* (1894), strong and passionate, or Faulkner's Dilsey, superior to the white Compsons in her patience, her love, her wisdom, her endurance. Rather than portraying Janie in *Their Eyes Were Watching God* as a tragic mulatto or turning her into a mammy, Hurston develops her as an independent woman with love for and commitment to a strong black man. Gaines's Miss Jane, old and wise, is in no sense a stereotyped mammy; in fact, like Janie, she is not even a biological mother. Rather, Gaines gives her an identity as a strong, brave, loving, free black woman. In Alice Walker's *Meridian* (1976), the title character emerges as an independent woman fighting for the rights of African Americans after the dissolution of the civil rights movement. In her neo-slave narrative *Dessa Rose* (1986), Sherley Anne Williams creates the feisty, enduring Dessa as a direct challenge to the wench or mammy.

Although southern race and class systems supported images of the gentlemen, belle, uncle, and mammy, these systems also assigned heterosexual identities to such images. The southern man and woman were expected to marry and produce children. Southern writers challenge the heterosexual norm through depictions of "queer" characters. Often, these writers critique southern society as offering either acceptance or intolerance of homosexuality.

Truman Capote interrogates white, male, heterosexual norms in his first novel, *Other Voices, Other Rooms* (1948). The youth, Joel, uncovers the secret past of his cousin, Randolph, and his love affair with an abusive boxer, Pepe Alvarez. When Joel falls in love with Randolph, Joel's individual identity evolves as he connects with a "queer" southern community. In much of her fiction, Carson McCullers interrogates homosocial and homosexual relationships. In *The Heart Is a Lonely Hunter* (1940), McCullers depicts John Singer's undying devotion to his companion, Spiros Antonapoulos. In *The Ballad of the Sad Café* (1951), McCullers creates a love triangle among Amelia, Lymon Willis, and Marvin Macy, blurring the boundaries between heterosexual and homosexual love.

In Tennessee Williams's plays, white male characters suffer the consequences of their attractions to other men. In *Cat on a Hot Tin Roof* (1955), Brick's prejudices against homosexuality lead his best friend, Skipper, to commit suicide. As Brick tries to come to terms with his own sexual confusion, he turns to alcohol, mistreats his wife, Margaret, and generally abuses his family. In *Suddenly, Last Summer* (1958), Catherine Holly battles against her aunt, Violet Venables, who wants her lobotomized so that Catherine cannot reveal the homosexual desires responsible for her cousin Sebastian's death. While on vacation, Sebastian is literally torn apart and consumed by a mob of local boys, whom he previously uses for sexual favors. Williams's plays expose the destruction caused by an intolerant southern society that views heterosexuality as the norm.

From the 1970s to the present day, southern authors write about homosexuality with frequency and openness. Often homosexual characters are shunned by the larger southern community. Rita Mae Brown's novel *Rubyfruit Jungle* (1975) charts Molly Bolt's coming of age as a lesbian in a South that refuses to accept her. When Molly's lesbian relationship with her college roommate is discovered, she loses her scholarship and leaves the South for New York. In *A Visitation of Spirits* (1989), Randall Kenan exposes the conflicts between black masculinity and homosexuality. Sexual discrimination intersects with racial conflict when Horace becomes friends with white boys who accept him as "queer" when his own zealously religious family will not. Horace eventually commits suicide. In Harlan Greene's novel *What the Dead Remember* (1991), the narrator describes growing up gay in Charleston, S.C. After escaping the South for a time, the narrator returns to a homophobic South dealing with the AIDS crisis of the 1980s. Similarly, Allan Gurganus's *Plays Well with Others* (1997) reveals the struggles of gay southerner Hartley Mims Jr. as he searches for a tolerant society in New York and ends up caring for his friends who contract AIDS. Like Williams's plays, these novels critique the persistence of an intolerant southern society (even in the face of a national epidemic).

As in the works of Capote, homosexuality often creates strong southern communities. In Alice Walker's novel *The Color Purple* (1982), Celie learns to value herself outside of her abusive husband's expectations through her relationship with the bisexual Shug Avery. Walker subverts portrayals of black women as sexual objects through the women's mutual love for one another. Fannie Flagg's popular novel *Fried Green Tomatoes at the Whistlestop Café* (1987) alludes to a love relationship between Idgie Threadgood and Ruth Jamison that engenders a tolerant community as the women, without discrimination, serve all customers at their café. In her novel *Bastard out of Carolina* (1992), Dorothy Allison explores the sex roles of "white trash" women through characters Bone Boatwright and her aunts. In Bone's Aunt Raylene, Allison posits a queer woman free from men and their patriarchal conscriptions (such as the lady-mother). John Berendt's best seller *Midnight in the Garden of Good and Evil* (1994) celebrates "queer" characters like Jim Williams and the Lady Chablis. In *The Promise of Rest* (1995), Reynolds Price shows how the AIDS crisis reunites a family when Hutchins Mayfield nurses his dying son, Wade. Jim Wilcox's comic novel *Plain and Normal* (1999) tells the tale of Lloyd Norris, whose wife outs him in order to divorce him. Although Wilcox's portrait of Lloyd's struggle with aging and romance inspires laughter, Lloyd also faces prejudice and stereotyping from his community at times. Although southern writers sometimes uphold southern sex roles, such authors also faithfully test the bounds of women's and men's assigned places. Depictions of these mutable roles reflect not only the ever-changing southern literary canon, but also the evolution of southern social norms.

MARTHA E. COOK
Longwood College

COURTNEY GEORGE
Louisiana State University

Francis Pendleton Gaines, *The Southern Plantation: A Study in the Development and the Accuracy of a Tradition* (1924); Anne Goodwyn Jones, *Tomorrow Is Another Day: The Woman Writer in the South, 1859–1936* (1981); Richard H. King, *A Southern Renaissance: The Cultural Awakening of the American South, 1930–1955* (1980); Gary Richards, *Lovers and Beloveds: Sexual Otherness in Southern Fiction, 1936–1961* (2005); Anne Firor Scott, *The Southern Lady: From Pedestal to Politics, 1830–1930* (1970); Mab Segrest, *My Mama's Dead Squirrel: Lesbian Essays on Southern Culture* (1985); William R. Taylor, *Cavalier and Yankee: The Old South and American National Character* (1961); Patricia Yaeger, *Dirt and Desire: Reconstructing Southern Women's Writing, 1930–1990* (2000).

Sexuality

The South is often portrayed as a subculture obsessed with sexual repression yet charged with undercurrents of sexual tension. Little concrete social science evidence exists, however, for evaluating the uniqueness of sexual attitudes and behaviors among southerners, despite widespread attention to the study of human sexuality in the 20th century. Many social science researchers either do not control for or do not consider regional differences in analyzing their data. In addition to the limited data from social science, however, many insights about southerners and sexuality can be found in the region's history, literature, music, and oral folklore.

Richard Godbeer's 2004 study, *Sexual Revolution in Early America*, details regional differences between southern and northern colonists and how those changed over time. Catherine Clinton and Michelle Gillespie argue that "sex and race must be situated at the heart of southern colonial history," and recent work has shown how Anglo-American laws prohibiting interracial sex were important in reinforcing slavery and racism. From early southern history on, sexuality was intertwined with issues of not only race but also gender and social class, within an emerging hierarchical, patriarchal society. Violence was an everyday part of life in the early South and proved a powerful weapon enforcing racial and gender dichotomies. Scholars document incidences of rape, castration, murder, infanticide, and physical brutality.

Probably the best-known images of southern sexual relations are the portrayals of steamy antebellum-era trysts in the vein of Kyle Onstott's *Mandingo*, emphasizing miscegenation and brutal control and use of sexuality. Historians generally agree that certain codes of behavior dominated the antebellum South: white men had the greatest latitude in fulfilling their sexual desires; black women were expected to be sexually accessible and more sexually expressive than white women; black men's sexuality was viewed as threatening and was tightly controlled; and white women were expected not to have sexual desires and to stand as asexual paragons of virtue. These cultural assumptions reflected the reality of power and dominance in a hierarchal society. Sociological studies such as John Dollard's *Caste and Class in a Southern Town* (1937) confirmed the persistence of some of these attitudinal and behavioral patterns during the early 20th century.

The household was a defining institution in the antebellum South, tying together whites across social class and providing an ideological justification for the presence of blacks in southern society. The transformation of the household in the postemancipation years led to legal and political debates about governance of sexuality in the new society. Peter Bardaglio sees "a new paternalistic ideal of government regulating the treatment of dependents" replacing an older model of the patriarchal head of the household, who governs it with undisputed authority. White anxiety about black male sexuality in this era led to increased violence against black men. Observers have long written of the "southern rape complex," which represented an unyielding white racial solidarity in the face of any black male challenges to white male sexual dominance. Diane Miller Sommerville has recently questioned this complex, arguing that white elites were often able to protect black men accused of rape. In addition, poor white women and black women were viciously stereotyped as sexually depraved, leading to a misogyny that prevented successful prosecution in rape cases brought by poor white and black women.

Aspects of the striking gender- and race-based double standards were not endemic to the South but represented national trends as well. Nineteenth-century physicians, moralists, and social commentators were obsessed with appropriate channeling of men's sexual urges and with suppression of women's sexuality. Physicians writing in the *New Orleans Medical and Surgical Journal* in the mid-1850s, for example, recognized men's strong sex drives but warned against masturbation because it drained men of the will for self-sufficiency. Women were exhorted to be virtuous, chaste, and pious—to keep their minds above sexuality. Married women, though, were also duty-bound to be available sexually to their husbands. Historian Barbara Welter refers to this view as "the cult of true womanhood," which flourished nationwide between 1820 and 1860. Although historian Carl N. Degler and others question the extent of actual acceptance of such exhortations, a strong double standard prevailed and was probably intensified by the chivalric code in the South.

Some examples of brutal repression of sexuality in the South exist. The 18th- and 19th-century trend was toward disapproval of the use of castration as a legal punishment. Eugene D. Genovese notes, however, that "scattered evidence suggests that some masters continued to apply it [castration] especially to slaves who had become their rivals for coveted black women." Female castration became common throughout the country after 1872, when Georgia physician Robert Battey developed the surgical techniques for "normal ovariotomy," a procedure he enthusiastically endorsed for "problems" ranging from "erotic tendencies" to "troublesomeness." As G. J. Barker-Benfield notes, this technique remained popular until about 1921, and numerous female circumcisions and clitoridectomies were also performed.

Scientific studies of sexual behaviors and attitudes began in the late 1800s. Unfortunately, no regionally specific data are available from such early studies as those of Dr. Clelia Mosher and Katherine Davis. Even Alfred Kinsey and associates employed no regional identifiers in analysis of the data from their landmark 1948 study, *Sexual Behavior in the Human Male*. Other demographic variables such as religion, education, and urban-rural residence that are confounded with region of residence were the primary bases for analyses. According to Kinsey and associates' *Sexual Behavior in the Human Female* (1953), approximately 3,600 of their total male and female samples of 16,392 cases were southerners. Nevertheless, the researchers commented in the 1953 volume that despite widespread assumptions about regional differences in sexual behavior, "we have an impression, as yet unsubstantiated by specific calculations, that there are actually few differences in sex patterns between similar communities in different portions of the United States." This impression seems to have guided much subsequent research.

As the so-called sexual revolution gained momentum, interest grew in the changing rates of premarital intercourse, and regional comparisons became more common. One important early investigation was Winston Ehrmann's 1959 study of premarital sexuality among students at the University of Florida. In the sample, 65 percent of the 576 males and 13 percent of the 265 females reported having had premarital intercourse. In a major 1964 study, Ira Reiss concluded that there was a nationwide trend toward acceptance of premarital intercourse on the basis of affection but not necessarily commitment to marriage, though in behavior the double standard still prevailed. In Reiss's Virginia sample, 16 percent of the high school and college students accepted the "permissiveness with affection" standard, compared to 72 percent of the respondents in New York.

Attention to regional differences heightened with publication in 1968 of Vance Packard's *The Sexual Wilderness*. Packard reported results of a study of college juniors and seniors nationwide, with a total of 185 respondents from three southern institutions represented. Among the southern respondents, about 69 percent of the males and 32 percent of the females reported having had premarital intercourse. This rate for males was the highest in the country; the rate for southern females was next to the lowest. Furthermore, southern males were the most likely to have taken part in a one-night affair with someone they never dated again. "The South has the nation's strongest reputation for a double standard in regard to sexual behavior," said Packard. "That reputation receives support in the survey results." Regarding attitudes, Packard found the strongest support of the double standard among females from the South and the Midwest. Commented Packard, "A major surprise (to us) was that next to the Easterners the males most untroubled by the idea of courting a nonvirginal girl were the Southerners (36 percent responding 'no')." More recent investigations have shown that southerners are now following the trend toward "permissiveness with affection." For example, researchers who compared data from 1965, 1970, and 1975 samples of students at one major state university in the South found trends congruent with national ones, particularly in the "dramatic liberalization in both premarital sexual behavior and attitudes for college females."

Beyond the information on premarital sexual standards, especially among the college educated, however, little reliable information exists about regional variations in sexual behavior and attitude, whether normative (for example, sexual relations among married couples) or nonnormative (for example, extramarital sexual relations, homosexual relations, or lesbian relations). Most recent large-scale studies of sexuality have not dealt with regional patterns. Laws in the South regarding sexual activities, however, provide valuable insights into the mixture of attitudes regarding sexuality.

For a brief period during the Civil War, Nashville registered and periodically inspected prostitutes, the first such system in the nation. As of 1885, Louisiana, Arkansas, and New Mexico were the only three states in which "red light" districts for prostitution were legal. New Orleans's notorious district, Storyville, was such an accepted institution in the late 1800s that guidebooks were distributed at restaurants, taverns, and other tourist attractions. As of 1975, Mississippi was the only state that allowed conjugal visits for married prisoners and provided cottages for such meetings. As of 2005, the state is one out of only five in the nation that permit the practice and one of two that distribute condoms to participating married inmates. When the streaking craze hit the country and many locales prosecuted the participants for indecent exposure, the Louisiana Legislature "excluded from prosecution streakers who did not attempt to arouse the sexual desires of their viewers." Also, southern states legalized the use of birth control by married couples and interracial marriage before some other states.

On the other hand, although many states in the 1960s and 1970s revised their penal codes to allow adults to engage in any sexual acts in private, Georgia doubled its penalties for consensual sodomy. Georgia, Kentucky, South Carolina, and Wisconsin stood out for years as the few states specifically penalizing both female and male homosexual practices (most states overlooked lesbian activities). In 1986 national attention focused on the Georgia sodomy statutes when the U.S. Supreme Court heard the case of a homosexual man from Georgia and upheld the state's right to define sodomy (oral or anal sex) as a felony punishable by 20 years in prison. As of 1986, 12 of the 24 states that had criminal penalties for sodomy were southern, with maximum penalties in the South ranging from a $200 fine in Texas to Georgia's 20-year prison term. Southern laws gained further attention in 1986 when a federal appeals court panel upheld Virginia's laws against fornication and cohabitation, enacted in 1829 and 1860, respectively. *Lawrence v. Texas* in 2003 was the Supreme Court ruling that overturned state sodomy laws and expanded the right to privacy.

Impressionistic information about southern sexuality abounds, in anecdotal accounts, literary images, and representations in television, movies, and popular music. According to historian Thomas L. Connelly, southern folklore contains a variety of sexual stereotypes, such as "the high school bad girl," who dresses provocatively and undulates rather than walks, and the "good old boy tribal shouter," who hangs out of his pickup truck to "deliver ancient Celtic tribal shouts such as 'who-oo-wee'" when an attractive girl passes by. Southerners have not been reticent about examining sexuality's role in their lives. Writers such as Florence King, author of *Southern Ladies and Gentlemen* (1976), and Rayna Green, a contributor to *Speaking for Ourselves: Women of the South* (1984), provide lively personal observations on southern morals, sex roles, and sexual behaviors. For decades, southern poets and novelists have grappled with "sin, sex, and segregation," according to Richard H. King, and examples of southern writers' struggles with the theme of sexuality are innumerable.

Anne Goodwyn Jones and Susan V. Donaldson use the body as a defining concept in exploring how cultural texts can reveal continuing intersections of sexuality with other central themes of southern culture. "From the body of the white southern lady, praised for the absence of desire, to the body of the black lynching victim, accused of excessive desire," they write, "southern sexuality has long been haunted by stories designating hierarchical relationships among race, class, and gender." Southern newspaper columnists write openly about sex and social relationships in the region; country music and blues lyricists have long incorporated many frank sexual themes, and hip-hop contests feature sex as a key part of "The Dirty South"; "common folk" readily swap sexual tales and advice; and such celebrities as Jessica Simpson, Britney Spears, and Billy Bob Thornton provide images of southern sexuality. Suzi Parker's *Sex in the South: Unbuckling the Bible Belt* (2003) is a state-by-state chronicle of sexual sites, institutions, and experiences. "The region is a full-to-capacity carnal playground," Parker writes, "where the den mother buys dildos, the principal is a swinger, and the preacher is a porn fiend."

Finally, the increasingly public presence of lesbian, gay, bisexual, and transgender (LGBT) people and the growth of the Religious Right movement opposing that public role has contributed to a new frankness in the discussion of sexuality in the contemporary South. A lesbian/gay rights movement is nationwide, but with distinctive southern dimensions. Queer studies scholars examine the historical and cultural role of LGBT people who have lived within a regional context dominated by evangelical religion, racial obsessions, and gender dichotomies. A considerable body of scholarship and memoirs demonstrates the long role of LGBT people in the region and their distinctive place within the national LGBT community. The Religious Right, on the other hand, makes sexual issues the core of their efforts to use political successes to change southern life. Pornography, premarital sex, the Equal Rights Amendment, and gay marriage are central elements of the Religious Right agenda. Passage of constitutional amendments prohibiting gay marriage in many southern states in 2004 reflects a new militancy by conservative religious groups in attempting to restore traditional moral strictures in southern public life.

SHARON A. SHARP
Boone, North Carolina

Edward G. Armstrong, *Journal of Sex Research* (August 1986); Peter W. Bardaglio, *Reconstructing the Household: Families, Sex, and the Law in the Nineteenth-Century South* (1995); G. J. Barker-Benfield, in *The American Family in Social-Historical Perspective*, ed. Michael Gordon (2d ed., 1978); Catherine Clinton and Michelle Gillespie, *The Devil's Lane: Sex and Race in the Early South* (1997); Thomas L. Connelly, *Columbia Record* (30 August 1985); Carl N. Degler, in *The American Family in Socio-Historical Perspective*, ed. Michael Gordon (2d ed., 1978); John R. Earle and Philip J. Perricone, *Journal of Sex Research* (August 1986); Winston Ehrmann, *Premarital Dating Behavior* (1959); Paul H. Gebhard, *Sexual Behavior in the Human Female* (1953); Eugene D. Genovese, *Roll, Jordan, Roll: The World the Slaves Made* (1972); Rayna Green, in *Speaking for Ourselves: Women of the South*, ed. Maxine Alexander (1984); Martha Hodes, *White Women, Black Men: Illicit Sex in the Nineteenth-Century*

South (1997); John Howard, *Men Like That: A Southern Queer History* (2001), *Carryin'
On in the Lesbian and Gay South* (1997); Anne Goodwyn Jones and Susan V. Donald-
son, *Haunted Bodies: Gender and Southern Texts* (1997); Herant A. Katchadourian and
Donald T. Lunde, *Fundamentals of Human Sexuality* (2d ed., 1975); Karl King, Jack O.
Balswick, and Ira E. Robinson, *Journal of Marriage and the Family* (August 1977);
Richard H. King, *A Southern Renaissance: The Cultural Awakening of the American
South, 1930–1955* (1980); Alfred C. Kinsey, Wardell B. Pomeroy, and Clyde E. Martin,
Sexual Behavior in the Human Male (1948); *Newsweek* (14 July 1986); Tara McPher-
son, *Reconstructing Dixie: Race, Gender, and Nostalgia in the Imagined South* (2003);
Vance Packard, *The Sexual Wilderness* (1968); Suzi Parker, *Sex in the South: Un-
buckling the Bible Belt* (2003); Ira L. Reiss, *The Social Context of Premarital Sexual
Permissiveness* (1967); Bradley Smith, *The American Way of Sex* (1978); Diane Miller
Sommerville, *Rape and Race in the Nineteenth-Century South* (2004); Barbara Welter,
in *The American Family in Socio-Historical Perspective*, ed. Michael Gordon (2d ed.,
1978); John Wheeler and Peter Kilman, *Archives of Sexual Behavior* (June 1983).

Single Mothers

Remember Claudine—that black, self-possessed Diahann Carroll character
who was a single mother, had six children, and "cheated" the welfare system
because she did not report her wages as a maid in Harlem in the 1970s? A filmic
attempt to present black single mothers' humanity and struggles, *Claudine*
(1974) did not have the cultural power to dismantle the increasingly popular caricature of single mothers that derogated female-headed households as
problematic and costly to the nation. By the 1970s the phrase "single mother"
powerfully evoked reproachful images of poor, black, lazy, welfare cheaters
who, according to apocryphal Reaganite lore, even bought Cadillacs with their
government checks.

Such societal and political preoccupation with single mothers reveals relatively little about actual lives and more about cultural anxieties regarding race,
gender, age, work, poverty, family values, sexuality, fertility, conformity, and
nationalism in specific historical eras. Some single mothers and their families
have been judged more worthy than others in different historical moments,
but all of them appeared at best inadequate or at worst pathological in a male-
centered world where the father-dominated breadwinner family model represented normality. Southern realities have long reflected national patterns in this
regard.

The use of the phrase "single mothers" to mean supposedly unworthy black
welfare recipients occurred only after World War II. From the mid-1800s

through the early 1900s, when black people's emancipation and foreign immigration conjured up questions of racial purity and national identity, public attention focused on white and European immigrant women as dangerous
single mothers. Such worry reflected the dominant gendered expectation that
white women should operate not only as the moral centers of families but also
as mothers responsible for reproducing the nation. For these reasons, those
single mothers deemed "good" or "worthy" were white widows—for, like their
wedded sisters, they had followed the socially acceptable path toward marriage
and motherhood. In contrast, unwed white and European immigrant single
mothers were considered fallen women, akin to prostitutes.

Single mothers became the targets of interventionist campaigns that relied
upon the cultural myths of their day. For instance, between the late 19th and
early 20th centuries, white and black clubwomen and social reformers established homes and provided resources for unwed mothers in their communities.
Reformers established southern missions for white fallen women in Tennessee, Georgia, Maryland, Washington, D.C., and West Virginia. Called "refuges,"
with women residents considered "inmates," these mission homes attached
shame (versus joy) to motherhood. Local communities exhibited hostility to
their very presence. Because Jim Crow realities excluded black single mothers
from white missions, black middle-class women started their own homes to
serve the unwed of the race.

At the same time, middle-class and elite white women sought to secure pensions for white widowed mothers in order to subsidize "appropriate" mother-
ing roles. Progressive-era pension campaigns, which excluded most black and
Latina single mothers, as well as the unmarried, deserted, or divorced, reinforced the idea of white, widowed motherhood as worthy and deserving. In
1935 the federal Aid to Dependent Children (ADC) program replaced the public welfare programs that operated in over 40 states and in Washington, D.C.,
Hawaii, and Alaska. Under the 1935 Social Security Act, ADC provided these
white widowed single mothers with a minimal federal social safety net. Only
after World War II, when many white widows began to receive subsidies from
survivors' benefits instead of ADC, did white women who gave birth to children
out of wedlock and black single mothers begin to access ADC (which was renamed Aid to Families with Dependent Children [AFDC] in 1962).

Although black and white unwed mothers gained increased access to ADC,
in other ways they received disparate treatment based on their race. While
white single mothers still experienced disgrace, blame, or reprimand, they
were potentially "salvageable." Influenced by dominant cultural forces, social
workers judged out-of-wedlock white mothers, particularly teenage girls, as

making personal mistakes. As a result, these mothers could be fixed by therapy or a conjugal relationship, or even by giving their babies up for adoption. At the same time, a language of pathology stigmatized black single mothers and their families as an intrinsically disorganized collectivity. Deemed culturally deficient, black single mothers needed punishment, not therapy.

When black women, then, began to assert their rights and receive ADC, stigmatizing portraits of single mothers replaced the image of the worthy unfortunate on ADC. In 1961 Louisiana public officials purged ADC roles, arguing that black single mothers were "a bunch of prostitutes." In 1965 the government-commissioned Moynihan Report reified such cultural images by blaming black maternal heads of households for their families' poverty. This specific incarnation of the black single mother as a matriarch assumed massive cultural and political proportions, so much so that white single motherhood disappeared from the public imagination. By the late 1960s, racialized welfare discourse with its loaded cultural assumptions about single motherhood went national.

Moreover, in post–World War II America, the increasing percentage of unwed teenage mothers, especially black and Latina ones, stoked public debates about population control, contraceptives, and fertility, as well as exacerbated public concern about the assault on "traditional" (or "white") family forms and values. Teenage pregnancy signified the dangers of inappropriate youthful sexuality and freer sexual mores. As a result, expectant teenage mothers were often expelled or attended special schools in the 1960s.

Although images of single mothers have had untoward cultural power and policy ramifications, real single mothers were never these one-dimensional or disfigured persons. As race, ethnicity, class, and age, for instance, have dictated the social construction of motherhood and real access to public support and jobs, most single mothers have had to figure out how to make ends meet in a patriarchal society that has resisted seeing them as heads of households and economic breadwinners. Moreover, popular depictions of single mothers have masked the varied and complicated reasons, beyond a spouse's death or extramarital sex, behind single status. Mistreatment by men—such as neglect, abandonment, rape, and domestic abuse—along with rigid state policies that deter men's presence in families have often remained hidden. Just as invisible have been the varied identities of single mothers, their daily lives, networks, relationships to the labor market and families, and ideas about caregiving and motherhood.

The caricaturing of single mothers, as well as the casting of them as social problems, has not only occluded their personal travails and masked political economy but has also preempted their societal role as agents. By the mid-

1960s, single mothers, especially poor black ones, led grassroots battles for poor people's political and economic rights. As public housing residents, welfare recipients, and low-wage workers, single mothers engaged in community-building efforts, demanded jobs and adequate incomes, and organized activist campaigns on the local and national levels. Founded in 1966, the National Welfare Rights Organization had a multiracial membership of black, white, Latina, and Native American women in local chapters across the country, including in the South, and yet the myth of the welfare queen has blotted out this activism.

In the early 21st century, a growing societal acceptance of female-headed households exists, especially those led by white middle-class women or single women who adopt. These are single mothers by "choice." Low-income black female-headed households, however, are still cast as the purveyors of social ills and an economic drain on society. In 1995 congressional debates over welfare reform, for instance, U.S. Representative John L. Mica (R-Fl.) described recipients as "alligators." The demonizing of recipients in this way helped to justify the dismantling of AFDC and the social welfare safety net in 1996.

RHONDA Y. WILLIAMS
Case Western Reserve University

Bette J. Dickerson, *African American Single Mothers: Understanding Their Lives and Families* (1995); Ruth Feldstein, *Motherhood in Black and White: Race and Sex in American Liberalism, 1930–1965* (2000); Linda Gordon, *Pitied but Not Entitled: Single Mothers and the History of Welfare* (1994); Elna C. Green, ed., *Before the New Deal: Social Welfare in the South, 1830–1930* (1999); Ange-Marie Hancock, *The Politics of Disgust: The Public Identity of the Welfare Queen* (2004); Elaine Bell Kaplan, *Not Our Kind of Girl: Unraveling the Myths of Black Teenage Motherhood* (1997); Regina G. Kunzel, *Fallen Women, Problem Girls: Unmarried Mothers and the Professionalization of Social Work, 1890–1945* (1993); Jennifer Mittelstadt, *From Welfare to Workfare: The Unintended Consequences of Liberal Reform, 1945–1965* (2005); Annelise Orleck, *Storming Caesars Palace: How Black Mothers Fought Their Own War on Poverty* (2005); Rickie Solinger, *Wake Up Little Susie: Single Pregnancy and Race before Roe v. Wade* (1992); Rhonda Y. Williams, *The Politics of Public Housing: Black Women's Struggles against Urban Inequality* (2004).

Slavery

Gender shaped slavery in the American South in many ways: it animated the making of racial slavery, it determined the kinds of work a person would perform, and it created ideas about manhood. In the 16th and 17th centuries, European male travelers to West and Central Africa were struck by a number of things, but skin color was not the most prominent among them. European men took greater note of the fact that most of the people they encountered were not Christian and were therefore "heathens" and that they were organized into groups that to them appeared to be lacking any form of governance and civilization. At least as remarkable to European travelers were African women: they did agricultural work, unlike European women, who—in the ideal—stayed out of the fields as much as possible. Not only did African women (and not men) do field work, but they seemed to give birth without any pain and with little or no need for postpartum rest. These two points seemed to suggest that field work was not only easier for African women but *natural* for them. European travelers to Africa noticed other things, as well. European men were especially awed by African women's bared breasts, which they described as "dugs" that were large and droopy, "like the udder of a goate," as one traveler put it. Such descriptions made African women seem more like animals than people. African women, then, seemed naturally fit for grueling agricultural and reproductive labor on the plantations of the Americas. African women, and by extension African men, were, in European eyes, inherently laborers—they were heathens, they were uncivilized. They were natural slaves.

Still, Europeans were only beginning to think of Africans that way. Their perception of Africans was still fluid and even vague. And it was mostly based on cultural differences. But in the 1660s, things shifted. In 1662 the Virginia colonial legislature acted to resolve the problem of the condition of children born to enslaved mothers and English fathers. In English tradition, children took the status and names of their fathers. Yet the legislature decided that children in Virginia would "follow the condition of the mother." In breaking with English tradition, Virginia's planter elite were able to reconcile their competing desires to have sex with their slave women and to own as many slaves as possible, including their own children. The principle of matrilineal descent made slavery *racial*. It made slavery in the South a condition based on biological descent—not, for instance, on criminal acts, defeat in war, or resistance to colonization, as had been the case in earlier forms of slavery in Africa, Rome, and Greece. During the 1600s, English people and their descendants moved away from relatively vague ideas of difference that separated them from Africans and toward a concrete perception of a deep and permanent gap between them.

In 1670 lawmakers forced the non-Christian servants who had arrived in Virginia "by shipping" (Africans) to be "slaves for their lives," while those who had "come by land" (Indians) served limited terms of service. This law combined with an earlier law (from 1667) banning the manumission of converted Christians to make slavery in Virginia an institution based not on religion or other changeable differences but on African descent per se. By 1700 the perception of difference was no longer based on cultural difference but on ancestry ("blood"), skin color, and other supposed physical and biological characteristics. It was based on the idea of race.

Gender determined, in conjunction with race and class, if a person worked and the kinds of work she or he would perform. It has been said that "slaves did little that was not work," and this was particularly true for enslaved women, from whom slaveholders demanded not only productive work but also reproductive work. Compared with other modern slave societies, in the American South reproductive work was an especially significant part of enslaved women's lives because the enslaved were able to form families. Slave family formation, which satisfied slaveholders' ambitions by creating more slave wealth, depended on women's reproductive labor. This dependence was deepened after the abolition of U.S. participation in the Atlantic slave trade in 1808, when the only (legal) source of more slaves was women's wombs.

Once enslaved people in the British mainland colonies were reproducing themselves after about 1750, their family formation was implicitly, from slaveholders' point of view, "breeding." Enslaved women's reproductive lives bore a direct, not an indirect, relationship to the production of crops and people for the market. Thus reproduction was fundamental to the perpetuation of racial slavery. It was equally fundamental to enslaved women's experience of bondage in the Americas.

Enslaved women also performed the reproductive (domestic) labor that kept slaveholding households running. On elite plantations, a few enslaved women engaged in specialized jobs such as cook, lady's maid, nurse maid to infants and children, housekeeper, seamstress, weaver, and knitter. (Men performed a number of servant functions as well, including valet, driver, messenger, cook, carriage driver, gardener, groomsman, livestock tender, or watchman.) Enslaved women also engaged in work beyond the purview of their owners, notably in health care, as midwives, herbalists, and root doctors. Slaveholders did not call women's specialized work "skilled" or "specialized," since they reserved these designations for the specialized tasks assigned to men, like blacksmithing, leatherworking, and coopering. Household work for women was further degraded by an unspoken demand: to satisfy the sexual demands of the master and his sons and guests.

Most enslaved women, however, did not perform specialized work. Instead, most worked steadily in the fields from dawn to dusk only to come home to a second shift of more work. Most had to cook a meal for their families from the meager rations they were allocated and from the produce they and their families raised in their gardens (the exception was those living on a large plantation, where sometimes a cook prepared meals for the slaves). Enslaved women also had to use evenings to make, clean, and repair the family's ragged clothing and make candles and soap if they could. Enslaved women also had child care responsibilities, often made more extensive by the fact that many husbands lived elsewhere.

The concept of "women's work" both did and did not apply to bondwomen in the Americas. The production of rice in South Carolina was probably the most gender-stratified field work in the Americas. As had been the case in the rice-growing regions of Africa, men often controlled the irrigation systems that watered the plants, while women cultivated it: women sowed the seeds, hoed the seedlings, transplanted them to drier land at just the right moment, hoed weeds, then harvested and processed the rice.

The influence of gender was more subtle in other crops. Some slaveholders expected somewhat less from women than from men and classified women in the prime of life as only a "3/4 hand," compared to a "prime" man's "full hand." Some gave enslaved women smaller daily quotas and tasks; some shortened those days even more when enslaved women were pregnant and for some time after they gave birth. Many did not. Nursing mothers worked in the hot fields carrying their infants on their backs or left the babes at the ends of rows. The mothers of young children hoped they would be well cared for when left in the care of older women who no longer worked in the fields and of children around the age of 10 who had not yet entered the fields.

And gender shaped *how* agricultural work was done. No doubt following the gender norms of the enslaved, hoeing was typically considered women's work, while plowing was men's work. Gender shaped when girls and boys entered the field: perceptions that girls had higher motor skill development at an earlier age led many enslavers to begin their training (with their parents) in field work around 10 to 12 years of age, whereas boys, on average, began their training between 11 and 13.

The enthronement of white women as delicate and ill-suited to field work was dependent on enslaved women's labor. Without black women's labor in the fields, English colonists would not have had the luxury of deeming white women to be unsuitable workers; they would have needed them too much. And indeed, white women were needed too much to stay out of the fields entirely, so an important minority of white women continued to work in the fields throughout the slavery era. Moreover, all but the most elite white women did at least some household production.

Black and white standards of masculinity were shaped, at the deepest levels, by the existence of slavery. Among white men, masculinity emphasized control of people (self, family, male peers, and subordinates), land, and nature. At the very least, white men enjoyed the status of free people and were therefore masters of themselves. Beyond that, whether or not they owned slaves, most white men could marry and have a family to rule over and profit from. The more ambitious would build their masculinity on property ownership as well as on possession of self and family. Thus even self-working (yeoman) farmers could become masters, if only of the "small worlds" of their households — their modest landholdings, families, and perhaps a few slaves.

Elite men epitomized, in their own minds, the masculine ideal of mastery: they owned property of many types (slaves, land, homes, luxury goods) and ruled over large households of family members and slaves. Slave ownership, in particular, provided much of the material out of which elite men made their masculinity. Power over and control of self and others spelled honor. Slave-made profits provided elite men with the money to support their families in comfort and to give their wives a measure of leisure, thus making them good husbands. Slave ownership gave them the opportunity to display their efficient and disciplined management of others, as well as their generosity (displayed, for example, with the distribution of weekly, monthly, and/or yearly clothes and food rations). Good management of slaves commanded respect from peers and made them honorable gentlemen.

Violence was the key to all of these forms of mastery, but elite and nonelite white men differed in the style of their violent acts. Elite men valued disciplined acts of violence to passionate ones — the latter suggested undignified and feminine impulses. They aspired to hold themselves above the fray when enslaved people were "punished," although they did not always succeed in doing so. They ordered overseers or other enslaved men to carry out whippings and other tortures while they either observed and put an end when they deemed it right (often fully expecting to be seen as beneficent and merciful) or absenting themselves altogether. Conflicts with peers, other men of honor, were to be resolved with duels, highly formal and disciplined rituals of violence and murder. The principle governing elite violence was honor. Honor demanded a disciplined and hyperdignified self-presentation to the world, one that emphasized mastery of one's emotions and body. In the world of honor, men presented themselves with a mask on, a mask that obscured human foibles and imperfect manhood and insistently featured only a seamless appearance of control. Many nonelite men did not share that appreciation for restraint in all arenas; indeed, many would have seen it as timid. Nonelite men often addressed conflicts through passionate and unstaged brawls.

Above all, slavery gave enslavers that which they valued more than anything else: "independence." Independence—without which no white person could truly be a man—came to be inextricably intertwined with property ownership in the United States, in no small part because of the existence of slavery. The ideal independent man owed no man his labor; he was a producer of his own accord. He owed no man money and avoided debt; he owed neither a king nor an employer his allegiance. He worked for himself. In the South, all of these attributes were obtained through the ownership of slaves. Though elite men considered themselves to be the most independent people, aspiring yeoman farmers and working men shared their preoccupation with independence, detested the yoke of obligation, and often coveted dependents, who would underscore their status as men capable not only of independence but of patronage and means.

Thus, manly American "independence" was spun out of slave labor and all that it made possible for elite and nonelite whites alike. Slaves made cotton, tobacco, and other crops that made profits. Profits bought land that would, whites hoped, produce more profit, pay debts, purchase store-bought necessaries, and subsidize slave labor in kitchen gardens, out of which slaveholding tables were laid and pantries stocked. This is to say nothing of the slave-grown produce and sugar that filled white bellies, the slave-derived cotton and wool and hemp that clothed white bodies, or the slave-raised tobacco whose smoke was a simple pleasure. In short, slaves made every aspect of economic independence possible for their owners.

Black manhood, by definition, could not be defined in the same ways. By white standards, enslaved men were not men. They were not citizens in the republic of men. Worse, they "allowed" themselves to be enslaved—something no real man would have permitted. They did not own property that white people and law recognized. As slaves and as the objects of violence, they were dishonored people, not real men. Nonetheless, black men did possess standards of masculinity, although their definition of it both overlapped with and departed from white norms. Enslaved men shared with white men a desire to protect their families from pain and want. Unlike white men, they were prevented from being able to act on this desire. When white men sold members of black families and communities, when they sexually preyed on black women, when they physically assaulted wives, children, mothers, and sisters, they simultaneously acted on their own vision of powerful manhood and assailed black men's masculinity. But while black men could not protect their families from sale, physical violence, and day-to-day exploitation, they could offer the salve of caring and compassion. In addition to caring, enslaved men valorized other "ordinary virtues," such as holding themselves to a high moral code in the creation of their manhood.

For some men, the higher moral code to which they held themselves extended to superhuman expectations of heroic behavior. Like many whites, some black men believed that real men did not submit to enslavement. Such men honored black heroes like runaways and strove to become like them, usually by attempting to run away themselves. If they made it to the North, some were able to author autobiographies or give speeches to abolitionist societies in which they expressed the idea that a slave could not be a man and in which they recounted their own manly resistance to slavery. The most heroic of all acts was open rebellion. Throughout the Americas, and with very few exceptions, slave rebellions were led and peopled by men; women had no place in this, for war was men's business.

STEPHANIE M. H. CAMP
Rice University

Cara Anzilotti, *Journal of Southern History* (May 1997); Kathleen M. Brown, *Good Wives, Nasty Wenches, and Anxious Patriarchs: Gender, Race, and Power in Colonial Virginia* (1996); Herbert G. Gutman, *The Black Family in Slavery and Freedom, 1750–1925* (1977); Peter Kolchin, *American Slavery, 1619–1877* (1993); Deborah White, *Ar'n't I a Woman? Female Slaves in the Plantation South* (1985); Betty Wood, *Women's Work, Men's Work: The Informal Slave Economies of Lowcountry Georgia* (1997); Jeffrey Young, *Domesticating Slavery: The Master Class in Georgia and South Carolina, 1670–1837* (1999).

Sports

The oldest sports in the South joined productive labor with male leisure. Hunting and fishing were primary activities of most American Indian groups, and they became crucial to the survival and enjoyment of many southerners of all ethnicities throughout the history of the region. In most of those groups, hunting was a male activity, with the pleasure of conquest combining with the centrality of game for the table. Male rituals marked successful hunts and successful initiation of young males into the men's world of the hunt. Fishing was less clearly marked as a male pastime.

A few sports were part of southern male identity as those identities were forming in the 1700s and early 1800s. Early southern sports followed class lines but often blurred them. Horse racing was an intriguing blend of English tradition and novelty, with men racing their own horses or, increasingly, gambling on horses bought and bred by the gentry. Historian Rhys Isaac describes "the role of the steed as an adjunct to virile self-presentation" in a society that welcomed aggressive competition among all free men, as long as they recognized the boundaries of a class system. The old English sport of cockfighting also brought together men in flamboyant competition, with the wealthy providing the setting—and the birds, slaves, and lower-class white men usually doing the actual fighting. For many southern males, the line between fighting as violence and fighting as sport was unclear, as understandings of male honor required violence in response to challenges to one's dignity.

The rise of organized sports has been fairly slow in the South, coming through educational institutions and commercial expansion. As baseball grew in popularity in more urban parts of the country, it was slow to move into the South, in part because, as Kenneth Greenberg argues, it put men in positions they found uncomfortable and even dishonorable. Factory life, military life, and an expanding college population brought more organized sports, in part because factories, military units, and colleges had clear routines, lots of young people, and authorities who hoped to keep people happy and, perhaps, build their character through sport.

The series of authors who tried to define southern identity in the middle decades of the 20th century rarely mentioned sports, and their brief references characterized sports as part of a newly organized world of consumption and spectacle that differed from past understandings of southern culture. The writers in *I'll Take My Stand* (1930) mentioned no sports except hunting, and Donald Davidson worried that modern forms of recreation in industrial society were "undertaken as nervous relief." For writers like William Faulkner, W. J. Cash, Will Percy, and James Agee, sports other than hunting were either anomalies or were irrelevant to the broader concerns of rural life and white supremacy. In 1961 historian Thomas Clark described high school and college basketball and football not as regional tradition but as modern innovation that reflected an important change in understandings of manhood. "Today most southern communities have developed a local mania over their athletic teams. Even hardened old rednecks who have wandered in from the cotton fields have caught the fever. Fifty years ago they would have regarded these sports as either effeminate or juvenile."

In the 20th century, most sports in the South have come to emphasize and even to glorify male competition. Individual athletes have exemplified a range of masculine identities: baseball star Ty Cobb and base-running that moved beyond determination to actual violence; Shoeless Joe Jackson and his unsophisticated willingness to take money from gamblers; golfer Bobby Jones and genteel sportsmanship; baseball player/announcer Dizzy Dean and his use of the language and grammar of plain southern folks; football coach Bear Bryant (and the coaches who aspire to be like him) and the call for personal sacrifice and honor in a team setting; baseball's Hank Aaron and tennis star Arthur Ashe and their workingmen's dignity in the face of opposition; NASCAR drivers Dale Earnhardt and Richard Petty and boxer Muhammad Ali and their competitive recklessness about personal safety; and Ali's ability to use words and the tendency of Earnhardt and Richard Petty to avoid them. In many communities, sports fans believe that the athletes who play for their high school, college, amateur, or professional teams exemplify virtues they associate with ideal manhood and, far less often, womanhood, even if some of those virtues may seem to us complicated or contradictory.

The rise of organized sports encouraged a kind of merging of southern and national trends. On one hand, the organized part of organized sports demanded rules, rote repetition, and acceptance of authority, including the authority of northern-born Ivy League coaches who came South to teach football. Colleges and the newly consolidated high schools trained their players to aspire to the Anglo-American ideal of the well-rounded scholar athlete, often with added touches of local or regional pride. On the other hand, winning at such sports allowed southerners to overturn stereotypes as being backward or lazy or, maybe more to the point, poorly organized. In the early years of southern football, defeating a better-funded northern opponent seemed a major victory for southern manhood. Historian Andrew Doyle notes that when the University of Alabama defeated the University of Washington in the 1926 Rose Bowl, newspapers described the victory as "another reminder that the South is in its manhood." At African American colleges and high schools, leaders urged players to succeed for the pride and dignity of both their own schools and more broadly of African Americans.

The majority of the region's sporting opportunities—colleges, high schools and colleges, textile mills, town teams, and the like—were more for men than for women. But women's sports have long had a place in the South, despite recurring concerns that female sports were unladylike, too aggressive, perhaps too violent, and certainly too physical. For years, a crucial issue in women's sports involved the relationship between physical activity and ladylike decorum. In the 1890s, Clara Baer started a physical education program for women at Sophie Newcomb College in New Orleans. She devised a form of basketball that, according to historian Paula Dean, "divided the court into zones with players assigned to each to reduce the unseemly rushing about the boys' full-court rules encouraged." Baer hoped to eliminate dribbling and any defensive guarding, emphasizing instead passing and shooting. Pamela Grundy argues that "learning to win" was part of becoming a sporting culture, and that many young women, trained as ladies not to be overtly competitive, faced opposition to their participation in sport. Physical education leaders and numerous college and university administrators feared that the game was too strenuous, competitive, and unladylike for polite young women and discouraged its growth as a competitive school sport, especially at the college level. From the 1930s through the 1950s, women's basketball became a game for working-class people, supported by factories, churches, and vocational schools (like Nashville Business College, a powerhouse in that era). Only in the 1960s and 1970s did women's programs, some of them at smaller southern institutions, start aggressively supporting women's basketball. The stars of southern basketball have tended to be coaches, like Margaret Wade at Delta State University, Sue Gunter at Stephen F. Austin and Louisiana State University, and above all the University of Tennessee's Pat Summitt, probably the most accomplished basketball coach in American history.

Racial segregation required separate coaches, teams, and, usually, playing fields for whites and African Americans. Many whites and African Americans took note of sporting heroes—heroes they could not legally or acceptably play in the same events. Negro League baseball stars knew their counterparts in the all-white major leagues, and many, like pitcher Satchel Paige, took pride in knowing he was as good or better than any of them. White southerners tended to disrespect African American sports in broad terms but to respect specific players and specific abilities—many whites believed black men ran faster than whites but chose not to imagine that they could play as well at supposedly thoughtful positions like quarterback. Some African American athletes, Olympian Jesse Owens and boxer Joe Louis, for example, faced the challenge of first using their abilities to overturn racist stereotypes and then dealing with some whites' expectations that they should never do or say anything controversial and some African Americans' expectations that they become vocal critics of white supremacy.

One of the most intriguing and important intersections of gender, sport, and race in the 20th-century South involves the dramatic increase in African American athletes on what were once white-only sports teams. The desegregation of team sports came shortly but not immediately after the desegregation of all-white colleges and high schools. In public schools, many white and black young men and women got to know each other as teammates, and many adults for the first time cheered for the same teams.

All-white colleges began recruiting African American players in basketball, football, track, and some other sports, and in the space of a generation, some teams at once-segregated colleges had African American majorities. Critics worry that the process of desegregating college sports, so celebrated by some fans, has in fact diminished the importance of sports at historically African American colleges and, moreover, that the white southern celebration of sports with large numbers of African American athletes may replicate an old and troubling tradition in which whites identified blacks as being gifted only in ways involving physical competition.

Stock car racing is a sport dominated by whites, especially white southern men, and its fans and participants delight in the (partially true) idea that their sport derives from the fearlessness of Appalachian men who learned their driving skills eluding federal agents trying to enforce prohibition laws. Celebrating the heroic individual male even as it relies on extraordinary technical expertise, teamwork, and corporate sponsorship, NASCAR is one of the South's most prominent contributions to modern sport. Like other sports that have become popular fairly recently in the South (for example, golf, tennis, soccer, and competitive bass-fishing), stock car racing has done relatively little to break down boundaries of gender, race, and ethnicity.

TED OWNBY
University of Mississippi

Kenneth S. Greenberg, *Honor and Slavery* (1996); Pamela Grundy, *Learning to Win: Sports, Education, and Social Change in Twentieth-Century North Carolina* (2001); Rhys Isaac, *The Transformation of Virginia, 1740–1790* (1992); Patrick B. Miller, ed., *The Sporting World of the Modern South* (2002); Ted Ownby, *Subduing Satan: Religion, Recreation, and Manhood in the Rural South, 1865–1920* (1990); Nicolas W. Proctor, *Bathed in Blood: Hunting and Mastery in the Old South* (2002).

Suffrage and Antisuffrage

Prior to the Civil War the South showed little interest in woman's enfranchisement. During Reconstruction the issue was raised in several constitutional conventions, but in no state were women granted the right to vote. After Reconstruction woman suffrage became associated with the South's desire to reduce the importance of the black male vote. A widely discussed proposal was the enfranchisement of women with educational and/or property qualifications. This extension of the franchise would include black as well as white women. Fewer black women would be able to meet these requirements, so the proportion of white voters would be increased. The strength of the black vote would be diluted, and white control of southern politics would be assured.

Proposals to enfranchise women meeting certain qualifications were introduced in constitutional conventions in Mississippi (1890), South Carolina (1895), and Alabama (1901). None of these proposals was adopted, however. Involving women in politics was contrary to southern cultural traditions, and southern men were unwilling to use this stratagem even for the purpose of coping with the vexing race issue.

In 1892 the National American Woman Suffrage Association established a special committee on southern work. Laura Clay of Kentucky chaired the committee, composed of southern women. The committee endeavored to influence public opinion through the distribution of literature and sponsoring lectures. Due largely to its efforts, suffrage organizations formed in all the southern states before the end of the decade.

When crusading for the ballot, southern women followed the guidelines of the National American Woman Suffrage Association. They conducted their agitation with dignity and restraint, avoiding the militant tactics advocated by Alice Paul's National Woman's Party. This party organized branches in the southern states, but its following there was small. It conducted no militant agitation in the area, but some southern women participated in such activities in the nation's capital. The oldest of the White House pickets and suffrage prisoners, for example, was a southern woman, 73-year-old Mary C. Nolan of Jacksonville, Fla.

The suffragists assured the public that enfranchisement would enable women to be better wives, mothers, citizens, and taxpayers. They would use their votes for the general betterment of society. The antisuffragists countered by arguing that enfranchisement would constitute a threat to the home and the family. Participation in politics would coarsen women and cause them to lose their femininity. It would also cause them to neglect their household duties and would lead to quarrels between husbands and wives.

The "antis" did little organizing in the South and can hardly be considered to have had a movement there. Their strength lay in their appeal to traditional prejudices and to generally established values. They were endeavoring to maintain the status quo while the suffragists were working for change.

The suffragists established lobbies in state capitals. Bills to enfranchise women were introduced in state legislatures, but they were seldom passed. In only three states were significant gains made. In Arkansas in 1917 the legislature passed a law permitting women to vote in primary elections. The following year Texas passed a similar law. In 1919 Tennessee granted women the right to vote for presidential electors and also the right to vote in municipal elections. No southern state, however, allowed full enfranchisement.

When the federal woman suffrage amendment was submitted to the states

Suffragists in early 20th-century Kentucky
(Photographic Archives, University of Louisville, Louisville, Ky.)

for ratification, it encountered its strongest opposition in the South. Many southerners considered suffrage a state, not a federal, matter and feared that ratification would mean federal control of elections. Others held that the enfranchisement of black women would reopen the entire issue of the African American's role in politics. Some predicted that it would usher in another era of Reconstruction.

In June 1919 Texas became the first state in the South to ratify the Susan B. Anthony Amendment. A few weeks later, Arkansas followed. Kentucky ratified in January 1920. In July 1919 Georgia became the first state in the Union to reject the proposed amendment. Georgia's example was soon followed by Alabama, South Carolina, Virginia, Mississippi, and Louisiana.

By August 1920, 35 states had ratified. The approval of only one more was needed. The governor of Tennessee submitted the question to a special session of the legislature. A bitter controversy ensued. Those opposing ratification called the proposed amendment a peril to the South and urged its rejection. Those in favor maintained that eventual ratification was a certainty and that

Tennessee's refusal could only delay it. After much emotional debate and political maneuvering, both houses of the legislature approved, and on 26 August 1920 the Nineteenth Amendment became part of the U.S. Constitution.

Two southern states refused to accept woman suffrage as the supreme law of the land. Mississippi and Georgia did not allow women to vote in the general election of 1920, claiming that the Nineteenth Amendment had been ratified too late to permit women to comply with state election laws. Georgia's leading suffragist, Mary Latimer McLendon of Atlanta, telegraphed the secretary of state in Washington, seeking his opinion in regard to her eligibility to vote. Her effort was in vain, however, because he refused to become involved.

During the months that followed, Mississippi and Georgia yielded, and woman suffrage prevailed throughout the South. Women voted and held office. And the fears of the "antis" were not realized. Women did not lose their femininity, nor did they neglect their homes for politics. Only a few aspired to political careers.

The South's strong opposition to woman suffrage was a result of the South's basic conservatism, its devotion to the ideal of the patriarchal family, and its fear of federal interference in elections. Having no alternative, the South accepted enfranchisement but remained conservative in its attitude toward women and the family. The advent of woman suffrage apparently resulted in no appreciable change in the fundamental nature of southern culture.

A. ELIZABETH TAYLOR
Texas Woman's University

Clement Eaton, *Georgia Review* (Summer 1974); Paul E. Fuller, *Laura Clay and the Woman's Rights Movement* (1975); Elna C. Green, *Southern Strategies: Southern Women and the Woman Suffrage Question* (1997); Kenneth R. Johnson, *Journal of Southern History* (August 1972); Suzanne Lebsock, in *Visible Women: New Essays on American Activism*, ed. Nancy Hewitt and Suzanne Lebsock (1993); Anne Firor Scott, *The Southern Lady: From Pedestal to Politics, 1830–1930* (1970); A. Elizabeth Taylor, *Journal of Mississippi History* (February 1968), *South Carolina Historical Magazine* (April 1976, October 1979), *The Woman Suffrage Movement in Tennessee* (1957); Rosalyn Terborg-Penn, *African American Women in the Struggle for the Vote, 1850–1920* (1998); Mary Martha Thomas, *The New Woman in Alabama: Social Reforms and Suffrage, 1890–1920* (1992); Marjorie Spruill Wheeler, *New Women of the New South: The Leaders of the Woman Suffrage Movement in the Southern States* (1993); Marjorie Spruill Wheeler, ed., *Votes for Women! The Woman Suffrage Movement in Tennessee, the South, and the Nation* (1995).

Visiting

Human beings have probably "visited" ever since they developed enough language and leisure to communicate about something other than access to food, safety, and a mate, but southern Americans have tended to make visiting especially central to their lives. Joe Gray Taylor quotes an Alabaman who, in the 1920s, described visiting as a "happy recreation," which was, nevertheless, taken "very seriously." Southern newspapers still include reports about people visiting from out of town, whether in a society column focused on the local elite or in reports from small-town church congregations. Certain common expressions of hospitality have long reflected the belief that southerners should always give the appearance of being willing to set aside whatever they are doing to visit with someone: "Y'all come to see us sometime"; "Come again real soon"; and "Come set a spell." Southerners announce that they have "had a good visit" with someone and usually mean that their conversation made them feel closer and that they are looking forward to seeing each other again.

The primary purposes of any visit have usually been to have fun and escape daily worries, to help each other solve problems, and/or to establish and reinforce personal ties. There has not been enough research to determine what visiting traditions, if any, have been exclusively southern, but many practices have been affected by their cultural and historical contexts. Until the 20th century, most southerners lived in relatively isolated rural settings, making them especially appreciative of any opportunity to talk with anyone, whether neighbors or strangers. Until the spread of air-conditioning, people wishing to escape both the summer heat and the isolation of their houses would sit on front porches where they could invite passersby to join them for a chat. The Sunday highlight for many churchgoers has been the chance to visit after the service either outside or in a "fellowship hall." At weddings, funerals, revivals, and other special gatherings, southerners have talked around tables "groaning" with massive platters of food (or, before football games, by the "tailgates" of each other's cars and trucks). Small sets of people wishing to be alone, particularly courting couples, have, throughout southern history, "gone for a ride," whether on horseback, in a carriage, or in an automobile.

The enduring social hierarchies in the South inspired complex regulations about who can see whom under what circumstances and how each individual should behave. Men have staked out special contexts for stag visits, including fishing, hunting, militia musters, political meetings, business luncheons, private clubs, locker rooms, bars, brothels, gambling, and various sports venues. Small-town men have gathered to chat and play cards or checkers in front of courthouses, in barbershops and country stores (sometimes open late to serve as a male community center), and, in recent decades, at a common table in "meat and three" restaurants. Melton McLaurin noticed that men in his grandfather's store kept rehashing the same subjects rather than approaching topics that might stimulate tensions, but many male conversations have ended in fights, especially when they were fueled by alcohol.

Women have been most apt to visit in each other's kitchens or parlors, in beauty shops (significantly called "beauty parlors" by many southern women), or while shopping together. Urban ladies of the 18th century followed the English pattern of holding "tea-tables," at which they discussed fashions and people who were not present. Gossip has often been the special purview of females, allowing them to share opinions on who needed to be helped, reined in, or shunned. The primary "work" for the wives and daughters of wealthy planters, besides making sure that their servants did as bid, was to nurture relationships with other elites through frequent visits. One young antebellum wife complained about having to give up her quiet days at home "to pay morning calls" but acknowledged that it was "a duty we all owe society, and the sacrifice must be made occasionally."

Heterosexual visits have occurred most often at parties, whether casual and spur of the moment or formal and planned. Each generation of southerners in each class has set standards for what kind of visiting was suitable for young men and women with romance on their minds. Until they were ready to court seriously one special female, 19th-century young males tended to gather in small groups and then visit a series of young women. Young people of the New South spent entire evenings riding a streetcar, much as their great grandchildren would "hang out" at a mall. For most of the 20th century, however, couples went on formal "dates," during which the young women were expected to feign interest in whatever fascinated their male companions.

Although visiting has never been an exclusive class privilege, access to particular gatherings has often been restricted. The wealthy have always had more leisure time, as well as more money to spend on food, drink, servants, and congenial private and public spaces in which to entertain, but this may have made opportunities to visit more precious to people who had to spend most of the day working. Zora Neale Hurston, in *Their Eyes Were Watching God* (1937), describes members of an all-black community who "had been tongueless, earless, eyeless conveniences all day long" enjoying "the time for sitting on porches" when they might "hear things and talk." Members of the lower classes have faced restrictions on their ability to unify through visiting since the earliest slave traders prevented Africans with the same language from being chained next to each other. Mills and other workplaces have been decorated with "no talking" signs. In spite of this, workers have met clandestinely in the woods and swamps of plantations, at times when overseers were out of sight, in workplace and school bathrooms, and during coffee and smoking breaks. Such visits have often included making jokes about the authorities.

The most significant visiting taboo in southern history has been against people of different "races" interacting as if they were peers. White men could have sex with both willing and unwilling black women, but they were never to be caught eating at the same table with African Americans. White women and their enslaved or free black servants might gossip together and help each other in childbirth, but they were never to let their "friendships" develop to a point that might challenge their social differences. Byron Bunch, in Faulkner's *Light in August* (1932), criticized Lena Grove, the daughter of humanitarian carpetbaggers, for visiting sick black people "like they was white."

In the 20th century, historical developments such as the civil rights movement and the migration of northerners to the South eroded some of the restrictions concerning who can interact with whom. Visiting practices among 21st-century southerners are probably less distinctive than in earlier times, but visiting, for whatever reasons and in whatever form, remains a favorite pastime across the South.

CITA COOK
State University of West Georgia

John W. Blassingame, *The Slave Community* (1979); Joyce Donlon, *Swinging in Place: Porch Life in Southern Culture* (2001); Elizabeth Fox-Genovese, *Within the Plantation Household: Black and White Women of the Old South* (1988); Jacquelyn Dowd Hall et al., *Like a Family: The Making of a Southern Cotton Mill World* (1987); Crandall A. Shifflett, *Coal Towns: Life, Work, and Culture in Company Towns of Southern Appalachia* (1991); Joe Gray Taylor, *Eating, Drinking, and Visiting in the South* (1982).

Womanism

The majority of African Americans live in the South, and African American communities throughout the United States are influenced substantially by southern culture and its racialized history. Movements for social change and organizations advancing African American interests often survive and succeed because of the presence of black southerners, usually women. African American women are recognized as consummate organizers in their churches and communities, and it is said that one civil rights leader commented, "If the women ever leave the Movement, I'm going with the women because nothing is going to happen without the women."

The civil rights movement brought a variety of activists to the South, including large numbers of white women. In its aftermath, white women, including some civil rights activists, sparked a feminist movement that challenged patriarchy and generated new modes of thinking about gender and women's experience. Although white feminists claimed black southern women like Fannie Lou Hamer, Gloria Richardson, Rosa Parks, and Daisy Bates as their role models, feminism emerged as a primarily white movement. In the words of some black feminist critics, "All the women are white." Consistent with American racial hierarchies, white women's experiences provided the foundation for feminist thought; the problem of racism was presumed to be subsumed within the problem of patriarchy.

Alice Walker (b. 1944), black woman and southern writer, created the term "womanist" in 1981. Novelist, poet, essayist, literary critic, and feminist, Walker discovered the limits of feminism as she sought to relate the issues and ideas identified by white women to the lived experience of black women. Seeking to integrate human liberation and self-definition, Walker eventually fashioned a succinct but very rich dictionary-style definition of her new term as a preface to *In Search of Our Mothers' Gardens: Womanist Prose*, her 1983 book of essays. With that definition, she provided the foundations for a theory of black women's history and experience that highlighted their significant roles in community and society. Heavily and enthusiastically appropriated by black women scholars in religious studies, ethics, and theology, womanist ideas became important tools for understanding black women's perspectives and experiences from a standpoint that was self-defined and that resisted the cultural erasure that not only was a destructive component of American racism but was also rapidly being replicated in American feminism.

In all of her writings—fiction, poetry, and prose—Walker struggled against the invisibility of black women. She brought ordinary southern black women into the foreground in her novels and recovered the writings about black southern women by black writers like Zora Neale Hurston, a southerner, and Jean Toomer, a traveler in the South. Inspired by Hurston, who was not only a novelist but also an anthropologist, Walker's novels and poems offered close and thick descriptions of southern black culture and connected that culture to national and global issues. In her short stories, especially in the volume *You Can't Keep a Good Woman Down*, Walker used issues raised by white feminists to raise questions about the contradictions surrounding gender in African American life and culture. At the same time, Walker also examined the intricate contradictions of white and black women's behavior in a system of white privilege, most dramatically in a short story titled "The Welcome Table" in *In Love and in Trouble.*

Walker used black women's history, black women's various forms of solidarity, and African American spirituality to construct her very complicated novel *The Color Purple.* That novel contains a tremendous amount of detail about black southerners and the complicated world they faced as they sought to survive with a degree of economic self-sufficiency, autonomy, and self-respect in the face of the violent opposition of the late 19th and early 20th centuries.

Walker was critical of the ways in which white feminists used their own experiences to interpret black women's experiences, thus ignoring or misinterpreting black women's history.

Walker first used the term "womanist" in a 1981 review of Jean Humez's book, *Gifts of Power: The Writings of Rebecca Jackson, Black Visionary, Shaker Eldress.* The review was reprinted in *In Search of Our Mothers' Gardens.* Shakers built a religious movement that required its members to be celibate. On becoming a Shaker, Rebecca Cox Jackson left her husband and assumed a life of celibacy. Because, like most black women missionaries, evangelists, and club women of the 19th and early 20th centuries, Jackson traveled with a woman partner, Humez chose to call Jackson's lifestyle "lesbian." Walker objected to Humez's use of a term that was not grounded in Rebecca Cox Jackson's definition of the situation. Walker questioned "a non-black scholar's attempt to label something lesbian that the black woman in question has not."

Within the review, Walker laid the foundations of her definition. She rejected a term for women's culture based on an island (Lesbos) and insisted that black women, regardless of how they were "erotically bound," would choose a term "consistent with black cultural values"—values that emphasized communality—"*regardless* of who worked and slept with whom." "Womanist," as defined by Alice Walker, clearly "affirmed connectedness to the entire community and the world, rather than separation." Humez's choice of labels was an example of the ways white feminists perpetuated an intellectual colonialism. This intellectual colonialism reflected the differences in power and privilege that characterized the relationships between black and white women.

With the term "womanist," Walker provided a word, a concept, and a way of thinking that allowed black women to name and label their own experiences. The invention of the term was an act of empowerment and resistance, which addressed and challenged the dehumanizing erasure of black women's experience. Walker's more elaborate definition provided a more extensive view of Walker's understandings of the experiences and history of black women as a distinctive dimension of human experience and a powerful cultural force.

First of all, Walker defined a "womanist" as a "black feminist or feminist of color," thus including the liberationist project of feminism in her definition. However, Walker gave the term an etymology rooted in the African American folk term "womanish," a term African American mothers often used to criticize their daughters' behavior. Traditionally "womanish" meant that girls were acting too old and engaging in behavior that could be sexually risky and invite attention that was harmful. Walker, however, co-opted "womanish" and used it to highlight the adult responsibilities that black girls often assumed in order to help their families and liberate their communities. Rebecca Cox Jackson lost her mother at age 13 and helped raise her brothers and sisters along with one of her brother's children. As a civil rights worker in Mississippi Freedom Schools, Walker taught women whose childhoods ended early, limiting their educations. Walker also observed the participation of young people in civil rights demonstrations and was aware of the massive resistance of children in places like Birmingham and Selma, Ala. Walker described the term "womanish" as being opposite of "girlish," subtly hinting that the pressures of accelerated development were the facts of black female life, which were not understood by white women's experiences or their meaning of "feminist." Walker's term "womanist" implied a desire to be "responsible. In charge. *Serious.*"

A womanist, according to Walker, loves other women and prefers women's culture, a very antipatriarchal orientation. However, womanists also evince a commitment "to survival and wholeness of entire people, male *and* female." A womanist is "not a separatist, except periodically, for health," and, as a "universalist," a womanist transcends sources of division, especially those dictated by color and class. Walker offered a new approach to the antagonisms of class and color among African Americans, problems often overemphasized by black nationalists. For a womanist, these issues were differences among family members. A womanist also has a determination to act authoritatively on behalf of her community. Walker evoked very specific black women role models, like Mary Church Terrell, a club woman whose politics transcended color and class, and Harriet Tubman, famous for her exploits on the underground railroad and the Civil War battlefield.

Finally, Walker offered a description of black women's culture that was at odds with some major emphases in white culture. Walker's key word was "love," and she linked it to spirituality, creative expression, and political activism. Her definition included a love of "food and roundness," which stood in stark contrast to the body images and gender norms of the dominant culture, a culture that celebrated pathologically thin white women and socially produced eating disorders. Finally, Walker emphasized self-love, a woman "loves herself, *regardless*," a direct challenge to the self-hatred that was a consequence of racism.

Although "womanist" has not displaced the terms "feminist" and "feminism," the womanist idea resonated with many black women as a grounded and culturally specific tool to analyze black women's experiences in community and society. Walker's idea was particularly useful for black women in religious studies and theology, where the confrontation between black and white theologies, in the context of debates over liberation theologies, was particularly vibrant and direct. In normative disciplines such as ethics, theology, and biblical studies, the idealism and values in Walker's idea were especially helpful. Ironically, all of the pioneering black women scholars who first used the term "womanist" in their work were southerners: Katie Geneva Cannon, author of *Black Womanist Ethics*; Jacqueline Grant, author of *White Women's Christ and Black Women's Jesus: Feminist Christology and Womanist Response*; Renita Weems, author of *Just a Sister Away: A Womanist Vision of Women's Relationships in the Bible*; and Delores S. Williams, author of "Womanist Theology: Black Women's Voices" and *Sisters in the Wilderness: The Challenge of Womanist God-Talk*. These scholars used Walker's perspective to explore the relationship of African American women's experiences to the construction of ethics, to theological and Christological ideas, and to the meaning and importance of biblical stories about women.

Although bell hooks (also a southerner), in her book *Talking Back: Thinking Feminist, Thinking Black*, suggested that some women used the term "womanist" to avoid asserting they are "feminist," the issue is more complex. Many black women who were self-identified as feminists found that the emphases of late 20th-century white feminists did not match their own concerns and experiences.

Although Walker did not indicate a desire to create a womanist movement, the term "womanism" was a natural corollary and extension of "womanist." Walker's writings and ideas, however, emphasized black women's creativity, enterprise, and community commitment, and "womanist" linked these specifically to feminism. Womanism was used to identify both the activism consistent with the ideals embedded in Walker's definition, as well as the womanist scholarly traditions that have grown up in various disciplines, especially religious studies. "Womanism is," as Stacey Floyd-Thomas points out, "revolutionary.

Womanism is a paradigm shift wherein Black women no longer look to others for their liberation."

CHERYL TOWNSEND GILKES
Colby College

Stacey Floyd-Thomas, ed., *Deeper Shades of Purple: Womanism in Religion and Society* (2006); Alice Walker, *In Search of Our Mothers' Gardens: Womanist Prose* (1983).

Workers' Wives

Although attention has been given to upper-class southern women (for example, the "southern belle") and slave women (for example, the "black mammy"), the wife of the southern worker has often been neglected. Not bound by the restrictions of racism or social demands to appear "ladylike," the worker's wife has been a significant contributor to southern history and society.

On the southern colonial farm, work was divided along gender lines. In addition to cooking, cleaning, and rearing children, women had responsibility for small animals, the dairy, gardening, and the orchard. Men cared for large animals, planted and harvested crops, and did general field work. But, in times of need, for example, during harvest season, sex roles on the colonial farm merged, as children and wife helped the husband bring in the crops.

The preindustrial work patterns continued into the antebellum South. As Frank L. Owsley noted in *Plain Folk of the Old South*, the wife of the yeoman farmer "hoed the corn, cooked the dinner or plied the loom, or even came out and took up the ax and cut the wood with which to cook the dinner." The Civil War revealed both her productivity and her endurance; after her husband went off to fight, often with her encouragement, she took over the farms and shops, and women provided the bulk of the urban labor force.

As scholars have discovered, southern women have had a more active and important role in southern politics than has been traditionally assumed. The Women's Christian Temperance Union (WCTU), antilynching crusades, and the progressive reform movements of the 19th and 20th centuries involved wives of southern workers, as well as middle- and upper-class women. But their role as political activists dates back even further. Workers' wives, for example, were politically active in the 1600s in Bacon's Rebellion in Virginia, and women such as Harriett Tubman were later involved in resistance to the slave system.

The industrialization of the South transformed to some extent the economic and social functions of women as well as men. In order to support their families, both husband and wife left the farm and took factory jobs. In Alabama, the number of men drawn into industry between 1885 and 1895 increased 31

Rural married couple, Bateville, Miss., 1968 (William R. Ferris Collection, Southern Folklife Collection, Wilson Library, University of North Carolina at Chapel Hill)

percent, but the number of women increased 75 percent. In 1890 women constituted 40 percent of the workforce in the four largest southern textile plants. But their level of political activity did not change. Women, particularly wives of workers, were active in protesting child labor, and, like Ella May Wiggins of the Gastonia strike, they were heavily involved in southern industrial struggles.

Nowhere was the importance and influence of workers' wives more vividly revealed than in the southern coalfields. By law and superstition (a mine would supposedly explode if a woman entered it), women were prohibited from industrial work, that is, working in the coal mines. And because southern coal towns were usually in isolated, rural areas, women were not able to find employment in other industries, as did miners' wives in northern coalfields. They hardly submitted, however, to the life of Victorian domesticity.

In the era before unions (1880–1933) men worked in the mines 10–14 hours a day, 6 days a week. Hence, their wives essentially controlled the domestic economy and ran the family. To assist the husband in supporting the family, wives continued their preindustrial roles of caring for the family garden, taking in boarders, and doing the laundry of company officials and single miners. And it was the wife who dealt with the daily frustration of keeping the house clean and sanitary in a town filled with coal dust and grime because the company refused to install sanitary facilities such as running water and sewers.

In the company towns that predominated in the southern coalfields, the home was hardly a "separate sphere" sheltering women from the cruelties of the competitive, "public" world, as was said to have been the case in northern urban areas. With her husband down in the coal mines, a wife dealt with the company store and had direct, day-to-day contact with company officials. Consequently, she most keenly and intensely felt the coal company's abuse of power, especially its exploitation in the form of low wages, monopolistic prices, and the lack of sanitary facilities.

Women expressed their anger toward the coal operators in a number of ways, including song. Florence Reece, who wrote the classic labor song "Which Side Are You On?" after company police had driven her husband out of their company town, was but one of many female coalfield troubadours, a list that includes Aunt Molly Jackson, Sarah Gunning, and, more recently, Hazel Dickens.

Women expressed their desire for improved living and working conditions in the coalfields, as well as their anger, by becoming major advocates for unionization. The exploits of the legendary union organizer Mother Jones are well known. But Ralph Chaplin (author of "Solidarity Forever") captured Jones's appeal when he wrote, after hearing her speak: "She might have been any coal miner's wife filled with righteous fury." The miner's wife helped ease the effects of labor strife by planting larger gardens and canning more food. Wages stopped, the usual source of food and clothing (the company store) was gone, and shelter was denied (miners were thrown out of company houses during strikes), and miners could not have succeeded in any coal strike without this extensive preparation.

Miners' wives formed auxiliaries to the United Mine Workers of America to promote the union cause. These organizations, sometimes denigrated as separate, sexist, and unequal, nevertheless increased social awareness and camaraderie among coalfield women and provided needed moral and financial support for organizing the southern coalfields. And wives of miners fought, often violently, for the union. After witnessing a gun battle during a coal strike in West Virginia in 1912, a San Francisco journalist reported, "In West Virginia women fight side-by-side with the men." Indeed, the wife's hostility to the company and her role in strikes were so important that coal company officials often took elaborate measures to encourage women's involvement in company-town life.

As the Academy Award–winning movie *Harlan County, USA* revealed, wives of miners still play a significant role in the unionization of the coalfields. The relative ease with which women have entered the coal mines as workers suggests that the coalfields may be a less "macho" culture than once assumed. Wives of workers in other southern industries and occupations have faced obstacles similar to those faced by miners' wives and have made similar contributions.

DAVID A. CORBIN
Washington, D.C.

David A. Corbin, *Life, Work, and Rebellion in the Coal Fields: Southern West Virginia Miners, 1880–1922* (1981); Margaret J. Hagood, *Mothers of the South: Portraiture of the White Tenant Farm Woman* (1939, reprint 1977); Lu Ann Jones, *Mama Learned Us to Work: Farm Women in the New South* (2001); Lorraine Gates Schuyler, *The Weight of Their Votes: Southern Women and Political Leverage in the 1920s* (2006); Anne Firor Scott, *The Southern Lady: From Pedestal to Politics, 1830–1930* (1970); Julia Cherry Spruill, *Women's Life and Work in the Southern Colonies* (1938); Melissa Walker, *All We Knew Was to Farm: Rural Women in the Upcountry South, 1919–1941* (2000).

Ali, Muhammad

(b. 1942) BOXER.

"Float like a butterfly, sting like a bee" are the words most often attributed to Muhammad Ali, the Olympic gold medalist and three-time World Heavyweight Champion boxer. Graceful yet powerful, as his catchphrase implied, Ali became just as famous for his stance against racial intolerance and his outspokenness against American society—in which he felt black men and women were treated as less than equal to whites—as he did for his outstanding success in the ring. Named Cassius Marcellus Clay Jr. when he was born— Ali's father was named after the ardent 19th-century, Madison County, Ky., abolitionist Cassius Marcellus Clay— Ali's destiny as social critic seemed fated from birth. Ironically, however, Ali changed his name to Muhammad Ali after embracing the Nation of Islam, insisting that Cassius Clay was his "slave name."

Ali began his boxing career as a 12-year-old boy in his hometown of Louisville, Ky. When his new bicycle was stolen, he reported the theft to the first police officer he found, crying, and claiming that he would beat up whoever it was who had stolen the bike. As it happened, that officer was Joe Martin, a boxing coach at the Columbia Gym in Louisville. Martin told the distraught boy, "Well, you'd better come back here and learn how to fight," thus beginning his and Ali's trainer/boxer relationship.

"I was Cassius Clay then," Ali said years later in a *Sports Illustrated* story. "I was a Negro. I ate pork. I had no confidence. I thought white people

were superior. I was a Christian Baptist named Cassius Clay." But by the time Ali was a high school senior he had begun exploring Islam, writing a senior paper on Black Muslims that nearly kept him from passing the class. He boxed as an amateur for six years, winning the Light Heavyweight gold medal in the 1960 Olympics in Rome, turning professional that same year and winning his first Heavyweight Boxing Champion title in 1964 against Sonny Liston. Shortly thereafter he changed his name to Muhammad Ali, symbolizing his new identity as a member of the Nation of Islam.

The shift in Ali's religious faith came at a volatile time in American civil rights history. Ali became famous after winning the gold medal in Rome, and after winning his first boxing championship and announcing his conversion to Islam, Ali became an outspoken critic of American racial injustice, a message in line with his new Muslim faith. Ali's obvious prowess in the ring made him a highly visible symbol of black masculinity, and his comments outside the ring became a source of black pride, propelling him into the role of a strong, straight-talking black leader. At a time when violence across the South was raging, Muhammad Ali was speaking out unambiguously against racism, violence, and injustice, and he often preached against social integration as a means to equality: "We who follow the teachings of Elijah Muhammad don't want to be forced to integrate. Integration is wrong. We don't want to live with the white man; that's all." His rhetoric was often so exaggerated, going so far as to con-

President Jimmy Carter greets Muhammad Ali at a White House dinner, 1977
(Marion S. Trikosko, photographer, Library of Congress [LC-U9-35102-20], Washington, D.C.)

done lynching as a way to keep the races separate, that he sometimes offended both sides of the race argument, from white supremacists to members of the NAACP.

In 1967, Ali refused to fight in the Vietnam War, claiming conscientious objector status on the basis of his religious beliefs. He later said to a *Sports Illustrated* reporter, "Why should they ask me to put on a uniform and go ten thousand miles from home and drop bombs and bullets on brown people in Vietnam while so-called Negro people in Louisville are treated like dogs?" As a result of his refusal to serve, Ali lost his boxing license and was stripped of his Heavyweight Boxing Champion title.

In 1970, Ali regained his boxing license, and although he made millions in the ring, he was ostensibly opposed to the sport: "We're just like two slaves in that ring. The masters get two of us big old black slaves and let us fight it out while they bet: 'My slave can whup your slave.' That's what I see when I see two black people fighting." Nevertheless, Ali went on to fight in some of the most famous and highly promoted boxing matches in history, such as "The Fight of the Century," fought in Madison Square Garden against Joe Frasier; "The Rumble in the Jungle," fought in Zaire, Africa, against George Foreman; and "The Thrilla in Manila," fought in the Philippines, again against Joe Frasier. Ali lost the first bout by unanimous decision but won the latter two, further cementing his reputation as the epitome of black masculinity.

In time, as public support waned for the war in Vietnam and as the pace of violence against blacks in America slowed, Ali's antiwhite rhetoric diminished. But his passion for racial justice continued. When asked how he would like to be remembered, he remarked, "As a man who never looked down on those who looked up to him and who helped as many of his people as he could—financial and also in their fight for freedom, justice, and equality. As a man who wouldn't embarrass them. As a man who tried to unite his people through the faith of Islam that he found when he listened to the Honorable Elijah Muhammad. And if all that's asking too much, then I guess I'd settle for being remembered only as a great boxing champion who became a preacher and a champion of his people."

JAMES G. THOMAS JR.
University of Mississippi

Gerald Early, ed., *The Muhammad Ali Reader* (1998); Thomas Hauser, *Muhammad Ali: His Life and Times* (1991); Hunt Helm, "The Making of a Champ," Louisville (Ky.) *Courier-Journal* (14 September 1997); David Remick, *King of the World: Muhammad Ali and the Rise of an American Hero* (1998).

Ames, Jessie Daniel

(1883–1972) SOCIAL REFORMER.
Jessie Daniel Ames, born 2 November 1883, had moved three times within Texas by the time she was a teenager. Her father, a stern Victorian eccentric, had migrated from Indiana to Palestine, Tex., where he worked as railroad station master, and in 1893 the Daniels moved to Georgetown, Tex., the site of Southwestern University, from which Ames later graduated.

The brutal Indian Wars and vigilantism of the period created a violent atmosphere, which strongly affected the sensitive young Jessie. A strong-willed child, she had resisted the perfect table manners expected of her and often was sent to the kitchen. In the Daniel kitchen, young Jessie heard about a lynching nearby in Tyler, an event she remembered for years and that influenced her lifelong efforts to abolish lynching.

In June 1905 Jessie Daniel married a handsome army surgeon, Roger Post Ames, who later died in Guatemala. In 1914 she rose to prominence in Texas as an advocate of southern progressivism and woman suffrage. Unlike most suffragists in the early 1920s, she understood the grave injustice against blacks in this country. She served as a vital link between feminism and the 20th-century struggle for black civil rights.

In 1924 she became field secretary for Will Alexander's Atlanta-based Commission on Interracial Cooperation, and immediately began organizing against lynching in Texas, Arkansas, and Oklahoma. Alexander brought her to Atlanta in 1929 as Director of Women's Work for the Commission, and in 1930 she founded Southern Women for the Prevention of Lynching, which within nine years had 40,000 members. Alerted by sympathetic law officers and her contacts in the press when a lynching threatened, Ames contacted women in that county who had pledged to work against violence. Her work was not always appreciated, and opposition came from women as well as men—the Women's National Association for the Preservation of the White Race claimed that Ames's women "were defending criminal Negro men at the expense of innocent white girls."

Ames did not support the federal antilynching law in 1940, believing it to be impractical. She said the bill would pass the House and southern senators would then defeat it. She was soon at odds with her boss, Dr. Alexander, as well as her old allies in the NAACP.

From May 1939 to May 1940 in the South, for the first time since records had been kept, not a single lynching occurred. World War II, however, meant the end of Southern Women for the Prevention of Lynching, just as it did to the attempt to abolish the hated poll tax in the South. The alliance between women and victimized blacks, which Ames had hoped for, was postponed.

In 1943 Southern Women for the Prevention of Lynching was absorbed by the newly formed Southern Regional Council, as was the Interracial Commission. Ames wanted to work for the new agency but found that her services were not needed.

In the foothills of the Blue Ridge Mountains, Ames set about rebuilding her life. Elected superintendent of Christian Social Relations for the Western North Carolina Conference of the Methodist Church, she welcomed the opportunity "to get back into public life and be remembered." She later returned to Texas and was honored in the 1970s as a pioneer who combined feminism with civil rights activism. Jessie Daniel

Ames died on 21 February 1972 at the age of 88.

MARIE S. JEMISON
Birmingham, Alabama

Association of Southern Women for the Prevention of Lynching and Commission on Interracial Cooperation Papers, Trevor Arnett Library, Atlanta University; Jacquelyn Dowd Hall, *Revolt against Chivalry: Jessie Daniel Ames and the Women's Campaign against Lynching* (1979); Jessie Daniel Ames Papers, Texas Historical Society, Dallas, Texas State Library, Austin, and Southern Historical Collection, University of North Carolina, Chapel Hill; Jon D. Swartz and Joanna Fountain-Schroeder, eds., *Jessie Daniel Ames: An Exhibition at Southwestern University* (1986).

Atkinson, Ti-Grace

(b. 1939) FEMINIST.

Ti-Grace Atkinson captured public attention between 1966 and 1972 as one of the most articulate and radical speakers for the women's movement in the United States. She was a protégé of Betty Friedan, who promoted her in the National Organization for Women (NOW) because her "lady-like blond image would counter-act the man-eating specter." Yet Atkinson, who was described by the media as "softly sexy," "tall," and "elegantly feline," came to stand for all that Friedan saw as most damaging to the movement: total separation from men, advocacy of abortion on demand, and the destruction of marriage and the family.

Atkinson was born in 1939 to an established Baton Rouge family. Had she remained at home, she might have become the family eccentric, an acceptable, though not desirable, role for southern women of her class. But she was one of those southerners whom Roy Reed described as born afire, who spend their days looking elsewhere for something to ease the burning. Although Atkinson virtually disowned and never discussed her southern upbringing, she always insisted that interviewers record her name as the Cajun "Ti-Grace."

Married at 17, Atkinson went to Philadelphia. By the time she was divorced five years later, she had earned a B.F.A. degree at the University of Pennsylvania and was establishing a career as an art critic, writing for *Art News* and acting as the founding director of the Philadelphia Institute for Contemporary Art. Then Simone de Beauvoir's *The Second Sex* converted her to a new philosophy. In 1966 Atkinson joined the nascent NOW, where her appearance, manners, and genteel Republican connections were put to use in national fund-raising.

A year later, Atkinson moved to New York City to pursue graduate study in political philosophy at Columbia University. As president of the local NOW chapter, she generated conflict within the group with her demands for changes not only in the organization's goals and programs but also in its internal structure. Failing to achieve her aims within NOW, she resigned in 1968 to start the October 17th Movement, later modestly renamed the Feminists—a small group of 15 to 20 women who were to separate totally from men. Although frequently described as a lesbian, Atkinson was in fact an advocate of celibacy. It was, she

acknowledged, a model for which most women were not ready.

Atkinson's distinctive position in the women's movement was characterized by her exceptional intelligence, her uncompromising radicalism, and her willingness to follow any position to its logical conclusion. She took the Mafia as a model of resistance, living outside the law, and formed an alliance with the Italian American Civil Rights League of reputed mobster Joseph Colombo. This affiliation was widely attacked, and on 6 August 1971 Atkinson separated herself from the rest of the women's movement.

Despite this breach, in November 1971 she helped organize the Feminist Party, which attempted to get the major political parties to incorporate feminist positions into their 1972 platforms. After publication in 1974 of *Amazon Odyssey*, a collection of her speeches and other writings from 1967 to 1972, Atkinson faded from public view. She continues to live in New York City.

JORDY BELL
Croton-on-Hudson, New York

Ti-Grace Atkinson, *Amazon Odyssey: The First Collection of Writings by the Political Pioneer of the Women's Movement* (1974); Maren Lockwood Carden, *The New Feminist Movement* (1974); Betty Friedan, *New York Times Magazine* (4 March 1973); Martha Weinman Lear, *New York Times Magazine* (10 March 1968); *Newsweek* (23 March 1970).

Baker, Ella Jo

(1903–1986) CIVIL RIGHTS ACTIVIST. Ella Jo Baker, the daughter of Georgianna and Blake Baker, was born in

1903 in Norfolk, Va. When she was seven, Baker's family moved to Littleton, N.C., to live with her maternal grandparents, who owned a plantation where they had previously worked as slaves. The absence of adequate public school for blacks in rural North Carolina and her mother's concern that she be properly educated resulted in Baker's attending Shaw University in Raleigh. There she received both her high school and college education. Following her graduation in 1927, she moved to New York City to live with a cousin, working as a waitress and then in a factory.

The product of a southern environment in which caring and sharing were facts of life and of a family in which her grandfather regularly mortgaged his property in order to help neighbors, Baker soon became involved in various community groups. In 1932 she became the national director for the Young Negroes Cooperative League and the office manager of the *Negro National News*. Six years later, she began her active career with the NAACP, working initially as a field secretary in the South. In 1943 she was appointed national director of the branches for the NAACP. In both capacities Baker spent long periods in southern black communities, where her southern roots served her well. Her success in recruiting southern blacks to join what was considered a radical organization in the 1930s and 1940s may be attributed, in part, to her being a native of the region and, therefore, able to approach southern people. Baker, who neither married nor had children of her own, left active service in the NAACP in 1946 in order to raise a niece.

A short while later she reactivated her involvement with the NAACP, becoming president of the New York City chapter in 1954.

In 1957 Baker went south again, this time to work with the Southern Christian Leadership Conference (SCLC), a newly formed civil rights organization. The student sit-in movement of the 1960s protested the refusal of public restaurants in the South to serve blacks and resulted in Baker's involvement in still another civil rights group. As the coordinator of the 1960 Nonviolent Resistance to Segregation Leadership Conference, which brought together over 300 student sit-in leaders and resulted in the formation of the Student Nonviolent Coordinating Committee (SNCC), Baker is credited with playing a major role in SNCC's founding. Severing her formal relationship with SCLC, she worked with the Southern Conference Educational Fund. In recognition of her contribution to improving the quality of life of southern blacks and to the founding of the Mississippi Freedom Democratic Party, she was asked to deliver the keynote address at its 1964 convention in Jackson, Miss.

Baker spent the remainder of her life in New York City, where she served as an adviser to a number of community groups. Prior to the release of Joanne Grant's film *Fundi: The Story of Ella Baker*, few people outside of the civil rights movement in the South knew about Baker's long career as a civil rights activist, but since then a number of leadership programs and grassroots organizations, such as the Children's Defense Fund's Ella Baker Child Policy

Training Institute and the Bay Area's Ella Baker Center for Human Rights, have been named in her honor. Nevertheless, she is probably less well known than many other civil rights workers, because she was a woman surrounded by southern men, primarily ministers, who generally perceived women as supporters rather than as leaders in the movement, and because of her own firm belief in group-centered rather than individual-centered leadership.

SHARON HARLEY
University of Maryland

Ellen Cantarow and Susan Gushee O'Malley, *Moving the Mountain: Women Working for Social Change* (1980); Clayborne Carson, *In Struggle: SNCC and the Black Awakening of the 1960s* (1981); Joanne Grant, *Ella Baker: Freedom Bound* (1999); Barbara Ransby, *Ella Baker and the Black Freedom Movement: A Radical Democratic Vision* (2003).

Bethune, Mary McLeod

(1875–1955) EDUCATOR.

On 10 July 1875, future educator, federal government official, and club woman Mary McLeod Bethune was born near Mayesville, S.C., one of 17 children born to former slaves and farmworkers Samuel and Patsy (McIntosh) McLeod. In 1882 Bethune left behind many of her farm chores to attend the newly opened Presbyterian mission school for blacks near Mayesville. With the help of a scholarship, she left South Carolina in 1888 and continued her education at Scotia Seminary (later Barber-Scotia College) in Concord, N.C., completing the high school program in 1892 and the Normal and Scientific Course two years

later. Hoping to become a missionary in Africa, she studied at the Moody Bible Institute in Chicago, but in 1895 the Presbyterian Mission Board turned down her application for a missionary post.

A disappointed Mary McLeod returned to her native South Carolina and began her first teaching job at Miss Emma Wilson's Mission School, where she had once been a student. Shortly thereafter, the Presbyterian Board appointed her to a teaching position at Haines Normal and Industrial Institute, later transferring her to Kindell Institute in Sumter, S.C.

Following her marriage to Albertus Bethune in May 1898, she and her husband moved to Savannah, Ga., where their only child, Albert McLeod Bethune, was born in 1899. Later that year, the family moved to Palatka, Fla., where she established a Presbyterian missionary school. Five years later, after separating from her husband, Bethune realized her lifelong ambition to build a school for black girls in the South and with her son moved to Daytona Beach, Fla., where in October 1904 the Daytona Literary and Industrial School for Training Negro Girls opened with Bethune as its president. Like most black educators in the post-Reconstruction South, Bethune emphasized industrial skills and Christian values and appealed to both the neighboring black community and white philanthropists for financial support. As a consequence of Bethune's unwavering dedication, business acumen, and intellectual ability, the Daytona Institute grew from a small elementary school to include a high school and a teacher training program. In 1923 Bethune's school merged with Cookman Institute, a Jacksonville, Fla., college for men, and became the Daytona-Cookman Collegiate Institute. Six years later, the school's name was changed to Bethune-Cookman College, in recognition of the important role that Mary McLeod Bethune had played in the school's growth and development.

As an educator in the South, Bethune had concerns that extended beyond campus life. In the absence of a municipally supported medical facility for blacks, the Daytona Institute, under Bethune's guidance, maintained a hospital for blacks from 1911 to 1927. During much of this same period she also operated the Tomoka Mission Schools, for the children of black families working in the Florida turpentine camps. Ignoring threats made by members of the Ku Klux Klan, Bethune organized a black voter registration drive in Florida, decades before the voter registration drives of the 1960s. As a delegate to the first meeting of the Southern Conference for Human Welfare, Bethune voiced her opposition to degrading southern racial customs.

Bethune joined and held official positions in a number of organizations, but she is best known among club women and the public at large for her monumental work with the National Council of Negro Women, which she founded at age 60 in 1935, serving as its president until 1949. Dedicated to meeting the myriad needs of blacks in all walks of life, the council grew under Bethune's leadership to become the largest federation of black women's clubs in

the United States. Headquartered in Washington, D.C., and with chapters throughout the country and abroad, this association published the *Aframerican Woman's Journal*, established health and job clinics throughout the South, and educated a number of black youths from poor families in the South.

In 1935 President Franklin D. Roosevelt appointed Bethune as one of his special advisers on racial affairs, and four years later she served as the director of black affairs for the National Youth Administration. In May 1955, at the age of 79, one of the South's most well-known women died. The unveiling of a statue of Bethune in a federal park located in the nation's capital in 1974 and the opening of the Mary McLeod Bethune Museum and Archives for Black Women's History in Washington, D.C., in 1979 are lasting testaments to Bethune's intelligence and determination.

SHARON HARLEY
University of Maryland

James J. Flynn, *Negroes of Achievement in Modern America* (1970); Rackham Holt, *Mary McLeod Bethune: A Biography* (1964); Barbara Sicherman and Carol Hurd Green, eds., *Notable American Women: The Modern Period: A Biographical Dictionary* (1980); Emma Sterne, *Mary McLeod Bethune* (1957).

Boggs, Lindy

(b. 1916) POLITICIAN.
Marie Corinne Morrison Claiborne ("Lindy") was born 13 March 1916 at Brunswick Plantation, near New Roads, in Pointe Coupee Parish, La. She graduated from St. Joseph's Academy at New Roads in 1931 and earned her B.A. de-

gree from Sophie Newcomb College of Tulane University in 1935, after which she became a teacher. She married Thomas Hale Boggs Sr., and, after his presumed death in an airplane that disappeared, she was selected in a special election in 1973 to succeed him as Democratic U.S. representative from the Second District in New Orleans. Boggs was elected, with 82 percent of the vote, to a full term in 1974 and served nine terms. Boggs had 30 years of behind-the-scenes political activism before her election, working with her husband to raise money, run campaigns, and manage his Washington office.

While in Congress, Boggs served on the House Appropriations Committee and the Select Committee on Children, Youth, and Families, and she chaired the Joint Committee on Bicentennial Arrangements and the Commission on the Bicentenary of the U.S. House of Representatives. Boggs promoted legislation on civil rights, children and families, and equal pay for women. She was one of the founders of the Women's Congressional Caucus and was the first woman to chair the Democratic National Convention. President Bill Clinton appointed her the U.S. Ambassador to the Vatican, where she served from 1997 to 2001. In 2006 Boggs received the Congressional Distinguished Service Award. Her political and family life is documented in *Lindy Boggs: Steel and Velvet*, a 2007 film by Louisiana Public Broadcasting and Blackberry Films.

CHARLES REAGAN WILSON
University of Mississippi

Lindy Boggs, with Katherine Hatch, *Washington through a Purple Veil: Memoirs of a Southern Woman* (1994); Thomas H. Ferrell and Judith Haydel, *Louisiana History* (Fall 1994).

Brown, Charlotte Hawkins

(1883–1961) ACTIVIST AND EDUCATOR.

Regarded as the "First Lady of Social Graces," Charlotte Hawkins Brown spent more than 50 years guiding the education and social habits of southern black youth at her Palmer Memorial Institute in North Carolina. The descendant of slaves, Brown was born Lottie Hawkins on 11 June 1883 in Henderson, N.C. Lottie's grandmother, Rebecca Hawkins, descended from English navigator Sir John D. Hawkins. At an early age, Brown saw the importance of education and cultural aspirations as embodied in her mother and grandmother. Lottie's 18-member family moved to Cambridge, Mass., in 1888 for better social, economic, and educational opportunities. At Cambridge, the young Brown attended the Allston Grammar School and cultivated a friendship with Alice and Edith Longfellow, children of Henry Wadsworth Longfellow, who lived in her neighborhood near Harvard University. Demonstrating early proclivities for leadership, Brown, at age 12, organized her church's Sunday school kindergarten department. At Cambridge English High School, moreover, she proved herself an excellent scholar and artist, rendering several crayon portraits of classmates. Considering "Lottie" too ordinary, she changed her name to Charlotte Eugenia Hawkins upon graduation. Observing Brown in 1900 reading Virgil while babysitting two infants, Alice Freeman Palmer, humanitarian and president of Wellesley College, became her benefactor.

Influenced by educator and power broker Booker T. Washington, Brown sought to teach blacks in the South. To further this goal, she enrolled, with the help of Palmer, in the State Normal School at Salem, Mass., in the fall of 1900. Having been approached by a field secretary of the American Missionary Association, a white-led group that administered and financed southern black schools, Brown eagerly accepted an invitation to teach in her native state. Barely 18 years old, Brown emerged from a Southern Railway train in the fall of 1900, where she was confronted with the unfamiliar terrain of Guilford County, N.C. Suspending her junior college education at State Normal School, she began her first teaching job at Bethany Institute in Sedalia — a small, dilapidated, rural school for African Americans. Securing money from northern friends and donations from the Sedalia community, Brown soon raised funds to erect a campus with more than 200 acres and two new buildings. Alice Freeman Palmer Institute, named in honor of her benefactor, opened on 10 October 1902. It was later renamed the Alice Freeman Palmer Memorial Institute upon Palmer's death.

Distinguished among its contemporaries, Brown's private finishing school for rural African Americans provided college preparatory classes for upper-level high school students. Such instruction fitted the school's dual ambitions: to undo common assumptions of African American inferiority and to provide an expansive education beyond vocational studies. At Palmer, classes included art, math, literature, and Romance languages.

In addition to academic training, Brown outlined an exacting program of etiquette, involving lessons in character and appearance, for black boys and girls. Brown expected her students to abide by a strict code of Victorian moral conduct. She worked to smooth "the rough edges of social behavior" by producing graduates who were educationally sound, religiously sincere, and "culturally secure." This cultural regime, in part, took the form of small discussion groups for boys and girls, the boys led by an adult male counselor and the girls by an adult female counselor, in which students received individual attention in matters of etiquette. In one boys' session, discussion centered on the best manner in which to obtain "culture," along with clean minds and bodies. Students also participated in "wholesome" fitness activities designed to nurture habits of self-reliance, self-control, and fair play. Palmer girls played basketball and volleyball. The young men's sports repertoire was more expansive and included basketball, football, baseball, and track and field.

Perhaps Brown's most noted contribution to her student's cultural education was her etiquette manual, *The Correct Thing to Do, to Say, to Wear*. In it, she succinctly defined good manners for boys and girls, at home and outside of the home. Proper introductions, boy-girl relationships, and dress were also addressed. Palmer's curriculum and Brown's writings mirrored her race philosophy, which sought a holistic education for black youth based on the uplift of the individual. Charlotte Hawkins Brown and fellow black educators Mary McLeod Bethune and Nannie Helen Burroughs became collectively known as the "Three B's of Education," stressing liberal arts and cultural training for race uplift. The school's political and cultural legacy largely hinges on Palmer's credo, "Educate the individual to live in the greater world." Brown's shepherding of Palmer, which survived a major fire in 1917, ended in 1952. She died in 1961 and is buried on the Palmer campus, now a state historic site.

ANGELA HORNSBY-GUTTING
University of Mississippi

Charlotte Hawkins Brown, *The Correct Thing to Do, to Say, to Wear* (1941); Colonel Hawkins Jr., in *The Heritage of Blacks in North Carolina*, vol. 1, ed. Philip N. Henry and Carol M. Speas (1990); Tera Hunter, *Southern Exposure* (September/October 1983); Marsha Vick, in *Notable Black American Women*, ed. Jessie Carney Smith (1992); Charles Wadelington, *Tar Heel Junior Historian* (1995); Charles W. Wadelington and Richard F. Knapp, *Charlotte Hawkins Brown and Palmer Memorial Institute: What One Young African American Woman Could Do* (1999).

Burroughs, Nannie Helen

(1879–1961) EDUCATOR AND SOCIAL ACTIVIST.
As a church and organization leader, school founder and educator, women's advocate and race champion, Nannie Helen Burroughs was a pragmatic warrior and outspoken public intellectual who defied conventional female confinements of her era. Through her newspaper commentary, speeches, and writings, she inserted herself into the male-centered discourse on race advancement. Her work paralleled that of better-known black women predecessors and contemporaries, including Annie Julia Cooper, Mary Church Terrell, and Mary McLeod Bethune, and her accomplishments and zeal for race uplift were equally impressive. She brought into the public sphere a deep concern for black workers who lacked "social or economic pull" and a belief in self-help that caused people to compare her to Booker T. Washington. Burroughs, however, was more like W. E. B. Du Bois in her belief that blacks must demand their full rights, including woman suffrage, and must keep agitating for justice. "Hound dogs are kicked, not bull dogs," she wrote.

Burroughs's unique contribution to black female empowerment was in her understanding that black women needed both "respectability"—sometimes oversimplified by scholars as a middle-class notion—and economic self-sufficiency. In her view, one was not possible without the other. Her school, the National Training School for Women and Girls in Washington, D.C., was the realization of her dream of providing a practical education that would make black women economically self-sufficient and beyond spiritual and moral reproach. It was founded in 1909 with the help of the Women's Auxiliary of the National Baptist Convention, where Burroughs was the long-serving corresponding secretary. Graduates were expected to become community-minded wage earners who would counter the prevailing negative stereotypes of the black race—particularly of its women. Burroughs's grand vision was reflected in the fact that in naming the school she left out "Baptist," although she was supported by that denomination, and included "National" to signify the school's nonsectarianism and her own independence. Women wrote to Burroughs from across the nation seeking admission for themselves or their daughters and expressing delight in the prospect of living in such a protective enclave and reaping its many benefits.

Burroughs believed that women were the linchpins of race progress, and the curriculum stressed Christian-inspired precepts about the dignity of all work. By training black women to be skilled workers and "professionalizing" their work, including domestic work, she sought to raise women's self-esteem, race pride, and wages. Her school offered a mandatory black history course, courses in music, public speaking, secretarial skills, the Bible, and hygiene, plus nontraditional courses in shoe repair and printing. Using student labor, successful commercial ventures such as the Sunlight Laundry were launched. The school's creed—the three B's, "the Bible, the Bath, and Broom, clean life, clean body, clean house"—was infused into every aspect of school life. So was Burroughs's defiant certitude about black female education, captured in the famous declaration that became the school's motto: "We specialize in the wholly impossible."

In establishing the National Training School for Women and Girls (renamed the National Trade and Professional School for Women and Girls in 1939), Burroughs challenged the male leadership of the National Baptist Convention, which was wary of women leaders, and Booker T. Washington, who opposed locating black schools outside of the South for fear of losing support from white northerners. Burroughs realized the importance of having a black female presence in the nation's capital and used that visibility to attract a national and international student body. In addition to her long tenure as founder and principal of the National Training School for Women and Girls, Burroughs helped to organize the National Association of Wage Earners in 1921 to support better wages and living conditions for domestic workers.

Following her death in 1961, the school was renamed in her honor, and it continues as a kindergarten through sixth grade Christian day school on that same Washington, D.C., hillside from which Burroughs looked out into the world and sought to change it.

AUDREY THOMAS MCCLUSKEY
Indiana University

Sharon Harley, *Journal of Negro History* (Winter/Autumn 1996); Evelyn Brooks Higginbotham, *Righteous Discontent: The Women's Movement in the Black Baptist Church, 1880–1920* (1993); Audrey Thomas McCluskey, *Signs* (Winter 1997); Nannie Helen Burroughs Papers, Library of Congress Manuscript Division; Victoria W.

Wolcott, *Journal of Women's History* (Spring 1997).

Carter, Rosalynn

(b. 1927) FORMER FIRST LADY OF THE UNITED STATES.

Like First Lady Eleanor Roosevelt, Rosalynn Smith Carter played a major role in national affairs during her tenure in the White House. Since then, she has acted as a partner in many of former president Jimmy Carter's political and business endeavors, and she has strongly promoted mental health and women's rights issues. Her autobiography, *First Lady from Plains* (1984), has been warmly received by political analysts and literary critics.

Born in Plains, Ga., on 18 August 1927, Rosalynn Smith enjoyed a relatively carefree childhood until her father died of leukemia when she was 13. The following years were lean ones for her family—her mother, Allie Smith, was forced to make ends meet by taking in sewing and selling extra eggs and butter from the family's farm. Rosalynn helped her mother by working part time after school in a beauty salon. After her graduation from Plains High School as valedictorian of her class, Rosalynn Smith entered Georgia Southwestern College, a two-year college in Americus, Ga. In 1944, while visiting her best friend, Ruth Carter, Rosalynn spied and admired a picture of Ruth's brother Jimmy, a U.S. Naval Academy student. The couple married two years later. Ambitious and intelligent, she viewed her husband's naval career as her ticket out of Plains. Jimmy Carter's career took the young couple as far as Hawaii before his father died in 1953, when he resigned his commission to return to Plains to take over the family peanut business. Although she opposed his decision to return to Plains, Rosalynn Carter soon plunged into keeping books for the business, raising her family, and, eventually, taking accounting courses.

Politics has been the lifeblood of the Carter family. Rosalynn Carter's first taste of public life occurred in the early 1960s during her husband's stint on the local school board. His liberal political stances often brought threats to her family and the peanut business from area residents. In Jimmy Carter's 1962 bid for the Georgia state Senate, Rosalynn Carter handled all of his campaign correspondence. By 1970, when Carter was elected governor of Georgia, she had gained experience and, thereby, a reputation as a "steel magnolia"—a warm, gracious woman who was also politically astute. Eager to move beyond the boundaries of the governor's mansion, she worked with the Georgia Governor's Commission to Improve Service for the Mentally and Emotionally Handicapped, as a volunteer at the Georgia Regional Hospital in Atlanta, and as honorary chairman of the Georgia Special Olympics, and over the next four years she helped establish 134 daycare centers for the mentally retarded.

From 1973 to 1976 Rosalynn Carter campaigned independently in 96 cities and 36 states in Governor Carter's bid for the presidency. Once the Carters reached the White House, the new first lady took an active interest in national

Rosalynn Carter, first lady of the United States, 1977–81 (Carter Presidential Library, Atlanta)

policy making, attending cabinet meetings, holding weekly working lunches with President Carter, heading a diplomatic mission to South America, and attending the Camp David Mideast Peace Summit. She continued to pursue mental health reform on a national level while serving on the President's Commission on Mental Health and on the Board of Directors of the National Association of Mental Health. Her support of the Equal Rights Amendment won her a merit award from NOW.

Rosalynn Carter again took to the campaign trail in President Carter's reelection drive of 1980. His defeat was particularly devastating for her, and after two decades of public service she initially found it difficult to adjust to private life. After her return to Plains, she renewed her focus on mental health and women's rights. Numerous speaking engagements and promotions of her autobiography, *First Lady from Plains,*

and of *Everything to Gain: Making the Most of the Rest of Your Life,* written with her husband, allowed Rosalynn Carter to talk publicly and candidly about her life as first lady and to raise social and political issues of concern to her. In 1982 the Carters founded the Carter Center, a not-for-profit, non-governmental organization whose mission it is to "wage peace, fight disease, and build hope" worldwide. She has worked to promote the mental health and well-being of individuals, families, and caregivers through the Rosalynn Carter Institute for Caregiving at Georgia Southwestern State University, an institute founded in her honor on the campus of her alma mater in Americus, Ga., and she continues to contribute her time and efforts to Habitat for Humanity, a network of volunteers who build homes for the needy, and Project Interconnections, a public/private non-profit partnership to provide housing for homeless people who are mentally ill. Rosalynn Carter has received countless honors for her work. In August 1999 President Clinton awarded Rosalynn and Jimmy Carter the Presidential Medal of Freedom, America's highest civilian honor, and in 2001 Rosalynn was inducted into the National Women's Hall of Fame.

ELIZABETH MCGEHEE
Washington Post

Carl Sferrazza Anthony, in *American First Ladies: Their Lives and Legacy,* ed. Lewis L. Gould (2001); Patricia A. Avery, *U.S. News and World Report* (25 June 1984); Rosalynn Carter, *First Lady from Plains* (1984); Phil Gailey, *New York Times Book Review* (15 April 1984); *Who's Who in America* (1980–81).

Chesnut, Mary Boykin

(1823–1886) DIARIST AND AUTHOR.
Mary Boykin Miller Chesnut was
born 31 March 1823 in Stateboro, S.C.,
the eldest child of Mary Boykin and
Stephen Decatur Miller, who had served
as U.S. congressman and senator and
in 1826 was elected governor of South
Carolina, as a proponent of nullifica-
tion. Educated first at home and then in
Camden schools, Mary Miller was sent
at age 13 to a French boarding school in
Charleston, where she remained for two
years, broken by a six-month stay on
her father's cotton plantation in frontier Mississippi. In 1838 Miller died and
Mary returned to Camden. On 23 April
1840 she married James Chesnut Jr.
(1815–85), the only surviving son of one
of South Carolina's largest landowners.

Chesnut spent most of the next 20
years in Camden and at Mulberry, her
husband's family plantation. When
James Chesnut was elected to the
Senate in 1858, his wife accompanied
him to Washington, where they began
friendships with many politicians who
would become the leading figures of
the Confederacy, among them Varina
and Jefferson Davis. Following Lincoln's
election, James Chesnut returned to
South Carolina to participate in the
drafting of an ordinance of secession
and subsequently served in the Pro-
visional Congress of the Confederate
States of America. He served as aide to
Gen. P. G. T. Beauregard and President
Jefferson Davis, and he achieved the
rank of general. During the war, Mary
accompanied her husband to Charleston, Montgomery, Columbia, and
Richmond, her drawing room always
serving as a salon for the Confederate
elite. From February 1861 to July 1865
she recorded her experiences in a series
of diaries, which became the principal
source materials for her famous portrait
of the Confederacy.

Following the war, the Chesnuts
returned to Camden and worked unsuccessfully to extricate themselves from
heavy debts. After a first abortive attempt in the 1870s to smooth the diaries
into publishable form, Mary Chesnut
tried her hand at fiction. She completed
but never published three novels and
then in the early 1880s expanded and
extensively revised her diaries into the
book now known as *Mary Chesnut's
Civil War* (first published in truncated
and poorly edited versions in 1905 and
1949 as *A Diary from Dixie*).

Although unfinished at the time of
her death on 22 November 1886, *Mary
Chesnut's Civil War* is generally acknowledged today as the finest literary
work of the Confederacy. Spiced by the
author's sharp intelligence, irreverent
wit, and keen sense of irony and meta-
phorical vision, it uses a diary format
to evoke a full, accurate picture of the
South in civil war. Chesnut's book,
valued as a rich historical source, owes
much of its fascination to its juxtapo-
sition of the loves and griefs of individuals against vast social upheaval and
much of its power to the contrasts and
continuities drawn between the antebellum world and a war-torn country.

ELISABETH MUHLENFELD
Sweet Briar College

Mary A. DeCredico, *Mary Boykin Chesnut:
A Confederate Woman's Life* (1996); Elisa-

beth Muhlenfeld, *Mary Boykin Chesnut:
A Biography* (1981); C. Vann Woodward, ed.,
Mary Chesnut's Civil War (1981); C. Vann
Woodward and Elisabeth Muhlenfeld, eds.,
*The Private Mary Chesnut: The Unpublished
Civil War Diaries* (1985).

Conroy, Pat

(b. 1945) WRITER.

Pat Conroy has spent his career crafting personal trauma and abuse into rich, romantic, and often painfully autobiographical fiction. Along the way, he has become famous nearly as much for his contentious battles and reconciliations with his alma mater and his father as for his artistic and phenomenal commercial accomplishments.

Born in 1945 to Donald N. Conroy, a Marine fighter pilot, and Frances "Peggy" Peek, a native Georgian with a love for Margaret Mitchell's *Gone with the Wind*, Donald Patrick Conroy was the eldest of seven children, nearly all of whom would struggle with the legacy of their domineering father's physical and psychological abuse.

The itinerancy of military life ended for Conroy in Beaufort, S.C., where he spent his final two years of high school. Here, Conroy discovered Thomas Wolfe, the writer to whom his fiction is most indebted. He also excelled in athletics and earned a basketball scholarship to the only school his father would allow him to attend, the Military Institute of South Carolina, popularly known as The Citadel.

Failing to rise above the rank of private, Conroy found far more success with a basketball in his hand than with a rifle on his shoulder. As a senior, Con-roy started at point guard and received the dubious honor of being named Most Valuable Player for the disappointing 1966–67 season, an experience described in the memoir, *My Losing Season* (2003).

The Citadel was fertile ground for Conroy. His first book, *The Boo* (1970), was a self-published collection of essays celebrating Lt. Col. Thomas N. Courvoisie, the recently fired assistant commandant of cadets at The Citadel. The publication of *The Lords of Discipline* (1980) drew the ire of the institution, blowing open the secrets of the lightly fictionalized "Carolina Military Academy" with the same veracity—and not dissimilar reaction—with which his other works described the Conroy family. The novel was awarded the Lillian Smith Book Award in 1981.

Following his graduation in 1967, Conroy returned to Beaufort as a teacher and coach. In the fall of 1969, Conroy met and married Barbara Jones, a Vietnam War widow pregnant with her second child. He also accepted a position at the two-room elementary school on nearby Daufuskie Island, an impoverished African American community that was accessible only by ferry and long neglected by the school district. Daufuskie became "Yamacraw Island" in *The Water Is Wide* (1973), a memoir that was a modest success and was adapted as the film *Conrack* (1974).

Conroy followed up the memoir with his first novel, *The Great Santini* (1976), the autobiographical tale of the traumatic abuse suffered by a teenaged boy and his family at the hands of a bullying Marine father. Its publication nearly destroyed both Conroy and his family. He collapsed in a parking lot on his book tour, his father's family quit speaking to him, and his marriage ended, as did his parents'. Peggy Conroy even entered the novel as evidence in her divorce proceedings.

In *The Prince of Tides* (1986), Conroy again used his and his family's tragic history, this time exploring the adult consequences of abuse, particularly in his sister's manic depression and his own history of depression. The novel became a national phenomenon, riding a wave of momentum from instant best seller to Academy Award–nominated film.

Conroy's next novel, *Beach Music* (1995), drew from subjects as disparate as the Holocaust, the Vietnam War, Conroy's first divorce, his time in Rome with his second wife and their children, and the depression and eventual suicide of his youngest brother, Thomas. Highly anticipated and long delayed, *Beach Music* was another commercial success, if not a critical one.

Throughout the 1990s, Conroy remained in the headlines, vocally and financially supporting attempts to force The Citadel to accept women into its corps of cadets. Ultimately, women were admitted into the institution, and Conroy even received an honorary degree. Likewise, Conroy reconciled with his father: "My father answered my first novel by setting out to prove I was a liar of the first magnitude," he wrote in *Atlanta Magazine* in 1999, shortly after his father's death. "He worked night and day in turning himself into a father even his own children could love."

He has returned to Beaufort and lives on nearby Fripp Island with his third wife, the author Cassandra King. Conroy has revealed that he had been engaged with the Margaret Mitchell estate in protracted discussions to write a sequel to *Gone with the Wind*, the novel worshipped by his mother, but that the negotiations broke off over issues of editorial control.

ANTHONY D. HOEFER JR.
Louisiana State University

John Berendt, *Vanity Fair* (July 1995); Landon C. Burns, *Pat Conroy: A Critical Companion* (1996); Robert W. Hamblin, *Aethlon: The Journal of Sport Literature* (Fall 1993); David Toolan, *Commonweal* (February 1991).

Cooper, Anna Julia Haywood

(1858?–1964) WRITER.
Annie Julia Cooper's extraordinary energy and long productive life propelled her from being the daughter of a bondwoman to a place among the most educated and articulate voices in America. She devoted her 105 years in North Carolina, Ohio, and Washington, D.C., to education, language, and social change.

Cooper's education in rhetoric at St. Augustine's Normal and Collegiate Institute in Raleigh, N.C., at Oberlin College, and in her faculty position as a teacher of Latin at the renowned M Street School in Washington, D.C., paved the way for her writings. Her education also created the subject and method she used to stand for asserting rights in the educational and gender politics of African American women.

Cooper's father was reputed to be

her mother's owner. After the Civil War, at age nine, she attended a school founded as an outgrowth of the Freedmen's Bureau, St. Augustine's Normal School, and made it her "world." At St. Augustine's, Cooper ignored school rules limiting Latin and Greek instruction to boys and finagled her way into classes. By the time she enrolled at Oberlin College in 1881, she had read a wide array of Greek and Latin texts, and Oberlin stoked those interests in classical literature. In 1887, Cooper began teaching Latin and Greek at the M Street School and taught there for nearly 40 years. Cooper used education to prepare students for leadership roles. Her focus on cultivating the minds of black children put her at odds with Booker T. Washington and those who believed blacks were suited only for manual work, and she temporarily lost her job at the M Street School when she insisted on an intellectually based curriculum for her students.

Cooper used her argumentative skills at a time when American racial ideologies and educational institutions specifically excluded blacks from the power of oratory and rhetoric. Popular culture framed blacks as incapable of delivering useful information or shaping the public discourse. Nevertheless, in *A Voice from the South* (1892), Cooper built tight deductive arguments using the skills of classical rhetoric that she had learned in her youth. She would quickly convince her audience to agree with her on some point about general moral standards, and then, with a swift turn of phrase, she would hijack the audience's assumptions governing women's rights and

even the definition of race. Cooper's collection of orations and essays demonstrates her command of argument and prose that she used to redefine the very foundations of race and gender in the United States.

While teaching at M Street, Cooper took a leave from her job and attended the University of Paris–Sorbonne, earning a Ph.D. in French with a 1925 dissertation on slavery and the French Revolution. In her 70s, Cooper served as the president of Frelinghuysen University in Washington, D.C. For 10 years she oversaw the school that offered adult education at night to working people in the city. She remained committed to education and the power to speak throughout her long life.

TODD VOGEL
University of Washington

Anna Julia Cooper, *The Voice of Anna Julia Cooper: Including "A Voice from the South" and Other Important Essays, Papers, and Letters*, ed. Esme Bhan and Charles Lemert (1998), *Slavery and the French Revolutionists, 1788–1805, Studies in French Civilization*, vol. 1 (1925, 1988); Leona C. Gable, *From Slavery to the Sorbonne and Beyond: The Life and Writings of Anna J. Cooper* (1982); Todd Vogel, *Rewriting White: Race, Class, and Cultural Capital in Nineteenth-Century America* (2004).

Davis, Jefferson, Capture of

When the Union army at last took possession of Richmond, Va., on 3 April 1865, the Confederate government, if not yet completely decimated, certainly could no longer function in its onetime capitol. Indeed, the previous evening, the Confederacy's chief executive,

THE CHAS-ED "OLD LADY" OF THE C.S.A.

Confederate president Jefferson Davis's capture by Union cavalry on 10 May 1865. Here the artist shows a camp in the woods, where Davis, wearing a dress, shawl, and bonnet and carrying a water bucket labeled "Mom Davis" and a Bowie knife, is accosted by Union soldiers. One Union soldier (center) lifts Davis's skirt with his saber, mocking, "Well, old mother, boots and whiskers hardly belong to a high-toned Southern lady." Davis implores, "I only wish to be let alone." At right, another soldier, speaking in a German accent, says, "Mein Gott, ter olt mutter vears ter pig gavalrie poots!" He may be intended to represent the Norwegian-born tanner who first spotted Davis. The soldier at left exclaims, "Jerusalem! her old Mother, hey! Its Leach in petticoats — That's so." Behind Davis, a woman warns, "Do not provoke the President, he might hurt some one." A black youth, presumably Davis's servant, looks on, exclaiming, "Golly Marse Yank, de old Missus is done gone shu-ah!" (Library of Congress [LC-USZ62-89591], Washington, D.C.)

Jefferson Davis, along with members of his cabinet and other Confederate officials, departed Richmond for points farther south. First, they decamped to Danville, Va., in a feeble attempt to reconstitute a seat of command. But as Confederate armies everywhere began to surrender, Davis and his diminishing entourage — still vowing to continue the fight — were forced to keep moving. By May, Davis and those who remained in his party had crossed into Georgia. By this time, too, Union soldiers began to search more intensively for the former

Confederate president, who was now wrongly suspected of having participated in the assassination of Abraham Lincoln.

Union soldiers, specifically the members of the Fourth Michigan Cavalry, came upon Davis's party on 10 May 1865, near the town of Irwinville in southern Georgia. Although historians disagree as to the details, the ex-Confederate leader apparently made some attempt to evade his captors and donned some type of garment that he may have hoped would conceal his identity. Reports quickly circulated, however, that Jefferson Davis had put on one of his wife's dresses (Varina Davis, in fact, was not with the captured party) and so tried to flee by disguising his sex. The extreme hostility that northerners felt toward Davis, the tradition of cross-dressing stories that had already become part of Civil War folklore, and the desire that many in the North felt to ridicule the previously highly touted manhood of southern men almost guaranteed the rumors that would fly during May and June of 1865 regarding "Jeff in Petticoats" and "Jeffie Davis—the Belle of Richmond." Stories, cartoons, even a display in P. T. Barnum's museum, all portrayed the Confederate president as arrayed in feminine finery but then discovered and subdued by his Union captors. The accounts offered war-weary northerners a moment of humor and a way to express their outrage at the South, now pictured as ludicrously defying all proper gender conventions. Moreover, this portrayal of Davis in drag did double duty in allowing northerners to give vent to feelings of hostility toward southern women, whom many believed had been unnaturally aggressive in their defense of the Confederacy, and toward white southern men, who had once bragged of having courage that was superior to their Yankee counterparts.

Confederates, for their part, no doubt felt an intense humiliation, not only from the ultimate defeat of their national enterprise, but also from the shameful depictions of their onetime national leader. Indeed, the desire to defend the honor and manhood of defeated southerners and his own manhood specifically prompted Jefferson Davis to have a photograph taken in 1869, in which he attired himself in the clothes he allegedly wore at his capture.

NINA SILBER
Boston University

Gaines Foster, *Ghosts of the Confederacy: Defeat, the Lost Cause, and the Emergence of the New South* (1987); Nina Silber, *The Romance of Reunion: Northerners and the South, 1865–1900* (1993); Jay Winik, *April 1865: The Month That Saved America* (2001).

Designing Women

The hit television series *Designing Women* aired on CBS from 1986 to 1993. The popular sitcom revolved around the work and personal lives of four feisty southern women and one African American man who worked together at Sugarbaker and Associates design firm in Atlanta. The principal characters were two sisters, Julia (Dixie Carter) and Suzanne Sugarbaker (Delta Burke), Mary Jo Shively (Annie Potts), Charlene (Jean Smart), and Anthony (Mesach Taylor). Smart and Burke left the show after the 1990–91 season and were replaced by Julia's cousin, Allison Sugarbaker (Julia Duffy) and Karlene (Jan Hooks), Charlene's younger sister. The series was nominated for several Emmy and Golden Globe awards and remained in or near the Top 10 in viewer ratings for much of its run.

Designing Women was particularly notable for its focus on four women and their friendship as well as for its pronounced political point of view. Much of the sitcom's appeal lay in its female characters: its plotlines revolved around the spaces they convened in, around their very southern ways of talking, around their interests in femininity, and around their friendships. The series also tackled a number of hot-button issues of its time, including domestic violence, sexual harassment, divorce, equal pay, weight gain, pornography, and the nomination hearings of Clarence Thomas. Like *Maude* before it and *Murphy Brown* and *Roseanne* after it, the show came to be seen as espousing a liberal feminist point of view, particularly through the lengthy monologues Julia was prone to deliver. But, unlike these other series, the soft-pedaled feminism of *Designing Women* adopted a distinctly southern perspective. The characters' accents, looks, and mannerisms consistently signified "southernness" and referred to the region. The character Suzanne, a former pageant queen, served as perhaps the most stereotypically southern of the women. She was often the catalyst for the show's explorations of femininity, an ongoing theme of the show that positioned femininity as a site of both oppression and potential power. *Designing Women* thus reworked southern womanhood for wider, national consumption.

Indeed, the series mediated the region for the United States as a whole and took up the New South almost as a character on the show, revamping a "moonlight-and-magnolia" take on southern femininity as well as the demonizing representations of the region popular in the 1970s in films such as *Deliverance*. The sitcom's representation of Atlanta, and the South more broadly, was adroitly designed to showcase the

region's recent growth (in both economic and "moral" terms) via a focus on progress and liberal values. Several key episodes addressed southern themes, including southern tourism, historical memory, and the lingering impact of earlier popular portraits of the South, including *Gone with the Wind*. The inclusion of Anthony also reworked certain stereotypical images of regional black masculinity, although the series was perhaps more successful in challenging certain images of gender than in dealing with race or class.

Designing Women was created by Linda Bloodworth-Thomason, who produced the series with her husband, Harry Thomason. The pair and the core cast are all native southerners, and the production company's strategy was to market its sitcom by region. The approach proved successful, as the series had notably higher rating averages in urban southern areas. The executive producers were also avowed Democrats with close ties to Bill and Hillary Clinton. The exterior shots of Suzanne's home in the series actually featured the Arkansas governor's mansion, home to the Clintons for much of the sitcom's airing, and Linda Bloodworth-Thomason created Bill Clinton's 1992 campaign film, *The Man from Hope*. Clinton's inauguration was worked into the plotline of one episode, and Charlene claimed in another to have worked for Clinton while he was governor.

The show narrowly escaped cancellation in its first season and was saved only after the executive producers and stars encouraged audience members to protest. This campaign, led by Viewers for Quality Television, generated 50,000 letters of support, and the series was renewed. By the end of *Designing Women*'s final season, reruns of the sitcom had been sold to 200 television stations in the United States, which at that time was the widest syndication distribution in history. It continues to air in rerun rotation, particularly on Lifetime Television, which hosted a reunion celebration of the series in 2003. During its run the series garnered several Viewers for Quality Television awards and even prompting a parody in MAD *Magazine*. Its legacy continues among an active fan base, ranging from women who write fan fiction based upon the series to gay men who have developed drag routines reviving the characters.

TARA MCPHERSON
University of Southern California

Bonnie Dow, *Prime-Time Feminism: Television, Media Culture, and the Women's Movement since 1970* (1996); Tara McPherson, *Reconstructing Dixie: Race, Gender, and Nostalgia in the Imagined South* (2003); Lauren Rabinovitz, in *Television History and American Culture*, ed. Mary Beth Haralovich and Lauren Rabinovitz (1999).

Dixon, Thomas, Jr.

(1864–1946) WRITER.

Thomas Dixon's views on gender cannot be separated from his repugnant ideas on race. Throughout his adult life he fixated on the apocryphal notion that black men yearned to commit sexual violence against white women, and that black temptresses lured white men into their embrace. In his mind, the mulatto children that resulted from white men and women's "forced" unions with black sexual predators spelled the death of American civilization and the Anglo-Saxon race. To Dixon, the decline of the United States rested upon the North's insistence on granting bestial black men political rights during Reconstruction, thereby unleashing their libidinous desires for white women and facilitating the transformation of the white nation into a "mongrelized" and vulnerable state.

Although Dixon's notions of gender were profoundly shaped by a rabid racism rooted in his southern heritage, he was piercingly attuned to the cultural beats of his time. Steeped in the moral intensity of both his Baptist background and Victorian America as a whole, he plied his cautionary tales about white and black men and women acting outside their gendered roles and racial hierarchies within the easily digested forms of popular romance and melodrama.

Dixon was born in 1864 in Cleveland County in the southwestern corner of North Carolina. His father was a minister and farmer, who belonged to the Ku Klux Klan, as did his father's Confederate veteran brother. Thomas Dixon Sr. seems to have been the source of many of his son's psychosexual perceptions. Not only did his son decry his mother's ostensible rape as a child-bride in his autobiography, but Dixon Sr. was rumored to have fathered a son with the family's African American cook.

Thomas Dixon Jr. attended the Baptist-run Wake Forest College at the age of 15, where he excelled academically. He attended Johns Hopkins University for four months in 1883, studying under Herbert Baxter Adams, who provided Dixon with a scholarly apparatus for embracing white superiority. After a series of false starts as an actor, state legislator, and lawyer, Dixon eloped with Harriet Bussey, a Georgia minister's daughter, had a conversion experience at Wrightsville Beach, and became an ordained Baptist minister known for his gilded tongue, serving in Goldsboro and Raleigh, before being called to the prestigious Dudley Street Church in Boston and the Twenty-third Street Church in New York City.

Dixon embraced the principles of white superiority that rationalized Jim Crow disfranchisement, segregation, and brutality against African Americans in the turn-of-the-century South. He believed that thousands of years of development separated Aryans from Africans, and that African Americans believed they could bridge that gap through interracial marriage. White men, Dixon argued, must stop this black press for miscegenation at all costs. Dixon's beliefs reflected a wider culture in which white southern manhood seemed under siege. A developing market economy and interracial political alliances, combined with a changing population in which young single white women could move to the cities for employment and black men could become urban entrepreneurs and businessmen, challenged traditional white patriarchal authority and served as a crucible for the myth of the black beast rapist.

Dixon played an unparalleled role in disseminating that myth throughout American culture. He portrayed black men as innate barbarians unable to restrain their lust for white virgins, a theme hammered home in his best-selling trilogy, *The Leopard's Spots* (1902), *The Clansman* (1905), and *The Traitor* (1907). He used inflammatory scenes of black men stalking unprotected white women to justify the resurrection of the chivalric Ku Klux Klan, charged with saving not only southern ladyhood but the country as a whole. America's future, Dixon was suggesting, depended on the heroism of southern white men, a point literally writ large in the sensationalistic film he cowrote with D. W. Griffith, *Birth of a Nation* (1915).

Dixon did not write exclusively about the South. As an advocate of the Social Gospel movement, he addressed the social problems of modernity. He condemned society's blind eye on poor working women's desperate lives and wished they were honored as mothers of civilization instead. Interestingly, Dixon did not see white women as passive victims in all contexts. He celebrated women's strong leadership in church, even as he sought more exemplifiers of Christian manhood in his pews. He believed strong women could prevent men from pursuing the twin dangers of radicalism and promiscuity, a theme he explored in several of his books, including his first best seller, *The One Woman* (1903). For Dixon, a white man and white woman's romantic love, made sacred by having a child, ensured a man's highest morality, and modern white women who pursued careers and independence must give up those aspirations to "save" their men. Black men and women, by comparison, lacked the capacity for romantic love, and therefore the capacity for true piety.

Dixon's preoccupation with the dangers of black sexuality never waned. In his final book, *The Flaming Sword* (1939), he tied the rape of a white Piedmont wife by a savage black man to Communist efforts to overthrow the United States with the support of a black army. Throughout his long career, Dixon appealed to a national audience of white men and women anxious about modernization and its impact on manliness, race, and white authority. In the end, it is important to recognize that Dixon's horrific stereotypes ultimately reflected the collective anxieties of white America as much or more than Dixon's own warped imagination.

MICHELE K. GILLESPIE
Wake Forest University

Michele K. Gillespie and Randal L. Hall, eds., *Thomas Dixon Jr. and the Birth of Modern America* (2006); Glenda Gilmore, *Gender and Jim Crow: Women and the Politics of White Supremacy in North Carolina, 1896–1920* (1996); Diane Miller Sommerville, *Rape and Race in the Nineteenth-Century South* (2004); Joel Williamson, *Crucible of Race: Black-White Relations in the American South since Emancipation* (1984).

Earnhardt, Dale

(1951–2001) NASCAR DRIVER.
Born in Kannapolis, N.C., Dale Earnhardt became one of the most successful stock car drivers in NASCAR Nextel (formerly Winston) Cup series history. The son of NASCAR driver Ralph Earnhardt, Dale Earnhardt grew up working on his father's cars, racing his own automobiles, and fighting to become a successful stock car driver. His struggles were compounded as Earnhardt dropped out of school, married and had children at an early age, and had to regularly borrow money to fund his race team.

In 1975 he made his first Winston Cup start, racing in the series infrequently until 1979, when, thanks to improved funding and equipment, he won one race and the Rookie of the Year award. Tremendous on-track success followed as Earnhardt won 76 races (now seventh all-time in the series) and a record-tying seven Winston Cup championships (1980, 1986, 1987, 1990, 1991, 1993, and 1994). He was recognized in 1998 by NASCAR as one of the 50 greatest drivers in the circuit's history.

His success on the track, aggressive driving style, unique charisma, and black number "3" Chevrolet earned Earnhardt the nickname "The Intimidator." Legions of fans, particularly blue-color southern males, embraced Earnhardt's style, success, and humble southern roots and made him one of the most popular Winston Cup drivers. Even though some fans detested his rough driving style and consistent success, Earnhardt became the face of NASCAR beginning in the late 1980s. He usually appeared in advertisements and promotional material dressed in all black, with a steely gaze encouraging viewers to buy Chevrolets, Wrangler jeans, Coca-Cola, or a host of other products.

In 2001, when Earnhardt died during

Dale Earnhardt Way, an exit off of Interstate 35, is one of the entrances to the Texas Motor Speedway. (Courtesy Douglas Hurt, photographer)

a last-lap wreck at Daytona International Speedway, NASCAR fans reacted with an outpouring of mourning and memorialization efforts, repeatedly stating that Earnhardt was one of them — an unassuming, hardworking southerner. Ironically, widespread national media coverage of Earnhardt's death attracted new fans to NASCAR, including nonsoutherners, females, minorities, and high-income followers.

Earnhardt's legacy includes his business, Dale Earnhardt Incorporated, which fields Nextel Cup race cars; his son, Dale Earnhardt Jr., who replaced his father as one of NASCAR's most popular drivers; and many media events chronicling his life and death, including two full-length films, several country music songs, and a romance novel about mourners taking a pilgrimage to NASCAR tracks in memory of Earnhardt. Since his death, Dale Earnhardt's name has been imprinted on the southern landscape in the form of roads, racetrack grandstands, and businesses in North Carolina. Even after death, his

racing merchandise continues to be a best seller among his loyal fans.

DOUGLAS A. HURT
University of Central Oklahoma

Peter Golenbock and Greg Fielden, eds., *Stock Car Racing Encyclopedia* (1997); Mark D. Howell, *From Moonshine to Madison Avenue* (1997); Douglas A. Hurt, *Southeastern Geographer* (May 2005); Joe Menzer, *The Wildest Ride: A History of* NASCAR (2001); Frank Moriarty, *The Encyclopedia of Stock Car Racing* (1998); Neal Thompson, *Driving with the Devil: Southern Moonshine, Detroit Wheels, and the Birth of* NASCAR (2006).

Edelman, Marian Wright

(b. 1939) CIVIL RIGHTS LAWYER. Marian Wright Edelman is founder and president of the Children's Defense Fund, based in Washington, D.C. Born 6 June 1939 to a Bennettsville, S.C., Baptist minister and his wife (who also raised her four brothers, her sister, and 14 foster children), Edelman in 1983 was named by *Ladies' Home Journal* as one of the "100 most influential women in

America." In 1985 she received a Mac-Arthur Foundation award of $228,000, which she promptly devoted to her Children's Defense Fund to make the needs of children—especially poor children—a top priority on America's agenda. She is a voice for children who cannot vote, lobby, or speak out for themselves. Edelman is concerned with every aspect of childhood health and education, infant mortality, teenage pregnancy, and child abuse. Her work graphically details the effect of poverty on the minds and future of America's children.

Awards and accolades for Marian Wright Edelman have cascaded in a steady stream since her undergraduate days at Spelman College in Atlanta, where a Merrill Scholarship afforded her a year's study at the University of Paris and the University of Geneva. She has served as chair of Spelman's Board of Trustees.

In the intervening years, she has fulfilled her early promise as one of *Mademoiselle* magazine's "four most exciting young women in America" (1965) and as *Vogue*'s "Outstanding Young Woman of America" (1965–66). During those years, many pieces of civil rights legislation were written under the force of her determination and penchant for detail. Her brilliant congressional testimony, her lobbying for and drafting of legislation, and her highly focused intellect and energy led former vice president Walter Mondale to call Marian Wright Edelman "the smartest woman I have ever met."

Marian Wright grew up in a close-knit southern family, for whom civil rights represented an American ideal. Her father's final days in 1954 were spent with a radio at his side, listening to *Brown v. Board of Education* being argued before the Supreme Court. His last words to Marian, a week before the decision came down, were "Don't let anything get between you and your education."

Edelman graduated from Spelman as valedictorian in 1960, won a John Hay Whitney Fellowship to Yale University Law School, received her L.L.B. in 1963, and joined the NAACP Legal and Education Defense Fund as staff attorney in New York. From 1964 to 1968 she served as director of the fund's Jackson, Miss., office, where in 1965 she became the first black woman admitted to the Mississippi Bar.

In Mississippi, during the height of the civil rights movement, she organized Head Start programs throughout the state for the Child Development Group of Mississippi and developed a keen awareness of the effect of poverty and hunger on the lives of young children. Her advocacy drew national attention to children suffering from hunger and malnutrition in America. As a Field Foundation Fellow and partner in the Washington research project of the Southern Center for Public Policy, she became a principal architect of and successful lobbyist for the Food Stamp Act of 1970. That year she became an honorary fellow at the University of Pennsylvania Law School and won the Louise Waterman Wise Award, and in 1971 *Time* magazine named her one of 200 outstanding young American leaders. From 1971 to May 1973 she served as director of the Center for Law and Education at Harvard University—a position she left to form the Children's Defense Fund.

Edelman's research on the plight of children in America is quoted in the major media, cited by congressional committees, and used in state and federal programming. She is the author of three books, *Children out of School in America* (1974), *School Suspensions: Are They Helping Children?* (1975), and *Portrait of Inequality: Black and White Children in America* (1980), all published by the Children's Defense Fund, as well as numerous articles and scholarly papers.

MARY LYNN KOTZ
Washington, D.C.

Harry A. Ploski and James Williams, eds., *The Negro Almanac* (1983); *Psychology Today* (June 1975); *Who's Who in America* (43d ed., 1984–85); *Who's Who in Black America* (4th ed., 1985).

Felton, Rebecca Latimer

(1835–1930) POLITICIAN AND WRITER.

Rebecca Felton embodied many of the tensions and contradictions of the New South, a crusader for women's equality who retained all the outward grace of a southern lady, a plantation mistress who supported industrial expansion, and an advocate for Progressive-era reforms who bitterly championed white supremacy. Felton was born in 1835 near Decatur, Ga., the first child of a wealthy slaveholder and proprietor, Charles Latimer. She was educated at the Madison Female College, where she graduated at the top of her class. At age 18, she married William Felton, a widower in his 30s, who was, at various times, a physician, a Methodist minister, and a prosperous planter in Cartersville. Before the Civil War, Felton confined herself to managing the household and raising her children.

The Civil War shocked her out of this world. With their plantation devastated and two sons dead from disease, the Feltons worked to remake their lives. They had five children in all, only one of whom survived into adulthood. In addition to rebuilding their plantation, they established a Methodist school and entered the postwar political fray. Her husband served in the U.S. Congress as an Independent from 1874 to 1880 and then served three terms in the Georgia state legislature. In these years, she began her public life, managing her husband's political career, helping him draft bills and write speeches, and penning biting critiques of the Bourbon Democrats for numerous newspapers. In 1885 she took over the *Cartersville Free Press* (renamed the *Courant*) and became the first woman in Georgia to edit her own newspaper.

Felton's reputation soon eclipsed her husband's. She represented Georgia as a "lady manager" at the 1893 World Exposition in Chicago and wrote a regular column on women for the *Atlanta Journal*, from 1899 through the 1920s. She became most renowned for her reform campaigns on behalf of Georgia's women, beginning with an effort to outlaw Georgia's convict lease system in the 1870s and to establish separate prison facilities for women. In 1886 Felton joined the Woman's Christian Temperance Union and soon became a leading spokeswoman for prohibition in Georgia. She also was an advocate for compulsory education in Georgia's common schools, for vocational education for poor white girls, and for agricultural reforms that would give women control over a portion of the family economy. She argued that marriage was a partnership that should accord women all the rights and liberties of their husbands. These beliefs led to her fervent support for woman suffrage in the 1910s, against widespread condemnation from conservative lawmakers. In September 1922, when U.S. senator Tom Watson died unexpectedly, Governor Thomas Hardwick selected Felton to take his seat, though the Senate was not in session at the time. When the Senate did reconvene after the November elections, Watson's elected successor, Walter George, agreed to be sworn in a day late. Felton thus became the first female senator to sit in the Senate chambers, albeit for only one day, largely as a symbolic affirmation of the Nineteenth amendment.

Rebecca Felton, the first female senator to sit in the Senate chambers, standing on the steps of the Georgia Senate, November 1922 (Library of Congress [LC-F8-21357], Washington, D.C.)

But Felton's progressive politics did not extend to race. Her advocacy on behalf of white women stemmed in large part from her desire to protect white southerners from the prospect of black equality. She believed that the white race needed the strengthening that white women's suffrage, educational reform, and economic uplift could bring. She defended her feminism against conservative attack by claiming that white women needed to forge their independence because white men had abdicated their chivalric roles as protectors—by bringing suffering upon white southern households in seceding from the union, by abandoning their paternal and marital duties by turning to drink and by satisfying their sexual desires with black women, and by fostering what she saw as a misguided sense of black equality in cynically courting the black male vote after the war. This view led to the most notorious statement of her career. In 1897, Felton made national news when she defended lynching in a speech to the Georgia Agricultural Society, declaring that if lynching could protect white women from black male rapists, "then I say lynch a thousand a week, if necessary."

Despite her advocacy for southern farmers and her defensiveness against northern criticism and intrusion, she strongly supported industrial expansion in the South, believing that sectional progress would come from capitalist growth. She herself was a shrewd and wealthy businesswoman.

Felton remained active in Georgia politics well into old age. She died in 1930 at the age of 94.

AMY LOUISE WOOD
Illinois State University

Rebecca Latimer Felton, *Country Life in Georgia in the Days of My Youth* (1919); John Talmadge, *Rebecca Latimer Felton: Nine Stormy Decades* (1960); Marjorie Spruill Wheeler, *New Women of the New South: The Leaders of the Woman Suffrage Movement in the Southern States* (1993); LeeAnn Whites, *Gender Matters: Civil War, Reconstruction, and the Making of the New South* (2005); Joel Williamson, *A Rage for Order: Black-White Relations in the American South since Emancipation* (1986).

Gibbons, Kaye

(b. 1960) WRITER.

While a student in Louis Rubin's southern literature class at the University of North Carolina at Chapel Hill, Kaye Gibbons showed him a manuscript of her novel, *Ellen Foster*. Shortly thereafter, in 1987, Rubin's Algonquin Press published the book. Its spare and focused scope reopened the interrogation of what John Crowe Ransom might call the "economy of the household" in southern life. With each subsequent novel, Gibbons continues to chronicle the voice of southern women speaking "in place."

Matriarchal lines ground Gibbons's novels. The women here, in the author's words, "remember conversations" and practice a creed of "self-reliance." Ellen Foster (*Ellen Foster*) matures through her own wits as well as in conversations with her friend, Starletta, the Brontë sisters, and a "laughing Middle Ages lady," in the "old stories" given to her by the librarian. Hattie Barnes (*Sights Unseen*, 1995) discovers the means to live with her mother's mental illness, as her mother stares down the men's family relationships, which are defined by pride, violence, and power. This self-reliance is a continual touchstone for Gibbons's women, a constant reassertion of the intrinsic value of their social place in the face of history.

In a Gibbons novel, each narrator seems "insulated" in life's domestic spheres; each account feels "overheard." Yet this is not a self-obsessed, regionalized fiction. Instead, examining Gibbons's *On the Occasion of My Last Afternoon* (1998), Matthew Guinn calls the novelist's project "deconstruction from within." For instance, although one has examined the "official account" of a story in the newspaper or history book, Gibbons gives the reader a way of narrating the South—one that does not simply throw the region back on itself in self-absorption. The narration never pretends to escape place, personal or social history, or even the body. Slowed of narrative momentum, the Gibbons narrator often finds herself in the position of Margaret Birch (*Charms for the Easy Life*, 1993), who, after her grandmother's death, "l[ies] down, rest[s] her head by her [grandmother's] feet, and wait[s]) to be found." In this densely textured "waiting," Gibbons delves into the layers of accumulated psychological experience. Here, she engages myths of the unity of that experience. Her "South" geographically breaks into region and neighborhood. Her women are rooted in voices and bodies in which they move through domestic and historical spaces, retell, and disappear. For example, a school counselor challenges Ellen Foster to recall her experiences of poverty and fear. She recounts, "I used to be [afraid] but I am not now is what I told him. I might get a little nervous but I am never scared. Oh but I do remember when I was scared."

When Gibbons was nine years old, her mother committed suicide. Gibbons herself has faced manic depression, but it is too easy to say that she simply chronicles her own experiences with the disease in her novels, marking some journey toward psychological wholeness. Instead, her characters move from experience to storytelling, with this sense of living as distant observers of their own lives. The effect is of a narrator intent on getting all the details right in the face of a generalized and misremembered story line. In *Sights Unseen*, Hattie tells the story of her own naming. While the woman who shares her mother's room in the obstetrics ward joins "the various voices from [her] mother's [psychologically broken] life now in unison, telling her how much joy she could have if she were normal, happy, and sane," Maggie Barnes insists that the child's name be "Hattie," in a defiant stance against the accumulated stubborn and racial angers

of the men around her. Each novel's story is obsessively told within these subsumed histories. The force of southern economics and society moves along, the mills and migrant farmworkers working in place. This is a reality of which Gibbons's narrators never lose sight. No one would presume to disturb the region's unbroken pastoral appearance. In Margaret Birch's telling of her neighbors' suicide threats, "they would walk fifty miles and jump in some other person's river, but not their own." Similarly, each narrator tells her story with full awareness of that stasis, speaking with a sense of deflected memoir, as she reconstructs these subsumed domestic histories.

Kaye Gibbons was born Bertha Kaye Batts on 5 May 1960 in Nash County, N.C. As of 2009, she continues to write, living with her three daughters in Raleigh, N.C.

GARIN CYCHOLL
University of Illinois–Chicago

Suzanne Disheroon-Green, in *Dictionary of Literary Biography, Twenty-First-Century American Novelists*, ed. Lisa Abney and Suzanne Disheroon-Green (2004); Jan Nordby Gretlund, *South Atlantic Review* (Fall 2000); Matthew Guinn, *After Southern Modernism* (2000).

Grimké Sisters

(SARAH, 1793–1874; ANGELINA, 1805–1879) ABOLITIONISTS.
The Grimké sisters, Sarah and Angelina, were unique in the American anti-slavery movement. They were southerners, women, and members of a family known to own slaves. Sarah was born in 1793 and Angelina in 1805, the last

of 11 Grimké children. Sarah virtually adopted her new baby sister, and they remained close throughout their lives. The Grimké family belonged to Charleston's elite upper class, whose children were reared in luxury and served by many slaves. They were city dwellers, but their large plantation in upper South Carolina and its numerous slaves were an important source of family wealth. The sisters' education in a select girls' academy stressing the social graces was slight and superficial. They were expected to marry well, bear children, and become successful matrons. However, the sisters lost interest in conventional life as each grew into adulthood.

Religion led them to reject slavery. Though the Grimké family church was St. Philip's Episcopal, each sister experienced conversion in revivals of other churches. Sarah, in time, became a member of the Society of Friends, Angelina an enthusiastic Presbyterian. Sarah came to know Friends during her father's final illness. In 1821, following his death, she moved to Philadelphia and joined the Friends' Society. She accepted the Friends' firm tenet opposing slavery as a sin and eventually won over her sister to the Quaker faith and the antislavery conviction. After her efforts failed to convert family and friends, Angelina left Charleston to make her home with Sarah in Philadelphia.

In early 1853 the more activist Angelina began to make contact with the antislavery movement. After William Lloyd Garrison published her letter in the *Liberator*, Angelina began to write her first tract, *Appeal to the Christian Women of the South*. The

American Anti-Slavery Society rushed it into print and then urged her to aid the cause by addressing women's groups in "parlor meetings" — Sarah went with her and remained at her side.

They were the only women asked to the Convention of the Seventy, which met in October of 1836 for the training of new agents to spread abolitionism. Theodore Weld, whom Angelina later married, was the leader in the sessions and gave the sisters special training for their coming lecture tours. They went from this convention to their crowded "parlor meetings," held in churches, and accepted invitations from other localities. The two sisters were swept into preparations for a forthcoming Convention of American Anti-Slavery Women, held in March of 1837. When it ended, the Grimkés had come to know most of the abolitionist leaders in the East, men and women, and were themselves regarded as belonging to the circle of female leaders. The Grimkés arrived in Boston in May 1837 and began their historic antislavery crusade. They also increasingly spoke out in favor of women's rights, despite criticism from antislavery leaders.

The spring months of 1838 saw Angelina Grimké's greatest triumphs. Twice in a crowded Massachusetts legislative hall she addressed a committee of the legislature, a sensational occasion headlined in the press. Also, Boston's antislavery women rented the Odeon Theater, and for five meetings, one a week, Angelina addressed an overflowing hall on the abolition of slavery. In Philadelphia, she calmly addressed a mass meeting of a convention of American Anti-Slavery Women with a threatening mob outside.

Angelina and Weld were married the day before the convention. When the sessions ended, Sarah accompanied them to their new home, and she stayed with them for the remainder of her life. Angelina fully expected to return to her work for the antislavery cause but did not do so. She and Sarah assisted Weld on his best-known tract, *American Slavery As It Is* (1839). Three children were born between 1839 and 1844, two boys and a girl.

In the late 1850s both sisters taught in the Eagleswood School, which Weld headed. Later the family lived near Boston, where Weld and Angelina continued to teach. When the Civil War came in 1861, Angelina Grimké, at the age of 56, returned to part-time public life. Garrison had persuaded Weld to lecture again, this time in aid of the war effort. Angelina now rejoined her old friends in forming an organization, Loyal Women of the Republic, and once again she was speaking for freedom of the slaves. Sarah was over 70 years old when the end of the war brought full emancipation. She died in 1874. Angelina suffered two strokes, the first of which occured in 1875, and was ill until her death in 1879.

KATHERINE DU PRE LUMPKIN

Angelina Emily Grimké, *Walking by Faith: The Diary of Angelina Grimké, 1825–1835*, ed. Charles Wilbanks (2003); Gerda Lerner, *The Feminist Thought of Sarah Grimké* (1997), *The Grimké Sisters from South Carolina: Rebels against Slavery* (1967); Katherine Du Pre Lumpkin, *The Emancipation of Angelina Grimké* (1974); Weld-Grimké Collection,

Clements Library, University of Michigan, Ann Arbor.

Hamer, Fannie Lou

(1917–1977) CIVIL RIGHTS ACTIVIST. The youngest of 20 children born to Jim and Ella Townsend, black sharecroppers in Montgomery County, Miss., Fannie Lou Townsend moved with her family to Sunflower County, in the heart of the Delta, just after her second birthday. She picked her first cotton harvest as a six-year-old. Townsend was a gifted student, but she left Sunflower County's inferior black schools after the sixth grade to work on the Brandon plantation because her family desperately needed the money. She married Perry "Pap" Hamer in 1944; they sharecropped on the Marlow plantation just outside of Ruleville, not far from the plantation of U.S. senator James O. Eastland.

Thousands of African American women in the Mississippi Delta had similar family and educational histories and therefore her life prospects. Taught by their own public school systems that educating them would be a waste of money, they certainly were not expected to bear the responsibilities of citizenship. Hamer, however, rose far above the expectations held by the white supremacist society into which she was born. By the time of her untimely death in 1977, Hamer had become the most influential poor person in America. The absolute embodiment of the mantra of the Student Nonviolent Coordinating Committee (SNCC), "Let the People Decide," Hamer voiced a homegrown critique of the American political system that made Mississippi's white

Fannie Lou Hamer at the Democratic National Convention, Atlantic City, N.J., August 1964 (Warren K. Leffler, photographer, Library of Congress [LC-U9-12470B-17], Washington, D.C.)

but she attempted to register again; she learned in 1963 that Sunflower County's registrar had accepted her application on her second attempt, though other would-be voters had to return to the county courthouse multiple times. Such was Hamer's determination and so fast was the pace of change during Mississippi's Freedom Summer that the first vote she cast, in 1964, was for herself— in a Democratic primary race against incumbent U.S. representative Jamie Whitten. Hamer lost that race, but she, Victoria Gray, and Annie Devine challenged Whitten and the rest of Mississippi's delegation to the House, on the grounds that African Americans had systematically been denied the ballot throughout the state.

Hamer was the recognized spokesperson of the Mississippi Freedom Democratic Party (MFDP), the integrated but majority-black group that organized during Freedom Summer to challenge the lily-white "regular" Mississippi delegation at the Democratic National Party Convention in Atlantic City in August 1964. Hamer and the MFDP lost the challenge, but, in a nationally televised, highly charged address before the party's Credentials Committee, Hamer rattled off a litany of injustices she had suffered simply because she wanted to vote. "All of this is on account [of] we want to register, to become first-class citizens, and if the Freedom Democratic Party is not seated now, I question America," she concluded. Hamer's electrifying testimony laid bare the radically democratic enterprise at the heart of the civil rights movement as she knew it. Her further

supremacy possible. In the process she became a standard bearer for the disfranchised and ignored black poor and provided an effective challenge to Mississippi elected officials, the leaders of the national Democratic Party, and President Lyndon B. Johnson. Millions of Americans came to appreciate her as what a fellow activist called the "prophet of hope for the sick and tired."

Hamer was 44 years old when she attended a SNCC workshop in Ruleville and learned she was eligible to vote. She was one of dozens of Ruleville-area blacks who attempted to register in 1962 and became an indefatigable canvasser for black voters. Hamer's initial application was denied, along with the others,

challenge of the congressional delegation kept Mississippi racism in the nation's consciousness after the conclusion
of Freedom Summer and highlighted
black disfranchisement, which kept
pressure on Johnson and Congress to
pass the Voting Rights Act of 1965.

Hamer remained a nationally recognized philosopher of the black freedom
struggle and a darling of the Left even
after much of the civil rights movement disintegrated. She was an effective
fund-raiser for civil rights and voting
rights causes and a sought-after speaker
among social justice and feminist organizations throughout the decades of
the 1960s and 1970s. The feminists, it
must be said, were not quite sure what
to make of Hamer when she told them
she was not "hung up on this thing
about liberating myself from the black
man. . . . I got a black husband, six feet
three, 240 pounds, with a 14 shoe, that
I don't *want* to be liberated from." She
also departed from feminist orthodoxy
on abortion but was fully committed to
the principle that women should control
their own lives and persons.

Hamer came to this position via
hard-lived experience. She had spent
her life in a society with an inhumanly
racist healthcare system, and being
a civil rights activist had taken a tremendous physical toll on her. She had
suffered from polio as a child and later
wrote of recurrent childhood dreams
about food, in which she found a piece
of cornbread or an apple or orange to
relieve her persistent hunger. Hamer
saw a local doctor for treatment of a
stomach cyst in 1961; he performed a
hysterectomy without her knowledge or
permission. She suffered with pain and
walked with a limp for the rest of her
life following a beating she received in
a Winona, Miss., jail on the way home
from a citizenship education school in
1963. One of Hamer's adopted daughters
died from the effects of malnutrition at
the age of 22; her life might have been
saved had not a local hospital refused to
treat her because she was black. Hamer
herself succumbed to the effects of dia-
betes, hypertension, cancer, and heart
troubles at the age of 59, in 1977.

J. TODD MOYE
University of North Texas

Ed King, *Sojourners* (December 1982);
Chana Kai Lee, *For Freedom's Sake: The Life
of Fannie Lou Hamer* (1999); Kay Mills, *This
Little Light of Mine: The Life of Fannie Lou
Hamer* (1994); J. Todd Moye, *Let the People
Decide: Black Freedom and White Resistance
Organizing in Sunflower County, Mississippi,
1945–1986* (2004); Charles Payne, *I've Got
the Light of Freedom: The Organizing Tradition and the Mississippi Freedom Struggle*
(1995).

Home Extension Services

The U.S. Department of Agriculture
(USDA) developed the Home Extension
Services to disseminate information
to the farming community. Home Extension has its roots in the Progressive
era and the Country Life movement.
Theodore Roosevelt authorized the
Country Life Commission to investigate rural life. The committee's report
paid special attention to farm women,
finding that they were overworked and
lacking in modern technologies, and
recommended improving their conditions. In order to improve agricultural

scientific study, Congress passed the Morrill Acts of 1862 and 1890, which established land-grant colleges. Agricultural reformers eager to spread helpful information to farmers published bulletins and spoke at farmers' institutes, conferences, and agricultural fairs. Still, only a minority of farmers gained access to new scientific knowledge. Eventually, reformers realized they had to take the information to the farmer.

Seaman A. Knapp, a professor at what is now Iowa State University, was instrumental in developing the concept of demonstration work. Knapp helped draft the first experimental station bill, which was the precursor to the Hatch Act of 1877. This legislation appropriated federal funding for experimental stations to gather and disseminate practical scientific knowledge to farmers. In 1903 the Mexican boll weevil threatened Texas cotton production. Using five demonstration farms in Texas and Louisiana, Knapp was able to convince farmers that using good farming practices—crop rotation, deeper plowing, fertilizers, and improved seed selection—could prevent crop destruction. Seeing that these improved techniques worked, farmers immediately implemented them and saved their cotton crops. Impressed by Knapp's success, the USDA earmarked $40,000 to expand demonstration programs and created the Cooperative Demonstration Work of the USDA.

Knapp saw the advantages of expanding the demonstrations work for women, boys, and girls. In the early 1910s, agriculture agents organized girls into Tomato Clubs, boys into Corn Clubs, and women into Canning Clubs. The benign names of these organizations belie the lofty and transforming goals of the reformers, who wanted to educate the rural populations and lift them out of poverty through scientific farming, efficiency, mechanization, and improved profits. Later the organizations were renamed as Home Demonstration and 4-H Clubs.

In 1914 Congress passed the Smith-Lever Act, which provided federal money to land-grant universities to establish and administer the Extension Services. The universities provided training in the latest agricultural scientific knowledge to agents, who then educated the rural population, using demonstrations and USDA publications. The agents were assigned to counties, with the expectation that local governments would pay up to 50 percent of their salaries. The Rockefeller General Education Board also provided substantial funding. County agents reported to district agents, who in turn reported to state directors, who were usually responsible to the dean of the agricultural state college. Smith-Lever shared the goals of the Country Life movement of rural uplift and efficiency, working to improve the living conditions of rural women. Importantly, Smith-Lever mandated policies based on a gendered division of labor—men as farmers growing crops, women as homemakers taking care of domestic needs. But this division did not reflect the reality of farm life.

Tuskegee Institute pioneered demonstration work for African Americans, but this work developed slower because many county governments refused to fund demonstration programs for blacks. Authority over black extension work was centered in three black colleges, Tuskegee and Hampton Institute and briefly at Prairie View State Normal and Industrial College in Texas. Programs directed at black southerners had contradictory goals. In the segregated South, the Extension Service wanted to improve conditions for blacks without developing greater independence. Throughout the first decades of extension work for blacks, the programs were underfunded and agents were overworked, with responsibility for much larger districts than those of their white counterparts.

Today the Extension Service works with local governments and community leaders to improve rural life through a broad range of educational programs in agriculture, community resource development, nutrition, family issues, lawn and garden programs, and youth development. Membership in Home Demonstration Clubs has declined as women have left the farm to work outside the home. 4-H clubs are still an important aspect of rural life, adapting and changing to stay relevant.

MINOA D. UFFELMAN
Austin Peay State University

Laurie Winn Carlson, *William J. Spillman and the Birth of Agricultural Economics* (2005); Mary S. Hoffschwelle, *Rebuilding the Rural Community: Reformers, Schools, and Homes in Tennessee, 1900–1930* (1998); Jeannie Whayne, in *African American Life in the Rural South*, ed. R. Douglas Hurt (2003).

"I AM A MAN"

When black sanitation workers in Memphis, Tenn., went on strike in 1968, they carried placards with the slogan "I AM A MAN." The strike and slogan would capture national attention at a time when the civil rights movement was evolving from a quest for social equality to a more comprehensive campaign for economic justice.

In the context of the labor movement, the men in Memphis were demanding a living wage, one that would enable them to support their families as traditional male breadwinners. In 1968 many of the black sanitation workers in Memphis qualified for welfare, despite the fact that they worked full-time for the city (and many held second jobs). Racial divisions in the Memphis labor market and antiunion policies kept wages low, not only for black workers in the city but for whites as well. The sanitation strikers hoped that their demands for recognition of black manhood and of a union for city employees might break the hold that paternalistic politicians and employers had long had on the city.

In the context of the civil rights movement, the Memphis sanitation strikers' demand for respect and recognition as men tapped into a long history of African American dissent. Abolitionists like Frederick Douglass demanded that black men be allowed to serve in the U.S. army and vote during the Civil War era. A generation later, scholars like W. E. B. Du Bois recognized that black manhood was under direct attack because of the lynching in the Jim Crow era. The civil rights movement brought

Sanitation workers on strike in Memphis, 1968
(Courtesy Mississippi Valley Collection, University of Memphis Libraries)

issues of race and masculinity to the forefront of America's consciousness once again in the 1950s and 1960s. The "I AM A MAN" slogan captured this moment perfectly, calling attention to the ways that racism and poverty undercut black men's ability to achieve the American ideal of manhood.

At the request of labor and civil rights activists in Memphis, Martin Luther King Jr. linked the 1968 sanitation strike to his nationwide Poor People's Campaign. King traveled to Memphis twice in the spring of 1968 to support the strike. A march that he led during his first visit ended in violence and rioting. Shaken but undeterred, King promised to return to Memphis to lead a nonviolent march. In early April he did return. Speaking to thousands about the future direction of the civil rights movement, King said that he had been to the mountaintop and seen the promised land of freedom. Yet King's optimism was tempered by an eerie, almost prophetic, sense that he might not live long enough to get to the Promised Land himself. The next day King was assassinated.

Still, the sanitation workers soldiered on, despite the loss of King's leadership. By the end of the spring, the city agreed to address many of the sanitation workers' demands. The workers received higher pay, a guarantee of safer working conditions, an end to racist promotion practices, and a memorandum of understanding regarding the union's ability to bargain collectively with the city.

The quest for recognition and definition of black manhood continued. With the Million Man March in 1995, black leaders characterized the struggle for racial uplift in the gendered language of claiming manhood once again. There were questions from feminists (both women and men) about framing the struggle for racial equality and uplift in terms of masculinity, specifically the implication that traditional (and perhaps unequal) gender roles might be the foundation for such a movement. But few would debate the fact that this march and the "I AM A MAN" slogan point to complex relationships between race and manhood in southern culture—and, for that matter, in American culture.

STEVE ESTES
Sonoma State University

Joan Turner Beifuss, *At the River I Stand* (1985); Steve Estes, *I AM A MAN! Race, Manhood, and the Civil Rights Movement* (2005); Michael Honey, *Going Down Jericho Road: Martin Luther King, Black Workers, and the Memphis Sanitation Strike* (2007).

Jordan, Barbara

(1936–1996) LAWYER AND POLITICIAN.

Barbara Charline Jordan first came to national prominence in November 1972 when she was elected to the U.S. House of Representatives from the 18th Congressional District in Houston, Tex. She and Andrew Young, who was elected that same year from Atlanta, Ga., were the first two blacks from the Deep South to win national office since the turn of the 20th century.

Born 21 February 1936, the youngest of three daughters, to Ben and Arlyne Jordan, in Houston, Barbara Jordan grew up in a devoutly religious environment. Her parents and grandparents were lifelong members of the Good Hope Baptist Church in Houston's predominantly black Fifth Ward. As a child, she was a bright student with a natural flair for speaking. Her high school teachers encouraged her to develop her talent by participating in various oratorical contests. Although the Houston school system was segregated, the precocious youngster took many honors in citywide matches. She graduated magna cum laude from Texas Southern University and earned her law degree at Boston University in 1959.

Returning to Houston, the fledgling barrister worked three years before being able to open her law office, but politics was already drawing her, and she became active in the local Democratic Party. In 1966, following redistricting, Barbara Jordan was elected to the Texas Senate, the first woman to win a seat in the upper chamber of that legislature. During her six years in the Senate, she earned the admiration of her white male colleagues for her many accomplishments, which included setting up the Texas Fair Employment Practices Commission, improving the Workmen's Compensation Act, and sponsoring the state's first minimum wage law. In 1972 Barbara Jordan made history when the Senate unanimously elected her president pro tempore. On 10 June 1972, in the traditional "Governor for a Day" ceremonies, she became the first black woman governor in U.S. history.

Barbara Jordan, U.S. representative from Texas and educator, 1980s (News and Information Service, University of Texas at Austin)

In 1971 her supporters in the state Senate carved out a new congressional district to include a majority mixture of blacks and Hispanics. In November 1972 that electorate gave her a sweeping victory as their representative to Congress from the 18th District. She was assigned to the important House Judiciary Committee. In the wake of the scandals growing out of the Watergate break-in on 17 June 1972, the Senate Select Committee on Presidential Campaigning, under the chairmanship of Sam Ervin of North Carolina, began holding hearings in May of 1973. One year later, on 9 May 1974, the House Judiciary Committee under Peter Rodino opened impeachment hearings against President Richard Nixon.

During the House hearings, Barbara Jordan became a household name throughout America. As *Time* magazine said, "She voiced one of the most cogent and impassioned defenses of the Constitutional principles that emerged from the Nixon impeachment hearings." Opinion polls soon listed her as among the 10 most influential members of Congress, and Democratic Party leaders chose her, along with Senator John Glenn, to give a keynote address to its 1976 national convention.

Always realistic, Barbara Jordan firmly resisted all efforts to draft her as a candidate for the vice presidential nomination that year. She believed the country was not ready for such a development, although it was slowly inching toward the goal of equality in race relations. For personal reasons, Jordan retired from politics in 1978, accepting a position as the Lyndon B. Johnson Centennial Chair in National Policy at the LBJ School of Public Affairs at the University of Texas at Austin. Barbara Jordan has left a legacy of great accomplishments in public service, both legislatively and personally. President Bill Clinton awarded her the Presidential Medal of Honor in 1994. She died in 1996. *Texas Monthly* magazine in 1999 named her the Role Model of the Century for the state she served.

ETHEL L. PAYNE
Washington, D.C.

Ira B. Bryant, *Barbara Charline Jordan: From the Ghetto to the Capitol* (1977); *Ebony* (February 1975); *Houston Post*, 21 July 1976; Sandra Parker, ed., *Barbara C. Jordan: Selected Speeches* (1999); Mary Beth Rogers, *Barbara Jordan: American Hero* (1998).

Loving v. Virginia

In the 1950s Richard Perry Loving was a white man in the Jim Crow South, and thus it was not among his choices to marry Mildred Dolores Jeter, a woman classified under Virginia law as non-white. On the surface, the law was even-handed in its treatment of interracial couples, imposing the same rules and penalties on a black man and a white woman wishing to marry. Across time and space, in law and in culture, such dominant attitudes and behavior embodied a fundamental premise underlying the regulation of social life: racial equality was not to be demonstrated in so graphic a way as by an interracial couple's formal marriage. Nor were the benefits of marriage available. In a variety of states across the nation, not just in Virginia, white men had long faced impediments in passing along property to their mixed-race children, and white women had long been denied inheritance under a marriage to a non-white man.

When the couple wanting to be Mr. and Mrs. Loving drove from their native Caroline County, Va., north to Washington, D.C., in June 1958 to get married, they violated a Virginia statute that made it a felony to go out of state to marry, if they then returned to Virginia, in evasion of the law against their marrying in Virginia. Back home in Virginia, asleep in bed late one night the next month, the couple awoke to find three law officers in their room. Arrested for the felony of their marriage and subsequently convicted, they accepted an offer of exile rather than prison. Eventually they contested the constitutionality of the law, their convictions, and their exile. In March 1966 the Virginia Supreme Court upheld the law — and the Lovings' convictions — against this challenge. On 12 June 1967, however, the U.S. Supreme Court ruled that the Virginia law could not meet the Fourteenth Amendment's demands of due process and equal protection of the law. The Lovings could live as husband and wife, together with their three young children, back home in Virginia. The same ruling struck down similar laws across the South.

Laws of this sort dated back as far as the 17th century — Virginia first enacted such a law in 1691. The statute under which the Lovings were charged dated in its essentials from 1878, though some important modifications had taken place in 1924 and 1932. At the time that the Lovings had their marriage ceremony in the nation's capital in 1958, 24 of the nation's 48 states (down from 30 as late as 1948) had laws against interracial marriage, though these laws ranged widely in their definitions of interracial marriage and in the penalties prescribed. By the time of the Lovings' court victory nine years later, only 16 states retained such laws, all of them in the South. (From the 1890s into the 1960s, the South was solid in its maintenance of laws against interracial marriage, but many states outside the South had such laws as well, so they were hardly a uniquely southern phenomenon.)

In the 1970s, same-sex couples went to court (in Kentucky as well as in some northern states) in efforts to have the reasoning and law of *Loving v. Virginia* applied to them, but nowhere did they prevail. The Supreme Court had emphasized racial identity as a uniquely privileged category, on the basis of which states could no longer discriminate. The 1967 decision left intact all other powers of the states to regulate marriage. The federal courts' new interpretation of the Fourteenth Amendment trumped state legislatures' efforts to control marriage, but with regard only to race and not gender.

PETER WALLENSTEIN
Virginia Polytechnic Institute and State University

Phyl Newbeck, *Virginia Hasn't Always Been for Lovers: Interracial Bans and the Case of Richard and Mildred Loving* (2004); Peter Wallenstein, *Tell the Court I Love My Wife: Race, Marriage, and Law—An American History* (2002).

Lumpkin, Katherine Du Pre

(1897–1988) WRITER AND ACTIVIST. Born on 22 December 1887 in Macon, Ga., to Annette and William Lumpkin, a Confederate Civil War veteran and lawyer, Katherine Du Pre Lumpkin grew up in a household that adamantly embraced the ideology of the Lost Cause. Her memoir, *The Making of a Southerner* (1946), portrays a southern tradition that she herself was very much a part of, and as such, it provides unique insights into the perspectives of white, southern, elite families, detailing the system of slavery, the hardships of the Civil War and Reconstruction, and the rationale behind Jim Crow from their point of view. After laying out this mentality and how it affected her childhood, Lumpkin then describes how she,

as an individual, came to question and then to ultimately reject the mythology of the Lost Cause, which had served to buttress southern hierarchies of gender, race, and class.

In Richland County, S.C., where she and her family moved to farm when she was 11 years old, Lumpkin came into close contact with economically exploited working-class whites. Her contact in South Carolina with white poverty ignited what would later become her critical stance toward the ideology she was taught as a child. Additionally, her education played a large role in her thoughtful analysis of oppression in the South. From 1912 to 1915, Lumpkin attended Brenau College, in Gainesville, Ga., where she earned a bachelor's degree, before attending Columbia University to study sociology. After earning a master's degree from Columbia, Lumpkin moved to the University of Wisconsin and earned a doctorate in economics in 1928. Although she received her postgraduate education outside of the region, Lumpkin periodically returned to the South, and for a time she worked as the national student secretary for the southern region of the YWCA, an interracial organization that further challenged many of the biases and taboos Lumpkin learned as a child.

After earning her doctorate, Lumpkin lived most of her adult life in the northeastern United States, and she taught economics and social science at several women's colleges, including Mount Holyoke and Smith. Much of her academic research and writing deals with labor issues and social reform, and

Lumpkin herself spent periods of time working in mills and factories in order to inform this research. She used her position as a social scientist to argue against white supremacy, the devalued status of women, and economic exploitation in the United States.

Lumpkin's memoir, *The Making of a Southerner*, remains an essential work for anyone seeking to understand the ways in which white supremacy was justified and accepted by elite white southerners, as well as the roles white women played in this process. As such, her memoir is often compared to Lillian Smith's *Killers of the Dream*, as it not only provides insight into this process but also details the difficulties of rejecting an ideology that was so thoroughly ingrained.

AMY SCHMIDT
University of Arkansas

Darlene Clark Hine, foreword, in Katherine Du Pre Lumpkin, *The Making of a Southerner* (1991); Fred Hobson, *But Now I See: The White Southern Racial Conversion Narrative* (1999); Carolyn Perry and Mary Louise Weaks, eds., *The History of Southern Women's Literature* (2002).

Lynn, Loretta

(b. 1937) ENTERTAINER.
Country music is an essential accompaniment to contemporary images of the South and is the source for regional mythology. Loretta Lynn is a rural southerner who celebrates the traditional values of the South through her original compositions and her authentic folk style. She has created and portrayed the "coal miner's daughter," a popular myth of the working-class southern woman

that may become as pervasive as the myth of the antebellum southern belle, Scarlett O'Hara.

Born in the small community of Butcher Holler, Ky., on 14 April 1937, Loretta Lynn is the second of eight children born to Clara Butcher and Ted Webb. When she was 13, she married Mooney Lynn, a soldier who had recently returned from World War II. The first of her six children was born when she was 14, and she was a grandmother by 28. Loretta Lynn had been married over 10 years before she began singing for audiences other than her family. She was successful almost immediately after the release of her first record, "I'm a Honky Tonk Girl" (1960), which was her own composition. Neither the small recording company, Zero, nor the Lynns could finance promotion of "I'm a Honky Tonk Girl," so Loretta and Mooney mailed copies of the record, along with a short letter of explanation, to disc jockeys across the nation. When they realized that the record was a hit, the Lynns sold their home in Washington state and drove to Nashville in a 1955 Ford to sign a contract.

Since then, Loretta Lynn has written over 160 songs and released 70 albums. Based upon *Billboard*'s year-end charts of hit songs, among her most successful singles have been "Success" (1962), "Wine, Women, and Song" (1964), "Blue Kentucky Girl" (1965), "Happy Birthday" (1965), "You Ain't Woman Enough" (1966), "Dear Uncle Sam" (1966), "If You're Not Gone Too Long" (1967), "Fist City" (1968), "You've Just Stepped In (From Stepping Out on Me)" (1968), "Woman of the World—Leave

My World Alone" (1969), "That's a No, No" (1969), "You Want to Give Me a Lift" (1970), "I Know How" (1970), "I Wanna Be Free" (1971), "You're Looking at Country" (1971), "One's on the Way" (1972), "Rated X" (1973), "Hey, Loretta" (1974), "She's Got You" (1977), and "Out of My Head and into My Bed" (1978). Her most recent Top 20 hit was "Making Love from Memory" in 1985. Loretta Lynn has won a number of awards, including four Grammy Awards, three awards from the Country Music Association for top female artist, 10 awards from the Academy of Country Music, two awards from Record World, three from Billboard, and four from Cash Box. In 1961 she received an award as the Most Promising Female Artist, and by 1972 she had become the first woman to be honored as the Country Music Association's Entertainer of the Year. In 1980 the album soundtrack of the film *Coal Miner's Daughter*, which featured Loretta's hit songs sung by actress Sissy Spacek, was named Album of the Year by the Country Music Association. She was inducted into the Country Music Hall of Fame in 1989.

Lynn did not tour or record during much of the 1990s, but she returned to performing after her husband died in 1996. She wrote or cowrote the songs on her latest album, *Van Lear Rose*. She is the author, with George Vecsey, of *Coal Miner's Daughter* (1976) and wrote another memoir, *Still Woman Enough* (2000), and a cookbook, *You're Cookin' It Country* (2000).

RUTH A. BANES
University of South Florida

Ruth A. Banes, *Canadian Review of American Studies* (Fall 1985); Nicholas Dawidoff, *In the Country of Country: A Journey to the Roots of American Music* (1998); Peter Dogget, *Are You Ready for the Country? Elvis, Dylan, Parsons, and the Roots of Country Rock* (2001); Dorothy A. Horstman, *Stars of Country Music*, ed. Bill C. Malone and Judith McCulloh (1975); Loretta Lynn with George Vecsey, *Coal Miner's Daughter* (1976); Vertical file, "Loretta Lynn," Country Music Foundation Library and Media Center, Nashville.

McCord, Louisa S.

(1810–1879) WRITER.

Paradox pervades attempts to understand and weigh properly Louisa S. McCord. All wish to claim her; none knows how. She tempts irony at every turn. Like Dr. Sloper in Henry James's *Washington Square*, she addresses to us what the doctor addressed to his daughter Catherine—utterances shrewd, wise, valuable, but "with portions left over, light remnants and snippets of irony, which she never knew what to do with." Literary historians, especially historians of women's literature, should be glad to have her, but the poems filling her single book of verse, *My Dreams* (1848), are slyly, cunningly enigmatic, full of striving intellect, but from what and for what always kept hidden. She wrote a tragedy, *Caius Gracchus* (1851), irreproachably classical and thus, surely, safely southern, but women did not write plays in the Roman republic (the few others we have are snug in the domestic calamities of imperial Rome). She seems to be a conservative writer— favoring woman's traditional role and lauding slavery—but what conservative writer would exalt a hero of Roman radicalism, who, like his equally radical brother Tiberius, was murdered by ferocious and frightened aristocrats? And what kind of conservative woman was this who subscribed to the *Journal des économistes* from Paris, who translated a work of French laissez-faire economics, and who wrote her own essays on political economy in the *Southern Quarterly Review*?

McCord defended slavery and the life that could not live without it, seeing slavery as good for the slave, whom its laws and conventions protected from abuse by a more powerful race, but not good for the slaveholder. Although her own plantation—as a northern visitor reported—was "considered rather a model place even in South Carolina where there are so many fine ones," McCord confessed to another admiring visitor, from Rhode Island (where she and her family frequently summered), that "she would prefer to have $25,000 in good bank stock rather than $100,000 in negroes and plantations."

McCord saw woman's lot as an exploited one in her slave society. "The positions of women and children are in truth as essentially states of bondage as any other," necessitated by the superior strength and, at their will, the brutality of men. "Many a woman of dominant intellect is obliged to submit to the rule of an animal in pantaloons, every way her inferior," although her marriage might be a coequal one. Of a planter neighbor, however, Louisa McCord wrote: "He died horribly, (raving mad), I am told. Poor Mrs. Stark was up at her sister's here for a week or two after

his death, looking wretchedly. . . . I was sorry for her but really thought some kind of illumination or rejoicing would have been more suited to the circumstances."

McCord had begun life not unlike Scarlett O'Hara, for her father was a self-made man and her mother was the beautiful and sheltered daughter of a wealthy Charleston merchant. Exhausted by the birth of 14 children, her mother died young, and Louisa, left in charge of the household, soon came to know various claims of duty, for her father was successful at everything he did, law in South Carolina, politics in Philadelphia, where Louisa was schooled, and planting back home, and the plantations were many. One, Lang Syne, not far from Columbia, became Louisa's portion and remained so even after she married, unfashionably late, in 1840. Three children followed, and after them the literary career—poems, drama, essays—was battered, then terminated, by her husband's death in 1855 and the death, prolonged by senile dementia, of her revered father, Langdon Cheves, in 1857. Her sight had been failing for some time; a trip to Europe brought a partial cure and, as her daughter said later, the only accurate likeness of her mother, a bust carved by Hiram Powers in Florence. She supported South Carolina's secession and earned glory in the hospitals of Columbia, but she saw no romance in war. The war took her only son and devastated her property. Unable to endure Reconstruction, she spent five years in exile in Canada, before returning to her birthplace, Charleston, to live with her surviving daughter. Her own death, which was hard, she bore as the Romans she admired would have.

RICHARD C. LOUNSBURY
Brigham Young University

Leigh Fought, Southern Womanhood and Slavery: A Biography of Louisa S. McCord, 1810–1879 (2003); Elizabeth Fox-Genovese, Within the Plantation Household: Black and White Women of the Old South (1988); Jessie Melville Fraser, "Louisa C. McCord" (M.A. thesis, University of South Carolina, 1919); Eugene D. Genovese and Elizabeth Fox-Genovese, Washington and Lee Law Review (Winter 1984); Archie Vernon Huff Jr., Langdon Cheves of South Carolina (1977); Richard C. Lounsbury, ed., Louisa S. Mc-Cord: Selected Writings (1997), Louisa S. McCord: Poems, Drama, Biography, Letters (1996), Louisa S. McCord: Political and Social Essays (1995); Richard C. Lounsbury, in Intellectual Life in Antebellum Charleston, ed. Michael O'Brien and David Moltke-Hansen (1986); Michael O'Brien, Conjectures of Order: Intellectual Life and the American South, 1810–1860 (2004); Margaret Farrand Thorp, Female Persuasion: Six Strong-Minded Women (1949).

Charlotte Digges "Lottie" Moon, Southern Baptist missionary, 1840–1912 (© International Mission Board)

Moon, Charlotte Digges "Lottie"

(1840–1912) SOUTHERN BAPTIST MISSIONARY.

For four decades Lottie Moon was a pioneer missionary in China of the Southern Baptist Convention (SBC). Her life is celebrated by denominational literature, which has described her as the most famous individual in Southern Baptist history and the human symbol of her church's ongoing commitment to overseas missionary work.

Growing up on a plantation near Charlottesville, Va., Lottie Moon de-veloped marked interests in religion and in the study of foreign languages and cultures. Following the Civil War, she taught school in Kentucky and Georgia, until 1873, when a deepening spirituality led her to enter missionary service. From that point until her death 40 years later Moon worked as an evangelist and teacher at Tengchow (known today as Penglai) and at other Southern Baptist stations in Shandong province, northeast China. In addition to demonstrating compassion for the Chinese and skill in adapting to their culture, she displayed considerable courage and professional resourcefulness. All these qualities were particularly evident in her life during the late 1880s at Pingdu, an isolated city in the Shandong interior. Working alone under difficult circumstances, Moon initiated at Pingdu a successful mission at a time when Baptist efforts in north China were otherwise near collapse.

Moon's unique reputation among Southern Baptists, however, is a product of the Lottie Moon Christmas Offering for Foreign Missions. Inspired by an 1888 effort to raise money in the United States to help her work at Pingdu, the Christmas Offering became a church-wide institution and in 1918 was named specifically for her. An extensive promotional literature developed, which over the years has idealized Moon in books, poems, pamphlets, motion pictures and filmstrips, portraits, photo albums, tape cassettes, dramatic scripts and impersonations, greeting cards, and website features and even a Lottie Moon cookbook. The Christmas Offering, with annual collections now well over $100 million, has long provided over 40 percent of the annual funding of the SBC's Foreign Mission Board (renamed the International Mission Board in 1995) and is indispensable to American Protestantism's largest foreign missionary program.

Any explanation of Lottie Moon's status among Southern Baptists is inevitably subjective. Her story, as told by the SBC, however, contains at least two themes that are interesting in terms of southern culture. One is a traditional theme that W. J. Cash called southern gyneolatry, or the "pitiful Mother of God" image, centering on white women of intelligence, courage, and high capacity for self-sacrifice. The other theme, also strongly present, is of Lot-

tie Moon as an undeclared feminist—single, self-reliant, wiser, and stronger than male associates, pushing in "her own way" (the title of one of her SBC biographies) to advance Christianity and the status of women, both in China and within the Southern Baptist Convention. Rather than being mutually exclusive, these contrasting themes seem instead to have extended Lottie Moon's range and enduring influence.

Within the SBC, Lottie Moon has always been linked particularly to the Woman's Missionary Union (WMU), the denomination's most important organization for women and for broad support of mission work. New scholarship by Regina D. Sullivan details how in the 19th century Lottie Moon's story tied into the birth of the WMU as a woman's movement within the male-dominated SBC and how, a century later in the 1990s, control of Moon's image became part of a new struggle between SBC moderates, represented by the WMU, and a conservative denominational leadership represented by the International Mission Board. Reshaped to fit changing needs and times, the Lottie Moon story is shown by Sullivan to be "endlessly malleable" and a *lieu de memoire*, or memory site, where Southern Baptists continue to define their identity and future.

IRWIN T. HYATT JR.
Emory University

Catherine B. Allen, *The New Lottie Moon Story* (1997); Irwin T. Hyatt Jr., *Our Ordered Lives Confess: Three Nineteenth-Century American Missionaries in East Shantung* (1976); Una Roberts Lawrence, *Lottie Moon*

(1927); Regina D. Sullivan, "Woman with a Mission: Remembering Lottie Moon and the Woman's Missionary Union" (Ph.D. dissertation, University of North Carolina, 2002).

Moynihan Report

Published in 1965 by a group in the U.S. Department of Labor, the Moynihan Report, officially entitled "The Negro Family: The Case for National Action," raised controversial questions about the relationships among gender, family life, and African American life that lasted for more than a generation. Daniel Patrick Moynihan, a committed anti-poverty activist in the Lyndon Johnson administration, viewed the report as a way to dramatize serious problems that plagued African Americans, even after the *Brown v. Board of Education* decision and the Civil Rights Act of 1964. Responses to the report ultimately had more significance than the report itself. Critics condemned it for blaming poverty and other social problems that so many African Americans faced on the weaknesses among African Americans themselves.

The report was a short document with succinct writing, containing statistics comparing African Americans to other groups in the United States and occasional references to works by historians Stanley Elkins and Frank Tannenbaum and sociologists E. Franklin Frazier and Nathan Glazer. According to the report, African Americans were struggling economically and becoming more involved in crime because of a combination of centuries of injustice and exploitation and—the real emphasis of the report—the increasing instability of family life in urban ghettoes. The report emphasized high divorce rates, the large numbers of children born to unmarried couples, and the resulting high numbers of households headed by women as the immediate cause of the continuing and growing struggles that African Americans faced in cities.

The report mentioned the South primarily in its depiction of slavery as an institution that damaged people's psyches, worked against ambition and innovation, divided families, and gave men no role in leading those families. Thus, a weakened institution had never recovered in the decades after slavery and, according to the report, had become even weaker amid multiple migrations, poverty, and criminal behavior in northern cities. Moynihan and other figures in the Labor Department called for national action to help strengthen African American family life by some kind of unspecified guarantee of a family income.

Appearing at a time when much of the civil rights movement was turning away from optimistic national action and toward community empowerment and varieties of Black Power, the report came off as condescending toward African Americans. Critics offered two main responses to the report. Many argued it confused the causes of social problems with their consequences and insisted that the real causes of poverty were present and past forms of discrimination—not a flawed family structure.

Some critics were incensed that a government report that was ostensibly on the side of African American improvement could blame, or seem to blame, those problems on African Americans themselves. Sociologists such as Joyce Ladner and Carol Stack and historians, most obviously Herbert Gutman, took up the challenge to write a counternarrative, producing studies arguing that the history of African American family life, far from a story of crises and instability, showed the resiliency to adapt to various challenges. A second criticism addressed the assumption that men needed to be in charge of families, and that all families, to be successful, should aspire to middle-class norms of small numbers of children living with two permanent parents in individual homes. In 1971, for example, Albert Murray showed his scorn for the patriarchal and condescending elements of the report by twice referring to Big Daddy Pat Moynihan in his book *South to a Very Old Place*.

Support for the report came from a surprising and unwanted source. The Citizens' Councils claimed that the Moynihan Report documented a moral weakness and social breakdown among African Americans and dramatized why white children should not be forced to attend school with black children. Although criticizing the policy conclusions of the report, the Citizens' Councils bought numerous copies to distribute to their members.

Debates of course continue over welfare policy, a living wage, and the definition of family life, but the significance of the Moynihan Report continues almost exclusively in the irony of a leftist effort that failed because it blamed problems on the people it intended to be helping.

TED OWNBY
University of Mississippi

Herbert G. Gutman, *The Black Family in Slavery and Freedom, 1750–1925* (1976); Robert A. Katzmann, ed., *Daniel Patrick Moynihan: The Intellectual in Public Life* (1998); Joyce A. Ladner, *The Death of White Sociology* (1973); Lee Rainwater and William L. Yancey, eds., *The Moynihan Report and the Politics of Controversy* (1967); Daryl Michael Scott, *Contempt and Pity: Social Policy and the Image of the Damaged Black Psyche, 1880–1996* (1997); Carol B. Stack, *All Our Kin: Strategies for Survival in a Black Community* (1974) .

National Association of Colored Women

The National Association of Colored Women (NACW) was founded in 1895 to provide a national structure for African American women's organizations. Established as a federation of local and state women's clubs, NACW developed an agenda for improving conditions within African American communities and provided a forum for black women to promote national programs on parenting, antilynching, and education.

The NACW grew out of the organizational experiences of African American women in the 19th century. In northern and some southern towns and cities, black women established mutual aid and social welfare societies, as well as literary and cultural clubs, to respond to the needs of their communities. Three centers of organizational strength had emerged by the late 19th century: Washington, D.C., Boston, and New York. Educated and professional women from the middle and upper classes generally led the clubs in their communities, although working-class women headed some church clubs or mutual aid societies. Prominent clubwomen included Mary Ann Shadd Cary, Hallie Q. Brown, Mary Church Terrell, Fannie Barrier Williams, Josephine Bruce, and Anna Julia Cooper in Washington, D.C.; Victoria Earle Matthews, Maritcha Lyons, Sarah Smith Garnet, and Susan Smith McKinney in New York; and Josephine St. Pierre Ruffin, her daughter Florida Ridley, and Maria Baldwin in Boston.

In 1892, three events led clubwomen to create a national federation that could serve as the voice of black women—the exclusion of African American women's groups from the Board of Lady Managers of the Columbian Exposition in Chicago; the appearance of *Woman's Era*, the first monthly magazine by and for black women; and the publication in that magazine of an inflammatory letter from James Jacks, the white president of the Missouri Press Association, to British antilynching activist Florence Belgarnie.

In 1893 clubwomen in Washington, D.C., led by Hallie Q. Brown and Josephine Bruce, organized the Colored Women's League (CWL). Two years later, an alliance of clubwomen from Boston, Washington, D.C., and Tuskegee, Ala., convened the First National Conference of Colored Women, which met in Boston, with 104 delegates from 54 clubs in 14 states and the District of Columbia

attending the conference. Josephine St. Pierre Ruffin served as conference president, with vice presidents Helen Cook of Washington, D.C., and Margaret Murray Washington of Tuskegee; Elizabeth Carter of New Bedford, Mass., served as secretary. The conference led to the organization of the National Federation of Afro-American Women (NFAAW). Its principal goal was to stand up to assaults on the popular image of black women.

The NFAAW and the CWL both held their 1896 national conventions in Washington, D.C., and a joint committee, chaired by Mary Church Terrell, voted to merge the two organizations into the National Association of Colored Women (NACW). Terrell served as the first president, with vice presidents from Boston, Kansas City, New Orleans, and Philadelphia. The second convention, held in Nashville the following year, established the structure of the organization and created the national publication, *National Notes*. Biennial meetings over the next four decades charted the focus for the organization and created or consolidated its departments. NACW's work was similar to that of the national organization of white clubwomen, the General Federation of Women's Clubs (GFWC). But NACW's activities consistently centered on self-help, the protection of women, and the mission of elite, educated black women to foster "racial uplift." White clubwomen assumed no special mission to protect or improve conditions for their race as a whole. However, despite the unifying nature of NACW's goals, conflicts emerged within the organization over issues of the regional domination of the organization's leadership, personality, and color consciousness.

In 1924, under the presidency of Mary McLeod Bethune, NACW established a national headquarters at Twelfth and O Streets in Washington, D.C. The organization also assumed responsibility for saving and restoring the Frederick Douglass home and created a junior division to attract younger members. Although the biennial conferences in the 1930s attempted to address the needs of black women during the Great Depression, the organization continued to focus on its traditional mission to "standardize the home; create a good environment for the child; train girls to be industrious, artistic and gracious; improve working conditions for women and girls; and increase community service." But Bethune, now head of the Negro division of the National Youth Administration, was convinced that black women's organizations needed a united coalition that could represent their issues on the political front. NACW's tenure as the premier national organization of African American women's clubs ended in 1935 with Bethune's creation of the National Council of Negro Women.

BEVERLY GREENE BOND
University of Memphis

Alfreda Duster, ed., *Crusade for Justice: The Autobiography of Ida B. Wells* (1970); Tullia Hamilton, "The National Association of Colored Women, 1896–1920" (Ph.D. dissertation, Emory University, 1978); Sharon Harley and Rosalyn Terborg-Penn, eds., *The Afro-American Woman: Struggles and Images* (1978); Dorothy Salem, "National Association of Colored Women," in *Black Women in America*, vol. 2, ed. Darlene Clark Hine, Elsa Barkley Brown, and Rosalyn Terborg-Penn (1993), *To Better Our World: Black Women in Organized Reform, 1890–1920* (1990); Mary Church Terrell, *Colored Woman in a White World* (1940); Charles H. Wesley, *The History of the National Association of Colored Women's Clubs: A Legacy of Service* (1984); Debra Gray White, *Too Heavy a Load: Black Women in Defense of Themselves, 1894–1994* (1999).

Newcomb, Josephine

(1816–1901) PHILANTHROPIST.
Josephine Louise Newcomb was the founder of H. Sophie Newcomb Memorial College, the first degree-granting college for women established within a previously all-male major university. Born in Baltimore, Md., on 31 October 1816, she was the daughter of Alexander Le Monnier, a prominent Baltimore businessman. Orphaned in 1831, Josephine Louise moved to New Orleans to live with her only sister. While summering in Louisville, Ky., she met and married Warren Newcomb, a successful businessman who lived in New Orleans most of the summer because his wholesale business was located there.

In 1866 Warren Newcomb died, leaving to his wife and daughter, Harriott Sophie, born to the couple in 1855, an estate valued at between $500,000 and $850,000. Under her own direction Josephine Newcomb increased her inheritance to over $4 million by her death in 1901. In 1870, at age 15, Harriott Sophie died of diphtheria. Devastated by the loss of her child, Newcomb began to search for a suitable memorial to her daughter. An Episcopalian, she donated generously to the support of her church. A native southerner, she gave to numerous causes to assist in the recovery of the war-torn South. She contributed to the library of Washington and Lee University. She founded a school for sewing girls and supported a Confederate orphans' home, both in Charleston, as well as a school for deaf children in New York. In 1886, at the behest of Ida Richardson, a wealthy New Orleans woman, and Colonel William Preston Johnson, president of the recently established Tulane University of Louisiana, Newcomb agreed to found a college for women as a memorial to her daughter.

Although coeducational colleges and independent women's colleges existed, the H. Sophie Newcomb Memorial College was a unique experiment, the design of which influenced Barnard at Columbia, Radcliffe at Harvard, and the Women's College of Western Reserve. Part of, and yet separate from, Tulane University, the college had a separate administration and faculty and was empowered to formulate its own academic policy. The college's stated aim—to offer a liberal arts education for women equal to that available for men—represented a departure in the history of female education in the South. In an age when higher education for women was viewed with indifference, Josephine Louise Newcomb initiated significant change in the patterns of women's education.

Tulane University dissolved Newcomb as a separate entity in 2006, in the reorganization that took place in the aftermath of Hurricane Katrina. The heirs of Josephine Newcomb have mounted legal challenges to this plan, hoping to keep Newcomb a degree-granting college within the university.

SYLVIA R. FREY
Tulane University

Brandt V. B. Dixon, *A Brief History of H. Sophie Newcomb Memorial College, 1887–1919* (1928); John P. Dyer, *Tulane: The Biography of a University, 1834–1965* (1966).

Pringle, Elizabeth Allston

(1845–1921) PLANTATION MISTRESS. Elizabeth Allston Pringle exemplified the resourcefulness of elite southern women during and after the Civil War. She was born near Pawley's Island, S.C., to Robert Allston, a successful rice planter and future governor of the state, and Adele Petigru Allston. In her memoir, *Chronicles of Chicora Wood*, Pringle devoted no fewer than 100 pages to her family background, demonstrating the concern with lineage and heritage characteristic of wealthy 19th-century southerners.

Initially taught at home by a governess, Pringle was sent at age nine to join her sister at a small, select Charleston boarding school, which "finished off" young ladies by teaching them the fine arts and French, as well as basic subjects. The Allstons displayed considerable ambivalence about the education of their daughters, insisting that the girls study at home during the summer yet acknowledging that by age 16 "balls, receptions, and dinners" made it "impossible" for a young girl to "keep her mind on her studies." Elizabeth Pringle was too young to attend social events before the Civil War, but she recalled her sister's gowns and beaus and parties with keen interest.

The war, of course, was a central experience in Pringle's life. Through her youthful eyes, the excitement of seeing the men march off with banners waving was a strong early impression. But she also recalled her father's death, the steady reduction in food and clothing, the looting of the family residence, and tense confrontations with the now-free blacks on the family's various plantations. Clearly, Elizabeth Allston derived much of her later strength and independence from watching her mother cope with these trying circumstances and from facing up to them herself.

In the fall of 1865 Elizabeth Allston's mother decided to support herself by opening a school in Charleston. Initially afraid to teach, her daughter was ashamed of her weakness. "Am I really just a butterfly?" she asked herself. "Is my love of pleasure the strongest thing about me? What an awful thought." After three months of teaching, she was ecstatic about her work and confident in her abilities.

In 1868 she accompanied her family back to Chicora Wood, where she married John Julius Pringle two years later. Her memoir is characteristically discreet on the subject of their relationship, but the marriage appears to have been a happy one, until Pringle's untimely death in 1876. In a bold move, Elizabeth Pringle acquired her husband's plantation and elected to run it herself, growing rice and fruit and raising livestock. When her mother died in 1896, she took over Chicora Wood as well. Thus, she became a substantial rice planter, an unusual venture for a woman to undertake alone.

Elizabeth Allston Pringle pursued this occupation with vigor. She became deeply involved in agricultural techniques and in the often frustrating management of her workers. She enjoyed years of prosperity, but she succumbed to failure early in the 20th century, when severe weather and competition from other regions ruined many Lowcountry rice planters. But she voiced no regrets. "I have so loved the freedom and simplicity of the life, in spite of its trials and isolation," she asserted, noting too "the exhilaration of making a good income myself." In the last two decades before her death, in 1921, she turned to writing, and her gracefully penned recollections add much to the understanding of southern womanhood and southern life during the important transitional period in which she lived.

LAURA L. BECKER
University of Miami

Patience Pennington, *A Woman Rice Planter* (1961); Elizabeth A. Pringle, *Chronicles of Chicora Wood* (1922).

Prostitution (New Orleans)

In the antebellum period, numerous travelers commented on New Orleans's reputation as the South's Babylon. Many of them, like James Davidson and Rachel Jackson, referred to the city's well-known culture of sensual excess in biblical terms. The first lines Davidson wrote after arriving in the city in 1836 were "I am now in this Great Southern

Babylon—the mighty receptacle of wealth, depravity and misery." Fifteen years earlier, Jackson had expressed strikingly similar sentiments while on a visit to the city with her husband, Andrew. She wrote, "Great Babylon is come up before me. . . . Oh the wickedness, the idolatry of the place! Unspeakable the riches and splendor." Many other writers captured the contradictory nature of the city's appalling appeal as well, pointing out the city's sins and scandals while simultaneously being charmed by its aura of disorder and its culture of sexual permissiveness and sensual excess.

For most antebellum visitors, New Orleans's reputation as the South's Babylon sprang from its reputation as a center of tolerated prostitution and its position as the region's largest slave market. And, as many antislavery writers were anxious to point out, those two functions sometimes overlapped in the city's notorious fancy girl auctions, which featured the sale of light-skinned female slaves for implicitly sexual purposes. The city's reputation as a bastion of commercial sexuality and sex across the color line survived the Civil War and emancipation and, in the years that followed, generated enormous economic dividends and considerable controversy.

The city's reputation, combined with its location in an otherwise overwhelmingly rural and Protestant region, set it apart from the rest of the South, as did numerous attempts by local authorities to control prostitution while still profiting from it. Between 1857 and 1897 the city acted at least eight times to establish vice district boundaries. Ironically, the last and smallest of these districts, which came to be known as Storyville in mock-homage to the city councilman who drafted the ordinance, became its most notorious and well known. Storyville, which existed from 1897 to 1917, became an economic powerhouse that generated graft, enhanced the city's erotic reputation, and helped it to become one of the South's most popular tourist destinations.

Even as debates about the necessity of racial segregation raged, whites from all over the region and the rest of the nation descended on New Orleans in droves. Storyville provided a space where almost anyone might indulge in activities that were taboo outside the vice district's boundaries, including crossing the color line sexually and socially. The district was one of the few places in the turn-of-the-century South where people from all social classes, ethnicities, and races mingled so intimately, casually, and freely in the pursuit of sex and leisure activities. In fact, the existence of a ribald, racially mixed place like Storyville allowed white visitors to take a vacation from the so-called requirements of Jim Crow, yet maintain the pretension that white supremacy and racial segregation were absolute necessities in their own communities. In many ways, Storyville was a geographical expression of the 19th-century belief that male sexuality required an outlet in order to protect respectable white women. Like the city's reputation as the South's Babylon,

Storyville has remained an icon of the city's sybaritic appeal and a sexually alluring beacon to tourists from the Bible Belt and beyond.

ALECIA P. LONG
Louisiana State Museum

Alecia P. Long, *The Great Southern Babylon: Sex, Race, and Respectability in New Orleans, 1865–1920* (2003).

Richards, Ann

(1933–2006) TEXAS POLITICIAN. Ann Richards, the energetic and quick-witted feminist Texas Democrat, first burst onto the national political stage when she delivered the keynote address during the 1988 Democratic National Convention in Atlanta. Speaking of the wealthy incumbent U.S. vice president, George H. W. Bush, also a Texan, Richards quipped, "Poor George. He can't help it. He was born with a silver foot in his mouth." The line would become one of her most memorable, and the popularity she gained from it perhaps helped propel her to the highest office in the state of Texas.

Born Dorothy Ann Willis in Lakeview, Tex., to a father who, Richards always claimed, came from Bugtussle and a mother who, as she also claimed, came from Hogjaw, Richards moved with her family to Waco so she could attend Waco High School. While at Waco High School, Richards attended Girls State, a summer citizenship and leadership conference, in Austin. She also attended Girls Nation in Washington, D.C., where she toured the White House and met President Harry Truman.

After high school, Richards dropped the name Dorothy and married her high school sweetheart, Dave Richards. The couple enrolled at Baylor University in Waco the following fall, and Richards earned her B.A. degree in 1954. The couple moved to Austin following graduation, where Richards taught government at a junior high school and her husband attended law school at the University of Texas. After her husband earned his law degree, the couple moved again to Washington, D.C., where he worked for the U.S. Civil Rights Commission, and then to Dallas, where she settled in as a homemaker and became politically active as a campaigner for gubernatorial candidates Henry B. Gonzalez and Ralph Yarborough.

In the early 1970s, Richards went on to do campaign work for Texas candidates, including Sarah Weddington, a lawyer running for a seat in the Texas House who had successfully argued *Roe v. Wade* before the U.S. Supreme Court. In 1976 Richards decided to stage her own campaign for public office when she ran for Travis County commissioner and won. She was reelected to the position in 1980, won an election for state treasurer in 1982, and was reelected in 1986. But during this period of political ascension, Richards's personal life was plummeting into ruin. Her marriage had ended in divorce, and her drinking grew out of control. She entered and completed rehabilitation, and in 1990 Richards succeeded in becoming the second-ever woman governor of Texas (the first being Miriam "Ma" Ferguson in the 1920s and 1930s). During the first few years of her governorship, "a New Texas," Richards claimed, had been born.

Ann Richards, the boisterous Texas governor, obtained a license to ride a motorcycle at the age of 60. (Courtesy Texas State Library and Archives Commission, Austin)

A slew of achievements characterized Richards's term as an effective, progressive, and culturally liberal Texas governor, including increasing the number of women and minorities appointed to state government posts, revitalizing the Texas economy, instituting the state lottery, introducing insurance and environmental reform, establishing a substance-abuse program for inmates, and lowering the number of violent inmates released.

In what was widely considered an uninspired reelection campaign, Richards lost the governorship to the son of the vice president whom she had jokingly put down in 1988, George W. Bush. Although George W. Bush was inexperienced as a politician, despite his paternal background, he ran a cunning and successful campaign that used a number of Richards's liberal, still-popular, achievements against her. Republicans who had crossed the party line to elect her as governor returned to their GOP roots, citing fiscal irresponsibility and a lax attitude toward criminal punishment as among their reasons for abandoning her.

After leaving office, Ann Richards worked as a public speaker and as a lobbyist for a high-profile Washington, D.C., law firm. In 2006 she died of esophageal cancer and was laid to rest in the Texas State Cemetery in Austin.

JAMES G. THOMAS JR.
University of Mississippi

Ann Richards and Peter Knobler, *Straight from the Heart: My Life in Politics and Other Places* (1989); Mike Shropshire and Frank Schaeffer, *The Thorny Rose of Texas: An Intimate Portrait of Governor Ann Richards* (1994); Sue Tolleson-Rinehart and Jeanie R. Stanley, *Claytie and the Lady: Ann Richards, Gender, and Politics in Texas* (1994).

Scottsboro Boys

In the Depression-era South, an Alabama rape case tried in Scottsboro came to symbolize to much of the world the racism and injustice afforded blacks in southern society. The case galvanized protest among not just Americans but the international community as well. On 31 March 1931 several white men riding the Southern Railroad from Chattanooga to Memphis told authorities in Jackson County, Ala., that blacks had thrown them off the train. The sheriff telegraphed ahead to the next stop, Paint Rock, and when the train stopped the authorities arrested the nine youths. Two white women dressed in men's clothing also got off the train and told the sheriff that they had been raped by the group. The teenagers were taken to the county seat of Scottsboro and charged and jailed. Southern society considered the rape of a white woman by black men to be a most heinous atrocity and often used the charge as justification for lynching. That night the local white community rose up in outrage, but the sheriff called the governor for guardsmen to protect the youths from the mob.

The nine youths represented the lowest rungs and least powerful of southern society: black, transient, illiterate, and impoverished. Their trial was held within three weeks, and the defendants received inadequate legal council. They met only briefly with the two attorneys minutes before the trial. Despite the prosecution's lack of witnesses and the testimony of two doctors that there was no physical proof of rape, the all-white jury swiftly convicted all nine. White supremacy dictated that the honor of white women, even of questionable moral standing, trumped a black man's life. Outside of the South, the Scottsboro case caused immediate protest, due to the number of participants, their youth, the swiftness of the trial, the lack of evidence, the obvious insufficient defense, and their death sentences. Additionally, both the NAACP and the legal branch of the Communist Party—the International Labor Defense (ILD)—wanted to defend the youths in the appeal. The Communists convinced the boys' parents that they would mount a vigorous defense, and the ILD hired a talented northern Jewish lawyer, Samuel Leibowitz. Although indisputably a brilliant attorney, Leibowitz came to represent the southerners' animosity toward the North.

Throughout the next several years,

a series of trials at both the state and federal levels wound through the legal system. In 1932 the U.S. Supreme Court, in *Powell v. Alabama*, overturned the convictions because the defendants had received inadequate counsel. Undeterred, Alabama retried and convicted one of the defendants. In *Norris v. Alabama*, the U.S. Supreme Court overturned this conviction because Alabama systematically excluded African American jurors. Both the rulings chipped away at legal injustice long practiced by southern courts.

Eventually, one of the accusers recanted her story and went on a speaking tour with a defendant's mother. By 1937 the public had tired of the series of state and federal trials, and the prosecution settled with the defense to free four of the defendants. They traveled north and were feted as heroes. The other five received long prison terms, and four were quietly released through the 1940s. In 1950 the last prisoner escaped and traveled to Michigan, where the governor refused to extradite him to Alabama. The defendants grew from youth to manhood in the brutal Alabama penal system and were denied even the most basic education. Most worked low-paying menial jobs, drifted, and were in and out of jail. In 1976 Clarence Norris traveled to Alabama, where Governor George Wallace issued him a full pardon.

The Scottsboro case had tragic consequences for the nine innocent young men. Significantly, the case represented the worst aspects of southern racism and demonstrated the region's extreme regional animosities. Throughout the years, the case inspired poems, songs, plays, short stories, and novels.

MINOA D. UFFELMAN
Austin Peay State University

Dan T. Carter, *Scottsboro: A Tragedy of the American South* (1979); James Goodman, *Stories of Scottsboro* (1994); Michael J. Klarman, *From Jim Crow to Civil Rights: The Supreme Court and the Struggle for Racial Equality* (2004); Hugh T. Murray Jr., *Phylon* (1st Qtr., 1977).

Smith, Lillian

(1897–1966) WRITER AND SOCIAL CRITIC.

Internationally acclaimed as author of the controversial novel *Strange Fruit* (1944) and the autobiographical critique of southern culture *Killers of the Dream* (1949, rev. 1961), Lillian Eugenia Smith was the most outspoken white southern writer in areas of economic, racial, and sexual discrimination during the 1930s and 1940s. When other southern liberals—Ralph McGill, Hodding Carter, Virginius Dabney, and Jonathan Daniels—were charting a cautious course on racial change, Smith boldly and persistently called for an end to racial segregation. Furthermore, her work for social justice continued throughout her life. In 1955 she wrote *Now Is the Time*, urging support for the Supreme Court's decision on school desegregation. Her last published book, *Our Faces, Our Words* (1964), reflects her personal knowledge and experience with the young black and white civil rights activists of the 1950s and 1960s.

Lillian Smith was born on 12 December 1897, the seventh of nine children of Anne Hester Simpson and Calvin

Warren Smith, and grew up in Jasper, Fla., where her father was a prominent business and civic leader. Some of the richness of that childhood is portrayed in *Memory of a Large Christmas* (1962). Her life as daughter of upper-class whites in the small-town Deep South ended rather abruptly when her father lost his turpentine mills in 1915 and moved the family to their summer home near Clayton, Ga. Financially on her own, Smith attended the nearby Piedmont College for one year, was principal of a two-room mountain school, and helped her parents manage a hotel before she was able to pursue her interest in music. During the school terms of 1916–17 and 1919–22, she studied piano at Peabody Conservatory in Baltimore, spending summers working in the family's summer lodge and teaching music at Laurel Falls Camp for Girls, opened by her father in 1920.

In the fall of 1922 Smith accepted a three-year position as director of music at Virginia School in Huchow, China. But her ambitions for a career in music ended when her parents' ill health necessitated her return to direct Laurel Falls Camp. Under her direction, from 1925 through 1948, the camp became an outstanding innovative educational institution, known for its instruction in the arts, music, theater, and modern psychology. It was also a laboratory for many of the ideas informing Smith's analysis of southern culture, especially her understanding of the effects of child-rearing practices on adult racial and sexual relationships.

Through the camp, Smith also met Paula Snelling and began the lifelong relationship that encouraged and sustained her writing career. From 1936 to 1946, Smith and Snelling coedited a magazine, first called *Pseudopodia*, then *North Georgia Review*, and finally *South Today*, which quickly achieved acclaim as a forum for liberal opinion in the region.

A record-breaking best seller, *Strange Fruit* was translated into 15 languages, banned for obscenity in Boston, and produced as a Broadway play. But *Killers of the Dream*, an even more insightful exploration of the interrelationship of race, class, and gender in southern society, brought strong criticism from more moderate southerners. Though widely reviewed, none of her subsequent works achieved the popularity or financial success of her first novel.

Her more philosophical works, *The Journey* (1954) and *One Hour* (1959), demonstrate the extent to which Smith's concerns extended beyond race relations to encompass all aspects of human relationships in the modern world. In *The Journey* she wrote, "I went in search of an image of the human being I could be proud of." *One Hour*, Smith's response to the McCarthy era, is a complex psychological novel about the inevitable destruction unleashed in a community when the reality and power of the irrational are unacknowledged in human life.

Two collections of her work have been published posthumously: *From the Mountain* (1972), a selection of pieces from the magazine, edited by Helen White and Redding Sugg; and *The Winner Names the Age* (1978), a selection of speeches and essays, edited by Michelle

Cliff with an introduction by Paula Snelling.

MARGARET ROSE GLADNEY
University of Alabama

Louise Blackwell and Frances Clay, *Lillian Smith* (1971); Will Brantley, *Feminine Sense in Southern Memoir: Smith, Glasgow, Welty, Hellman, Porter, and Hurston* (1993); Margaret Rose Gladney, *Southern Studies* (Fall 1983); Fred Hobson, *Tell about the South: The Southern Rage to Explain* (1983); Darlene O'Dell, *Sites of Southern Memory: The Autobiographies of Katherine Du Pre Lumpkin, Lillian Smith, and Pauli Murray* (2001).

Terrell, Mary Church

(1863–1954) EDUCATOR AND SOCIAL ACTIVIST.

Mary Eliza Church was born in Memphis, Tenn., on 23 September 1863. She was the oldest child of Robert Reed ("Bob") Church and Louisa Ayers Church, who were slaves of Charles Church and T. S. Ayers, respectively, at the time of Mary's birth. Louisa and Robert had "assumed the relationship of man and wife" in 1862, and their relationship was legitimized under Tennessee law in 1866. Mary's family, which also included her younger brother, Thomas, continued to live in Memphis after the Civil War. Bob Church owned several businesses, and Louisa Church, with the financial backing of her former owner, opened a hairdressing salon. Mary ("Mollie" to her family and friends) enjoyed a life of relative economic security, despite the ever-present specter of racial animosity. Her parents and her maternal grandmother, Lisa, told her about their own and other family members' experiences as slaves and her father's injury during the 1866 Memphis Race Riot. Mollie remembered a train conductor's attempt to force her out of a first-class coach when she was only five years old. Only her father's drawn pistol prevented the conductor from carrying out his threat.

Mary's parents separated when she was six years old. After their divorce, Louisa Church sold her salon and moved to New York, where she opened a similar business. She sent Mary to Antioch School, in Yellow Springs, Ohio, rather than enroll her in the segregated New York City schools. Mary continued her early education in Ohio, graduating from Oberlin Academy in 1879 and entering Oberlin College in 1880. Her father's business interests expanded, and he was soon recognized as one of the wealthiest black men in the South. His connections with other "aristocrats of color" provided young Mary admission into a widening circle of influential black political and economic leaders. She met Frederick Douglass when she attended the 1880 presidential inauguration with Josephine Bruce, wife of Bob Church's friend (and the newly elected Mississippi senator) Blanche K. Bruce.

Mary Church graduated from Oberlin College in 1884 and briefly returned to Memphis before assuming a teaching position at Wilberforce College. Although her father opposed her decision, Mary felt that her education had prepared her to do useful work for her race. After two years at Wilberforce, she moved to Washington, D.C., to teach at the M Street School, the most prestigious public school for blacks in the city.

In 1888 she began a two-year sojourn in Europe, traveling in France, Italy, and Germany. She returned to her teaching position in Washington, D.C., and married fellow educator Robert Heberton Terrell in 1891. Robert Terrell served as principal of the M Street High School and was appointed judge of the Municipal Court in Washington, D.C., in 1902. Although her husband was a supporter of Booker T. Washington's educational philosophy and owed his judgeship to the black leader, Mary Church Terrell advocated liberal arts education and interracial cooperation.

Mary Church Terrell was a leading advocate for the civil rights of African Americans, particularly African American women, throughout the first half of the 20th century. She fought against lynching (after the 1892 murder in Memphis of her childhood friend Thomas Moss and two other black businessmen), disfranchisement, and segregation. Terrell believed that the key to the advancement of the race was recognition of the respectability of black women. In 1896 she became founder and first president of the National Association of Colored Women (NACW), and under her two-year tenure as president this organization of clubwomen adopted an agenda that supported black women's activities in progressive reform. She helped organize and was a charter member of the NAACP. She campaigned for woman suffrage, while calling attention to the racist agenda of some suffrage leaders.

Terrell supported efforts to pass federal antilynching legislation, campaigned for the Equal Rights Amendment, endorsed A. Phillip Randolph's March on Washington Movement, which led to President Franklin Roosevelt's executive order creating a Fair Employment Practices Committee, attacked court rulings in the Scottsboro Case, and fought for the integration of the Washington, D.C., chapter of the American Association of University Women. In 1950, at the age of 77, Mary Church Terrell began a three-year struggle to integrate restaurants in Washington, D.C. Terrell was a party in the case of *District of Columbia v. John Thompson*, which successfully forced Washington, D.C., restaurants to enforce 19th-century laws requiring that they serve "any respectable, well-behaved person regardless of race." Terrell died on 24 July 1954, two months after the Supreme Court handed down the *Brown v. Board of Education* decision.

BEVERLY GREENE BOND
University of Memphis

Darlene Clark Hine, Elsa Barkley Brown, and Rosalyn Terborg-Penn, *Black Women in America: An Historical Encyclopedia*, vol. 2 (1993); Beverly W. Jones, *Quest for Equality: The Life and Writings of Mary Church Terrell, 1863–1954* (1990); Jacqueline M. Moore, *Leading the Race: The Transformation of the Black Elite in the Nation's Capital, 1880–1920* (1999); Mary Church Terrell, *A Colored Woman in a White World* (1996).

Uncle Tom

In current usage, the term "Uncle Tom" is an epithet used for African Americans who are traitors to their race. However, when the abolitionist and novelist Harriet Beecher Stowe created the character for her 1852 novel *Uncle Tom's Cabin, or, Life among the Lowly*, she viewed him as the hero of her story. Stowe's book, a response to the Fugitive Slave Act, combined the genres of sentimental domestic novel and abolitionist polemic to convince public opinion that slavery was evil. By early 1853 more than a million copies of *Uncle Tom* had been sold in the United States and England. The book was translated into numerous languages and read throughout the world. The novel's immense popularity in the North was matched by virulent criticism in the South. Southern women writers penned novels about slavery from the southern perspective, though none approached the cultural impact of *Uncle Tom*. Other characters from the novel, Little Eva, Eliza, Topsy, August St. Clair, and Simon Legree, immediately became part of American culture. The book's melodramatic scenes lent themselves well to the stage, and hundreds of performances entertained thousands of audiences. Indeed, it was the most performed play in America until the 1920s. The story was filmed as early as 1903, and there were various remakes and spin-off films that created an Uncle Tom genre.

Criticism began from the moment of publication and ranged from Stowe's inaccurate portrayal of slavery and her lack of firsthand knowledge of the South to the book's poor literary merit. Subsequent generations have critiqued the novel, with much of the criticism reflecting the particular concerns of each period. Stowe, a deeply religious woman, was the daughter, wife, and sister of six ministers. She imbued Uncle Tom with Christ-like characteristics and made him virtuous, kind, selfless, loving, and peaceful. After Tom loses his family he becomes devoted to a young white girl named Little Eva. Later in the novel, Uncle Tom refuses to betray two runaway slaves and to renounce his Christian beliefs, knowing that Simon Legree will kill him. To Stowe, Uncle Tom was a Christian martyr for all to emulate.

Later generations did not see Tom's passive characteristics as noble. In 1949, writer James Baldwin scathingly criticized *Uncle Tom* in "Everybody's Protest Novel." During the civil rights movement, African Americans desired a different type of hero. The noble character in Stowe's novel was not suited for the times, which called for a more masculine, less compliant hero. Today the term "Uncle Tom" is a pejorative and has come to symbolize black impotence and a weak, obsequious, unmanly man who is too eager to please whites. Literary criticism and historical and cultural analysis of *Uncle Tom's Cabin* is vibrant and lively, indicating that the novel still inspires debate.

MINOA D. UFFELMAN
Austin Peay State University

Henry Louis Gates Jr. and Hollis Robbins, *The Annotated* Uncle Tom's Cabin (2007); Thomas F. Gossett, Uncle Tom's Cabin *and American Culture* (1985); Eric J. Sunquist, *New Essays on* Uncle Tom's Cabin (1986).

United Daughters of the Confederacy

Southern fiction frequently portrays indomitable southern women in the Civil War. Given the late 19th century's predilection for organizations, it was

A monument to Gen. John H. Morgan and members of the United Daughters of the Confederacy who commissioned it, c. 1911, Lexington, Ky. (R. L. McClure, photographer, Library of Congress [LC-LC-USZ62-95819], Washington, D.C.)

perhaps inevitable that real-life diehard women who saw themselves as guardians of the Lost Cause would create the United Daughters of the Confederacy (UDC), as they did in Nashville in September 1894. The roots of the UDC may be traced back to the wartime Ladies' Aid Societies that sprang up spontaneously throughout the South in 1861 to assist Confederate soldiers. Perhaps the earliest organized voluntarism among Victorian southern women, these societies began as sewing groups, many of them in the churches, to make socks, mufflers, gloves, balaclava helmets, uniforms, and blankets for Confederate soldiers. As war took its human toll, some societies changed into Women's Hospital Associations, which set up hospitals and convalescent homes for Confederate sick and wounded soldiers.

During the spring of 1866 many of these organizations reorganized as Ladies' Memorial Associations to ensure proper interments for hastily buried Confederate dead, to honor their graves on 26 April (Confederate Memorial Day), and then to raise funds for monuments and statues commemorating the Lost Cause, in settings ranging from courthouse squares to battlefields.

Many members of the Ladies' Memorial Associations joined the UDC when it was organized, with its founders' declared goal of obtaining an accurate history of the Confederacy. The UDC was and is a social, literary, historical, monumental, and benevolent association made up of widows, wives, mothers, sisters, and other lineal descendants of men who rendered military, civil, or other personal service to the Confederate cause.

Organized on 10 September 1894, the UDC was incorporated in the District of Columbia on 18 July 1919. It has erected numerous memorials, it presents Crosses of Military Service to lineal Confederate descendants who themselves have served in later American wars, and it presents awards to outstanding service academy cadets and midshipmen. At its height, in the early 20th century, the UDC totaled some 100,000 members and was a political force to be reckoned with. As the years took their toll and memories faded, its membership dwindled to about 20,000 in the 1950s. But after the Civil War Centennial in the 1960s, interest revived. Today there are chapters in southern, northern, and western states, as well as in Paris and Mexico City. Associated organizations include the Sons of Confederate Veterans, founded in 1896; the Children of the Confederacy, organized in 1899; and the Military Order of the Stars and Bars, begun in 1938 and made up of male descendants of Confederate officers.

CAMERON FREEMAN NAPIER
Montgomery, Alabama

Jerome Francis Beattie, ed., *The Hereditary Register of the United States of America* (1972); Karen L. Cox, *Dixie's Daughters: The United Daughters of the Confederacy and the Preservation of Confederate Culture* (2003); Wallace Evan Davies, *Patriotism on Parade: The Story of Veterans' and Hereditary Organizations in America, 1783–1900* (1955);
 Mary B. Poppenheim et al., *The History of the United Daughters of the Confederacy* (1956).

Walker, Alice
(b. 1944) WRITER.

Alice Walker's *The Color Purple* is saturated with the atmosphere of the South, the rural Georgia farmland of her childhood. Walker, who has written more than 29 books of poetry, fiction, biography, and essays, finds strength and inspiration in the land and the people: "You look at old photographs of Southern blacks and you see it—a fearlessness, a real determination and proof of a moral center that is absolutely bedrock to the land. I think there's hope in the South, not in the North," she says.

Alice Walker was born in 1944 in Eatonton, Ga., the youngest of eight children. Her parents were poor sharecroppers. As a child, she read what books she could get, kept notebooks, and listened to the stories her relatives told. She attended Spelman College in Atlanta and graduated from Sarah Lawrence College in Bronxville, N.Y., where her writing was discovered by her teacher Muriel Rukeyser, who admired the manuscript that Alice had slipped under her door. Rukeyser sent the poems to her own editor at Harcourt Brace, and this first collection of Walker's poetry, *Once*, was published in 1965. From 1966 through 1974 Walker lived in Georgia and Mississippi and devoted herself to voter registration, Project Head Start, and writing. She married Mel Leventhal, a Brooklyn attorney who shared her dedication to civil rights in his work on school desegregation cases. Their daughter, Rebecca, was born in 1969. After they left the South, Walker and Leventhal lived for a while in a Brooklyn brownstone and then separated. Alice Walker now lives in rural northern California, which she chose primarily for the silence that would allow her to "hear" her fictional characters.

Alice Walker is the literary heir of Zora Neale Hurston and Flannery O'Connor. Walker has visited O'Connor's home in Milledgeville, Ga., and Hurston's grave in Eatonville, Fla., to pay homage. Walker's novels *The Third Life of Grange Copeland* (1977), *Meridian* (1976), and *The Color Purple* (1982) and short stories *In Love and Trouble* (1973) and *You Can't Keep a Good Woman Down* (1980) capture and explore her experiences of the South. She draws on her memories and her family's tales of Georgia ancestors in creating the portraits of rural black women in *The Color Purple*. Their speech is pure dialect—colloquial, poetic, and moving. Walker's poems too are filled with the rich landscape and atmosphere of the South.

Consciousness of the South has always been central to Alice Walker. The flowers and fruits in her California garden recall her mother's garden back in Georgia, a place so important to Walker that it became the inspiration for her collection of essays entitled *In Search of Our Mother's Gardens: Womanist Prose* (1983). Her mother's creativity was a compelling example to Alice Walker, as well as a constant source of beauty amid the poverty of rural Georgia. Her

mother died in 1993 at the age of 80. The headstone reads "Loving Soul, Great Spirit."

Among her many accomplishments and honors, Alice Walker has been Fannie Hurst Professor of Literature at Brandeis University and a contributing editor to *Ms.* magazine. In her writing and teaching she continually stresses the importance of black women writers. She edited a Zora Neale Hurston reader and wrote a biography of Langston Hughes for children. In 1984 Walker launched Wild Trees Press in Navarro, Calif., and published the work of unknown writers until 1988. The film version of *The Color Purple* was released in 1985 to much acclaim. In 2004 the musical version of *The Color Purple* premiered in Chicago, and it opened on Broadway in 2005. Alice Walker continues to highlight vital issues, such as female genital mutilation, which is central in her 1992 novel, *Possessing the Secret of Joy*. Alice Walker's literary awards include the Rosenthal Award of the National Institute of Arts and Letters, the Lillian Smith Award for her second book of poems, *Revolutionary Petunias* (1972), and the American Book Award and the Pulitzer Prize for fiction for *The Color Purple* (1983).

ELIZABETH GAFFNEY
Westchester Community College,
SUNY

David Bradley, *New York Times Magazine* (January 1984); Robert Towers, *New York Review of Books* (12 August 1982); Alice Walker, *Atlanta Constitution*, 19 April 1983; Evelyn C. White, *Alice Walker: A Life* (2004).

Walker, Maggie Lena

(1867–1934) BANKER.

Maggie Lena Walker, born in Richmond, Va., founded the Saint Luke Penny Savings Bank in Richmond in 1903, becoming the first woman bank president in the United States. Before her death she helped to reorganize it as the present-day Consolidated Bank and Trust Company, the oldest continuously existing black bank in the country. The bank, like most of Walker's activities, was the outgrowth of the Independent Order of Saint Luke, for which she served as Right Worthy Grand Secretary for 35 years. Under her leadership, this female-founded but previously male-run mutual benefit association established a juvenile department, an educational loan fund for young people, a department store, and a weekly newspaper. Growing to include 80,000 members in 2,010 Councils and Circles in 28 states, the order demonstrated a special commitment to expanding the economic opportunities within the community in the face of racism and sexism. It sought to develop interdependence among black women as a positive response to their problems and a step toward collective well-being.

Walker believed that black women had a "special duty and incentive to organize." And her work as a founder or leading supporter of the Richmond Council of Colored Women, the Virginia State Federation of Colored Women, the National Association of Wage Earners, the International Council of Women of the Darker Races, the National Training School for Girls, and the Virginia Industrial School for Colored Girls resulted from that belief. Additionally, Walker and others of the Saint Luke women were instrumental in political activities of the black community, including the struggle for woman suffrage, voter registration campaigns after the passage of the Nineteenth Amendment, and the formation of the Virginia Lily-Black Republican Party, which nominated Walker for state superintendent of public instruction in 1921. Throughout the 1920s Walker handled the finances of the National League of Republican Colored Women.

As a contributor to the ideological perspectives and political strategies of the black community, Walker symbolizes the growing belief in the early 20th century in economic development and self-help. All of her activities were motivated by a profound belief in the necessity to create an independent, self-sustaining community. Walker also helped direct the NAACP, the National Urban League, and the Negro Organization Society of Virginia.

Throughout her life and career, this daughter of a washerwoman developed a distinct understanding of what it meant to be wife, mother, businesswoman, and female activist. It was this perspective that shaped her struggle to expand notions within the black community of the proper role of women and within the larger society of the proper place of blacks.

ELSA BARKLEY BROWN
University of Maryland

Wendell P. Dabney, *Maggie Walker and the I. O. of Saint Luke: The Woman and Her Work* (1927); Sadie Iola Daniel, in *Women Builders*, ed. S. Daniel (1931); Maggie Lena Walker Papers, Maggie Walker National Historic Site, Richmond, Va.

Wells-Barnett, Ida B.

(1862–1931) JOURNALIST AND SOCIAL ACTIVIST.

For Ida B. Wells-Barnett, "southern culture" was an embattled site of identification. She was a native of Holly Springs, Miss., born a slave in 1862. There she attended Rust College, which was run by the American Missionary Association, and was strongly influenced by its "Yankee" teachers. Wells-Barnett was baptized in the Methodist Episcopal church. After her parents' death in the yellow fever epidemic of 1878, she moved to Memphis, Tenn., around 1880 and lived there until 1892. In that year she published her most important writing, a pamphlet entitled "Southern Horrors: Lynch Law in All Its Phases." This essay placed southern codes of honor in the horror of the lynching-for-rape scenario, part of a violent, morally hypocritical, crassly economic system of white supremacy. White men justified the murder of "bestial" black men by claiming the role of protectors of "weak" white women. But Wells-Barnett proved that, statistically, the rape charge was rarely in play during actual, documented lynchings. Instead, the cry of rape was often a cover to punish black men who in any way challenged the social, political, or economic status quo of the South. She also pointed out that white women sometimes participated in both mob activity and consensual sex with black men. When a death threat appeared in print in 1893 because of Wells-Barnett's newspaper criticism of lynching and southern honor, she had to leave for the North. She returned only once, in disguise, in 1917, to investigate the plight of 16 Arkansas farmers imprisoned for labor-organizing activity and sentenced to die in Helena.

Ida B. Wells-Barnett became famous—to opponents, infamous—for her critique of the South, but she accomplished the work largely outside of it. In 1895 she settled in Chicago, married lawyer Ferdinand L. Barnett, and raised four children. She died there in 1931. She perhaps achieved greatest prominence outside the United States, during 1893 and 1894, when she traveled to England and Scotland to mobilize opposition to lynching in the United States. At strategic points, however, she referred to herself as a "southern girl, born and bred," or by the pen-name "Exiled." Such identifications established her credibility as a native witness to history, especially since a black woman's moral authority was by definition suspect in American society. After a difficult period of political retrenchment in Chicago and the brutal race riot of July 1919, Wells-Barnett again reached out to the progressive elements of the white South in renewed efforts toward interracial understanding in the region (probably through the Commission on Interracial Cooperation), but this offer likely did not reach ears that had long since tuned her out.

Ironically, some of the best evidence of Ida B. Wells-Barnett's sparsely documented personal life dates from the 1880s, when she lived in Memphis and participated in a wide array of activities that mark her as a product of the post-Reconstruction New South. She left a diary dating from December 1885 to September 1887, and it provides vivid details of her life during this dynamic period. Entries describe a context not, perhaps, stereotypically "southern" or dominated by folkways. She studied Shakespeare and elocution, attended lectures by national figures like Dwight Moody, and was present at gender- and racially inclusive meetings of the Knights of Labor. The diary further documents her anger at injustice and violence directed at African Americans, some of which touched Wells-Barnett directly, as in her forced removal from a railroad "ladies" car. She was also the godmother of a child whose father, along with two business associates, was murdered, during a conflict in the spring of 1892. This triple lynching in Memphis was a life-changing event that directed her attention to full-time protest against mob violence protest.

Ida B. Wells-Barnett organized against southern violence outside of the region, resulting in scores of local anti-lynching committees and the founding of the National Association of Colored Women (1896) and the NAACP (1909). Her efforts successfully positioned antilynching as a legitimate focus of national reform, although based in the urban North. In that context, individuals and groups more securely positioned than she—by academic credentials, social status, or political connections in publishing, philanthropy, and govern-

ment—assumed leadership of the issue in the World War I era. Although Ida B. Wells-Barnett's southernness enabled her powerful voice to emerge in the 1890s, she came to be eclipsed by the competitive, money-driven, and con-solidating trends that came to charac-terize social reform in the United States over her lifetime.

PATRICIA A. SCHECHTER
Portland State University

Miriam DeCosta-Willis, ed., *The Memphis Diary of Ida B. Wells: An Intimate Portrait of the Activist as a Young Woman* (1995); Trudier Harris, ed., *Selected Words of Ida B. Wells-Barnett* (1991); Patricia A. Schechter, *Ida B. Wells-Barnett and American Reform, 1880–1930* (2001); Ida B. Wells-Barnett, *Crusade for Justice: The Autobiography of Ida B. Wells*, ed. and introduced by Alfreda M. Duster (1970).

Winfrey, Oprah

(b. 1954) TALK SHOW HOST AND ACTRESS.
Oprah Winfrey was born on 29 January 1954 in Kosciusko, Miss., to Vernita Lee and Vernon Winfrey, who never married. When Oprah was a baby her mother moved to Milwaukee, Wis., in search of better economic opportuni-ties. Winfrey spent her formative years in Kosciusko with her maternal grand-mother, who taught her to read at an early age and enrolled her in kinder-garten. Oprah attended church with the deeply religious woman and began her public speaking at a young age in her grandmother's church. When she was six, Winfrey moved to Milwaukee to be with her mother. These were difficult years for Oprah because her mother

worked long hours as a domestic and came home exhausted to their tiny apartment. Additionally, when she was nine years old, Oprah was raped by a teenage cousin, and another family member and a family friend continued the sexual abuse. In response, Oprah became so rebellious that her mother could not control her, and she sent Oprah to Nashville to live with her father and his wife. Her father proved to be a strict disciplinarian, and Oprah responded favorably. She focused her talents in a number of extracurricular activities at East High School, including theater, debate, and student council. A local radio station sponsored Oprah in a Miss Fire Prevention contest, which she won, and when management heard her speak, they hired her to read the news on the radio after school. Winfrey earned a scholarship to Tennessee State University in Nashville, and during her college years she entered and won the Miss Black Nashville and Miss Black Tennessee contests and competed in the Miss Black America Pageant. When she was 19, the local CBS affiliate named her coanchor, making her the first woman to hold that position.

In 1976, during her senior year, Oprah relocated to Baltimore to the ABC affiliate to become the anchor for the evening news. Soon thereafter she began providing updates for ABC's *Good Morning America*, and later she hosted a morning talk show called *Baltimore Is Talking*. After eight years in Baltimore, Oprah moved to Chicago to host *A.M. Chicago*, the lowest-rated talk show, opposite the popular Phil Donahue. Within a month, her show's

ratings equaled Donahue's. After several months, the show was extended to an hour and renamed *The Oprah Winfrey Show*. In 1985, while on a business trip to Chicago, movie producer Quincy Jones saw Winfrey's show, was impressed by her talent, and offered Oprah the role of Sophia in *The Color Purple*. Oprah eventually performed in several movies, including *Native Son* and *The Women of Brewster Place*. In 1986 Oprah started HARPO, Inc., to produce videos, films, and television shows. That same year, King World Productions syndicated the talk show, making it the highest-rated show in its time slot in virtually every city in the country. Oprah's popularity crosses racial and class lines, and she even has immense international appeal. Her show is seen in 107 countries.

As Oprah has grown and matured, so has the show. Earlier themes were sometimes sensational in nature; later shows stress how to improve lives in a variety of ways. With her willingness to explore the emotional aspects of life, critics have sometimes decried the "Oprahization" of American society. In 1996 Oprah launched the Oprah Book Club, and any writer whom Oprah featured became an instant best seller. To promote philanthropy, she created Oprah's Angel Network, which has raised over $50 million for charities. To further her commitment to improving education for impoverished African girls, she built the Oprah Winfrey Leadership School in South Africa. Winfrey entered the publishing world with a popular magazine called *O, The Oprah Magazine*. The international version is published bimonthly. Winfrey invested in the cable network Oxygen.

Throughout her career, the *Oprah Winfrey Show* has won dozens of Emmys, and she was nominated for an Academy Award for her role in *The Color Purple*. She has received numerous humanitarian awards and honorary degrees and is consistently chosen by magazines as one of the most influential people in America. She has the distinc-tion of becoming the first black billion-aire in the United States.

MINOA D. UFFELMAN
Austin Peay University

Helen S. Garson, *Oprah Winfrey: A Biography* (2004); Henry Louis Gates Jr., *Finding Oprah's Roots: Finding Your Own* (2007); Kathryn Lofton, *Journal of Popular Culture* 39, no. 4 (2006).

INDEX OF CONTRIBUTORS

INDEX

Page numbers in boldface refer to articles.

Baptist Convention, 335; International Mission Board of (formerly Foreign Mission Board), 336; and Southern Baptist Theological Seminary, 326

Baptist Young Peoples' Union, 234

Barber-Scotia College (Scotia Seminary), 297

Barber Shop (film), 42

Bardaglio, Peter, 258

Barker-Benfield, G. J., 259

Bates, Daisy, 220, 283

Baton Rouge, La., 294

Battey, Robert, 259

Baylor University, 344

Bazile, Leon, 186

Bealts, Anne, 138

Beaufort, S.C., 306–7

Beauty, cult of, **30–40**, 40–42, 170, 208

Beauty pageants, 30, 31, 34–39, 86, 124; black, 34. *See also* Miss America; Miss Black America Pageant

Beauty queens, 8, 35–38, 311

Beauty shops and barbershops, 33, **40–42**, 281

Beauty Trade, 34

Beauvoir, Simone de, 295

Beavers, Louise, 172, 250

Belgarnie, Florence, 339

Bell, Carrie, 51

Bell, Lurrie, 51; "I'll Be Your .44," 51

Belles and ladies, xviii, 1, 30, 31, 38, **42–49**, 51, 85, 126, 156–59, 188, 191, 192, 195, 209, 212, 230, 252–53, 255, 287, 313, 332. *See also* Ladies and gentlemen; Respectability, politics of

Belzoni, Miss., 52

Bennettsville, S.C., 315

Bentley, Gladys, 52

Bentsen, Lloyd, 222

Berendt, John, 30, 256; *Hiding My Candy*, 30; *Midnight in the Garden of Good and Evil*, 30, 256

Berger, John, 206

Berkin, Carol Ruth, 1, 4

Berry, Halle, 197

Bethany Institute, 300

Bethune, Mary McLeod, 219, **297–98**, 300, 301, 340; and Mary McLeod Bethune Museum and Archives for Black Woman's History, 298

Bethune-Cookman College (formerly Daytona Normal and Industrial Institute for Girls), 85, 219, 297–98

Betts, Doris, 138, 253; *Heading West*, 253; *The River to Pickle Beach*, 253

Beulah (television show), 172, 250

Beverly Hillbillies, The (television show), 196

Bible Belt, 13, 29, 34, 213, 221, 262, 343

Birmingham, Ala., 125, 285

Birney, Alice M., 76

Birth control, 2, 55, 261, 265

Bisexual and bisexuality, 29, 52, 122–25, 262

Black, Hugo, 219

Black and White Men Together (BWMT), 125

Black Codes, 63

Blackface minstrelsy, 81

"Black is Beautiful," 34

Black Panthers, 69

Black Power movement, 181, 182, 337

Blanton, Annie Webb, 76, 215

Blassingame, John, 183

Blease, Cole, 165

Bloodworth-Thomason, Linda, and Harry Thomason, 311; *Designing Women* (television show), 311; *The Man From Hope* (film), 311

Blount, Roy, Jr., 126

Blues, xviii, **49–53**, 261; bluesmen, 33, 50–51; blueswomen, 50–52; lyrics, 33, 52, 261

Board of Home Missions, 74

Bodies, 6, 9, 22, 41, 50, 130, 131, 132, 210, 228, 261, 286

Bogan, Lucille, 52

Boggs, Hale, 221

Boggs, Lindy, 221, **298–99**; *Lindy Boggs: Steel and Velvet* (film), 299

Bogle, Donald, 197

Old Screamer Mountain, Ga., 123
Oliver, Paul, 33
Olympic Games, 226, 275, 291
Onstott, Kyle, 257; *Mandingo*, 257
Order of Eastern Star, 76
Orlean, Susan, 36
Orr, Pauline, 213
Ortega, Gregoria, 237
Outlaw Movement, 80. *See also* Haggard, Merle
Owens, Buck, 79, 80
Owens, Jesse, 275
Owsley, Frank L., 287
Ozarks, 129

Pace v. Alabama, 22
Packard, Vance, 259, 260; *The Sexual Wilderness*, 259
Page, Thomas Nelson, 158, 252; "Marse Chan," 252; "Social Life in Old Virginia Before the War," 158
Paige, Satchel, 275
Palatka, Fla., 297
Palestine, Tex., 293
Palimpsest Prize, 29
Palmer Memorial Institute (Alice Freeman Palmer Memorial Institute), 214, 299–301; and Alice Freeman Palmer, 300
Parker, Idella, 246
Parker, John, 217, 218
Parker, Suzi, 262
Parks, Rosa, 67, 69, 193, 220, 283
Parton, Dolly, 80, 156, 192; *Best Little Whorehouse in Texas* (film), 80; "Coat of Many Colors," 192; "9 to 5," 80; "The Rosewood Casket," 80
Paternalism, 6, 7, 93, 103, 140, **201–4**, 211, 232, 318, 326
Patriarchy, 6, 22, 28, 29, 44, 46, 47, 71, 83, 85, 101, 102, 103, 106, 107, 181–82, 190, 211, 230, 232, 257–58, 265, 279, 283, 338
Patriot and patriotism, 8, 43, 54, 80, 106, 126
Paul, Alice, 277; National Woman's Party, 277

Paycheck, Johnny, 192; "I'm the Only Hell My Mama Ever Raised," 192
Peabody Conservatory, 348
Pearl, Minnie, 78
Pecknold, Diane, 79
Pennsylvania, 185, 295, 339
Pennybacker, Mrs. Percy, 75
Pentecostal, 36–37
Pentecostal-Holiness groups, 36, 237; Church of God, 237; Church of the Nazarene, 237; Pilgrim Holiness, 237
Percy, Walker, 252, 253, 273; *The Last Gentleman*, 252; *The Moviegoer*, 253; *The Second Coming*, 252
Petersburg, Va., 232
Petty, Lee, 199
Petty, Richard, 199, 200, 274
Philadelphia, 185, 295, 334, 339; Institute for Contemporary Art, 295
Philippines, 292
Phillips, John, 53
Phillips, Lena Madesin, 76
Phillips, Ulrich B., 202
Photography, xviii, **205–11**, 353
Piedmont College, 348
Pilot International, 76
Plains, Ga., 303
Planters and planter class, xvii, 4, 46, 47, 63, 92, 101–4, 107, 108, 116, 144, 158, 168, 175, 192, 196, 267, 281, 334, 341–42
Pocahontas, 9
Poitier, Sidney, 197
Politics, women in: 1700s to 1920, **211–16**; 1920 to present, **216–23**
Politics of respectability. *See* Respectability, politics of
Populists and populist movements, 5, 19, 153, 213
Porter, Edwin S., 194; *Uncle Tom's Cabin* (film), 194
Porter, Gregory, 52
Porter, Katherine Anne, 253; "The Old Order," 253
Potter, David, 188
Poverty, 4, 19, 74, 79, 94, 97, 109, 136, 178,

Williams, Hank, 79, 80, 192; "Message to My Mother," 192
Williams, Sherley Anne, 255; *Dessa Rose*, 255
Williams, Tennessee, 29, 170, 255–56; *Cat on a Hot Tin Roof*, 255; *Memoirs*, 29; *Streetcar Named Desire*, 170; *Streetcar Named Desire* (film), 195; *Suddenly, Last Summer*, 255
Williams, Vanessa, 39
Williamson, Joel, 242
Willis, Deborah, 210
Wilmington, N.C., 63, 217
Wilson, Gretchen, 8
Wilson, Woodrow, 217
Wiltz, Christine, 248–49; *Glass House*, 248–49
Winfrey, Oprah, 250, **357–59**; HARPO, 358; Oprah's Angel Network, 358; Oprah Book Club, 358; Oprah Winfrey Leadership School, 358; *The Oprah Winfrey Show*, 358–59; *O, The Oprah Magazine*, 358
Wisconsin, 261, 357
Wiseman, Lulu Bell, 78; "Hayloft Sweetheart," 78
Withers, Ernest, 210
Witherspoon, Reese, 195
Wolcott, Victoria, 240
Wolfe, Tom, 126, 199, 306; "The Last American Hero," 199
Womanhood, xvii, 2, 31, 42–48, 52, 88, 90, 130, 156–59, 171, 173, 191, 208, 209, 231, 234, 243, 245–46, 274, 311, 342; "true," 47, 258
Womanism, 10, **282–87**
Woman's Christian Temperance Union (WCTU), 74, 213, 218, 287, 317; and Grange coalition, 213
Woman's Era, 339
Women and work, 17–21, 150–56, 161–62, 168, 170–73, 178, 192, 193, 263, 265, 268–69, 287–90
Women of Brewster Place (film), 358
Women's College of Western Reserve, 341

Women's Congressional Caucus, 299
Women's Foreign Mission Board, 236
Women's Hospital Associations, 352
Women's Missionary Union (WMU), 74, 235–36, 336
Women's National Association for the Preservation of the White Race, 294
Women's rights, 13, 150, 212, 303, 307–8, 321; language, 13; movement, 110, 138, 231, 294, 295
"Wonderful Hair Grower," 41
Wood, Amy Louise, 209
Woodward, C. Vann, 5, 104, 242, 244–45
Workers' wives, **287–90**
Workmen's compensation, 328
Works Progress Administration, 206, 220
World War I, 19, 41, 76, 101, 151, 196, 357
World War II, 19, 25, 67, 78, 107, 118, 155, 165, 247, 250, 263, 264, 265, 294, 332
Worley, Anna Lee, 217
Worley, Darrel, 80, 81
Wright, Frances, 212
Wright, Richard, 10, 94, 109, 254; *Black Boy*, 94, 109; *Native Son*, 254; *Native Son* (film), 358; *12 Million Black Voices*, 94
Wrightsville Beach, N.C., 313
Wyatt-Brown, Bertram, 46, 107
Wynette, Tammy, 79

Yaeger, Patricia, 9
Yale University Law School, 316
Yankee, 84, 106, 192, 310, 356
Yarborough, Cale, 200
"Year of the Woman," 80
Yearwood, Tricia, 80
Yeomen, xvii, 8, 18, 93, 141, 145, 151, 270–71, 287
Yoknapatawpha County, 158
Young Negroes Cooperative League, 296
Young People's Society of Christian Endeavor, 234
Young Women's Christian Association (YWCA), 331

Zealy, J. T., 206